Community
Health and Wellness
a **Socioecological** Approach

For Kate and Emily, and their generation

Community
Health and Wellness
a **Socioecological** Approach

Anne
McMurray

Faculty of Nursing and Health
Griffith University

M Mosby

Mosby
is an imprint of Elsevier Science

Elsevier (Australia) Pty Limited
30–52 Smidmore Street, Marrickville, NSW 2204

Second edition © 2003
First edition © 1999

Published by Elsevier (Australia) Pty Limited
ACN 000 910 583

Every attempt has been made to trace and acknowledge copyright, but in some cases this
may not have been possible. The publisher apologises for any accidental infringements
and would welcome any information to redress the situation.

National Library of Australia Cataloguing-in-Publication Data

McMurray, Anne.
Community health and wellness: a socioecological approach.

2nd ed.
Includes index.
ISBN 0 7295 3673 4.

1. Public health. 2. Social medicine. 3. Public health –
Social aspects – Australia. 4. Health promotion. 5.
Health promotion – Social aspects – Australia. 6. Social
Medicine – Australia. I. Title.

362.120994

Publishing Editor: Vaughn Curtis
Publishing Services Manager: Helena Klijn
Edited by Kay Waters
Index by Max McMaster
Cover and internal design by Vivien Valk
Typeset by Sun Photoset Pty Ltd, Brisbane
Printed in Australia by Southwood Press

 Mosby

Sydney Edinburgh London New York Philadelphia St Louis Toronto

Contents

Section 1: Community health and wellness

Section 3 Promoting community competence

About the author

Anne McMurray is Dean of the Faculty of Nursing and Health at Griffith University, and is a fellow of the Royal College of Nursing, Australia, and the Institute for Healthy Communities. Anne has practised in a range of nursing and community health settings in Canada and Australia, and has been an academic for over 15 years. Her research interests lie in continuity of care across the hospital, home and community, and family adaptation to illness and life events.

Anne is a member of several state, national and international committees, and serves on a number of advisory boards including the ICN's Leadership for Change evaluation committee and the WHO Western Pacific Advisory Committee on Health Research, and is Expert Advisor on Primary Health Care to the International Council of Nursing.

Preface

This second edition of *Community Health and Wellness: A Socioecological Approach* has been written to extend the contention introduced in the first edition: that health is the product of interactions between people and their many environments. We are primarily social creatures who live in communal environments, each with distinct physical, psychological, social, spiritual and cultural features. Interactions between members of the community and these environments have the capacity to shape the conditions of people's lives in ways that can either enhance or constrain health and well-being. At the same time, the community itself may become transformed through interactions between and among the people who reside there. The health and well-being of a community is therefore ecological: the product of dynamic interrelationships between people and their environments.

Throughout the past few decades there has been greater recognition that interrelationships between people and their social environments represent an extremely important element of health and well-being. For this reason, this edition has attempted to focus on a wider range of social conditions, or determinants of health, than the first edition. As we unravel the myriad influences of the social world, it is clear that, as health professionals, we must work toward greater understanding of how health can be enhanced and sustained in the settings of people's lives—the workplaces, schools and neighbourhoods of our communities. The key to achieving this is to foster 'health literacy' wherein people are sufficiently knowledgeable about health to feel empowered to make healthy choices and/or alter the circumstances of their lives where necessary.

For those of us who work with communities to promote health and well-being, there is a need to be responsive to the peculiarities of the community. However, there are also common goals for all communities, such as ensuring accessibility to health care, using appropriate technology, fostering community empowerment to promote health, intersectoral collaboration and encouraging community participation. In this increasingly globalised world, there is greater opportunity to share information and insights into ways of achieving these goals, and for this reason the second edition has a stronger international focus. The common elements in this international body of work show that greater gains can be achieved from conceptualising practice within the principles of primary health care using the guidelines of the Ottawa Charter for Health Promotion. This text is offered as a guide to assisting communities everywhere to build healthy public policies, create supportive environments, strengthen community action, develop personal skills and reorient health services in a way that creates and sustains health and well-being.

Anne McMurray
July 2002

Acknowledgments

I would like to acknowledge a number of people who contributed to this book, especially the students who stimulate my thinking, and my friends and colleagues who provide lively critique and help shape my consideration of communities and community health. I would also like to acknowledge Samantha Bray's expert assistance, and Susan Griffith's masterful approach in searching for all the right resource materials and then taking the time to talk through the various issues with me.

Vaughn Curtis and Kay Waters once again provided invaluable assistance and advice in the production of the book, as did Helena Klijn and Rhiain Hull, who kept the project flowing in the right direction. Thanks to all of you for your support and understanding. Finally, I would like to acknowledge my children and their enthusiasm for this work, which helps keep me motivated to be curious about the world and its communities.

Community
Health and Wellness

Section

Introduction
to the Section

The four chapters in this first section of the book are designed to lay a foundation from which the health of a community can be created, supported and sustained. The first aspect of this foundation, as described in Chapter 1, is the ecological perspective that conceptualises health as being at the centre of a reciprocal process, where people interacting with their environment build both human and environmental capacity. Included in this chapter is a discussion on the way this process can be empowering for the community and the individuals who live in it. The contemporary concept of health literacy is introduced as one aspect of community empowerment. The discussion captures the importance of sustaining health and the environment, focusing on the centrality of place in people's lives. The social determinants of health are introduced, paving the way for detailed examination of social and environmental factors later in the section. To further entrench the idea that health is basically a social construct, this chapter also introduces primary health care as a mechanism for social justice and valuing social and human capital. The chapter concludes with an introduction to community health promotion and health education from the perspective of the Ottawa Charter for Health Promotion.

Chapter 2 explores the principles of primary health care in depth. Distinguishing features of primary care, primary health care and primary, secondary and tertiary prevention are explained. Each primary health care principle is then examined in relation to current issues of equity, access, self-determinism, cultural sensitivity and intersectoral collaboration. The impact of globalisation on equity and access is included in this discussion. The chapter then takes a closer look at social determinants of community health, particularly in urban environments. The healthy cities movement is outlined, with regard to the interplay of social determinants and the challenges faced by city dwellers.

Chapter 3 begins with an examination of the concepts of risk and risky behaviours. This is linked, once again, to the determinants of health and the way these form a data base for change. Without a solid base of evidence that change is required for community health promotion, resources will not be forthcoming to aid the process. Nor will there be any convincing arguments for people, cultures or governments to change their risky behaviours and unhealthy systems, and work towards increasing levels of personal and community health. The chapter briefly outlines the biomedical model of data gathering through epidemiological studies, providing a critique of the shortcomings of this approach. The notion of global risk is introduced, with examination of the Global Burden of Disease studies and the way they are informing World Health Organization (WHO) strategies for the future.

The final chapter in this section provides an historical look at the way health promotion has evolved from the epidemiological beginnings of the last century, through the mass media campaigns of the 1970s and 1980s, to the current era of the Ottawa and Jakarta charters. Conceptual models used to evaluate health promotion in the 1980s and 1990s are outlined, with a critique of their limitations. The healthy settings approach adopted by the WHO in the late 1990s is discussed, leading to an analysis of contemporary health promotion approaches. The notion of risk is revisited from the perspective of proximal and distal factors. Included is a report card on health promotion efforts in the last century. The chapter ends with a commentary on health promotion strategies for the future, linked to the rapidly evolving body of knowledge on how health can be created and sustained in diverse communities throughout the world.

CHAPTER 1

The community
of the twenty-first century

introduction   The twenty-first century has begun with a stark revelation that we are all members of a global community. Thanks to technological developments in the twentieth century, our communications systems today bring us closer together, allowing us to share common problems, common solutions, strengths and vulnerabilities. Information technology has shown us possibilities for change, the potential of creative imagination and new pathways for educational and economic development. But the technology has also sharpened the focus on inequities between communities at varying levels of development. Common public images have changed perceptions and expectations of social life, diminishing the uniqueness of some communities, venerating others. Information literacy has been gained, yet languages have been lost. Knowledge has been shared, including knowledge of the widening gap between the health status of the rich and that of the poor. As a result, the world has a common understanding of the desperate expectation of continuing poor health for those born into poverty, and the enhanced potential of those born into more privileged situations.

New skills have been developed to replace those made redundant by technologies. The world has greater access to consumer goods, medicines and health experts, and yet, as a global population we remain no healthier than in the past and no less threatened by the conflicts and compromises to health created by human behaviours. The rapidly evolving technological changes have therefore rendered us a double-edged sword, one side slicing efficiently through the challenges of daily living, the other deleting the social elements that previously served to sustain community life and community health. Because global developments have touched all our communities in some way, it is timely to reassess notions of community and community health from the global to the local context and to anticipate the myriad ways in which we, as health professionals, can promote the health of our communities in the years ahead.

objectives   **By the end of this chapter you will be able to:**

1   Define health in relation to community health, community development
    and primary health care

2   Explain the different philosophical approaches of community health and
    public health

3   Discuss health from a social and ecological perspective

4   Explain the concept of health literacy

5   Identify the difference between health education and health promotion

6   Discuss the health promotion implications of a socioecological model
    of health.

Your
community

You find yourself in a geographic space, by choice or by chance. Looking
around, you see features of the physical environment: air and water, filled with
harmful or vitalising elements; mountains or an ocean; lush, watered lands or
parched brown earth; tall shade trees, the harbour of bushland; or a desolate
expanse of desert devoid of firewood but with rocks that provide shelter from
the burning sun. Your health, and that of your family, is profoundly affected
by these geographic features. Comfort, nourishment and freedom from illness
are to a large extent determined by the environment and the choices and
opportunities it affords to create and maintain a healthy lifestyle.

Consider, for a moment, the effect of space on health. Those who
work indoors may be affected by ambient air carrying dangerous chemicals
or agents of respiratory illness. They may work with constant noise in a
crowded environment, precipitating a rise in blood pressure. Artificial lighting
may be depriving them of the vitamin D found in sunlight. Uncomfortable

workstations or repetitive movements may be causing postural problems or strain injuries. Outside in the street, workers providing services to their workplaces are being affected by a different kind of environment. Air streaked with dust particles, street noise and constant demands on their musculoskeletal systems may be wearing down their bodies. Others may be driving a taxi, a bus or a train, or working a harvest, all to a tight schedule, all under the pressures of customer demands or the vagaries of the weather. They work in the same streets where homeless people sit or walk in discouraged silence or in search of numbing agents to provide momentary respite from the reality of their lives. In addition to the physical and emotional stresses, their health is severely compromised by the social milieu. In the suburbs, a different kind of stress overshadows the health of the young parent confined inside by the responsibilities of caring for young children and, in many cases, elderly, incapacitated family members. For many in this situation, life is a constant battle to balance paid work and family responsibilities, with little opportunity for physical exercise or social exchange beyond the family. Another kind of isolation affects those with disabling conditions, depriving them of the vibrancy and enthusiasm of lives shared with others.

What these examples illustrate is that health is clearly a *socioecological* construct. It begins from a base of biologically influenced physical and emotional characteristics that are shaped by the social and environmental elements of our lives. Added to this equation is personal choice. Health-seeking or health-compromising behaviours may be a function of attitudes that embrace healthy choices, or those that diminish or negate their importance. Attitudes are, in turn, a product of the biological, social and environmental influences on our lives and those of our forebears. This cycle explains the ecological focus of health. The term *ecology* refers to the balanced interrelationships between living things in their environment. It is an ideal way to think of health. For each of us, health is the product of interactions between people and their many environments in ways that, by design or inadvertently, conserve and sustain health and well-being.

What is
a community?

As members of a community, our lives are closely interwoven with the lives of others, some living in close proximity to us, others sharing common characteristics but not inhabiting our geographical space. We also hold membership in various population groups on the basis of gender, age, physical capacity or culture. In the context of all these group memberships, we interact with a moveable feast of other richly diverse communities. To these interactions we bring our own individuality—the combination of genetic predispositions, history, knowledge, attitudes, preferences and perceptions of capacity. Each community in turn brings to each of its members a set of distinct environments: physical, psychological, social, spiritual and cultural. Interactions between people and their environments provide the dynamic forces that shape community character and determine the extent to which community members will be able to create and sustain health. Each of these interactions, whether with our families, our social groups or our physical environment, is *ecological* in that there is an opportunity for exchange of ideas or energy. As a result, we and the environment are transformed, even in a small way. Bandura (1977) called this *reciprocal determinism*. By this he meant that both the behaviours of people and the characteristics of their environments are determined by the set of dynamic exchanges between them. It is a useful way to explain the socioecological nature of community health, as the health of any given community is embedded in, and transformed in the context of, its social and ecological exchanges.

Ecological exchange can yield both constraints and enhancements to personal and community health. Some of the more familiar constraints on health and well-being arise from the effects of contaminants in the physical environment, such as air and water pollution, as well as infectious diseases and/or injury. Some degree of risk to health and well-being is also present in the social environment, in the workplace, school and neighbourhood. Interactions with our environment in recreation, education and social interchange present opportunities for achieving higher levels of health and well-being. Interactions between community members and the health care system are also imbued with challenges and opportunities for illness prevention and health improvements. For those of us whose role involves helping people achieve and maintain good health and protection from illness or injury, it is important to understand the many types and levels of interactions that occur in a community.

In the most basic terms, the word *community* simply means that which is common. We often think of a community as the physical or geographical place we share with others, but an *ecological* view takes this a bit further by defining a community as an *interdependent* group of plants and animals inhabiting a common space. People depending on each other, and interacting with each other and with aspects of their environment, distinguish a living community from a collection of inanimate objects. Communities are thus dynamic entities that pulsate with the actions and interactions of people, the spaces they inhabit and the resources they use.

Some communities are also defined on the basis of personal factors such as age or gender, and some by virtue of their vulnerability to a health concern (Barnes et al 1995). So, in addition to belonging to a certain neighbourhood or city, a person may be a member of a community of females, a community of adolescents or a community of middle-aged workers. In many cases, a person decides to become a member of a certain community by choice. For example, people may see themselves as members of the cycling community when they decide to engage in that sport. What is *communal* or *common* is the sport of cycling. Similarly, those of us who surf, swim, fish, jog or walk along the beach share the communal bonds of the beach community by choice. Online communities are also formed this way. The internet is host to millions of communities, some on the basis of information seeking, some designed for sociability, perhaps for making new friends, and others simply to share resources and help meet one another's needs (Preece 2000).

When you think about communities in this way, the reciprocal relationship between people and their environment is readily apparent. Community health, then, is a *synthesis* or *creation* of people interacting with their environments. Of course, some environments are better endowed than others with natural resources that encourage healthy lifestyles. However, communities with few resources but a high commitment to health and wellness can also achieve a high level of community health. Before examining the notion of community health and how it can be achieved, we first need to be clear on what we mean by health.

What is
health?

The classic definition of health is that adopted by the World Health Organization (WHO) in which health is defined as 'a state of complete physical, mental and social well-being and not merely the absence of disease or infirmity' (WHO 1974, p 1). What is useful about this definition is that it encompasses a holistic view of health. *Holistic* means encompassing the *whole*, not just the physical components. So the WHO definition is holistic in that it refers to physical, psychological, cultural and social factors. However, it fails to capture the dynamic or *action-oriented* nature of being healthy and well. Health is not a static entity; it is ever-changing according to the environments in which it occurs. According to WHO, 'health depends on our ability to understand and manage the interaction between human activities and the physical and biological environment' (WHO 1992, p 409).

This broad view of health and wellness is *socioecological* at the personal, group and environmental level. The social world provides the context within which people interact with the environment. When we define health from a social perspective we acknowledge the *social capital* of the community. In this context, the word 'capital' refers to something of value and therefore worthy of investment. Whereas economic capital refers to material wealth, social capital is 'the common currency of humankind—health' (Ratzan 2001, p 213). This means that health is valued, and people are valued in a climate of trust and mutual respect that extends to all facets of life (Cox 1995). The ecological part of the definition draws the diverse social and environmental aspects together into a whole, to work towards achieving equilibrium and harmony, even while aspects of the personal, social or physical environment may be changing.

Health is not always experienced as the ideal described above. It is also relative; that is, it is defined according to circumstances, context and perceptions. It is therefore interesting to examine individual perspectives on health, or the extent to which people define themselves as healthy. Examples abound of individuals who have some type of functional disability yet consider themselves healthy. Many people who have had surgery for an illness or injury (a mastectomy, or removal of a limb, or cardiac surgery), recover to a state of health wherein they describe their lives as extremely healthy. Not all people overcome adversity in this way, and some people react to illness or injury by tending to see themselves in terms of their disability. However, others use an illness or injury as a motivation to achieve higher levels of health than they had previously experienced. Terry Fox, for example, who lost his leg to cancer, refused to see himself as disabled, and ran across Canada to demonstrate the power of willpower and to raise funds for other victims of cancer.

Communities may also be faced with adversity and limitations. A community may have the disadvantage of isolation, or few natural resources conducive to health, yet community structures and processes may enable those who live in the community to achieve high levels of health. In this case, the community would be seen in terms of its potential for building and/or strengthening health capacity. Community health capacity emerges where there are supportive organisational structures, such as schools, workplaces and community planning mechanisms, that are conducive to health. Health capacity is also enhanced when health is included in a community's decision-making for other services, such as transportation, job training (and retraining), community policing, conserving the environment, and waste disposal, for example. Capacity building also occurs through programs that support disadvantaged people through affordable housing, employment opportunities and any measures to reduce discrimination (Bowen, Harris & Hyde 2001). In summary, where a community is committed to using whatever resources it has to improve the health of its people there is a greater likelihood of building both personal and community capacity.

Healthiness
and wellness

Two important elements of healthiness are *balance* and *potential*. When people are healthy, their lives are in balance. There is harmony between the physical, social, emotional and spiritual. When communities are healthy there is a balance between the various barriers to health (unemployment, poverty, lack of fresh vegetables) and those things that encourage health (sporting facilities, neighbourhood clubs, medical facilities). When people are healthy, they recognise the potential for higher levels of wellness. The term *wellness* was coined by Dunn (1959) to extend what seemed like a static notion of health to one that explained the dynamic relationship arising between people and their environment when individuals use that environment to maintain balance and purposeful direction (Dunn 1959). *High-level wellness* is considered by Dunn (1961) to be living life at maximum potential and in harmony with the circumstances of one's life. Current definitions of health try to capture Dunn's idea that being healthy encompasses much more than simply a healthy body at one point in time. Most definitions emphasise two major ideas: first, that health is dynamic rather than static; and second, that the environment or context of people's lives influences the extent to which they can reach their health potential. For example, healthy, fit people go to the gym and eat a nutritious diet, students balance study with recreation, young families immunise their children, older people keep active and socialise with others. Similarly, healthy communities participate in greening their environment, keep an eye on crime rates and make resources available for promoting physical fitness and healthy lifestyles in their schools and workplaces. However, these personal and group activities are only made possible in supportive environments, which include the social, cultural and physical elements that allow people to achieve the level of health to which they aspire.

The socioecological view of health and wellness goes beyond a simple or shallow ecology, which sees people conserving resources and recycling, for example, to a *deep ecology*, which requires collective questioning, at increasingly deeper levels, of our basic assumptions about the world, our culture, life and our everyday relationship with the natural environment (Lacroix 1996). Conservation and sustainability in this sense involve all the supports that enable people to draw maximum support from their environments and, in the process, ensure that these supportive elements also endure.

What determines
health and wellness?

Just as some people are healthier than others, some communities and societies are healthier than others. Population-wide studies suggest that the health of a population is influenced by social and economic conditions, by the psychosocial environment, and by the experiences individuals bring to those environments, which, in turn, are influenced by their early biological development (Hertzman 2001). The material wealth of a society and the way it is distributed among the population creates one aspect of the environment that is important to health. Socioeconomic factors that flow from the equitable distribution of wealth include such things as adequate housing, safe water, clean air, nutrition, education, working conditions that promote good health, and a range of services that support healthy choices for leisure activities and recreation. Most importantly, the extent to which these services and conditions are accessible by all members of the population is a powerful indicator of the community's health. Where there is a relatively healthy environment, and a sense of communal sharing or civic pride, people tend to work together to make sure their community or society is sustainable. Individuals who enter such a community from an enriched biological and social environment in the early stages of their lives have a strong chance of continuing on a path to good health (Hertzman 2001).

The key determinants of health therefore include: biological factors such as heredity and genetic constitution; individual behaviours, beliefs and responses; the social and physical environment, including early nurturing, cultural and economic conditions; and the accessibility and quality of health services. Each of these influences an individual's potential for health. Any combination of these factors may also interact to determine lifestyle choices, which also have a profound impact on health and feelings of well-being.

Personal concepts of health are also embedded in the values, norms and conditions of the family and the community. Many health scholars believe that the environments or *conditions* of a person's life are pre-eminent, that they shape and mould biological factors (Hertzman 2001). Because of this, the 'double jeopardy' of children born into families of low socioeconomic status is attracting research interest (Hardy & Miller 2000). Studies have shown considerable insight into the importance of education, nurturing and anticipatory guidance in overcoming the health hazards of being born into a relatively deprived social situation (Hardy & Miller 2000). This area of research is gathering momentum as we begin to let go of our rigid methods of measuring health status and examine the contexts of people's lives and the interactions between various factors. As the pieces of the puzzle begin to fit together, many permutations emerge. For example, social and demographic factors such as gender may affect a person's employability, which may determine family financial status, which may affect access to health or social resources, which may precipitate illness, which may influence family dynamics. Similarly, family structure may affect financial opportunities that impinge on geographical mobility, which may determine access to health services or parenting styles. Clearly, adequate assessment of the interplay of factors such as appear in Figure 1.1 is fundamental to planning appropriate and adequate health care.

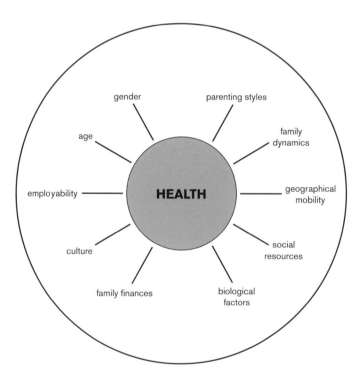

FIGURE 1.1 *Interactions between factors affecting health*

What is
community health?

A healthy community is one where there is a visible commitment to achieving the health and well-being of individuals, families and various groups of people. To begin with, there must be a common notion of health, one that is shared by community members as well as health professionals. From an ecological perspective, the first goal of community health must be *sustainability*; that is, the community must be able to continue indefinitely without causing excessive disturbance or damage (McMichael 2000). In today's society, where communities are interdependent upon one another and the global community, absolute sustainability represents an ideal. However, varying levels of sustainability can be achieved through *conservation* of both personal and physical resources, and by valuing *diversity*. Valuing diversity celebrates the different contributions that comprise the kaleidoscope of opinions, ideas and networks of the community. This means that the community is bound by a common commitment to conserve not only its natural habitat, but all aspects of the physical, social and cultural environment that enable both current and future inhabitants to maintain health and wellness.

The key to community health lies not so much in the provision of medical services or access to expert advice on how to live a healthy lifestyle, but in the quality and equality of sharing and caring that occurs in the community (Labonte 1997). Healthy communities are those that feel empowered to shape their own destiny. They enjoy broad participation in health policies and in developing appropriate conditions for living and working. By participating in decisions that affect daily life, members of healthy communities are able to feel they have some control over the design and sustainability of the community's current and future potential. In short, they feel a sense of commonality or cohesion with others, which becomes beneficial for all members of the community (Hertzman 2001).

Community
empowerment

Empowerment is a concept that is instrumental to understanding community health. As a psychological construct, empowerment is defined as having a feeling of personal control over the things that affect one's life (Rissel 1994). In order to make decisions for good health, individuals need to feel that sense of control. At the community level, empowerment extends beyond this feeling of self-empowerment, to participation in collective political action for the benefit of the community itself. In this respect, community empowerment occurs where members of a community gain influence over events and outcomes of importance (Fawcett et al 1995). Neighbourhood groups, for example, may become empowered by joining forces to improve the conditions of their neighbourhood, and in the process individuals become empowered. Self-help groups also support both personal and group empowerment. Consider, for example, what occurs when someone is diagnosed with cancer. In most cases, especially if the diagnosis is unexpected, there is a feeling of utter abandonment from all that is familiar. The person may have feelings of disbelief, and be stunned at her or his lack of knowledge and understanding of the condition. For at least a short time, they may flounder in a state of overwhelming confusion. Even after seeking information, people with cancer may not have the personal or organisational resources to help them deal with the condition, or to ensure that they are able to maintain a relatively normal life beyond the illness. In this state, an individual can be described as disempowered. Something beyond their control has overtaken their decision-making and their health-related actions. They have no point of reference, no guidelines with which to plan for the future, no sense of control. Psychologically, many of these people feel cast adrift from all that is meaningful and comfortable in their lives. They may also have family concerns ranging from child care to financial resources, to personal relationships. How, then, will empowerment assist them?

The concept of empowerment is based on the premise that if people are prepared for illness or rehabilitation from injury with both information and community support systems that help them chart their own course, they will be better able to recover from illness and/or maintain health. Controlling resources is one aspect of this process (Rissel 1994). If a person is able to identify the particular needs they have at any given time, and then access the resources to meet those needs, he or she could be described as empowered. Where health is concerned, being empowered to find the support to either get well or stay well is essential. As part of a self-help group or network, the individual has at their disposal all the benefits of people who have had a similar experience and their advice on how best to use available opportunities. This could involve access to community resources such as transportation services, accommodation close to the treatment centre, supportive environments wherein social services such as child care are provided, community structures to assist with physical or psychological needs, personal skills to monitor or evaluate progress, and health services that are responsive to needs and provided at an affordable cost.

Empowered communities are those where there is active participation in creating the conditions within which decisions are made and, where possible, resources are distributed accordingly. Describing a community as empowered therefore includes the psychological empowerment of individuals, as well as a collective political will to effect improvements to health or prevention of illness. This is not to suggest that empowered communities are *fully* empowered in relation to all health decisions, as this represents an unrealistic ideal (Rissel 1994). A particular community may be empowered on certain issues or circumstances, but recognise constraints on others, especially where there are unachievable or unsustainable resources involved. Because of the participation of community members in decision-making, there is a greater likelihood that development of the community will be undertaken according to an understanding of both strengths and constraints. So community empowerment may be seen in terms of developing the skills and abilities to build capacity and/or to manage community development (Kahssay & Oakley 1999). These skills in turn help to empower people to continue to influence administrative and political decision-making over time, and this is personally developmental. Personal and community empowerment operate in conjunction with one another to create and sustain the processes of community development. Once community residents feel empowered, any structural inequities that exist in the community can be overcome through a more inclusive, or partnership, approach to future decisions affecting health or development (Kahssay & Oakley 1999).

As a health professional, understanding empowerment is critical to helping people help themselves. Labonte (1994) describes the difference between a somewhat 'medicalised' and an empowerment approach to developing a heart health program. One approach sees the health professional develop a healthy heart program in terms of cardiovascular outcomes (number of people having cardiovascular incidents, treatment regimes, post-treatment indicators etc), while the empowerment approach plans the program in light of community members' family, community and economic lives. In the first case, heart health remains encased in the context of cardiovascular disease. In the second, heart health is only one entry point into people's physical, psychological, social and cultural experiences (Labonte 1994). A community empowerment approach would first consider participative structures within which members of the community could identify, then plan, their own heart health program using appropriate community resources. In this way, empowerment emerges from group participation that is developmental and appropriately tailored to group or community needs and desired directions.

Health
literacy

Literacy is one of the foundations of other life skills (Nutbeam & Kickbusch 2000). It is most often associated with education, but at a more critical level the term *health literacy* includes a wider awareness of the conditions that create and sustain health. The global health promotion community has identified 'Education For All' as a way forward in strengthening factors for the development of communities and empowering those who live in them (Nutbeam & Kickbusch 2000). For some people, a lack of education and the health literacy that would flow from this education prevents them from becoming empowered at any time during their lives. For many women especially, illiteracy prevents them from achieving adequate personal health, and from ensuring their family's access to good nutrition and freedom from illness, and exercising their developmental potential.

In any community, the potential for community health and wellness is enhanced once the community has achieved at least a functional level of health literacy (Nutbeam 2000). *Functional health literacy* means that individuals have received sufficient factual information on health risks and health services

available in their community so that they are free to participate in illness prevention and health protection activities, such as screening and immunisation
programs (Nutbeam 2000). To participate in this way, they need to be able to
read consent forms, medicine labels and other written health care information.
They also need to be able to understand and act on both verbal and written
instructions from healthcare practitioners, pharmacists and insurers (Kickbusch
2001). At a second level, *communicative or interactive health literacy* develops
personal skills to the extent that community members have developed their
capacity to influence social norms and to help others develop their personal
capacity for better health. This involves understanding how organisations
work, and communicating with others in the context of self-help or other
support groups, for example.

A third level of literacy, *critical health literacy*, improves individual
resilience to social and economic adversity. This paves the way for community
leadership structures to support community action and to facilitate community
development (Nutbeam 2000). Critical health literacy involves such things as
providing technical advice to support community action and community development. For example, when workers exert pressure on workplaces to reduce
hazardous risks, or when lobby groups attempt to gather support from others
in the community to preserve the environment, or lobby policy makers for
changes that would promote good parenting practices, they are demonstrating
critical health literacy.

Where there are adequate levels of health literacy—that is, where the population has sufficient knowledge and skills—and where members of a community have the confidence to guide their own health, people are able to stay
healthy, recover from illness and live with disease or disability (Ratzan 2001).
Education is therefore a powerful way of overcoming inequities and supporting community empowerment. It is also congruent with the way healthcare
professionals now address the challenges of promoting public health.

What is
public health?

Until the mid-1970s, there was no clear understanding of the distinction
between the terms 'public health' and 'community health'. From the turn of the
century, public health was primarily concerned with eradicating infectious
diseases using a regulatory approach of surveillance and control. The focus
was on tracking epidemics or potential epidemics and ensuring that government regulations were in place for the ongoing monitoring of illness in the population and to respond quickly to situations of need. For the most part, their
activities were unquestioned by the general public. Few references were made
in the professional literature to community health. From the 1930s to the
1970s, public health was defined according to a *biomedical model*, where
the emphasis was on understanding the causes of illness in order to apportion
resources appropriately. These resources were concentrated in hospitals and

acute-sector services that were in reality more concerned with public illness than public health (Davies & Kelly 1993). Medical and other public health professionals were specially trained to recognise patterns of disease, environmental hazards and models of health service delivery that would result in adequate levels of health for the largest number of people. This was, and continues to be, the goal of public health: to secure adequate health for as much of the population as possible.

Historically, the health-related decisions made by public health experts were guided by current medical knowledge, political factors and the availability of financial and personal resources. So, for example, in those parts of the world where health personnel and resources were plentiful, people were expected to have higher levels of health. Where vaccines were available, and where the politics of the day encouraged medical research through generous funding schemes, diseases should have been be curtailed. However, this has not always been the case. Despite a long history of eradicating some illnesses and improving health status in some populations, public health officials have realised for some time that there is only a tenuous association between the provision of services and achieving acceptable levels of health (Navarro 1993). In the 1950s and 1960s, communities were encouraged to take a more active role in urban and rural community development activities that would lead to better health, but this was not always successful. Technological complexity, increasingly sophisticated approaches to health decision-making and, in many countries, the centralisation of health services, created barriers to participation by communities with inadequate knowledge or skills development for participation (Kahssay & Oakley 1999).

For years there remained an expectation that achievements in medicine would eradicate disease, yet it became clear throughout the last century that medical advances explained very few improvements in the health of the population. This dilemma was the subject of heated discussion for much of the twentieth century, which led health planners and policy advisors in many countries to convene an international meeting to consider a new direction in health for all peoples of the world. Clearly, the public health or 'biomedical' approach had not been successful, and policy makers were searching for a new approach that would result in better health for more of the population.

Primary
health care

In 1978, the challenge of public health—that is, securing the highest level of health for the greatest number of people—formed the agenda for a meeting of public health delegates from 134 countries throughout the world. The meeting was held in Alma Ata, (a city in the former USSR) to develop new solutions and new directions in public health. The delegates' deliberations culminated in the Declaration of Alma Ata, which was essentially a commitment to embody public health goals within the philosophy of primary health care. The Declaration defined *primary health care* as follows:

> *Essential health care based on practical, scientifically sound and socially acceptable methods and technology made universally accessible to individuals and families in the community through their full participation and at a cost that the community and country can afford to maintain at every stage of their development in the spirit of self-reliance and self-determination. It is the first level of contact with individuals, the family and community with the national health systems bringing health care as close as possible to where people live and work, and constitutes the first element of a continuing care process. (WHO UNICEF 1978, p 6)*

The declaration represented a watershed in public health in that the focus was on empowering people to have control over decisions that affected health in their own families and communities. The primary health care approach conceptualised health as a fundamental right, an individual and collective responsibility, an equal opportunity concept and an essential element of socio-economic development (Holzemer 1992). This represented a stark contrast to the historical 'top-down' approach to planning for public health, in that people at the grass roots level of societies were now to have a greater say in planning from the 'bottom up', or 'inside out' instead of 'outside in' (Courtney 1995). As McMichael (1993) suggested, this new approach would see experts *on tap* rather than *on top*. Primary health care was not only a new vision for health; it was seen as a philosophy permeating the entire health system, a strategy for organising care, a level of care (primary, or first) and a set of activities (Chamberlain & Beckingham 1987).

Communities throughout the world embraced the concept of primary health care and the opportunity to become more involved in decisions affecting their health. The Declaration of Alma Ata thus signalled a shift in thinking from the 'old public health', where health professionals decided what was best for the community, to a 'new public health', where communities themselves would decide priorities and preferences for health from the grass roots, where people live, work and play. The consumer movement, which unified people with common health goals, and the information revolution, which brought people in touch with one another, both played a part in encouraging heightened awareness and greater community involvement in health. From the perspective of those at the top, it was a welcome change to have governments recognise the influence of all sectors of society on the health of the population, as the Declaration clearly acknowledged the importance of technology, community planning, economic factors and settings such as the workplace in securing and maintaining community health.

Perhaps most importantly, the declaration launched what is now commonly known as the 'Health For All' (HFA) movement, a global attempt to work towards health for all people by the year 2000. Health For All was not a call for global eradication of disease or an attempt to create similar levels of health for all people, but an attempt to reduce inequities. It was aimed at redirecting health policy to eliminate those differences that arise from either avoidable or unfair social and economic factors (Bowen, Harris & Hyde 2001). We have now passed the deadline for HFA, acknowledging that it was an unrealistic goal. However, primary health care has left a legacy to communities of the twenty-first century, wherein the *community*, rather than experts, lies at the centre of health care, and where community participation in health decisions is seen as more important to health than the dictates of experts. People in communities are now considered partners in creating and sustaining health, rather than recipients of health services.

This century dawned with a stark realisation that, for communities to be partners in health care, public health knowledge is crucial, particularly in relation to the new epidemics of HIV/AIDS, hepatitis B and social violence. Greater sharing of health knowledge and enhanced transparency of decision-making represents a more democratised approach to health, one that supports community development.

Community
development

Since the Declaration of Alma Ata, WHO has actively encouraged community involvement in health care and development, convening numerous meetings to study the relationship between community involvement and community development (Kahssay & Oakley 1999). If we accept the premise that the major obstacles to health and well-being are structural—that is, part of the economic and political conditions of people's lives—the need for community development becomes obvious (Kahssay & Oakley 1999). Poverty, for example, is the greatest threat to health and one of the most significant causes of child mortality (Akukwe 2000). If poverty can be overcome by building human and community potential, there will be a greater likelihood of sustaining long-term health gains. This approach lies in contrast to the dichotomy of consumer–provider, where one party (in this case, health professionals) provides, and the other (the public) consumes. In the consumer–provider model, there is a distinct power differential in that the provider holds the key to such resources as information, services or consumables, and the consumer must abide by the rules set down by the provider to gain the information, goods or services. The community development approach replaces this power structure with a partnership arrangement, where one person or group collaborates and negotiates with another for needed information, services or consumables. Today, recognising the features of our communities that enable health, and facilitating empowerment through coalitions for changing the conditions that would imperil us, are the most important directions for this century. And the pivotal element around which all our actions revolve is the 're-discovery after a century of medical reductionism that everything is connected to everything else' (Labonte 1997, p 64).

Helping
communities change

One of the challenges of community development is to ensure that health professionals do not impose their agenda on the community. Instead, members of the community should decide what they wish to change, what services they need to assist change, and what support mechanisms are required to maintain the change. The role of the health professional is to provide enough information so that the community will have the skills and knowledge to plan for improved health outcomes. The objective of this role is to foster *community competence*, the ability of community members to collaborate and negotiate effectively to get what they need (Goeppinger, Lassiter & Wilcox 1982). This is akin to *community health literacy*. The health professional fosters community competence and health literacy by *advocating* for people where necessary, assisting people to develop decision-making skills and encouraging *indigenous leadership* wherein decisions originate from local individuals (Courtney 1995; Ratzan 2001).

Helping communities involves trusting in their abilities and advocating on different levels. As social advocate, the health professional adopts a respectful and culturally sensitive approach. As political advocate, it is essential to become knowledgeable about the health and welfare systems and the processes that govern both resource allocation and policy development. As professional advocate, the health professional must preserve the professional competence and solidarity that will help him or her maintain credibility in the community, and therefore act as an effective resource (McMurray 1993).

This is the essence of working with communities: advocating for community health literacy, collaborating with community members, sharing information and resources and helping them construct pathways to change. The process is developmental in that by working together, people's skills, knowledge and self-confidence are developed, ultimately empowering them to go on to the next undertaking. Facilitating and enabling this type of change in communities also plays a role in developing the skills of the health professional. Each community and each community development strategy is unique, so every opportunity to work with a community yields new information that the health professional can use to consolidate and refine health promotion skills. In this respect, advocacy is a deliberate two-way process of mutual development.

Several principles guide community development:

1 *Integration* Community development must be accomplished with integration of social, political, cultural, environmental, personal and spiritual elements. By adopting a holistic approach, issues of class, gender, race/ethnicity, age, disability or sexuality can be considered for their contribution to health.

2 *Community ownership* The community, rather than health professionals, must own the structures and processes of change. This ensures independence of strategies and action, which empowers the community for

decision-making and the pace of development. It also circumvents any need for coercion or oppression from outsiders.

3 *Recognition of the political nature of community change* The links between individual and public issues are crucial and mutually dependent; an example is the case of political processes that give rise to unemployment, which in turn affects health and family functioning. Community development must not be oppressive or grounded in conflict.

4 *Advocacy and partnership* The role of the health professional is to preserve the human rights of community members, ensure the integrity of the processes of change, and strengthen social interactions by bringing community members together and helping them communicate with genuine dialogue, understanding and social action. Such an approach must be inclusive, so all community members are encouraged to participate. In addition, the health professional must help the community recognise and define need, by bringing together residents, service providers and researchers.

5 *Vision* Community development must be undertaken with a view towards sustainability and holistic nurturing, rather than mechanistic, linear solutions to health and developmental problems. Its overall purpose is to promote health and well-being for all people (Ife 1995).

If we accept the interrelationship between community health and community development, communities must be seen as dynamic, functional entities where thoughtful planning creates conditions within which people can strive for health and their preferred quality of life. Working effectively with communities to achieve health goals requires not only a focus on the people who live there, but the community as a whole. In effect, the role of the health professional is to work with not only the collective of people, but the physical space and social habitat with which they interact. This requires an understanding of the relationship between people and place.

People develop a sense of equilibrium within a defined context—whatever is defined as their *place*. This is an ecological relationship characterised by *mutuality*, where what happens in one aspect affects the other. People and their communal, physical environment operate in a kind of symbiotic relationship, which means that people and their environments are closely interdependent. A person's sense of place is an expression of communal culture and, as such, helps set the agenda for activities related to health and illness, and the way services are used to sustain each (Hudson-Rodd 1994). Culture, in turn, shapes the way people define health and the ways they interact within their place.

Health in relation to place is both a product and a resource. It is a product of all aspects of the environment, including the health care system, and an essential resource for living a full and rich life. As members of a certain community, most people recognise the elements that will contribute to their personal health or the health of their family, but few spend much time focusing on the strengths and weaknesses of the communal environment. So, in many cases, the first task of the community health professional is to heighten awareness among people of the linkages between community resources, community risk factors and health. This requires an ecological mindset wherein people incorporate an ecological perspective into their family and community culture.

Ecological
considerations

There are several ways people can be encouraged to focus on community ecology. One approach is to collaborate with local education, health, recreation, sporting and business groups to ensure that the younger generation develops an affinity with the environment and that all citizens are aware of the strengths and resources particular to their community. Another is to use the local media to raise public awareness of the importance of the environment in creating and sustaining health. This can be as simple as publicising the need for recycling among residents of a neighbourhood, or using the media to communicate to the local community what is happening in the wider arena. For example, newspapers, magazines and television broadcasts provide access to deliberations taking place at the major environmental meetings, whether these are international summits sponsored by the United Nations, the World Bank, or scientific meetings addressing the implementation of strategies for preserving the environment. These meetings signal to young people especially that people everywhere are taking the environment seriously. They also reflect an important sign of the times we live in: the increasing trend towards globalisation.

Globalisation refers to the interdependence of nations around the world. No one country can produce all the goods and services it needs to sustain its people and thus no one nation can afford to be insular in any policies affecting its people. We need one another, we must trade and barter with one another, and to do this, we must understand the nature of each other's resources, how they are allocated, and how they will be replenished. The environment is the most important resource in the world, and therefore all people interested in preserving the future must become aware of how environmental issues in one place affect all others. The most essential consideration in globalisation must be the environment, yet, on the agenda of world leaders, it is often subjugated to economic concerns. For example, questions must be posed as to who conserves the health of those who labour for multinational corporations, and who is responsible for ecologically sound decisions over waterways that may run through more than one country.

Some of the most important environmental discussions of our time took place in the last decade of the twentieth century. The 1990s saw the first large summit on the environment, the Rio Summit of 1992. This meeting of nations was to be a watershed for the environment. People around the world believed that such a visible discussion of environmental preservation would signal a commitment to action, yet in 1997 a new summit had to be convened to further warn all nations of the world about the lack of progress in devising a plan for sustainability. The Kyoto Protocol emerged from this meeting and was to be a blueprint for decreasing automobile emissions into the atmosphere and setting standards on acceptable methods of waste disposal. However, even today, countries have failed to ratify the protocol. It appears that the environment has come second to the economy in developed countries such as the United States, Canada, Japan and Australia. Yet these are the countries that disgorge most of the carbon emissions into the atmosphere.

The mass media is keeping the environment on the global agenda and having some effect at the local level, primarily in the industrialised nations, particularly in emphasising the environmental effects of various patterns of consumption and waste disposal. The internet has become an invaluable medium for these types of messages—there are now numerous websites devoted to articulating principles of sustainable health and development. A well-prepared article linking health and environmental issues can often provide the impetus for public debate, especially when the author is a credible source and where people are empowered to respond through such mechanisms as letters or chat rooms. One such article from the Better World website advises that:

Becoming sustainable individually and collectively requires all of us to commit our lives to building communities of fully empowered, com-passionate, non-violent, honest, loving human beings who live joyfully and beautifully within the limits of their physical environment. (Leland 1996, p 2)

This is the broader picture of sustainable health.

Sustainability

Lowe (1994) describes the sustainable community as one that has at its dis-posal an amount of land that supplies all the resources it consumes, and the ability to absorb all the waste it produces. Likewise, sustainability in commu-nity health can be taken to mean that the community has a type of health–illness carrying capacity—that is, all the health resources it needs and the capacity to respond to all the illness it produces. The United Nations (UNFPA 2001) is concerned that the world is exceeding its carrying capacity, primarily due to overpopulation in the developing countries. Some countries, primarily the industrialised nations, consume significantly more than their sus-tainable share of the global environment, and if this continues, the earth's ecosystems will be doomed to fail in a relatively short time. Clearly, sustaining the environment in one country is fundamental to the health of all people.

Another threat to sustainability in health is the degradation of our natural resources. It is ironic that people are living longer these days because of eco-nomic and technological developments, yet it is these very developments that have exploited, and thus degraded, the environment so necessary to their sur-vival (Evans, Barer & Marmor 1994). Perhaps the most significant example of this is the gradual decline in water quality and availability in developing nations. In many countries, the need for fresh water is both crucial and criti-cal. Water scarcity leads to food scarcity, and some predict that this will lead to even more wars and conflicts than we are experiencing at present. The problem for the future is that, as competition for land, water, food, trees and minerals continues to destroy large chunks of our civilisation, people will be displaced from their environments and become 'eco-refugees' (Hancock & Davies 1997; Nelder 1996).

In the most overpopulated countries, over-reliance on pesticides and herbicides, wasteful or improper irrigation, unsustainable growing practices and overproduction have diminished topsoil and the productive capacity of the land. Global warming has the capacity to produce massive floods, the withdrawal of forests and the death of species or entire ecosystems, leading to massive extinctions regardless of conservation efforts (McMichael, Smith & Corvalan 2000). We may lose 20 per cent of all the species on the planet within the next twenty to forty years, most from the tropical rainforests, yet we continue to burn fossil fuels and spill carbon dioxide into the air at unprecedented levels (Nelder 1996). The potential health effects of these practices are of enormous significance, and some will only be revealed in generations to come.

Global environmental changes have now been linked unequivocally to physical ailments. At present there appears to be an epidemic of acute respiratory disease responsible for up to four million deaths per year in children under age five. Air pollution, both indoor and outdoor, appears to play a central role in this epidemic, as researchers have found a direct link between hospital admissions for respiratory and cardiac diseases and increases in air pollution, particularly acid aerosols and ozone (Bascom et al 1996; McMichael et al 2000).

Early environmental studies identified a number of workplace hazards linked to various forms of chemical pollution, including silicosis in miners, scrotal cancers in chimney sweeps and pulmonary disease in those who worked with asbestos. These reactions occur because certain environmental agents may be acting as 'endocrine disruptors', affecting human endocrine systems in ways that lead to possible mental and reproductive abnormalities (Lee & Paxman 1997). Environmental changes have also caused numerous sociocultural changes, with land and water shortages causing forced migration, urbanisation and poverty, with consequent ill effects on health (McMichael et al 2000). The most important way we can address environmental issues is to ensure that sustainable health considerations are woven into all decisions for community development, and this is evident in the way we plan and implement health promotion activities (WHO 1992a).

What is
health promotion?

The term *health promotion* refers to the process of enabling people to increase control over and improve their health (WHO, Health and Welfare Canada 1986). Health promotion is part of the role of many health professionals, and encompasses a wide range of activities, from local initiatives to interacting with the global community. At the local level, strategies may involve lobbying the government for better roads or more parklands, or helping to institute a recycling scheme. At the global level, health promotion may involve becoming personally aware of the problems of other countries, and making sure their health issues are publicised. For example, toxic waste disposal is a global problem that should be a part of everyone's awareness (Chukwuma 1996).

Similarly, relaxed attitudes and non-stringent environmental controls have allowed multinational corporations to relocate polluting industries to non-industrialised countries, where hazardous trace elements are disposed of in the soil. These threats to the health and sustainability of the planet should also be of grave concern to health professionals (McMichael & Hales 1997).

In our own communities, we have a responsibility to do what we can to ensure that we, our communities and our policy makers understand the politics of sustainable health and to see the impact of local decisions on global health (McMichael 2000). Globalisation has brought with it many changes in contemporary life. Time and space have collapsed (Tesoriero 2001). Events such as nuclear accidents rebound across generations, including those not yet born. War and threats of war in one part of the world affect the economy of communities tens of thousands of kilometres away in ways ranging from changes in the price of petrol (Tesoriero 2001) to issues concerning safety and security, such as those posed by the 11 September 2001 acts of terrorism.

Promoting health in any setting, whether a city, village, school or organisation, is based on the premise that health development potential can be fostered through a series of defined strategies (Kickbusch 1997). The role of the health professional in promoting community health is to unravel available information on the factors involved in health, together with local knowledge and understanding of the community's health goals, and work in partnership with community members to achieve health. This also involves helping the community to identify, and thus overcome, any barriers or impediments to sustaining health and preventing illness. Health promotion activities may be individual or social—for example, working with young people to help them clarify values and goals for the future. They may be aimed at different population subgroups, such as creating day care centres for the elderly to prevent them from being socially isolated, or working with new parents to ensure they have the informal support systems they need. What all these activities have in common is commitment to being a *change agent*, or an *advocate* for health, 'initiating constructive social change' (Whitehead 2001, p 830). In some cases, the major focus of health promotion activities will be on facilitating structures and partnerships for change, while in others, the focus may be on health education. Most health promotion activities have at least some educational components, which leads to the need to understand the factors involved in planning and implementing appropriate educational strategies.

Health
education

According to Green and Kreuter (1991) *health education* refers to any planned educational intervention that is aimed at the voluntary actions people can take to look after their health or the health of others. There are several elements in this definition that are crucial to success. One is *planning*. Successful health education programs are carefully planned with respect to the audience, timing, setting, credibility of the health educator, and method of evaluation.

Without such planning, the information may fail to educate for several reasons. First, there may be less than optimal delivery of the educational material. Second, if the presentation does not occur when the audience is receptive to the message or when the environment is conducive to learning, the information may fall on 'deaf ears'. Third, if the information is not seen as coming from a reliable source it may be ignored. Finally, if there is no evaluation of the program or presentation, the health educator will have no way of knowing whether his or her efforts have been effective, or whether change may have merely occurred by chance. So the next time, a whole new approach will have to be devised rather than having the benefit of feedback on what did or did not work previously.

Another aspect of the definition of health education that is important to consider is that it must be *educational*. Many of today's health education presentations represent a combination of educational content and entertainment value. This 'mix' is sometimes called 'infotainment' and is based on the notion that people learn best when they are enjoying themselves. Such an approach to disseminating health information may fall within the realm of social marketing, an approach wherein the health educator identifies the determinants of behaviours for various market segments (such as adolescents), and targets the marketing strategies accordingly. The infotainment approach is visible on the internet, where health messages and health information are provided on websites designed to be people-friendly, or market-sector-friendly. This mode of transmission will likely be the most significant vehicle for encouraging health literacy in the twenty-first century, whether the messages are aimed at helping people stay well, detect illness or disease, or at helping those living with illness to make any necessary lifestyle modifications (Ratzan 2001).

The final important element within the definition of health education is that it is designed to bring about *voluntary* change. The implication of this for the health education planner is that the health education program or presentation will be designed to *influence*, rather than *coerce*, for change. People themselves will decide whether or not to make a change. The role of the health educator is to present a basis for *informed choice* by providing the options, choices and access to resources that will help people choose healthy pathways to living. In order for those choices to be sustainable, people in the community must feel a sense of investment, or ownership, in the changes and their effectiveness in meeting the long-term health goals of the community.

Community health promotion: the Ottawa Charter for Health Promotion

Promoting the health of a community extends individual health education and health promotion to a broader scope of activities. In most countries this level of health promotion is guided by the Ottawa Charter for Health Promotion (WHO-Health and Welfare Canada 1986).

In 1986, eight years after the Declaration of Alma Ata, the members of 38 nations met in Ottawa, Canada, to evaluate progress in achieving health for all by the year 2000. From this meeting, the Ottawa Charter for Health Promotion was developed as a blueprint for future community health promotion initiatives. The Charter emphasised the importance of promoting health at a global level and identified the fundamental conditions and resources for community health. These include peace, shelter, education, food, income, a stable ecosystem, sustainable resources, social justice and equity (WHO-Health and Welfare Canada 1986). The Charter identified five major strategies for health promotion that circumscribed the public health activities of disease control and resource allocation, yet adopted the primary health care approach of grass roots community development and an ecological view of health. The five strategies are as follows:

1 *Build healthy public policy*   This strategy is aimed at encouraging all those involved in health care to ensure that health is incorporated into all public policy decisions. This represents a change from the traditional approach, where decisions in the health sector were relatively confined to the health industry. The Charter suggested intersectoral collaboration, where there is mutual recognition that the policies of other sectors, such as education, housing, industry, social welfare and environmental planning, also affect, and are affected by, those that guide the health of our communities.

2 *Create supportive environments*   This strategy embodies the socioecological approach to health. The Charter encouraged all people to recognise the importance of conserving and capitalising on those resources that enable people to maintain health, whether they be physical or social resources.

3 *Strengthen community action*   The Charter identified information and learning opportunities as the focus for empowering communities to make informed choices for better health. This type of community action exemplifies the community development approach.

4 *Develop personal skills*   This strategy guides communities to provide adequate and appropriate education and opportunities for skills development so that people can influence their communities to make local decisions for effective use of resources in order to attain health. Today this is called health literacy.

5 *Reorient health services*   Those involved in decisions affecting community health must operate from a base of evidence on what works best to foster the health of people. Included in this strategy is the need for research and the dissemination of knowledge from the multiple perspectives of those concerned with social, political, economic and physical resources as well as health.

In 1997, the strategies of the Ottawa Charter were endorsed in the Jakarta Declaration on Health Promotion into the 21st Century (WHO 1997). The Jakarta Declaration, which emerged from the 4th International Conference on Health Promotion, directs health promotion toward the social, economic and environmental conditions that either constrain or facilitate health by focusing on social responsibility for health, re-framing health as an investment in the future, establishing partnerships for health, and empowering the community (WHO 1997).

FIGURE 1.2 *The Ottawa Charter for Health Promotion (WHO-CPHA 1986. Reproduced with permission.)*

Implications for
community health promotion

Effective health promotion requires access to information and some unique skills. To become knowledgeable in all health matters or to keep up to date on the latest research results would take nothing short of an encyclopaedic mind. However, the internet has now made it possible to access current information on a wide range of health-related topics almost instantaneously. This has significantly enhanced the ability of health professionals to assist communities, but it has also created a wide disparity between people with internet access and those without it. Health professionals must be aware of this type of inequity and ensure that information is provided from a range of sources. Appropriate use of technology means that the relevant technologies are used to support people in achieving health in ways that eliminate inequities.

Besides information, the most important element in health promotion is a broad understanding of human development and behaviour, and the ability to communicate well. These three characteristics are fundamental to the role of a health advocate. To work with a community requires a sensitive approach to different people's needs at different stages of their development. For example, the community resources for dealing with asthma may be somewhat similar to encourage both young and elderly asthmatics to cope with their conditions, but the strategic organisation of those resources, and the approach to health education for each group, will differ considerably. Similarly, promoting sexual health in small rural areas or within small enclaves of certain ethnic groups may require a vastly different approach from that used to reach the typical urban teenager. The most important issue is to start where the people are, allowing the community to become empowered by having a voice in all decisions that affect the health and well-being of its people.

Enabling and facilitating the development of community health also requires a commitment to the notion of health as a socioecological construct. As mentioned at the beginning of this chapter, we are primarily social creatures who live in communal environments. We energise and are energised by those environments, which are constructed on foundations layered by historical, personal and situational events. Within this framework, health is not given to people, but generated by them. Our role is therefore one of mediating, enabling and facilitating the processes, people and systems that can be mobilised to achieve health goals.

The promotion of health involves getting to know the will of the people and the resources unique to the community, and how these are linked with the wider context, even to the extent of the global community. The health promoter must form multiple partnerships for change, engaging with the immediate community, understanding and respecting local, immediate dynamics and needs, within a framework of sustainability. It is an approach that requires resourcefulness, information exchange, receptivity to new ideas and strategies, a tolerance for difference, a willingness to change and a common goal of community development. Within this framework, health can be generated and cultivated from within, rather than without, from bottom up rather than top down, as the community develops the will and the capacity for relevant and appropriate change.

---

case study...

Lusaka SOS Children's Village

In 1960, the Austrian group SOS-Kinderdorf International began a worldwide venture to establish children's villages, embodying the idea that 'it takes a village to raise a child'. To date, the villages have been developed in 131 countries. Since 1999, the SOS children's villages have succeeded in Zambia, a country where, like many other African countries, the need to care for orphaned children is acute. Zambia has been forced to deal with the reality that, since the advent of the HIV/AIDS epidemic, fewer adult parents are surviving long enough to raise their children. In this country of ten million people, one million Zambian children have already been orphaned, and the number is growing. In African societies the family is pre-eminent, and it is typical to live in a home where extended family members come and go and are always made welcome, however long they choose to reside in the family home. With so many young people of child-bearing age lost to AIDS, the African family is changing. Where once there were grandparents available to care for young children while their parents worked, surviving grandparents are now the ones looking for paid work outside the home. Many of the young men are dying or unemployed.

Life expectancy in Zambia has fallen from 56 to 37 years. Factories and merchants on the trade routes where their products were once sold have closed, due to both the recession in global markets and the unavailability of young men to support manufacturing. Although Zambia has a comprehensive AIDS prevention campaign, which has been partly responsible for slowing the rate of infection, AIDS has spread to young women at startling rates. The fact remains that many babies are born with AIDS, and many more are orphaned at a very young age. Zambia has been faced with the dilemma of accommodating these young people at a time when there is no one at home to care for them.

One solution has been found in the SOS Children's Village, where 175 children live in safe, loving families, within a permanent, home-like environment. Driving 6.5 km from Lusaka, the capital, the village can be seen from the Great North Road. It is a pretty village set in a beautifully tended twelve-hectare block with fifteen family houses, a house for visitors and staff, a multipurpose building for village activities, a kindergarten and a school. Each family consists of five or more children aged ten and under who grow up as sisters and brothers. If siblings are orphaned, the rules are relaxed to allow older children to remain with their younger brother(s) or sister(s). Every child is given a mother, as someone to turn to at all times. Mothers are recruited from the local community, most of them from Lusaka. The Village administrators ensure that each has the appropriate cultural background and is given training to allow them to meet the demands of their work. Educationalists and other resource people are employed by the village to assist them.

The overriding goal of the Village, as described by its founder, Hermann Gmeiner, is to give children a mother, brothers and sisters, a house and a village. An educationalist, Gmeiner established the Hermann Gmeiner Academy in Innsbruck, which supports the SOS Children's Villages that currently care for 300 000 children throughout the world. The focal point of his academy, and the SOS Villages, is to secure and develop quality educational standards, to train and follow up the skills of village mothers, to guide and care for adolescents from the villages so that they can grow to become independent and self-sufficient adults, and to provide comprehensive training courses for village staff.

For Zambia, the SOS Children's Village has been a remarkable community development. Health professionals throughout the country are confronted with the ongoing challenges of meeting the needs of a dwindling population. Medical doctors, nurses, social workers and other allied health professionals suffer enormously from the stress of extraordinary efforts to maintain the health of surviving family members when their loved ones are suffering from AIDS, malaria and cholera. Yet it is part of the nature of African people to be optimistic, and the locals speak with pride about the Children's Village. The Zambian people are cheerful, hopeful, skilful and committed. They understand better than any of us fortunate enough to live in a developed country, how building local capacity to nurture and care for the young can be empowering for the entire community. The Children's Village is providing accommodation, employment, education, health care and health literacy, life skills and community competence to deal with one of the most tragic situations a community must confront. At present, they rely on benefactors from SOS Kinderdorf International, but in future, building this type of capacity from within the community will have an enduring effect on all the next generations (SOS Children's Villages Zambia 2002).

thinking critically

Community health

1   What are the three most important resources for health that are evident in your community? In what way is each of these resources dependent on other factors in the environment?

2   To what extent is your community's environment sustainable?

3   Identify a group in your community who share a common vulnerability to a health issue.

4   How would you address this vulnerability, using the Ottawa Charter as a guide?

5   List two approaches to developing community competence.

6   Analyse your community in relation to the three levels of health literacy.

7   Identify two major threats to the global community's health. Consider how Nutbeam's (2000) 'critical' level of health literacy can be used as a guide to overcoming these threats to health.

8   Explain the relationship between health literacy, community empowerment and community development.

REFERENCES

Akukwe, C. (2000). Maternal and child health services in the twenty-first century: critical issues, challenges, and opportunities. *Health Care for Women International*, 21: 641–53.

Bandura, A. (1977). Self-efficacy: toward a unifying theory of behavioral change. *Psychological Review*, 84: 191–215.

Barnes, D., Eribes, C., Juarbe, T., Nelson, M., Proctor, S., Sawyer, L., Shaul, M. & Meleis, A. (1995). Primary health care and primary care: a confusion of philosophies. *Nursing Outlook*, 43(7): 7–16.

Bascom, R. et al (1996). Health effects of outdoor air pollution. *American Journal of Respiratory and Critical Care Medicine*, 153(3): 50.

Bowen, S., Harris, E. & Hyde, J. (2001). Capacity building: just rhetoric, or a way forward in addressing health inequality? *Health Promotion Journal of Australia*, 11(1): 56–60.

Chamberlain, M. & Beckingham, A. (1987), Primary health care in Canada: in praise of the nurse? *International Nursing Review*, 34(6): 158–60.

Christiani, D. (1993). Urban and transboundary air pollution: human health consequences. In: E. Chivian (ed), *Critical Condition*. Cambridge MA: MIT Press.

Chukwuma, C. (1996). Perspectives for a sustainable society. *Environmental Management & Health*, 7(5): 5–20.

Courtney, R. (1995). Community partnership primary care: A new paradigm for primary care. *Public Health Nursing*, 12(6): 366–73.

Cox, E. (1995). Changing patterns of work and living. *Proceedings of the Third National Women's Health Conference*, pp 274–6.

Davies, J. & Kelly, M. (1993). *Healthy Cities: Research and Practice*. London: Routledge.

Dunn, H. (1959). High-level wellness for man and society. *American Journal of Public Health*, 49: 789.

—— (1961). What high-level wellness means. *Health Values*, 1: 9.

Evans, R., Barer, M. & Marmor, T. (1994). *Why are Some People Healthy and Others Not?* New York: A. deGruyter.

Fawcett, S., Paine-Andrews, A., Francisco, V., Schultz, J., Richter, K. et al (1995). Using empowerment theory in collaborative partnerships for community health and development. *American Journal of Community Psychology*, 23(5): 677–98.

Goeppinger, J., Lassiter, P. & Wilcox, B. (1982). Community health is community competence. *Nursing Outlook*, 30: 464–7.

Green, L. & Kreuter, M. (1991). *Health Promotion Planning: An Educational and Environmental Approach.* Mountain View, California: Mayfield.

Hancock, T. & Davies, K. (1997). *An Overview of the Health Implications of Global Environmental Change: A Canadian Perspective.* Ottawa: Canadian Global Change Program, Royal Society of Canada.

Hardy, J. & Miller, T. (2000). Growing up healthy, wealthy, and wise. *Contemporary Pediatrics,* 17(2): 63–70.

Hertzman, C. (2001). Health and human society. *American Scientist,* 89(6): 538–44.

Holzemer, W. (1992). Linking primary health care and self-care through case management. *International Nursing Review,* 39(3): 83–9.

Hudson-Rodd, N. (1994). Public health: people participating in the creation of healthy places. *Public Health Nursing,* 11(2): 119–26.

Ife, J. (1995). *Community Development: Creating Community Alternatives—Vision, Analysis and Practice.* Melbourne: Longman.

Kahssay, H. & Oakley, P. (1999). Community involvement in health development: a review of the concept and practice. Geneva: WHO.

Kickbusch, I. (1997). Health promoting environments: The next step. *Australian and New Zealand Journal of Public Health,* 21(4): 431–4.

Labonte, R. (1994). Health promotion and empowerment: reflections on professional practice. *Health Education Quarterly,* 21(2): 253–68.

—— (1997). Community and public health: an international perspective. *Health Visitor,* 70(2): 64–8.

Lacroix, D. (1996). Awakening an ecological self in nursing. In: D. Lacroix (ed), *The Ecological Self in Australian Nursing.* Canberra: Royal College of Nursing, Australia, pp 1–26.

Lee, P. & Paxman, D. (1997). Reinventing public health. *Annual Review of Public Health,* 18: 1–35.

Leland, B. (1996). The heart of sustainability. Editorial, *Better World Zine:* 4(Jun/Jul): 1–4.

Lowe, I. (1994). 'Foreward: priorities for a sustainable future'. In: C. Chu & R. Simpson (eds), *Ecological Public Health: From Vision To Practice.* Canberra: ANZPHA, pp vii–viii.

McMichael, A. (1993). Public health in Australia: a personal reflection. *Australian Journal of Public Health,* 17(4): 295–6.

—— (2000). The urban environment and health in a world of increasing globalization: issues for developing countries. *Bulletin of the World Health Organization,* 78(9): 1117–24.

McMichael, A. & Hales, S. (1997). Global health promotion: looking back to the future. *Australian and New Zealand Journal of Public Health,* 21(4): 425–8.

McMichael, A., Smith, K. & Corvalan, C. (2000). The sustainability transition: a new challenge. *Bulletin of the World Health Organization,* 78(9): 1067–95.

McMurray, A. (1993). *Community Health Nursing: Primary Health Care in Practice,* 2nd edn. Melbourne: Churchill-Livingstone.

Najman, J. (1993). Health and poverty: past, present and prospects for the future. *Social Science and Medicine,* 36(2): 157–66.

Nelder, C. (1996). Envisioning a sustainable future. *Better World Zine:* 6(Oct/Nov): 1–15.

Nutbeam, D. (2000). Health literacy as a public health goal: a challenge for contemporary health education and communication strategies into the 21st century. *Health Promotion International,* 15(3): 259–67.

Nutbeam, D. & Kickbusch, I. (2000). Advancing health literacy: a global challenge for the 21st century. *Health Promotion International,* 15(3): 183–4.

Preece, J. (2000). *Online Communities: Designing Usability, Supporting Sociability.* Chichester: Wiley & Sons.

Ratzan, S. (2001). Health literacy: communication for the public good. *Health Promotion International,* 16(2): 207–14.

Rissel, C. (1994). Empowerment: the holy grail of health promotion. *Health Promotion International,* 9(1): 39–47.

SOS Children's Villages ZAMBIA (2002). Retrieved 10 January 2002, http://www.lecongo.com/zintro.htm.

Tesoriero, F. (2001). Partnerships in health promotion and the place of trust and equality as obstacles to promoting health. *Health Promotion Journal of Australia,* 11(1): 48–55.

United Nations Family Planning Association (UNFPA) (2000). The state of world population, 2000. New York: UN.

Whitehead, D. (2001). Health education, behavioural change and social psychology: nursing's contribution to health promotion? *Journal of Advanced Nursing,* 34(6): 822–32.

World Health Organization (WHO) (1974). Basic documents, 36th edn. Geneva: WHO.

—— (1992a). Health and the environment: a global challenge. *Bulletin of the World Health Organization,* 70(4): 409–13.

—— (1992b). Our Planet, Our Health: Report of the WHO Commission on Health and Environment. Geneva: WHO.

—— (1997). The Jakarta Declaration on Health Promotion into the 21st Century. Geneva: WHO.

World Health Organization-Health and Welfare Canada-CPHA (1986). Ottawa Charter for Health Promotion. *Canadian Journal of Public Health,* 77(12): 425–30.

World Health Organization UNICEF (1978) Primary Health Care. Geneva: WHO.

CHAPTER 2

Primary health care:
enabling health and wellness

introduction As mentioned in Chapter 1, primary health care is a framework for community health that fosters community competence to identify and meet health needs. The role of the health professional is one of advocacy, where the major focus is on providing whatever assistance is required to enable the community to build health capacity. Promoting primary health care therefore involves helping individuals and families achieve and maintain the skills, knowledge and experience to create and sustain the community, to develop sustainable resources that will support healthy lifestyles. This is accomplished through partnerships aimed at achieving the goals of the Ottawa Charter for Health Promotion: building healthy public policy, creating supportive environments, strengthening community action, developing personal skills, and reorienting health services towards the needs of the community (WHO Health and Welfare Canada-CPHA 1986).

Primary health care principles formed the basis for the Ottawa Charter for Health Promotion and, subsequently, the Jakarta Declaration for Health Promotion (WHO 1997). The Jakarta Declaration reiterated the need for a socioecological model of health, and emphasised that health should be considered an investment for the future. Both declarations hold common principles, which urge a social justice approach to health promotion, placing human rights and individual and community choice at the heart of healthy communities. Because the principles of primary health care are not uniformly understood, this chapter provides an explanation of these and other related terms. This is aimed at encouraging a common framework and common understandings in advocating for community health. The way health is determined by social factors is also explored, particularly in light of our increasingly urbanised world. The chapter culminates in a discussion of the Healthy Cities movement, which developed in response to the particular needs of urban communities.

objectives   **By the end of this chapter you will be able to:**

1   Explain the terms 'primary health care', 'primary care' and 'primary, sec-
    ondary and tertiary prevention'

2   Define the principles of primary health care

3   Explain the links between social justice and primary health care

4   Outline the characteristics of urban environments that affect the health
    of city dwellers

5   Discuss the application of primary health care principles to the strate-
    gies of the Ottawa Charter for Health Promotion

6   Devise a strategic plan to address the health of a given community
    using the Ottawa Charter as a guide.

Distinction between primary care
and primary health care

After more than two decades since Alma Ata, primary health care remains the
internationally accepted way of structuring community health promotion. The
main advantage of using primary health care as a framework lies in working
within a set of globally recognised principles and explicitly defined strategies,
such as the Ottawa Charter for Health Promotion. This adds consistency
across different programs and between different people developing similar programs. However, in some cases, the terms *primary health care* and *primary
care* are used interchangeably, and this occasionally causes confusion.

Primary care

When people require health care because of injury or illness, the *first* line of
care is *primary*. But primary care is more than just the initial decision as to

what must be done. It extends to the primary management of a person's condition. Primary care may involve only one intervention, or treatment over an extended period of time, but it is still primary, in that it is aimed at helping people with whatever problem required care in the first place. Physicians, nurses, dentists, physiotherapists and a range of other health professionals provide primary care in that, depending on the circumstances, they may be responsible for managing a health problem.

So, for example, if an athlete is injured on the sports field, the trainer will often provide *first aid* and then refer the athlete to a physician who will assume the role of primary care provider. Similarly, a nurse in a hospital emergency department or in a community clinic may provide initial treatment for an emergency, and then either refer the person to the local medical practitioner to manage the condition, or manage it her- or himself, depending on the situation. In the latter case, the nurse would be acting as a primary care provider, as often happens in remote locations where there is no medical practitioner.

Another situation where someone other than a medical practitioner acts as primary care provider is in the workplace. Many manufacturing and mining companies, for example, employ health professionals to undertake the management of occupational health and safety. For some workplace-based problems, the occupational health nurse or health and safety officer may be the most appropriate and available person to provide primary care.

Primary health care

Primary health care may include primary (initial) care to address a problem, and it may encompass a broad spectrum of activities to encourage general health and well-being. The goal of primary health care is to build community capacity to achieve sustainable health and wellness. This includes not only identification of the things that will make people healthy, but strategies for the prevention of illness, protection from harm, and those that help people adjust to or recover from illness or disability.

Primary, secondary
and tertiary prevention

The terms *primary prevention, secondary prevention* and *tertiary prevention* are commonly used to distinguish between the general health promotion approach described in the previous chapter, and preventative or rehabilitative actions. For community members, this translates into staying healthy (primary prevention), getting better or preventing further problems (secondary prevention) and living with disease or disability (tertiary prevention) (Ratzan 2001). From the health professional's perspective, at the community level, primary prevention activities could involve posters or television ads portraying the benefit to individuals of eating vegetables, or regular exercise to help them stay healthy. Or primary prevention may be offering encouragement for community residents to participate in the decisions of the local council, especially concerning community development plans. Secondary prevention includes such preventative activities as screening for skin cancer or conducting mammography clinics, or establishing drop-in centres for adolescents or isolated older people. Tertiary prevention typically involves providing assistance or information on coping with a potentially disabling condition. This could involve the establishment of walking programs for those who have had a cardiac incident, or support groups for family members coping with a loss. Whether the aim of the program is to promote health in general, address a specific health need, or minimise a particular risk, the actions of the health professional can be guided by the philosophical principles of primary health care.

Primary
health care principles

The way primary health care has been interpreted from the Declaration of Alma Ata has led to a number of primary health care principles. Halfdan Mahler, the former Director-General of WHO, summarised eight principles of primary health care as follows.

Primary health care should:

1 fit the life patterns of the community, meeting needs and demands
2 be part of the national health system, which should have responsibility for continuous technical and logistics support and referral
3 be fully integrated with other aspects of community development
4 assure population participation
5 place maximum reliance on community resources within stringent cost limitations present in each country
6 use an integrated and balanced approach of preventive, promotive, curative and rehabilitative services for the individual, family and community
7 choose health workers capable of intimate dialogue with the community and ensure that they have the skills to respond to priority needs of the community
8 assure the training and functioning of a health team in the specific tasks to solve community health problems and not perpetuate 'professional clubs' that subjugate the well-being of the individual to club rules (Mahler 1977, p 25).

Over the subsequent three decades, the principles of primary health care were condensed into as few as three principles (equity, intersectoral action and public participation) (WHO 2000). However, most interpretations of the Declaration of Alma Ata incorporate the following five principles:

1 accessibility
2 appropriate technology
3 increased emphasis on health promotion

4 intersectoral collaboration
5 public participation.

These are interconnected, but we will examine them separately here to underline the importance of each principle to the overall philosophy of primary health care.

Accessibility

Health for all people means equal access to opportunities for all people, whether they differ by geography, race, age, gender, language or functional capacity. The major objective of providing equity of access is, of course, allowing all people a fair opportunity to attain their full health potential (Whitehead 1995). This means that a major goal for health must be to eliminate disadvantage, whether it is related to social, economic or environmental factors. Conditions that create social disadvantage include such things as unemployment, lack of information pertinent to good health, or cultural or language difficulties that prevent an individual from accessing information or services required for health or to treat illness. Environmental factors can include geographical distance from services, for example, some of which may be directly related to health, or others that could provide education or training to support health. A broad perspective of environmental factors directs us to try to eliminate inequality of access to any supportive mechanisms for sustaining our environment. This could include the physical environment, or the cultural or social environment.

Because sustainability is as important as access to support systems, it is relevant to consider future as well as current needs. This means that any present measures taken to improve our environments must not compromise the ability of future generations to meet their needs (Lowe 1994). Within a socioecological framework, the notion of equitable access therefore includes consideration of the community in terms of future inhabitants. This, again, is relevant to globalisation.

Access, equity and globalisation

The world we live in today is uncertain, risky, inequitable, sometimes alienating, and most definitely influenced by globalisation (Tesoriero 2001). Despite greater wealth, income inequalities within and between nations are growing (Kawachi & Kennedy 1999; Keating & Hertzman 1999; Labonte 2001; Raphael 2001). The research evidence demonstrates conclusively that the greater the gap between the incomes of the rich and poor, the worse the health status of citizens (Kawachi & Kennedy 1999; Keating & Hertzman 1999). But this is not as simple a proposition as it first seems. Recent research indicates that it is not so much the creation of wealth as its equitable distribution that affects health (Keating & Hertzman 1999), and even this association is tenuous and complex. Studies of the linkages between financial resources and health status indicators in a number of communities show that health may be more clearly an outcome of education rather than income. Ratzan (2001) cites the comparison between the United States, where there is an average annual income of over

$20 000 but inequities in access to education, and a life expectancy of 77 years, and Costa Rica, the most educationally literate society in the Western world, where the average annual income is $2000 and life expectancy is almost comparable (only one year lower) to that in the United States. The point being made is that the distribution of wealth must be seen in conjunction with other opportunities this creates—namely, access to education and skills development.

Other societal factors, such as wars and conflicts, have also had a profound effect on the global community. The number of economic and political refugees has escalated beyond expectation in the first years of this decade, provoking fear, uncertainty and religious and ethnic-based disputes over resource allocation and social policy. The free trade agreements struck towards the end of the last century have also been less than successful in creating equal opportunities. In some cases they have accomplished the opposite, eroding opportunities for health, education and welfare, national economic development and environmental health policies (Labonte 2001). Many countries have retreated from the declarations of the past that were designed somewhat optimistically to preserve the future. For example, the Kyoto Protocol, devised for international cooperation in reducing harmful emissions into the atmosphere, has become so politicised that it has now been relegated to appeasing the automobile industry and those who favour individual rather than community rights, rather than preserving the environment. Similar tensions have been created around the world with respect to a number of global issues ranging from global warming to genetically modified food, to the use of reproductive technology.

The principle of accessibility requires us to include global issues in our community health promotion strategies to unravel the pathways to health for all of society. Global warming, overpopulation, the destruction of forests and the processing of industrial waste all affect the future disproportionately for those from the poorer levels of society to the top of the wealth hierarchy. Clearly, decisions for community health involve awareness of simultaneous assessment of the impact on other people and communities, future generations and the earth, our home.

The first requirement for primary health care is therefore to ensure refinement of our political and social consciousness—that is, deliberate consideration of the needs and agendas of *all* people. This is where the notion of *social justice* permeates all primary health care activities. Social justice, or equitable access for all, must supersede individual goals, so that the least advantaged people in a community receive care and service equal to that received by those who are advantaged by virtue of both tangible (finances) and intangible (knowledge) resources. A commitment to primary health care dictates that we remain aware of the health needs of our local community, and how they relate to the needs of others. It is also important to understand the capacity of both local and global resources to meet health needs across the spectrum of advantage and disadvantage. Only by approaching health planning in terms of the 'big picture' will we 'think global' and 'act local'.

The second element of accessibility requires that health care be available where people live and work (WHO-UNICEF 1978). One of the greatest barriers to access for rural dwellers is geographic location, particularly in the current climate of financial constraint. Historically, those who lived in rural and remote areas were included in public health service provision schemes that accommodated their needs for medical, dental and specialist care within an overall national, state or provincial budget. As health care costs have increased, the financing of health services has become more tightly controlled, and services that formerly served relatively few people have been rationed on the basis of their cost inefficiency. Consequently, many country people have witnessed the loss of existing services, or have failed to receive new services readily available to those living in urban centres.

Yet another barrier to access is a lack of education or information, in which case the question is, should the informed person who demands certain services from the health care system have an advantage over those ignorant of what is available? The internet poses a relatively new twist to this dilemma, as those who can afford internet access surely must have an advantage over those who are deprived by either finances or distance.

Many city dwellers also experience lack of access to services, but for different reasons. In some countries, labour regulations and fears over job security prevent people from accessing health services. This has a particularly negative effect on female workers who defer access to health care because of their fear of losing what is frequently the family's only means of financial support. In some cultures, where it is considered inappropriate for the male to assume household duties, these women experience even further compromises to their personal health as they spend long hours preparing meals and cleaning their homes prior to, and after, their paid work. In most cases, occupational health services are nonexistent in their place of employment and there is no out-of-hours community access to preventive programs such as cervical screening. As could be expected in this situation, rates of post-partum infections and other female problems have grown exponentially with socioeconomic factors that leave families either with no steady income or with migratory patterns of searching for work (UNFPA 2000; USOWH 2001). This lack of access to health services also occurs in industrialised countries, where many women especially, as the sole household wage earner, perform a 'double-shift', returning home from paid work to housework and child care responsibilities. These people have a particular need for health advocacy to ensure their access to services available after hours and at times when they can be absent from either the workplace or child care.

Appropriate technology

Another primary health care principle guides us to develop and use technology in the most appropriate way for the needs of the community. The issue of technology has been debated in many forums, and tends to polarise opinions, particularly in the ethical arena (Lee & Paxman 1997). We have the technology to keep very low birthweight infants alive, yet should we do so at the expense of others? Similarly, is it appropriate use of technology to sustain the life of the very oldest old? Is it appropriate to provide access to high tech medicine for very old or very young people if they have merely become part of clinical trials to test the devices? Is it fair to deny access to the type of health care provided in big cities to those who live at a distance? Should fertility treatment, for example, be allocated on the basis of gender or age equity, or on the basis of human desire for a child regardless of overpopulation problems? And the big questions looming on the horizon for this decade flow from dramatic developments in stem cell research. The question being debated in many corners of society, including the research, legal and political arenas, relates to whether medical scientists should be allowed to harvest organs or clone body parts to repair damaged bodies, or provide fertility treatments that would lead to greater selectivity or 'designer babies'.

From each new development, questions of social justice arise. Who will be the beneficiaries of technology? Who is in danger of being excluded? To what extent will community members be involved in decision-making related to technological innovations? What strategies will be included to ensure informed choices can be made? Are new developments achievable at a cost the community and the country can afford? What will be the opportunity costs involved; in other words, what will *not* be funded, if new technologies are developed?

These dilemmas are not new, as technological developments have had an impact on health for many years. For example, when the refrigerator was first invented it represented the single most important device preventing illness by guarding against contamination of foods. It was, however, accessible only to those who could afford it and no public health authority ever considered providing refrigerators for all people. Today, partly because of global communication and increased consumer sophistication, new technologies have become part of the public interest, and people everywhere tend to enter into debates over the ethics of resource allocation and their right to technological innovations (Shakespeare 1999). This type of involvement is healthy, in that it demonstrates not only social awareness, but growing community empowerment in decision-making.

Increased emphasis on health promotion

Promoting health involves enabling the conditions for healthy choices and ensuring that support systems are available to help people achieve the level of health to which they aspire, prevention of ill health or injury, and successful rehabilitation from illness. This places the emphasis in health care on community empowerment, with sufficient back-up from the health care system so that people do not feel abandoned in their quest for good health. As mentioned in Chapter 1, community empowerment can be equated with developing individual and community capacity (Kahssay & Oakley 1999). People become empowered when they believe in their ability to create change. Instead of being directed towards choices made by outsiders, empowered community change comes from within the community.

The role of the health professional in the change process is markedly different from the past, when at times people were coerced into changing their health behaviours on the basis that it was good for them. The fundamental flaw in this approach was the assumption that what was good for people could be described within standardised, generic prescriptions decided by experts who, despite being well versed in the latest medical literature, were field illiterate. Without knowledge of the 'field' or 'grass roots' it is impossible to incorporate cultural differences that provide wider and more relevant choices for people in achieving health and wellness.

To participate in securing health for people in an empowered community requires *cultural sensitivity*, one of the cornerstones of social justice. Cultural sensitivity is not simply tolerating differences between groups of people, but understanding the dynamics of another culture in a way that captures both the words and the music—that is, being able to assess elements within the behaviour patterns or social roles of a culture that make it special and that are, or can be, conducive to health. Some examples of cultural differences in health behaviours stand out clearly: for example, the way some ethnic groups use hot and cold foods to overcome various illnesses, and the reliance on kinship ties to support one another during rehabilitation. Others are subtle—for example, the way religious or spiritual beliefs contribute to mind–body–spiritual harmony or the wider 'world view' held by members of a particular cultural group (Brady 1995; Chatters 2000). Trudgen (2001) cites a life-threatening example of the importance of this type of cultural knowledge. He accompanied an Australian Indigenous man who had been suffering from a long-term kidney condition to see his medical practitioner. For thirteen years the man had been unaware of the serious side effects of his diet and tobacco smoking or how his illness was exacerbated by an excess intake of sugar and salt as well as the smoking. At no point during these years of medical treatment was he given a plausible explanation that fitted with his 'world view' of nature and the workings of his body, as to how any of these substances affect the circulatory system. Once he had a culturally sensitive explanation provided within his cultural framework or world view, his recovery was dramatic. He was able to re-frame the way he conceptualised his kidneys and his lifestyle, and immediately took steps to prevent what would surely have been lifelong dialysis treatment. This underlines the fact that various conceptions of health and healthful living can only be understood from within and alongside a community, which is where all health promotion interventions must begin.

Cultural sensitivity also plays a large role in helping people determine directions and strategies for change. For example, in some African countries, it is a cultural expectation for breastfeeding mothers to abstain from sexual relations. It is also customary, and a highly valued family tradition, that breastfeeding will continue for at least two years. To preserve the sanctity of the mother–child relationship there is also tolerance for the perceived need of males to satisfy their sexual needs outside the family during this time, and this is where the issue of culture becomes problematic. As we are now aware, the rate of HIV/AIDS infection in African countries (and elsewhere) is escalating and the transmission of the virus is clearly sexual. To further complicate the problem, many African males hold entrenched beliefs that prevent them from using protection during sexual intercourse. The dilemma is at once cultural, social and public health related: how does the community strike a balance between cultural sensitivity, community empowerment and saving lives? The answer lies in assisting the community to address issues of access (to information, in this case), equity, involving the rights of all members of the community including the unborn, and community empowerment to make and enact self-determined changes without overriding cultural norms. One of the ways this may be approached is by casting beyond the immediate problem to the wider environment, and enlisting the help of others in non-health sectors of society who may be able to work within the cultural and spiritual norms to facilitate a solution to the problem.

case study...

The Haida Gwaii Diabetes Project

The Haida Gwaii are members of two First Nations villages in the Queen Charlotte Islands, British Columbia, Canada. 'First Nations' is the term given to Indigenous or Aboriginal people, which signifies that they were the first, or original, inhabitants of Canada. Health researchers have known for many years that diabetes is a particularly prevalent problem among Aboriginal people worldwide, and that to be effective, prevention programs must be developed by members of the community in ways that are both culturally considerate and empowering. In response to this need, a group of researchers from the University of British Columbia devised a strategy for encouraging members of the villages to develop their own diabetes teaching and prevention program.

The researchers joined with local family physicians and Haida community health workers (CHR) to plan a research project on diabetes prevention that would be acceptable to the community. The community health workers acted as intermediaries between the researchers and the community, explaining the people's concerns about research that had been conducted in the past. Previously, researchers had been seen by the community to have 'parachuted' in, taking samples for research, then disappearing, with nothing returned to the local people. The residents felt strongly against the taking of blood, hair or other body substances, as these were

seen by the Haida people as subject to misuse and a violation of their cultural mores.

The CHRs also explained to the researchers the rich traditions of the Haida culture, including their approaches to healing and health maintenance, and commitment to sustaining health for the next generation. The CHRs then identified certain key leaders of the villages, provided assurances that no body substances would be taken, and ascertained their willingness to engage in discussion with the research team. After consulting with these key informants and attending traditional Haida feasts, the research team members were able to organise focus group discussions attended by many villagers to discuss the meaning of diabetes, how they felt about living with the illness, their ideas about causation and prevention, and their traditional approaches to healing.

During these interactions the researchers were able to answer questions, but more importantly, to convey the message that their role was one of partnership with the community; that they were there to help the community solve its own problems. The community then developed a framework for health promotion based on both traditional and acquired knowledge. Rather than simply 'parachuting' out, the non-resident team members formed a liaison with the community to act as external partners in any future endeavours (Herbert 1996).

Intersectoral collaboration

Intersectoral collaboration requires cooperation between different community sectors, including (but not limited to) those managing health, education, social services, housing, transportation, environmental planning and local government. Intersectoral collaboration involves a kind of fluid and flexible network of coalitions, where different alliances between sectors may respond to certain needs. In this case, they have a finite existence. Other alliances may be longer term, and still others may be part of a long-range plan that requires sequential activities. For example, if the Haida Gwaii community mentioned above decided to institute a campaign to examine family health issues while preserving the community's sense of cultural identity, an intersectoral group may begin planning for the changes by involving the spiritual elders first. After a series of conversations with these community leaders, a plan would be devised to educate adults and young people. Collaborative meetings would then include people responsible for workplace and school health, local and national political leaders and community health professionals, with roles and responsibilities apportioned according to the expertise of the various participants.

This type of collaboration is effective in most cases where a health issue may be putting community health in jeopardy. For example, in an urban community, where heart disease is prevalent, intersectoral collaboration could be used in developing a heart health program for males at risk of heart disease, and it might work something like this. For several months, the health department and various industries would work together to screen working males at risk. Then a government and employee group would liaise with community members to explore their preferences for developing exercise and nutrition programs or alternative plans to address the problem. Private enterprise may then enter into discussions between local government, fitness personnel and medical specialists to guide program implementation. Finally, the education department may be invited to work with the public media to promote whatever approach they decided to take.

Intersectoral collaboration also involves the provision of health information and programs to other sectors to help them see the value of adding health to their operations. Health professionals contribute to the education industry by integrating health issues into the curriculum. Health and safety personnel contribute to the environment and transportation industry by providing information on pollution hazards and road safety, and members of the recreation and fitness industries propound the merits of corporate health programs for private or public industry which, in turn, has a 'value added' effect of reducing absenteeism.

Intersectoral collaboration lies at the heart of community participation. It is a two-way process of planning for health goals with the participation of all aspects of the community and, in turn, adding value to the community by increasing health. It may include an 'all-in' approach, an 'all-at-once' approach or a series of small stages where smaller subgroups of people collaborate to achieve small gains that will contribute to larger solutions. For example, greening a neighbourhood can be done in a way that transcends organisational boundaries through liaison with community councils, housing authorities and such community groups as tenants' associations, gardening groups, parents' groups, and scouting or guiding associations.

At the global level, intersectoral collaboration involves various sectors collaborating to achieve a healthy society. This is an intensely political activity, in that state, provincial and national governments must be ready to allocate economic resources to health budgets and to respond to their local electorates. The essential elements for successful intersectoral collaboration at this level include national primary health care policies that support decentralised control, local goal-setting, service planning and provision, mutual accountability, responsibility, cooperation and respect (Barnes et al 1995).

As always, social justice concerns must supersede individual gain so that the least advantaged receive equitable and accessible health resources. At the global level this may require redeploying a portion of economic resources to aid developing countries or to absolve them of existing debt, even while there are unmet needs in domestic health. This is a contentious issue at a time of shrinking resources, but it is the ultimate expression of social justice, and in some cases a political necessity, as nations rely on one another's support in a range of areas.

Public participation

If we, as health professionals, are to encourage communities to become empowered participants in creating and sustaining health, it is important to understand human behaviour and some of the things that prevent people from, or encourage them in, taking responsibility for their own health goals. It helps to recognise that some people tend to seek out information about their health, while others prefer to leave health matters and various strategies for managing their health to professionals. Still others believe in fate—that relative states of health are predetermined and so there is little use in trying to change. This difference is illustrated in two Canadian studies. One used a primary health care approach to foster collaboration and empowerment in a nurse-managed centre in Comox, on Vancouver Island, where health-promotive, preventive, curative, rehabilitative and supportive services were identified and provided in collaboration with the community (Attridge et al, in Clarke & Mass 1998). Evaluation of the project revealed that community members were enthusiastic about taking a collaborative partnership role in their health. Most felt they had become more knowledgeable about their health, had improved physically and mentally, took action on their own, made better use of health care resources, communicated more confidently with health care providers and helped others through community action and group support.

The other study, conducted by one of the Ontario Health District Councils in preparation for instituting a participative community health approach, surveyed community members in a series of meetings prior to developing the health programs. The planning team found that, although the majority (72 per cent) of people were willing to play a role in overall decision-making, most shied away from specific programs, expressing the concern that they were ill-prepared for such a role (Abelson et al 1995). What this difference illustrates is the importance of working in partnership with the community long before programs are implemented, so that they can develop a sense of self-direction with the 'safety net' of access to professional help.

Individual preferences for decision-making must be respected. Information and options should be introduced slowly and sensitively, building community self-confidence in a way that will be readily understood. When resources are freed up to develop this approach in the time frame of community members, most people will choose to take responsibility for their health. This can sometimes be tricky, as different people's group allegiances may compete with various community health goals as defined by others. For example, a community may contain a mix of people who have different notions about nutrition. One group may want to establish a school canteen with fresh foods; another may want a cheaper, fast food option that will return revenue to the school to purchase exercise equipment, for example. To encourage both healthy eating patterns and exercise in the children who attend the school, competing agendas will need to be discussed, options considered, and information provided that will help the community make their decision.

In this and similar cases, the health professional can play an important advocacy role. This includes getting people together to explore their options, and adopting a role as a mediator and facilitator, ensuring that everyone has a say and that any required information is brought to the community to inform decisions. This has proved effective in many school-based programs, where the objective is to get young people to make healthy choices because they are informed, not coerced (St Leger 2001).

Community participation is more likely when there is equity in the relationship between the health professional and the community; that is, the health professional is clearly recognised as a partner, rather than the leader, in decision-making. The ultimate objective is to encourage empowerment, so that the community defines its priorities and identifies what is accessible, affordable and essential to achieve health goals (Kolbe, Kann & Brener 2001).

Community participation and empowerment rely on several considerations. People need to decide that they do indeed belong to the community, and this was one of the main conclusions of the Ontario study—that participation depends on how 'the community' is defined. The authors believe their results challenge the assumption that communities have a 'unanimous and perceptible interest in making decisions on health care and social services' (Abelson et al 1995, p 411). To enable community participation we need to work towards making community concerns and issues visible. Communities also need assistance in mapping out the way their concerns are communicated to others, including those with access to resources. They need to know who they can rely on for help with particular needs. Equally important, they need to be assured that different levels of participation are valued, so that different people may make a choice for participation that doesn't make unreasonable demands on their other responsibilities (Barnes et al 1995).

Health in the city:
the interplay of social determinants

Nowhere is the relationship between social and environmental factors and health more evident than in the urban community. In fact, urbanisation can be considered to have had the most 'decisive impact on public health in the second millennium' (Freudenberg 2000, p 473). The majority of the global population now live in cities or their surrounding metropolitan areas, and many are both poor and vulnerable to illness and injury (Freudenberg 2000). By 1980, 40 per cent of the world's population were urban citizens (Stephens 1996) and this number has continued to grow exponentially with the shrinking of employment opportunities and services in rural areas. Some of the more obvious health risks in cities include crowding, epidemics of virus infections and substance abuse, concentrations of pollutants, homelessness and greater risks of accidents, injuries and violence (Freudenberg 2000). However, industrialisation and urbanisation have also brought into focus such things as population ageing, patterns of immigration and migration, changes in the global economy and the increase in social support needs of isolated young families and the elderly. This is occurring at a time when many of the wealthier members of society have left cities for the suburbs, some because of a decline in manufacturing, which has left those remaining in the city relegated to either low-paying employment in the service sectors or no employment at all. One consequence of their leaving is that it has eroded the tax base of cities, revenues that in the past would have been used to support social services (Freudenberg 2000). As a result, those at the poorer end of society are left with few resources to change things and a level of need that outstretches urban capacity.

The urban environment contains many layers of health risk that are created by factors such as inequality in the distribution of risk, and inequities (injustices) in the distribution of control over how goods and risk exposures are created (Stephens 1996). Inequalities in health risk reflect both personal susceptibilities to illness and unequal exposure to risk. For example, research carried out over the past decades reveals a strong, persistent, hierarchical association between the health of people and their socioeconomic status. This has been explained as a type of social partitioning, called the gradient effect, where those of higher occupational status enjoy successively better health (Keating & Hertzman 1999; Hertzman 2001; Marmot 1993; Marmot et al 1987; Marmot & Shipley 1996; Wilkinson 1996). However, the gradient effect has been found to be more an indication of how a person's early childhood has prepared them to cope with their lives and their work, than their current lifestyle or occupational status (Hertzman 2001; Mustard 1996, 1999).

Urban health inequalities may also reflect the extent to which different groups of people have sufficient control over their lives to be able to avoid exposure to environmental risks and to treat illness when it occurs (Stephens 1996). For the poor, there is a double layer of inequity in that their health is jeopardised by the very things that benefit the wealthy. For example, the poor are less likely to own, drive or use cars, yet they are more likely to live on busy streets with considerable traffic and therefore be more exposed than those better off financially to local air and water pollution, proximity to waste disposal sites and the risk of accidents (Stephens 1996; Robert 1998). Those at the higher end of the socioeconomic scale imperil the poor in a number of other ways, in over-consumption of water for air conditioning or swimming pools, for example, or in burning fossil fuels to avoid extremes of weather, which adds pollution to the air of the impoverished, who have no choice over land use (Stephens 1996). The wealthy also tend to have greater political clout and often pressure governments for lower taxes and reduced public services (Kawachi & Kennedy 1999). Any attempt at addressing inequity must therefore target both ends of the socioeconomic spectrum: the rich as well as the poor.

Those living in poverty in the city also have an inflated risk of both communicable (HIV/AIDS, tuberculosis, hepatitis) and non-communicable disease, such as circulatory disease. This is related to a range of factors, from poor maternal nutrition to lifestyles that include smoking, drinking, substance abuse, fatty food consumption, social instability, unsafe sexual behaviour and low levels of education (Freudenberg 2000). There is now clear and undisputed evidence that those who live in high-risk conditions live, on average, shorter and more disabled lives (Labonte 1997). Young males among the urban poor are also at risk of a cycle of violence, both as victims and increasingly as perpetrators, an issue that has become a significant mental health concern throughout the world (Stephens 1996). To address violence and other socially destructive behaviours requires tackling the problems of social injustice and alienation. Stephens (1996, p 28) contends that this should begin with some recognition that the urban poor are sold 'the same signals of a global aspirational model (the Nike shoes and other consumer goods affordable only by the wealthy) and then told to suffice with basic needs'. The feelings of disempowerment engendered by these disparities often create a spiral of despair that leads to neglect and/or further risk taking. It is important to recognise that the widening gap between the poor and the wealthy erodes social capital, the 'glue' that holds communities together when they cooperate for mutual benefit (Hancock 2001; Kawachi & Kennedy 1999). Social capital is essential to democratic societies as it promotes trust, confidence in public institutions and political participation, all of which promote social cohesion (Hertzman 2001; Putnam 1993).

We need our economic and natural resources as two distinct kinds of capital, but human and social capital must also be considered as important components of wealth (Hancock 2001). Hancock explains that, in the past, we have not managed the balance between these four types of capital well. We have increased economic capital by decreasing funding for education, thus depleting human capital, or by laying off vast numbers of people. This has in turn disrupted the social capital represented by families and social networks. In some cases, economic capital has been amassed at the expense of depleting natural resources, especially in developing countries (Hancock 2001). None of these actions are helpful to sustaining societies, or to valuing people over material wealth.

The principles of primary health care guide us to recognise the inextricable links between patterns of community participation and patterns of risk at all levels of society. The goal is clear: we must foster empowerment for all members of our communities. The best approach to this is to create programs to address community problems in a way that builds both personal and community capacity. This may involve bringing groups of people together with shared interests and concerns, to strengthen their sense of struggle and community activism (Laverack & Wallerstein 2001). These small coalitions can be encouraged to work towards greater social cohesion through small group activities, the community's organisational structures, and external networks. In the process, they can explore the broader social and political aspects of their lives that can be maximised in achieving empowerment (Laverack & Wallerstein 2001).

In many cases, working with neighbourhood organisations, self-help groups, churches, political parties, advocacy organisations or unions helps to build a level of personal confidence that will stimulate continuing community involvement (Hancock 2001; Robert 1998). In this way, the reciprocity between the individual and the community can be optimised for mutual benefit. Different groups working within the community one step at a time can address the entire range of social inequities including education, employment, support for families, income redistribution, affordable housing, employment opportunities and personal security. Labonte (1997, p 66) considers this type of approach participatory politics: not the 'politics of parties and leaders but the politics of sharing that fragile space called community on an increasingly stressed planet of finite resources'. Perhaps the best example of this type of approach lies in the Healthy Cities movement.

The Healthy Cities
Movement

The Healthy Cities Movement was one of the first specific initiatives of the global Health for All campaign. In 1974, the Canadian Health Minister, Marc Lalonde, released a document on health called the Lalonde Report which, for the first time, identified the government's responsibility to create favourable environments within which people could achieve health gains (Hancock 1992). The report was based on the rationale that, without an environment conducive to health, it was futile to try to preach the gospel of healthy lifestyles to individuals. Others agreed and recognised that in many cases health promotion campaigns would be blaming the victim if they were not targeted at *both* the people *and* the environmental circumstances within which they were expected to make healthy choices. So public health initiatives began to adopt a wider focus and, finally, in 1986, representatives from seventeen European cities met in Lisbon to declare cities the prime targets for environmental change.

The cities that have chosen to participate have developed health goals in ways appropriate to their particular conditions; however, all are based on the premise that a healthy city is one where:

- health is a social rather than medical matter
- health should be the responsibility of all city services
- health should be monitored by physical, social, aesthetic and environmental indicators
- health must be the product of intersectoral collaborative efforts
- cities should be not merely survival units, but a cradle of good health. (Baum & Brown 1989)

Since the inception of the Healthy Cities Movement, health professionals have been instrumental in helping city residents launch and evaluate their various projects (Harpham, Burton & Blue 2001). This type of support makes visible the role of the health professional as a partner and advocate, particularly in the political arena, and it has also given many health professionals a comprehensive understanding of system-wide knowledge and strategies for intersectoral collaboration.

The Healthy Cities projects have expanded and become widely diverse, drawing support from health professionals, representatives of recreation, police, social services, voluntary organisations and people of all ages to effect changes that, in turn, have informed health policy. The movement now incorporates thousands of cities worldwide, all with a common aim of using intersectoral collaboration and community participation to reduce inequalities, strengthen health gain and reduce morbidity and mortality.

Since the mid-1990s, with support from WHO, the Healthy Cities movement has been gradually introduced into developing countries. Four of these projects, in Cox's Bazaar (Bangladesh), Dar es Salaam (Tanzania), Fayoum (Egypt) and Quetta (Pakistan) were evaluated by Harpham and colleagues (2001) on the basis of their awareness raising and environmental improvements, particularly solid waste management. The evaluation team found that, like other European Healthy Cities, some of the outcomes were limited, primarily by the lack of political commitment. One of the important lessons learned was that, in cities where there is political instability, high levels of community participation and adequate funding are imperative (Harpham et al 2001). Despite their mixed responses, it has been useful to have examples from the developing countries, of where small gains can be made and the elements that predict success in improving life in the city. This seems to have worked best when collaboration between government sectors is strong, and where there is strong political support for community empowerment (Harpham et al 2001).

Healthy Cities is a prime example of how intersectoral partnerships can effectively implement the principles of primary health care in partnership with local communities, using the strategies of the Ottawa Charter for Health Promotion. The developing countries mentioned in Harpham and colleagues' (2001) report also received assistance from the Local Initiative Facility for Urban Environment (LIFE)/United Nations Development Program (UNDP) and the Dutch bilateral aid agency. At the regional level, such powerful lobbies as The Council of Europe's 'Sustainable Communities' program and the OECD's 'Ecological Cities' project have also aligned themselves with the Healthy Cities projects (Hancock & Davies 1997). Such broad endorsement from the highest levels of society encourages collaborative alliances between local government and health councils to develop and manage health plans that underline the importance of the environmental movement to the quality of people's lives. However, the sustainability of these programs relies on continuing political commitment and support. Policy makers must understand the broad, community-oriented vision of health promotion, rather than place too great an emphasis on the epidemiology of disease and illness (Raphael 2001). Otherwise, resources may be allocated to projects that overlook the need for social infrastructure for those most in need (Raphael 2001). In the next chapter, we will take a look at the role of epidemiology in community health, with a view to examining the balance that must be maintained for both community-determined health developments and accurate indicators of need.

---

case study...

Cleaning up Australia

In 1989, a self-described 'simple Australian bloke' had a simple yet ambitious idea to clean up one of the great places in the world: Sydney Harbour. As a yachtsman, Ian Kiernan had been shocked by the pollution and rubbish he encountered in the world's oceans. Back in Sydney, he decided to do something about this, and set about promoting an annual campaign that has now attracted more than six million Australians to clean up their local environment. His idea of a 'clean up day' ignited the enthusiasm of the average Australian, and his vision galvanised the country into action. From its humble beginnings of 300 000 Australians, this man's dream has now gained the support of the United Nations Environment Programme (UNEP), which launched a Clean Up the World movement, attracting 30 million people in 80 countries in its first year (1993). By 2002, Clean Up the World had attracted 37.5 million people in 80 countries.

The communities that have stayed with Clean Up the World report that they feel empowered to act locally, and find sharing their achievements with other countries inspirational. All have shared the knowledge that, for the planet to survive, waste reduction strategies are needed in all the countries of the world.

Although the movement has touched a nerve in all age groups, all cultures and every walk of life, and cut across every socioeconomic group, the most heartening aspect of this work is the passion it has ignited among young people, for they hold the key to future sustainability. One important spin-off from the project is a series of Fix Up projects, wherein local schools, businesses and communities identify and fix up local environmental problems through partnerships between community members, government, industry and businesses. This has been so successful that Clean Up Australia's vision for beyond 2005 is nothing less than to be the most influential community-driven environmental organisation in the world.

Clean Up Australia (http://www.cleanup. com.au) intends to apply the principles of ecologically sustainable development, integrated catchment management, community empowerment, cooperative action, community participation and repairing the environment to make the community a better place for the present and future. In this respect, it is an excellent example of primary health care in practice: using community resources and local partnerships to make the world a better place.

---

thinking critically

Primary health care

1 Describe three elements of coping with the HIV/AIDS epidemic from the perspective of primary health care.

2 Discuss the term 'empowerment'. Is it possible to empower communities?

3 Explain the relationship between self-empowerment and community empowerment.

4 Identify at least two major issues that need to be addressed when planning for a Healthy City.

5 Identify four factors that compromise the health of urban dwellers.

6 Explain the cycle of poverty in relation to its negative health effects.

7 Explain three ways in which your own health has been compromised by access and/or equity issues.

REFERENCES

Abelson, J., Lomas, J., Eyles, J., Birch, S. & Veenstra, G. (1995). Does the community want devolved authority? Results of deliberative polling in Ontario. *Canadian Medical Association Journal*, 15 August, 153(4): 403–12.

Barnes, D., Eribes, C., Juarbe, T., Nelson, M., Proctor, S., Sawyer, L., Shaul, M. & Meleis, A. (1995). Primary health care and primary care: a confusion of philosophies. *Nursing Outlook*, 43(7): 7–16.

Baum, F. & Brown, V. (1989) Healthy Cities (Australia) Project: issues of evaluation for the new public health. *Community Health Studies*, XIII(2): 140–9.

Brady, M. (1995). Culture in treatment, culture as treatment. A critical appraisal of developments in addictions programs for indigenous North Americans and Australians. *Social Science and Medicine*, 41(11): 1487–98.

Chatters, L. (2000). Religion and health: public health research and practice. *Annual Review of Public Health*, 21: 335–67.

Clarke, H. & Mass, H. (1998). Comox Valley nursing centre: from collaboration to empowerment. *Public Health Nursing*, 15(3): 216–24.

Clean Up Australia, http://www.cleanup.com.au/Main.asp accessed 4 April 2002.

Freudenberg, N. (2000). Health promotion in the city: a review of current practice and future prospects in the United States. *Annual Review of Public Health*, 21: 473–503.

Hancock, T. & Davies, K. (1997). *An Overview of the Health Implications of Global Environmental Change: A Canadian Perspective*. Ottawa: Canadian Global Change Program, Royal Society of Canada.

Hancock, T. (1992). The healthy city: utopias and realities. In: J. Ashton (ed), *Healthy Cities*. Philadelphia: Milton Keynes, pp 22–9.

Hancock, T. (2001). People, partnerships and human progress: building community capital. *Health Promotion International*, 16(3): 275–80.

Harpham, T., Burton, S. & Blue, I. (2001). Healthy city projects in developing countries: the first evaluation. *Health Promotion International*, 16(2): 111–25.

Herbert, C. (1996). Community-based research as a tool for empowerment: the Haida Gwaii diabetes project example. *Canadian Journal of Public Health*, 87(2): 109–12.

Hertzman, C. (2001). Health and human society. *American Scientist*, 89(6): 538–44.

Kahssay, H. & Oakley, P. (1999). Community involvement in health development: a review of the concept and practice. Geneva: WHO.

Kawachi, I. & Kennedy, B. (1999). Income inequality and health: pathways and mechanisms. *Health Services Research*, 34: 215–27.

Keating, D. & Hertzman, C. (1999). *Developmental Health and the Wealth of Nations: Social, Biological and Educational Dynamics*. New York: The Guilford Press.

Kolbe, L., Kann, L. & Brener, N. (2001). Overview and summary of findings: school health policies and programs study 2000. *Journal of School Health*, 71(7): 253–63.

Labonte, R. (1997). Community and public health: an international perspective. *Health Visitor*, 70(2): 64–7.

Labonte, R. (2001). Health promotion in the 21st century: celebrating the ordinary. *Health Promotion Journal of Australia*, 12(2): 104–9.

Laverack, G. & Wallerstein, N. (2001). Measuring community empowerment: a fresh look at organizational domains. *Health Promotion International*, 16(2): 179–85.

Lee, P. & Paxman, D. (1997). Reinventing public health. *Annual Review of Public Health*, 18: 1–35.

Lowe, I. (1994). Foreward: priorities for a sustainable future. In: C. Chu & R. Simpson (eds), *Ecological Public Health: From Vision to Practice*. Canberra: ANZPHA, pp vii–viii.

Mahler, H. (1977). The meaning of primary health care, *The Australian Nurse's Journal*, 7(5): 22–5.

Marmot, M. (1993). Explaining socioeconomic differences in sickness absence. The Whitehall 11 study. Toronto: Canadian Institute for Advanced Research.

Marmot, M., Rose, G., Shipley, M. & Hamilton, M. (1987). Employment grade and coronary heart disease in British civil servants. *Journal of Epidemiology and Community Health*, 32: 244–9.

Marmot, M. & Shipley, M. (1996). Do socioeconomic differences in mortality persist after retirement? 25 year follow-up of civil servants from the first Whitehall study. *BioMedical Journal*, 313(7066): 1177–80.

Marmot, M., Shipley, M. & Rose, G. (1984). Inequalities in death-specific explanations of a general pattern, *The Lancet*, I: 1003–6.

Meleis, A. (1992).Community participation and involvement: theoretical and empirical issues. *Health Services Management Research*, 5(1): 5–6.

Momsen, J. & Kinnaird, V. (eds) (1993). *Different Places, Different Voices: Gender & Development in Africa, Asia and Latin America*. London: Routledge.

Mustard, J. F. (1996). Health and social capital. In: D. Blane, E. Brunner & R. Wilkinson (eds), *Health and Social Organization: Towards a Health Policy for the Twenty-First Century*. London: Routledge, pp 303–13.

Mustard, J.F. (1999). Social Determinants of Health. Presentation to University of Queensland Centre for Primary Health Care. Brisbane, 5 August.

Patz, J., Engelberg, D. & Last, J. (2000). The effects of changing weather on public health. *Annual Review of Public Health*, 21: 271–307.

Putnam, R. (1993). *Making Democracy Work*. Princeton, NJ: Princeton University Press.

Raphael, D. (2001). Letter from Canada: paradigms, politics and principles. An end of the millenium update from the birthplace of the Healthy Cities movement. *Health Promotion International*, 16(1): 99–101.

Ratzan, S. (2001). Health literacy: communication for the public good. *Health Promotion International*, 16(2): 207–14.

Robert, S. (1998). Community-level socioeconomic status effects on adult health, *Journal of Health and Social Behavior*, 39(March): 18–37.

Shakespeare, T. (1999). Manifesto for genetic justice. *Social Alternatives*, 18(1): 29–32.

St Leger, L. (2001). Schools, health literacy and public health: possibilities and challenges, *Health Promotion International*, 16(2): 197–205.

Stephens, C.(1996), Healthy cities or unhealthy islands? The health and social implications of urban inequality. *Environment and Urbanisation*, 8(2): 9–30.

Tesoriero, F. (2001). Partnerships in health promotion and the place of trust and equality as obstacles to promoting health. *Health Promotion Journal of Australia*, 11(1): 48–55.

Trudgen, R. (2001). *Why Warriors Lie Down and Die*. Darwin: Aboriginal Resource and Development Services, Inc.

United Nations Family Planning Association (UNFPA) (2000). *The State of World Population 2000*. New York: UN.

US Office of Women's Health (USOWH) (2001). *Women's Health Issues: an Overview*. Washington: US Department of Health and Human Services.

Whitehead, M. (1995). Tackling inequalities: A review of policy initiatives, In: M. Benzeval, K. Judge & M. Whitehead (eds), *Tackling Inequalities in Health*. London: King's Fund, pp 22–52.

Wilkinson, R. (1996). *Unhealthy Societies: The Afflictions of Inequality*. Routledge, London.

World Health Organization (WHO) (1997) The Jakarta Declaration on Health Promotion into the 21st Century. Geneva: WHO.

World Health Organization-Health and Welfare Canada-CPHA, (1986). Ottawa Charter for Health Promotion. *Canadian Journal of Public Health*, 77(12): 425–30.

World Health Organization-Regional Office for Europe (1993). Setting Standards for WHO Project Cities: The Requirements and the Designation Process for WHO Project Cities. Copenhagen: WHO.

—— (2000). Exploring Health Policy Development in Europe. Copenhagen: WHO.

CHAPTER 3

Determinants of
health, illness and disability

Introduction Although health is largely determined by community members and the way they interact with their environments, there are many ways in which health services and community support structures and processes can be planned to enhance community health. Health services, including intervention or illness-prevention strategies, must be based on a solid foundation of information related to the community's risk of illness, injury or disability. Planning goals must take into account local knowledge of available community resources and barriers to health, some of which may be related to the motivation and preferences of community residents. Equally important is information on the current health status of the people who live in the community, so that comparisons can be made with wider trends and patterns of health and illness or disability. This type of data gathering and analysis is aimed at making visible community strengths and resilience that will help people cope with risk factors, illness, injury or disability.

The first part of this chapter addresses health risk, including the way risk is measured for health planning. This is followed by an explanation of how epidemiological studies are used in analysing patterns of illness among the population. Next, global perspectives on health and health status are outlined, including a discussion of the way the Global Burden of Disease studies have fulfilled the need for population data bases of disease and disability. Finally, a framework is presented to illustrate how the socioeconomic determinants of health can be incorporated into comprehensive health planning for primary health care.

objectives **By the end of this chapter you will be able to:**

1 Explain the concepts of risk and populations at risk

2 Justify the need for epidemiological information as a basis for planning

3 Discuss the significance of the Global Burden of Disease studies

4 Explain the difference between population health and primary health care

5 Describe the Web of Causation model for epidemiological investigation

6 Explain upstream, midstream and downstream factors in health and illness

7 Discuss the pros and cons of using predictive models to calculate health risk

8 Conduct a community assessment.

Risk

The risk of ill health or injury is a prediction of the possibility of incurring illness or injury, given a set of predisposing factors in either the person or the environment (or both). These factors can be related to biology (including genetic predisposition), exposure to environmental elements that are potentially harmful, or human behaviour. Risky behaviours may be *intentional*, such as participating in extreme sports or failing to take precautionary measures to protect health, or *non-intentional*, such as occurs when a person has no knowledge of the particular risk. Failing to understand the need to eat sufficient fruit and vegetables, the benefits of exercise or the hazards of cooking over wood fires in poorly ventilated rooms, are some examples of non-intentional behaviours that place a person at risk of illness or injury. Risk may also occur because of a lack of resources, such as adequate health care services, or factors in the environment that are beyond a person's control (smoke from forest fires, for example).

Where a community has no regular and accessible health services, the population is at risk of inadequate treatment for illness and injury, and may also be at risk for diseases that could be prevented by early detection. The risks of ill health are greater in physical environments of extreme heat or cold, or those with high levels of air pollution, particularly if there is inadequate housing or alternative shelter. A further risk factor arises when people have no choice over the type of employment or working conditions available, especially for those who must work outdoors in extreme climatic conditions or in other conditions of risk to health or safety.

In general, risky behaviours include such things as unhealthy food consumption, engaging in a sedentary lifestyle, smoking, excessive use of alcohol and other harmful substances, unsafe sexual habits, participating in dangerous activities, and being exposed to such stressors as violent and abusive behaviours (McKie et al 1993). To this list could be added a person's unwillingness to look after personal or family health needs, or cultural taboos against healthy practices, such as maintaining sexual safety. Naturally, longer exposure to risky behaviours and the compound effects of multiple factors produce greater levels of risk of ill health or injury. However, there are some circumstances where risky behaviours are determined by social and cultural perceptions. For example, the elite athlete would not consider her- or himself to be engaging in a risky behaviour while running a rigorous marathon; nor would the person whose culture dictates a relaxed, sedentary lifestyle consider themselves at risk for failing to take up running or another vigorous form of exercise.

Measuring risk is of interest to health planners and policy makers to ensure that resources are used appropriately. Whether these measurements relate to the global or community level, they tend to be standardised according to the definitions explained below.

Measuring
risk

A *risk factor* is an attribute or exposure that is associated with an increased probability of a particular outcome, such as the occurrence of a disease (AIHW 2000). This does not mean that if the risk factor is present it will cause a disease, but it is a starting point for understanding the potential for illness or a condition that will jeopardise optimal health in the population. Risk factor indicators measure economic and other social determinants of health status, as well as individual factors. These could include genetic predisposition, attitudes and beliefs, lifestyle and behaviour, and/or biomedical factors such as unsafe drinking water or the presence of infectious agents (AIHW 2000). Community risk factors may include demographic factors such as fertility rates, migration trends, and the number of people who are overweight or 'at risk' for heart disease. These community factors could also include the rate of

unemployment, economic indicators such as the development of new industries, rates of participation in education, or the proportion of people engaging
in regular physical activity or eating a nutritious diet.

Epidemiological indicators
of health and illness

- *Epidemiology* is the study of the frequency, distribution and determinants
  of health and illness, the patterns of disease occurrence in human
  populations and the factors that influence these patterns. An *epidemic* is
  where a health problem or illness occurs in a population in excess of what
  would normally be expected. At the expected level, it would be *endemic*.
- *Morbidity* refers to the number of people in a certain population affected by
  an illness or condition. Morbidity is described in terms of incidence and
  prevalence.
- *Incidence* is the number of new cases of the condition occurring in a specific
  population during a specified period of time.
- *Prevalence* is the number of both old and new cases occurring in a
  population during a specified period of time.
- *Mortality* refers to the number of deaths from the illness or disease.
- The *population at risk* is the total number of those in the population who
  are susceptible to the condition. This may include the number of non-
  immunised children at risk for measles, or the rate of those who work in
  unsafe or unhealthy occupational environments, such as those with high
  noise exposure. This fraction is multiplied by a base number, which is
  usually expressed as 1000 or 100 000, depending on the size of the
  population.
- *Rates* are a mathematical computation of the frequency of occurrence of a
  condition in a population. The rate is expressed as an equation estimating
  the likelihood that the condition would occur in a member of the
  population. The most common rates are incidence and prevalence rates.
  These are calculated using incidence (the number of new cases) or
  prevalence (the number of both new and existing cases) as the numerator,
  and the population at risk as the denominator, as shown here:

Rate:

$$\text{Incidence} = \frac{\text{No new cases}}{\text{Population at risk}} \times 1000 \text{ (or } 100\,000)$$

$$\text{Prevalence} = \frac{\text{No existing cases (new and old)}}{\text{Population at risk}} \times 1000 \text{ (or } 100\,000)$$

Using epidemiological
information

Rates can be expressed as *crude rates*, which are computed for the population as a whole. They may also be *specific* to certain subgroups, or *adjusted* on the basis of demographic characteristics such as age, race or sex (AIHW 2000). For example, a community may choose to publish the crude rate of cancer among its population, but this information would not be specific enough to encourage women to have pap smears, or for males to be screened for prostate cancer. On the other hand, age- and sex-adjusted rates of cancer of the cervix and prostate cancer are more useful for health planning, to heighten awareness of the need for screening among the population at risk. Likewise, linking prevalence rates or local incidence rates of measles among children provides a useful base of information from which to encourage parents to have their children immunised against this disease.

One of the problems of population studies is the need to study patterns over time. This can best be done using *prospective* epidemiological studies that follow the pattern from one point in time using a *longitudinal* design, rather than adopting a method that studies the group of people or *case cohort* at only one point in time. The prospective study provides a more realistic view of the problem than would be captured at a single moment in time.

Other analytical tools can be used to provide more specific measures for health planning. For example, *relative risk* can be computed to show the extent to which a factor can be predictive of risk in a population. This is expressed as a ratio of the difference between the incidence rate in those who are exposed to the hazard, and in those who are not. If the difference between the two is significantly higher in the population exposed to the hazard, it is identified as a risk factor. In cases where no incidence rates are available but a disease or condition occurs, an *odds ratio* can be calculated retrospectively. This is done by comparing the mathematical odds of the condition occurring when the risk factor is present, and when it is absent.

Determining
causation

Despite having sensitive tools available to calculate risk, it is important to distinguish between *cause* and *association*. Health and illness are products of a complex web of factors, as indicated in Figure 3.1.

For a variable to be defined as a causative agent, several conditions must be met.

1 The cause and effect association must be coherent or logical in light of historical knowledge of the health condition.

2   The association between the factor and the illness or health condition that eventuates must be consistent over time and must occur in the same direction. For example, if many studies reveal that a large number of people become ill after ingesting food from a certain source, the source can be considered a causative agent of the illness.

3   The association must be significantly strong and the factor must consistently produce the condition.

4   The factor must always occur prior to the illness.

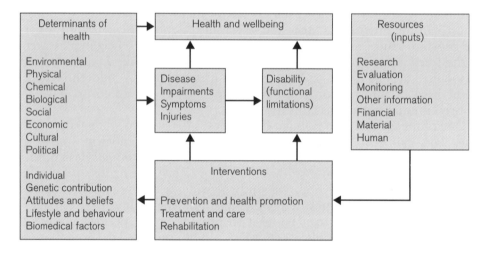

FIGURE 3.1 *Framework for health (AIHW 2000. Reproduced with permission.)*

In most cases, an illness is the result of interconnections and interplay between many elements, some of which have a *synergistic,* or combined, effect that can alter either the *latency* period (the lag between exposure and development of the condition) or *potency,* once the condition begins to develop. Attributing cause must therefore be done with caution and substantiated with careful documentation of what is occurring in various groups of people at particular times, or in relation to specific events. The measurement of risk is also tempered with information related to patterns of health, illness and behaviour in a constantly changing social environment.

The interactions between various risk factors are illustrated in Figure 3.2, which suggests a set of linkages between the things that influence health and illness—in this case, in a family. The links portrayed show, for example, that factors such as gender and education can have an effect on employability. Either or both of these factors may influence a person's (or family's) financial status, which may have an impact on where they live and their access to health resources or family support services. The extent to which health resources are used will depend on whether or not the family sees these resources or supports as culturally appropriate and adequate for their needs. The family's judgements of cultural appropriateness and adequacy of supports in their environment may dictate whatever choices are made to access services, which can have a direct effect on health.

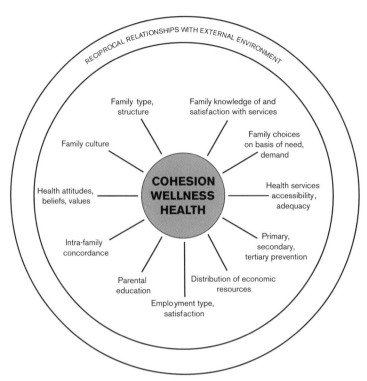

FIGURE 3.2 *Interactions between factors affecting family health*

Health and other support services therefore influence the health of all family members, including children. Whether children are healthy or constantly experiencing illnesses can have a significant impact on family dynamics. Another influence on family dynamics will be family members' lifestyles and employment. This often affects the way the children are nurtured and the extent to which they develop adequate coping skills to deal with their own life circumstances as adults. In early adulthood, some family members may straddle two or more cultures simultaneously, and this can further complicate developmental issues that affect family dynamics and, ultimately, family cohesion. Taken together, these factors have a cumulative effect on health status and health potential. Because there is no predictable sequence to these factors, families can have cycles of good health or ill health, and it is difficult to determine the extent to which any one factor may be affecting the health of the family or of their community. So this is where specific information is required.

The epidemiological
triad

One way of analysing health is within an epidemiological model, which configures the pattern of illness according to the triad of *host, agent* and *environment.*

For example, where there is an outbreak of salmonella poisoning in a certain group of people, the agent is the salmonella organism, the host is the group of people who ingest the organism, and the environment includes all the conditions that encourage people to consume the substance containing the organism, or that encourage the organism to thrive. These environmental conditions include the existing health status of the host, community resources needed to diagnose and treat the ensuing illness, and educational resources that will help people learn to take preventative precautions against future occurrences. Figure 3.3 illustrates the model.

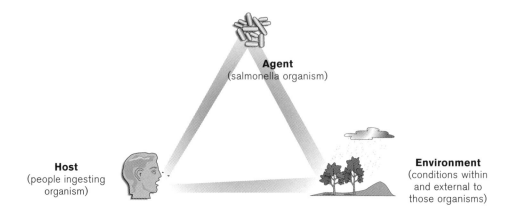

FIGURE 3.3 *The epidemiological triad model*

Agent

The agent in an epidemiological triad may vary according to *type*. It may be physical, chemical, biological or even the absence of a substance—for example, as occurs in a metabolic deficiency, like Type 1 diabetes. It may also be combinations of these. For example, a physical agent such as an extremely hot climate may combine with the type of chemical agents that are found in air pollution to create a potent substance that could poison a group of people, especially if they are susceptible hosts.

Transmission also varies, and is an important consideration when analysing the interaction between factors. The agent may be transmitted directly—for example, in semen or blood products, as occurs in the case of the HIV virus—or indirectly, through *vehicles, vectors* or *air*. Milk, for example, may transmit diptheria in babies, and food is a vehicle for salmonella. Lice, in some cases, can transmit typhus, and airborne agents may travel in dust or water droplets (Valanis 1988). Agents may gain *entry* to the host through a variety of methods, including inhalation (as occurs with the flu), ingestion (salmonella) or the transfer of body fluids (HIV).

Host

Characteristics of the host also vary. *Susceptibility* of the host is influenced by many factors. Some of these are *demographic* factors such as age, gender or marital status, *personal* factors including immunity or nutritional status, and *social* factors such as having a family or neighbourhood support system. Of course, the most important host factor is *exposure* to the agent, but exposure alone is not enough to guarantee that the condition or epidemic will occur, as there is never a foolproof way of predicting how an array of factors will interact.

Environment

Environmental factors may include geography and climate (physical factors), the presence of biological and chemical factors, or socioenvironmental factors such as whether the environment is rural or urban, crowded or isolated, supportive or non-supportive. The impact of the environment cannot be overstated, particularly in considering the synergistic effects of many environmental factors. Where it is warm, people are often inclined to go outside and exercise. Where there is social support, families can often overcome a lack of personal resources. Conversely, where there are extraordinary air pollution levels, even the strongest individuals may succumb to respiratory problems. Illnesses and epidemics thus grow out of unpredictable interactions, some within the host, agent or environment, and some between the three categories of factors.

The epidemiological triad model has been expanded in a more comprehensive format, the Web of Causation model. The web provides a more visual illustration of the interplay between factors affecting health, according to the original epidemiological triad of host, agent and environment. One environmental factor that is often overlooked in epidemiological studies is the policy environment. Since the inception of the consumer movement, lobby groups have emerged on a number of occasions to bring pressure to government departments to respond quickly to epidemics or potential epidemics. In many cases, these grass roots movements have been directly responsible for improvements in health through public awareness campaigns and informal investigations of factors related to health. This type of social determinant is often overlooked in traditional epidemiological models, which focus on biomedical rather than social factors. The Web of Causation allows these social and environmental factors greater visibility, and therefore has a better fit with a socioecological model of health, as seen in Figure 3.4.

Throughout the past decade, the scientific community has adopted a new approach to gathering and analysing population-based information. Globalisation and the need to justify strategies for health planning on a rational basis have led health planners to develop a consistent way of gathering evidence. The studies that have been conducted to provide this base of evidence for planning are called the Global Burden of Disease (GBD) studies (Michaud, Murray & Bloom 2001).

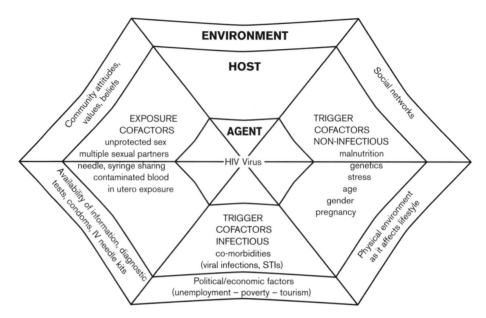

FIGURE 3.4 *The Web of Causation model, illustrating factors known to be associated with the HIV/AIDS epidemic (McMurray 1993)*

The global burden
of disease

In order to inform national and international health policies for prevention and control of disease and injury, in the early part of the 1990s researchers from Harvard School of Public Health and WHO began an investigation into the worldwide burden of illness. Their goal was to quantify the data on incidence, prevalence, duration, mortality and disease burden for disease and injury categories using the disability-adjusted life year (DALY) to measure the total impact of mortality and non-fatal health outcomes (Mathers, Vos & Stevenson 1999). 'One DALY is a lost year of "healthy" life and is calculated as a combination of years of life lost due to premature mortality (YLL) and equivalent "healthy" years of life lost due to disability (YLD)' (Mathers, Vos & Stevenson 1999, p xxiii).

The original GBD studies began with 14 groups categorised according to age and sex, in eight regions of the world, for 107 causes of death (Murray & Lopez 1997a). These studies revealed that in 1990 the major causes of death were ischaemic heart disease, cerebrovascular accidents (stroke), lower respiratory infections, diarrhoeal diseases, perinatal disorders, chronic obstructive pulmonary disease, tuberculosis, measles, road traffic accidents and lung cancer. Five of the 10 leading killers were communicable, perinatal and nutritional disorders, largely affecting children. Ninety-eight per cent of all deaths in children under 15 years occurred in the developing world, most related to childhood malnutrition, poor water and sanitation, and personal and domestic hygiene (Murray & Lopez 1997a,b). The prevalence of disability was highest in sub-Saharan Africa and lowest in established market economies (Murray & Lopez 1997c). Developed regions accounted for 11.6 per cent of the world-wide burden from all causes of death and disability, and for 90.2 per cent of health expenditure worldwide (Murray & Lopez 1997b).

The research group concluded that health trends in the next 25 years will be determined mainly by the ageing of the world's population, the decline in age-specific mortality rates from communicable, maternal, perinatal and nutritional disorders, the spread of HIV/AIDS, and the increase in tobacco-related mortality and disability (Murray & Lopez 1997d). This information provided the data for the WHO report on global risk, which serves as a basis for future WHO initiatives (WHO 1999).

Global
risk

Since the inception of the Health for All movement, WHO has been attempting to refine methods for measuring risk. The GBD studies have provided an invaluable set of global data for WHO to use as a basis for planning. At the close of the twentieth century, the conclusion drawn from this information was that primary health care and improvements in living standards have played a large role in the twentieth century's 'health revolution' (WHO 1999, p 1). The health revolution refers to the generation and application of new knowledge about diseases and their control. There has also been a revolution in treating some illnesses, and a number of successes were recorded in reducing mortality throughout the twentieth century, primarily from infectious disease (WHO 1999). Despite these gains, WHO predicted that over a billion people would enter the twenty-first century with lives shortened and scarred by disease. New problems confronting health planners this century include the rapid spread of the HIV/AIDS epidemic, the threat of resurgent malaria and the unexpected magnitude and consequences of the tobacco epidemic (WHO 1999).

The four major global challenges to be confronted this century are:

1 To reduce the burden of excess mortality and morbidity suffered by the poor. This will be addressed by giving renewed attention to diseases like tuberculosis, malaria and HIV/AIDS, which affect poor people disproportionately. A further step will be to urge governments to invest in reducing maternal mortality and improving maternal and childhood nutrition and immunisation.

2 To prevent premature deaths through a global commitment to tobacco control, countering specific threats such as the spread of resistance to antimicrobials, developing proactive strategies for risk reduction (including healthy lifestyles), cleaner air and water, adequate sanitation, healthy diets

and safer transportation. WHO claims that to address these threats requires stable economic growth and ensuring educational opportunities for females as well as males throughout the world.

3 To develop more effective health systems that can:
- improve health status
- reduce health inequalities
- enhance responsiveness to legitimate expectations
- increase efficiency
- protect individuals, families and communities from financial loss
- enhance fairness in the financing and delivery of health care.

4 To expand the health knowledge base that countries can use to shape the future of their health systems (WHO 1999).

GBD information
at the national level

Since the Global Burden of Disease studies began, many countries have adopted the DALY to measure the national burden of disease as a basis for their own health planning. Researchers in the Netherlands, for example, have estimated the burden of disease due to 48 causes, concluding that the GBD approach appears to be a feasible way to ascertain national health issues in Western Europe (Melse et al 2000). Australian researchers have studied mortality, disability, impairment, illness and injury for 176 diseases, injuries and risk factors between 1981 and 1996 (Mathers, Vos & Stevenson 1999). The Australian data revealed some interesting comparisons with those of other countries. For example, Australia ranks tenth in the world in terms of life expectancy at birth, but lags behind Japan, Greece, Sweden and Italy in terms of the probability of dying between ages 15 and 59. As in most other industrialised countries, cardiovascular disease is the most common concern.

Cardiovascular problems, along with cancers and injury, accounted for 72 per cent of the total Australian mortality burden in both females and males, but males lose 26 per cent more years of life than females (Mathers et al 1999). The Australian researchers also found that the age-adjusted mortality burden declined by 27 per cent between 1981 and 1996, with substantial declines in the mortality burden of cardiovascular diseases, road traffic accidents, low birthweight babies, and stomach cancer for both males and females. Importantly, they also found that the burden of smoking-related diseases had decreased in males, but increased substantially in females. Their analysis also revealed that the mortality burden is significantly higher among socioeconomically disadvantaged people (of both genders), with a spread of 35 per cent more years of life lost by the most disadvantaged quintile, compared with the least disadvantaged. These socioeconomic differentials have widened for boys and young men aged 15–24 because of motor vehicle accidents and suicides. On the other hand, the differences have narrowed for deaths from drug overdose, which means that rates have increased faster at the top socioeconomic quintile than at the bottom.

In terms of disability, mental disorders account for the highest non-fatal cause of years of life lost due to disability (YLD), amounting to 30 per cent of the non-fatal burden of disease. Depression causes 8 per cent of the burden for both males and females. The second- and third-highest burdens for males are hearing loss and alcohol dependence and, for females, dementia and osteoarthritis. Risk factors identified as smoking, physical inactivity, obesity, high blood pressure and high cholesterol were found to be responsible for a sizeable proportion of the total burden of Australian disease, even though the data do not capture the interactions between various factors. Tobacco smoking was found to be the risk factor responsible for the greatest burden of disease: 12 per cent in males and 7 per cent in females (Mathers et al 1999).

Implications
of the GBD data

The value of measuring the burden of disease lies in being able to collect information on the magnitude and impact of health problems to provide a basis for investments in health care. However, the GBD studies are also a lesson in the politics of research. In an increasingly politicised and corporatised health care environment, health planners and managers are held accountable for the cost-effectiveness of their actions as well as the quality assurance aspects of health coverage in the population. By calculating the burden of death and disability, the GBD approach provides information on the magnitude of health problems for population health planning—that is, the allocation of national health resources.

Despite the fact that information has also been collected on inequalities in health status and health determinants (Mathers et al 1999), the 'population health' approach of measuring the size of the problems has been criticised on the basis that it does not reflect a social justice or primary health care approach, particularly in relation to community-determined decisions for health spending (Poland et al 1998; Raphael 2001; Robertson & Minkler 1994; Robertson 1998). As advocates for community empowerment in Canada, Robertson and Minkler (1994) contend that all those involved in health promotion should be concerned with facilitating empowerment by assisting the community to articulate both their health problems and their solutions. One of their major concerns is that the research basis for change needs to be developed around the problem-solving abilities of communities rather than exclusively on the basis of biomedical indicators (Robertson & Minkler 1994). Similarly, Poland and colleagues (1998) argue that the population approach taken by researchers may decontextualise the social problems inherent in many communities, especially where there are economic disparities. They suggest that the emphasis on economic prosperity should be challenged and replaced with a stronger focus on equity.

Some critics believe that the measurement of DALYs and too great an emphasis on epidemiology may preclude local participation in planning. Raphael (2001, p 100) suggests that the population health approach has a fundamentally different vision of health than one that is 'values-based, pluralistic and community oriented'. He cautions that concentrating on large-scale quantitative surveys to identify risk and protective factors across the population may turn out to be more focused on restaurant and nursing home inspections than on addressing such things as poverty and social exclusion (Raphael 2001). In his view, governments have responded to large-scale data by adopting funding models that commodify health in terms of economic rationalism. This gives pre-eminence to market considerations rather than addressing the urgent need for spending on social infrastructure such as education, social and health services. Raphael (2001, p 101) concludes that it will be left to community activists to reverse this trend, through both electoral politics and the 'mobilization of community members in support of their own interests'.

Health planning
for the future

The challenge for those promoting the health of communities lies in greater understanding of *both* the biomedical indicators of health *and* its social determinants. In response to the need for a balanced approach, Turrell and colleagues (1999) devised a conceptual model to guide analysis of the multilevel and diverse determinants of socioeconomic health inequalities. Their framework consists of three discrete yet interrelated levels, called *upstream, midstream* and *downstream* factors. The model is presented in Figure 3.5.

Upstream factors are macro-level factors, which include international influences, government policies and the fundamental determinants of health (social, physical, economic and environmental). Included are such interrelated factors as education, employment, occupation and working conditions, income, housing and area of residence.

Midstream factors are intermediate-level factors, which include psychosocial factors, health-related behaviours and the role played by the health care system. Midstream factors show the influence of the contexts of people's lives in affecting health, either indirectly, through psychosocial processes and health behaviours, or directly, through such things as accidents, injuries and violence. Cultural factors cut across both upstream and midstream factors, in that culture affects both personal actions and behaviour, and such contexts as family, workplace and school.

Downstream factors are micro-level factors, including changes to physiological systems and biological functioning brought about as a consequence of those factors operating at the midstream and upstream levels. So illness and disease reactions and systems are identified in the framework as downstream factors.

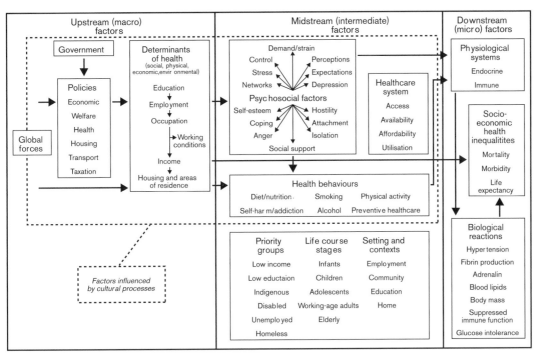

FIGURE 3.5 *Socioeconomic determinants of health (from Turrell, G., Oldenburg, B., McGuffog, I. & Dent, R. (1999). Socioeconomic determinants of health: towards a national research program and a policy and intervention agenda. Brisbane: Queensland University of Technology School of Public Health, Centre for Public Health Research. Reproduced with permission).*

Community
assessment

All the models presented in this chapter can be used to guide community assessment. It is important to have statistical information on epidemiological status and health indicators, but it is also crucial to understand how the characteristics of the people who inhabit the community might influence their health-related decisions. One such characteristic concerns whether the community generally feels ownership, whether community residents feel responsible for and will be accountable for health and to one another (Abel et al 1995).

Communities are inherently social organisations and, as such, community residents are instrumental in shaping community dynamics and cohesive environments. People contribute to the community through such things as their informal caring activities and their sense of community identity and belonging. Community networks, especially in village societies, allow community members to meet basic social needs by providing a sense of connection, opportunities to participate in decisions, a sense of safety and security, a buffer against stress, and leisure activities, all of which have the capacity to contribute to the quality of community life (Last 1998). So it is important to understand community dynamics—who the key players are and how people interact with one another.

It is also important to know the geography of a community. Some communities are bonded together by their seclusion, while others have features such as mountains, rivers or railway tracks that provide barriers to communication. Health planning cannot be done without understanding people's relationship with the land, and whether the majority of community members are long-term residents. The assumption may be made that if people feel a sense of long-term connection with the community, they may be more amenable to persuasions aimed at preserving the local physical environment.

People themselves often have a clear idea of the sustainability of their local environment and how it can circumscribe their lifestyle opportunities. This is exemplified in the struggle of Indigenous people to retain their land, and of rural communities to remain in their homes even when they cease to be economically viable. When health professionals gain an in-depth understanding of people's affinity with the land and their cultural history, they have greater insight into how to frame health promotion strategies. It is also necessary to know what age groups and family types comprise the community.

In the past, numerous inventories or checklists have been generated to guide community health assessment. However, these tend to approach assessment from predetermined assumptions and run the risk of failing to document unexpected issues. The following categories are therefore presented as an informal guide to community assessment, in the expectation that the processes of assessment will be developed in partnership with community members.

Some of the questions to ask community members include the following:

- Are there large proportions of elderly or young families who will require particular health services either in the present or in future?
- What is the cultural mix?
- How does the community see itself?
- What do people think of living in this community?
- Do they believe it is conducive to health?
- What is the level of awareness of health and ecological issues?
- What are the environmental strengths?
- What do they think the community needs most?
- Is there access to transportation for those who need health services?
- What should be sustained?
- What structural features exist and what social and structural changes do they think are required for sustainability?
- What notable differences in opinion exist?
- What is the level of volunteerism in the community?

Once this information is known, the next level of assessment should move on to community members' relationships with the external environment. These questions are as follows:

- Who are the gatekeepers or key funders of health?
- Are there adequate numbers and types of health professionals?
- What are their priorities for the short, medium and long term?
- In what way are these tied to political goals? What *are* the political goals?

All health programs, especially screening programs, require financial resources. Where a community has a visible problem that is high on the list of government health priorities, it is easier to argue for the necessary funds for an intervention program. However, many issues remain problematic to the community, yet invisible to or dismissed by government funding agencies because of the need, in a climate of economic restraint, to justify return on investment.

Tuberculosis is a case in point. A generation ago, tuberculosis occurred in many countries in epidemic proportions; however, the rate of infections subsided after worldwide chest X-ray screening brought those afflicted with tuberculosis into treatment. As the number of those with the illness declined, screening was thought to be cost ineffective, on the basis that funds could be better spent in other areas of health need and, of course, the HIV/AIDS epidemic has attracted a large portion of current resources. However, there is now a resurgence of cases of tuberculosis and it is of great significance in the developing countries, where it accompanies HIV/AIDS (WHO 1999). WHO is working with health authorities throughout the world to heighten awareness of the program, mobilise support on a major scale, and provide direct guidance and support to national programs.

Community assessment as a political activity

Because of competition for resources, community assessment must be conducted within the political and economic context of the community and the wider health-budgeting arena. This is reflected in the language of health promotion. It has become the norm in many parts of the world to describe health as an investment, especially where every government expenditure must be rationalised (Kickbusch 1997). Few health promotion investments are easily quantifiable, and in many cases it is extremely difficult to demonstrate return on investment in terms of human or other resources.

Part of the difficulty in demonstrating return on investments in health is the lag between health interventions and outcomes. For example, programs to counter domestic violence, which has profound effects on the health of many families, have a long period between innovation and outcomes. Family violence is rife in numerous communities throughout the world, yet many people complain of inadequate resources to respond to the problem with viable solutions. In some cases this is because of the problem being politicised to the extent that funding is often dependent on policy makers' ability to see a return on their investment within the term of their political appointment.

It usually takes years to see improvements in health, and it is often impossible to identify which health gains are due to particular interventions. It is interesting that the greatest return on investment in health comes from such simple forms of daily exercise as walking, but the gains in terms of cardiovascular health and prevention of bone disease take many years to demonstrate.

One of the problems encountered by health professionals wishing to establish intervention programs is the lack of specific information from which to argue the need. Where there is competition for funds between programs, an immunisation program, for instance, is readily measurable within a fairly reasonable time frame. A domestic violence program aimed at teaching young people about relationships is not. Sometimes this can be redressed by using a creative way of documenting assessment data. For example, a health education program aimed at teaching young people about violence could be argued on the basis of the prevalence of violence-related injuries, particularly when injury prevention is high on the list of government priorities for community health.

The final step in community assessment is therefore linked to identifying the key players within the community who will provide ongoing support for any necessary changes to community health, and those questions can be framed as:

- Who are the key players who will be willing to engage in serious resource dialogue to sustain both community health and economic viability?
- What networks and coalitions can be built?
- Who in the community are the opinion leaders?
- Who plays important roles in resource allocation?
- How does the community show its capacity for caring?
- What precedents have been set?

This line of questioning means addressing the issue of equity, but it also aims at making subtle aspects of the community *transparent*, so that the processes as well as the structures of change can be made visible. Then programs can be developed that tap in to the strengths of the community and acknowledge the constraints in the environment, whether these be personal, physical, social or financial.

Without this community ownership and commitment, sustainability in programs designed to meet local needs will be difficult to achieve. In the long term, only community involvement can sustain the supportive social networks, good jobs and safe neighbourhoods that are fundamental to good health (Freudenberg 2000; Stephens 1996). This is a type of *asset mapping*. When neighbourhood or other community groups can demonstrate their assets and the type of public resources they have and/or need, they will be more persuasive in convincing governments of the need for either ongoing support or additional services (Young & Gardner 1998). To ascertain the community's existing capacity, or the need for change, community assessment must revolve around the themes listed below.

Community assessment inventory

- People:
  - people–place relationships
  - networks for communication, volunteerism support systems, family caregivers
  - community leadership
  - psychosocial factors
  - cultural factors, ethnic 'mix'
  - demographic characteristics
- Place:
  - geographic area
  - natural resources
  - development base, including taxation
  - other structural features
  - access to welfare, housing, transportation

- Health patterns:
  - local burden of disease and disability
  - social determinants of health
  - quality of life
  - demographic patterns
  - access, availability, affordability of health services
  - local patterns of service utilisation
- Gatekeepers:
  - local, state, national health policies and priorities
  - financial resources
  - competing political, development goals
  - health professionals
  - global factors.

Community assessment is a bit like a SWOT analysis. The object of the exercise is to reveal the *Strengths, Weaknesses, Opportunities* and *Threats* to community health. Once that has been achieved, the information can be shared among members of the community, to look for acceptable solutions to existing problems and strategies for maintaining these over time. The health professional then acts as a community advocate, a resource person who *mediates* between people and those responsible for freeing up the resources they need, *enables* community groups to achieve their goals by helping to build coalitions for change, and *monitors* their progress by collecting information to inform them of the benchmarks they achieve along the way and to help them re-vision their goals for the future.

The key to accurate assessment is community participation. Planning for equitable, accessible and culturally sensitive health services and resources can only be achieved by incorporating local knowledge and insight into the risk factors and determinants of health that are peculiar to that community.

thinking critically

The determinants of health

1 What information would you need to conduct an epidemiological assessment of a mining community?

2 Generate a web of causation for occupational injuries in a migrant population.

3 Discuss risk and risky behaviours related to alcohol consumption.

4 Explain the relationship between epidemiological information and ensuring primary health care in a community.

5 Discuss the significance of the Global Burden of Disease study to health planning in your community.

6 Identify the socioeconomic determinants of health in one community known to you.

7 Conduct an assessment of your community using the community assessment inventory.

REFERENCES

Abel, P., Boland, M., Durand, B., Geolot, D., Goodson, J., Isham, G. & Steele, L. (1995). Work force and community health care needs: A model to link service, education, and the community. *Family and Community Health*, 18(1): 75–9.

Australian Institute for Health and Welfare (AIHW) (2000). *Australia's Health 2000*. Canberra: AGPS.

Freudenberg, N. (2000). Health promotion in the city: a review of current practice and future prospects in the United States. *Annual Review of Public Health*, 21: 473–503.

Kickbusch, I. (1997). Health promoting environments: the next steps. *Australian and New Zealand Journal of Public Health*, 21(4): 431–4.

Last, J. (1998). *Public Health and Human Ecology*, 2nd edn, Stamford, Conn: Appleton & Lange.

Mathers, C., Vos, T. & Stevenson, C. (1999). *The Burden of Disease and Injury in Australia*. Canberra: Australian Institute for Health and Welfare.

McKie, L., Al-Bashir, M., Anagnostopoulou, T.,Csepe, P., El-Asfahani, A., Fonseca, H., Funiak, S., Javetz, R. & Samsuridjal, S. (1993). Defining and assessing risky behaviours. *Journal of Advanced Nursing*, 18: 1911–16.

McMurray, A. (1993). *Community Health Nursing: Primary Health Care in Practice*, 2nd edn, Melbourne: Churchill-Livingstone.

Melse, J., Essink-Bot, M., Kramers, P. & Hoeymans, N. (2000). A national burden of disease calculation: Dutch disability-adjusted life years. *American Journal of Public Health*, 90(18): 1241–7.

Michaud, C., Murray, C. & Bloom, B. (2001). Burden of disease—implications for future research. *Journal of the American Medical Association*, 285(5): 535–63.

Murray, C. & Lopez, A. (1997a). Mortality by cause for eight regions of the world: Global Burden of Disease Study. *The Lancet*, 349(3 May): 1269–76.

—— (1997b). Global mortality, disability and the contribution of risk factors: Global Burden of Disease Study. *The Lancet*, 349(17 May): 1436–42.

—— (1997c). Regional patterns of disability-free life expectancy and disability-adjusted life expectancy: Global Burden of Disease Study. *The Lancet*, 349(10 May): 1347–52.

—— (1997d). Alternative projections of mortality and disability by cause 1990–2020: Global Burden of Disease Study. *The Lancet*, 349(24 May): 1498–1504.

Poland, B., Coburn, D., Robertson, A. & Eakin, J. (1998). Wealth, equity and health care: a critique of 'population health' perspective on the determinants of health. *Social Science and Medicine*, 46(7): 785–98.

Raphael, D. (2001). Letter from Canada: paradigms, politics and principles. An end of the millenium update from the birthplace of the Healthy Cities movement. *Health Promotion International*, 16(1): 99–101.

Robertson, A. (1998). Shifting discourses on health in Canada: from health promotion to population health. *Health Promotion International*, 13(2): 155–66.

Robertson, A. & Minkler, M. (1994). New health promotion movement: a critical examination. *Health Education Quarterly*, 21(3): 295–312.

Stephens, C.(1996). Healthy cities or unhealthy islands? The health and social implications of urban inequality. *Environment and Urbanisation*, 8(2): 9–30.

Turrell, G., Oldenburg, B., McGuffog, I. & Dent, R. (1999). Socioeconomic determinants of health: towards a national research program and a policy and intervention agenda. Brisbane: Queensland University of Technology School of Public Health, Centre for Public Health Research.

Valanis, B. (1988). The epidemiological model in community health nursing. In: M. Stanhope & J. Lancaster (eds), *Community Health Nursing: Process and Practice for Promoting Health*, 2nd edn St Louis: Mosby, pp 149–71.

World Health Organization (WHO) (1999). The World Health Report 1999: Making a Difference. Geneva: WHO.

Young, N. & Gardner, S. (1998). Children at the crossroads. *Public Welfare*, 56(1): 3–11.

CHAPTER 4

Health promotion:
concepts to practice

Introduction   As mentioned in Chapter 1, health promotion encompasses all activities that enable and facilitate health, including planned interventions aimed at the voluntary actions people can take to look after their health or the health of others. Health promotion programs may also encompass health education interventions and programs, or actions taken to encourage early detection of illness or its precursors. This chapter takes a closer look at the way health professionals attempt to promote health in communities. It will examine the ways in which the field of health promotion has evolved throughout the previous century on the premise that historical experience can be used to inform strategies for the future.

objectives **By the end of this chapter you will be able to:**

1 Explain the genesis of contemporary health promotion approaches

2 Plan a health promotion intervention guided by a conceptual model

3 Explain the merits of using a settings approach to health promotion

4 Analyse the differences between the Ottawa and Jakarta charters for health promotion

5 Explain the difference between proximal and distal risk factors

6 Develop a comprehensive strategy for promoting health in a specific population group in a community.

The evolution of
community health promotion

The way health promotion has been conceptualised by the health professions has changed dramatically over the years. The most significant change has been a shift in focus from teaching people how to manage their health (the 'top-down' model), to a more socially embedded approach that capitalises on the inherent capacity of community members to establish their own goals, strategies and priorities for health (the 'bottom-up' model). This is the socioecological approach to community health. It is based on the premise that if community members are provided with structural resources and information that is appropriate to their cultural, social and physical needs, they will make informed choices to improve their health and the health of their environment, which will lead to sustainable community health. The role of the health professional in this model of health promotion is not to persuade people to undertake certain behaviours because it will be 'good for them', but to help people recognise the personal, social and structural influences and elements of their lives and their environment that have a health-enhancing potential. Recognition of these factors is the first step towards community development.

The most important aim of community development is community competence. This does not imply that the community is *self-contained*. Instead, it suggests a community in which people are sufficiently health literate to capitalise on the resources within their own environment that can be used to improve health and reduce the risk of illness. Members of a competent community are also able to identify community needs, establish local goals and objectives for health, and identify the additional resources necessary to meet those goals. Such a community exemplifies the principles of primary health care. However, as previously mentioned, communities must also have access to epidemiological information as a basis for illness prevention and treatment.

Epidemiological knowledge has developed only throughout the past one hundred years. At the end of the nineteenth century, health was promoted on the basis of medical knowledge that was current at that time, and the opinions of medical experts were accepted without question. This created enormous pressure on scientists to advance the field of biomedical investigation. To a large extent, this was conducted in medical laboratories. However, laboratory medicine provided only partial reasons for why some people became ill in the prevalent conditions of the time, while others thrived. Obviously, factors outside the biological sphere, and in the context of people's lives, exerted some effect on health outcomes. One of the first medical experts to pursue this thesis was John Snow, a physician in London. His research into the causes of cholera in the residents of London was a significant event, in that it led to an important, if somewhat primitive, understanding of the links between people and their environment.

---

case study...

Epidemiology as a basis for health promotion

For many years, scientists have been attempting to find plausible explanations for the causes of disease. Some explanations have emerged through biblical myths and folklore, while others have been the product of careful observation and investigation. In the 1850s, John Snow, a London physician, began piecing together the likely reasons for a cluster of cholera cases. For months he treated numerous people for the dreaded disease, systematically recording aspects of his patients' lives that might indicate a common cause. He was aided by the advent of quantitative measures of recording disease frequency, called rates (Valanis 1986). Carefully, he compiled rates of infection among his patients, relating these to a wide variety of factors. Because those with the illness were of all ages and of widely varying general health status, he began to look beyond characteristics of the individual to those in the physical environment. As it turned out, the common thread in this cluster of cases was a water pump in the centre of town, shared by all those who became ill.

Once his documentation indicated a strong enough link between the pattern of using town water from the pump and development of the disease, Snow removed the pump handle to prevent further usage. He continued to record what would later be described as incidence and prevalence data related to the cholera cases. From his careful documentation, he was able to build an explanatory framework to be used for educating the local residents on preventive measures they should take to avoid contracting the infection. He recruited local community leaders from the church and schools to help explain to their families, neighbours and friends how the disease could be contracted from the water pump, and how to dispose of contaminated waste from those already infected. Although it was later found to be the cholera vibrio rather than the water itself that caused the disease, his work was a landmark in furthering our knowledge of health and disease (Valanis 1986).

Snow's epidemiological research heralded the beginning of a movement to provide a rational basis for health promotion. However, the intention of teaching people the causes of disease was to justify their compliance with expert advice. For many years this was the basis of health promotion. The health educator, usually the medical doctor, was expected to provide instruction to the public on what they should and should not do. In most cases, the scientific principles informing this expert opinion were considered beyond the comprehension of the public and thus not shared with them. This created a sense of medical mystique, which heightened with the rapid expansion of medical and epidemiological knowledge that occurred because of developments in biomedical and communications technology.

By the 1920s the so-called 'Golden Age of Medicine' was born, where medical doctors were considered privy to fascinating information inaccessible to the general public (Emanuel & Emanuel 1996). In this era, health promotion was health instruction, dominated by the medical profession, usually without public scrutiny. With the onset of the information age in the 1960s, medical and health information became readily available to all, and the public began to demand greater responsiveness from medical science. The information age ushered in an age of consumerism which advanced the cause of community involvement.

Consumerism:
health as a marketable commodity

The information revolution of the 1960s and 1970s transformed the world into a global village, where communities began to share ideas and to have a greater say over the conditions that affected their lives. Greater access to information led to greater critical awareness in many realms, including health, the environment and the politics of health care. The consumer movement was a product of this explosion of information. As active consumers (rather than passive recipients) of government policies and strategies, people began to see health as a commodity, and to exert their right to greater participation in matters concerning health and the conditions of their lives (Robertson & Minkler 1994).

Concomitant with the consumer movement was the growth of public advertising in the 1960s, reflecting in part most people's access to television. The field of marketing experienced unprecedented growth. By the 1970s, health began to be seen as a product, and health educators borrowed strategies from the marketing specialists, subsequently engaging in what was called *social marketing*. Social marketing uses the system of developing the right *product*, backed by the right *promotion*, put in the right *place* at the right *price* (Kotler 1975). The formula conceptualises health education messages as an almost tangible product that has some cost benefit to the consumer. Proponents of this approach were attracted to the idea of promoting health using public media campaigns, primarily because it allowed access to large numbers of the population, an outcome that is today called 'product reach'.

The major goal of the public health promotion era of the 1970s was to prevent people from adopting high-risk lifestyles. The underlying assumption, informed by the advertising specialists, was that if people heard a message often enough, behaviour change would follow. The scientific and professional basis for health promotion campaigns was a combination of behavioural epidemiology, preventive medicine and health education. In contrast to the medicalised 'old public health' (top-down) approach, it focused on 'bottom up' influences on the individual, which incorporated personal and family influences.

The field of health promotion burgeoned from the mid-1970s through to the early 1980s. Health educators used information from psychology and marketing to systematise the process of social marketing. They developed persuasive techniques for behaviour change, targeted to specific goals such as smoking cessation, reducing fat intake and increasing exercise. Although some health promotion programs were carefully conceived and researched, many were poorly evaluated, making it difficult to compare what was working with what was not. In addition, they were usually costly and, as government-funded programs, carried the additional challenge of having to demonstrate visible results within the time frame of a particular term in office.

The most effective health promotion campaigns used a community organisation approach, where the community was targeted in campaigns to heighten awareness and encourage behavioural change. Included were several large-scale longitudinal studies of health-related behaviour change in the United States (Maccoby & Solomon 1981; Lasater, Carleton & LeFebre 1988), Finland (McAlister 1981), Wales (Nutbeam & Catford 1987) and Australia (Egger et al 1983). Each of these studies reported substantial improvements in a range of lifestyle factors, with the largest gains evident in the extent to which community attitudes became more attuned to health issues. As community-wide programs, each was impressive from the perspective of general population awareness. Many health professionals (including this author) were attracted to the idea of widespread preventative programs, and we witnessed first-hand the way community members accepted the 'healthy lifestyle' messages with almost evangelical zeal (Esler-McMurray 1980). However, by the 1990s, the mass media campaign approach to health promotion had drawn considerable criticism.

Some criticised the mass health promotion approach on the basis that it was directed at the average or 'typical' person. Messages were often poorly constructed, ineffectively communicated and imprecisely focused (Mechanic 1999). Few campaigns were directed towards encouraging healthy lifestyles among the various sub-populations, segmented by different ages and cultural backgrounds (Young et al 1996). As a result, they were not able to counter the extraordinary amount of negative health programming that encourages drinking, fast driving, smoking, risk taking and violence. Another criticism of mass health promotion campaigns is that they did not incorporate a view of health issues in terms of social relations and their interdependence with the environment (Kickbusch 1997). Trying to reach large numbers of people using the media signalled that cost containment in health care systems had become more dominant a goal than peeling back the layers of need that existed in a community. Most of the criticism revolved around the fact that campaigns aimed at reaching the largest number of people resonate with the cost-constrained nature of health care delivery rather than with the primary health care goals of equity and cultural sensitivity to individual or group need (Iannantuono & Eyles 1997).

Mass media campaigns have not captured environmental issues well. Media coverage, primarily via television, has generally focused on dramatic visual opportunities, controversial health risk information, blaming someone (or some group) for the situation and political conflict (Greenberg & Wartenberg, cited in Labonte 1994a). As a result, many people tend to accept as truth information that is biased, because it seems 'scientific'. The single-issue focus that is portrayed in many of these television messages leads many to conclude that solutions are beyond their control and that, in time, the scientists will solve the problems. As a result, many are discouraged from seeking community solutions or engaging in local participatory networks (Labonte 1994a).

Despite these problems, the mass media have been useful in contributing to positive health education outcomes. An analysis of the research examining the influence of the mass media reveals the following:

- Campaigns combining media messages and securing 'commitment' such as pledges obtained in a door-to-door survey have produced significant behaviour changes.
- Mass media campaigns without community participatory or 'pledging' functions have produced poor and cost-ineffective changes.
- Media appeals that were personalised and which modelled specific behaviour changes have been more effective than general, non-role-modelling approaches.
- Feedback has been shown to be essential to reinforce and improve behaviour change.
- Specific, often financial, rewards or penalty-avoidance have been associated with behaviour change that was maintained over time (Labonte 1994a).

The health promotion rhetoric of the 1970s and 1980s has also been the subject of criticism by those advocating for the poor and other marginal groups. For those with few resources, the lifestyle approach wherein all people were urged to take up jogging, eat more vegetables and ensure more leisure time may have also *exacerbated* inequalities in health, given the possibility of unequal access to health services and recreational facilities that could support healthy lifestyles. Members of various consumer movements, such as the women's health movement, challenged the genuineness of health promotion campaigns. Women, especially, were attempting to articulate new forms of social and political relations with respect to health and healing. This meant regaining control over their bodies, their children's health and birthing practices. On one hand, they were hearing the rhetoric of empowerment, and on the other being urged to change their behaviour (Grace 1991).

The dichotomy between individual and social responsibility for health was also debated in the health promotion literature of the time. Labonte (1986) argued for a social model of health that would relieve the individual of exclusive responsibility for outcomes. For example, when a problem such as driving under the influence of alcohol is viewed from an individual perspective, the victim is blamed, and that person is urged to change his or her irresponsible behaviour. A social model of health includes consideration of the structural, environmental conditions within which behaviours occur, including alcohol advertising, regulatory control over liquor licensing, road conditions, public transport and workplace conditions.

Grace (1991) suggests that changes in health promotion from the 1980s to the 1990s have been only minimal. In her view, health promotion initiatives continue to be infiltrated by a contradictory logic wherein there is a promise of creating conditions for empowerment, yet health professionals continue to preach and control. Others agree. We continue to mandate immunisation and other programs aimed at personal safety, sanctioning those who disobey through such things as denying access to child care for those whose children are not immunised, or penalties for not wearing seatbelts or safety helmets (Falk Rafael 1999).

Health for all
and the Ottawa Charter

The next phase in health promotion attempted to respond to the criticisms by describing favourable environments within which health could be created (Hancock 1992). The rhetoric of the new public health to be enshrined in the Ottawa Charter met with general approval among health promotion specialists, particularly for its emphasis on the *creation* of health, and the role of the *environment* in health.

WHO saw this new approach as the key to tackling the problems of the twenty-first century, and as described in the 'Global Strategy of Health for All by Year 2000' document, health promotion is viewed as a process of enabling people to increase control over and improve their health. With the Ottawa Charter, health was no longer seen as a goal; instead it was a resource for living, and potentially available to all (WHO-CPHA 1986). This changed the emphasis from the provision of and access to health *services*, to a focus on accessing *health*, effectively shifting from service *input* to *output*. Being healthy, therefore, was seen to have less to do with the consumption of services than the choices made to lead a healthy life (Iannantuono & Eyles 1997).

The shift to a more global or comprehensive construct of health gradually gained wide acceptance among the international health promotion community. Health researchers began to adjust their models of documenting and measuring the achievement of specific health goals, to incorporate a wider range of factors influencing health, including the contexts of people's lives. The ultimate aim of health was seen not as increasing longevity, but enhancing quality of life (Raeburn & Rootman 1998). In North America, Evans and Stoddart (1990) described the key elements in quality of life outcomes within a framework that included culture, healthy public policies and economic activities that would shape the environments of people's lives. Individual responses were seen as a product of the social and physical environments which, in conjunction with appropriate health care services, could be expected to improve health status (Evans & Stoddart 1990).

Parallel developments in the United Kingdom realigned health promotion with the environment, the relationship between material deprivation and health, and growing recognition of the importance of democratic participation in building health strategies from the community's perspective (Whitelaw, McKeown & Williams 1997). Promoting health within such a framework was seen to include different combinations of strategies that could include any or all of the following:

- legislative change (compulsory wearing of seat belts)
- organisational change (parental leave for early child care)
- sociocultural change (restricting smoking in public places)
- environmental change (reducing automobile emissions or pesticide use in food)
- behavioural change (safe sexual practices)
- technological change (introduction of lead-free petrol)
- economic change (removing subsidies for tobacco producers) (Sindall 1992).

Another product of this health promotion era was the development of conceptual models to guide comprehensive needs assessment, such as the PRECEDE-PROCEED model (Green & Kreuter 1991). Like the approach of Evans and Stoddart, Green and Kreuter's model integrated individual and environmental elements into a set of specific factors.

The PRECEDE-PROCEED
model

Green and Kreuter's model was based on the premise that health promotion must adopt a systematic approach and be based on epidemiological evidence and local needs assessment. Diagnosing the community's education needs flows

from this assessment data, which provides the foundation for setting community health goals.

The first stage of needs assessment is called the *social* diagnosis. Assessment
at this stage includes such social variables as level of educational attainment,
crime, population density and unemployment. This is followed by an *epidemiological* diagnosis, which is intended to reveal rates of morbidity, mortality,
disability and fertility, complete with dimensions of each, such as incidence and
prevalence. Next, a *behavioural* and *environmental* diagnosis is undertaken.
Behavioural indicators include such elements as consumption patterns (healthy
diet), preventive actions (safe sexual practices), self-care indicators and coping
skills (stress management practices).

Green and Kreuter's model was the first to include environmental factors as
equally important influences on health. Environmental aspects were explained
in the model as economic indicators (a community's productivity), geographic
features (potable water, sewage) and services (health care and preventive services). Analysis of these factors is complemented by analysing those elements
in the social environment that would be predictive of a community's inclination to change. This phase of the model includes an *educational* and *organisational* diagnosis, which is aimed at identifying predisposing, reinforcing and
enabling factors that could lead to behavioural and environmental change.
Predisposing factors include individual knowledge, attitudes, values and perceptions that may hinder or facilitate motivation for change. Reinforcing
factors include the attitudes and behaviours of others. Enabling factors are
those skills, resources or barriers that could help or hinder the desired changes,
including environmental factors. Following this phase, an *administrative* and
policy diagnosis is conducted to examine organisational and administrative
capabilities and resources available to respond to identified needs. These elements include such things as current government policies, and organisational
or workplace trends.

Once these diagnostic phases have been completed, implementation can
begin. The implementation program and its constituent strategies are developed to correspond to all issues identified in the diagnostic phases.
Implementation of the strategies is also evaluated to compare the extent to
which the program's objectives were met (Green & Kreuter 1991).

The PRECEDE-PROCEED model quickly gained worldwide acceptance
and has been used in hundreds of health promotion programs (Green et al
1994). However, it has also come under criticism for its academic orientation,
primarily in its use of behavioural and social science jargon (Grace 1991;
Green et al 1994). One of its co-authors subsequently worked with the
Centers for Disease Control in the United States and with various health
departments and community groups, to develop a slightly more user-friendly
model to illustrate the application of the theories and procedures underlying
the PRECEDE-PROCEED model. This model, called PATCH (Planned
Approach to Community Health), has been used to guide risk reduction
related to such issues as physical activity, tobacco use, breast cancer, access
to health care, child abuse and cardiovascular disease (Freudenberg 2000;
Kreuter 1992).

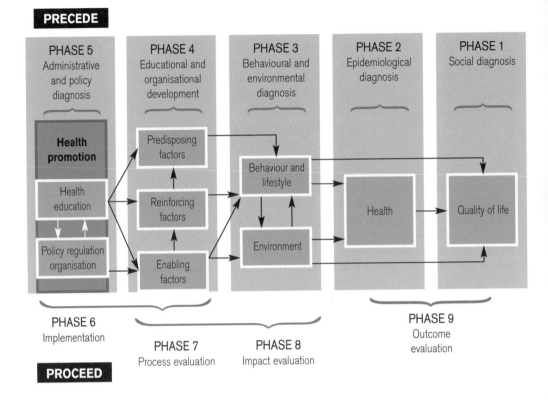

FIGURE 4.1 *The PRECEDE-PROCEED model for health promotion planning and evaluation (from: Green, L.W. & Kreuter, M.W. (1991).* Health Promotion Planning: An Educational and Environmental Approach, *2nd edn, Ca: Mayfield. Reproduced with the permission of McGraw-Hill Companies.)*

The PATCH
model

PATCH is based on the notion of community competence (Cottrell 1983; Goeppinger, Lassiter & Wilcox 1982). When a community is competent to manage and sustain its own structures and processes for sustaining health and a quality life for its residents, it is considered competent. However, this does not imply self-containment. Instead, the competent community relies on horizontal and vertical coalitions (Green et al 1994; Kreuter 1992). A horizontal coalition could be a group-to-group link, such as a men's or women's health group linking up with other similar groups for the purpose of sharing ideas, strategies or resources. At the government level, there is intersectoral collaboration, where horizontal linkages could involve several departments of a state or provincial government collaborating to improve a community service.

Transportation may join with education, health and recreational services, for example, to improve facilities for underprivileged youth. Vertical coalitions involve linkages between various levels of government (local, state, provincial and federal) or various levels of health services.

The primary goal of PATCH is to create a practical mechanism for responding to local-level health priorities. In this respect, the model is sensitive to the context in which health decisions are made. A second goal of the program is to offer a practical, skills-based approach of technical assistance to local people to develop health education programs that will help community development. Like its predecessor (PRECEDE-PROCEED), the model emphasises community participation and rigorous evaluation of information. Its basic concept is that of local ownership; that is, decisions for social change affecting lifestyle issues can be best made 'collectively, as close as possible to the homes and workplaces of those affected' (Kreuter 1992, p 136).

A series of evaluative studies was carried out for six programs in Maine (United States) that used the PATCH approach (Goodman et al 1993). Study results led the authors to a number of conclusions, including the need to: begin community health promotions with an assessment of community capacity; allow community members flexibility in prioritising health objectives; sustain technical assistance and coordination throughout the project, rather than just at the beginning; emphasise multiple interventions for each problem addressed; and ensure organisational commitment to continuing capacity-building efforts (Goodman et al 1993).

---

case study...

Drinksafe in the university community

A group of students at Perth's Edith Cowan University decided to test the usefulness of the PRECEDE-PROCEED model for health promotion planning and evaluation to address drinking behaviour in 18–25 year-old university students. They chose the Drinksafe program because it was being used by the local health department (HDWA) to promote healthy drinking behaviour throughout the community. Below is an account of their progress and success in the program.

Phase 1: Social diagnosis

From the literature and HDWA statistical data, the students identified increased absenteeism, decreased worker productivity and domestic violence (all related to alcohol use) as the major social implications of alcohol misuse in the general community. Studying the social effects of excessive drinking among members of the university community, the students identified poor attendance at classes, failing grades and difficulties with interpersonal relationships.

Phase 2: Epidemiological diagnosis

In the second phase, the students discovered from HDWA data that in the year prior to their program, 5 per cent of all deaths as well as a considerable burden of illness in the State of Western Australia were attributable to alcohol. They were, however, unable to segment out how many of these cases occurred among the student population, which they considered a limitation of their epidemiological investigation.

Phase 3: Behavioural and environmental diagnosis

The next phase revealed a high prevalence of 18–25 year olds regularly drinking alcohol to excess and a high incidence of 18–25 year olds being booked by the police for drink-driving.

Phase 4: Educational and organisational diagnosis

Predisposing factors: Through peer discussions, the students suspected that there existed a lack of knowledge about safe drinking levels among 18–25 year olds, and that many of this group held the attitude or belief that 'getting caught drink-driving won't happen to me'. Furthermore, the students hoped to overcome any incorrect perceptions of the amount of alcohol required to get drunk. They also considered the various beliefs related to alcohol use, such as cultural beliefs in some households that consuming alcohol with meals is beneficial.

Reinforcing factors: The factors familiar to the students that were sustaining drinking behaviour were identified as peer approval and, in some cases, parental approval, and the constant presence of alcohol portrayed in the media.

Enabling factors: The students identified the enabling factors as the availability of alcohol, its low cost, the proliferation of pub promotions offering free drinks and, related to the drink-driving factor, a lack of public transport.

Phase 5: Administrative and policy diagnosis

In order to mount an effective campaign, the students looked into the policies that would affect drinking behaviour. These included legislation for safe driving (0.05 blood alcohol limit) and the introduction of random breath testing, both of which were designed to act as deterrents to overuse of drinking and driving.

The Drinksafe campaign in the university community

The students organising the campaign decided to introduce the following health education strategies:

- **Individual.** Information booklets on safe drinking levels were distributed throughout the campus. These were readily available through the state Drinksafe campaign. In the campus primary health care clinic, the students also offered individualised computer assessment of alcohol use to students and staff wishing to take part. For this they used a health education program previously developed for public use, publicised through staff newsletters and the student magazine.
- **Group.** The students conducted an educational seminar on drink-driving. Educational videotapes on alcohol-related issues were shown in the campus cafeteria as well as in the primary health care clinic.
- **Mass media.** Posters and pamphlets supplied by the state Drinksafe campaign were displayed in campus libraries and other places such as the local pubs, where 18–25 year olds tend to gather.

The goal of the program was to bring about a reduction in the incidence and prevalence of illnesses, injuries and deaths associated with alcohol intake in 18–25 year olds. Specific program objectives included the following:

- **Educational objectives:** After some discussion, the students running the campaign decided that realistic expectations for change six months after implementation of the program would include the following:
  - 80 per cent of 18–25 year olds on campus would be able to state the safe drinking limits
  - 80 per cent of liquor outlets in the surrounding community would provide and advertise low alcohol beer
  - 80 per cent of 18–25 year-old students at the university would request and receive further information about alcohol use.
- **Behavioural objective:** The students decided that it would also be realistic to expect that six months after implementing the program there would be a 20 per cent reduction in the current number of 18–25 year-old university students booked for drink-driving.

The students suggested that these objectives be evaluated six months after the program's implementation, with evaluation data to be used as the basis for renewal or modification of the program. Because they were about to graduate and move on, they were unable to undertake the evaluation, but they studied the evaluation data from the state-wide program and set their expectations at the same level—that is, a total reduction in consumption, and a reduction in the average number of days on which community members reported drinking any alcohol at all (McMurray 1993, pp 166–8).

Although the students mentioned in the case study above were unable to follow through with their intended evaluation, they reported that the exercise was a valuable lesson in the systematic planning necessary for promoting health. They also learned that, irrespective of the indications of behaviour change, when a health education program is undertaken, there is some level of community or group development, often simply by increasing attention to the health issue. This is borne out by evaluations of both the PATCH and PRECEDE-PROCEED programs, both of which were designed to empower local residents to make health-enhancing choices while acknowledging the importance of the environment or context. However, these programs have been criticised as working against community empowerment in relation to the risk analysis components, which are biased towards identification of risk in professional terms, rather than in a context and language familiar to community residents (Labonte 1994b). Despite this criticism, one of the merits of PATCH is that it has drawn attention to the need to focus on the setting in community health and development, foreshadowing WHO's 'healthy settings' approach.

Health promotion as an investment:
the settings approach

In the 1990s, WHO's health-promotion approach was based on the assumption that health is an indication of the extent to which people are, on the one hand, able to develop aspirations and satisfy needs and, on the other hand, able to change or cope with the environment (Kickbusch 1997). The approach was built on three premises. The first is the fundamental question of *what creates health?* (Antonovsky, cited in Kickbusch 1997). Good health is a product of coherent interactions between people and their environments in the course of everyday life. Within this model, the most important strategies for health promotion are those that strengthen people's sense of coherence, and this can be achieved by supporting the environments of their daily lives: their schools, hospitals and workplaces (Kickbusch 1997).

The second element of this model is the public health premise: *which investment creates the largest health gain?* From a public health perspective, health is seen as an investment. Practically, it is achieved through community development, participation and partnership. The key resource questions revolve around the relationship between health investments and outcomes. Health policies address the ways in which resources can be deployed to lead to optimal health outcomes for the population. Community health gains are made possible from public investments in areas other than health; that is, the *settings* of people's lives (Kickbusch 1997).

The practical premise is the third aspect of the health-promoting environments approach, and this involves *community development and organisational development*. The settings approach broadens health promotion from the population level to the level of organisations and systems (Harris & Wills 1997). Healthy organisations are considered integral to community health, and they are also predictive of a community's capacity for sustainability because they respond to health needs at the environmental or service level (Kickbusch 1997). For example, where there is a constant influx of new people into the community, a healthy system of assisting the newcomers with the myriad of transitions would include providing assistance with language, education and workplace services, and culturally appropriate health care in the settings of their daily lives.

The settings of people's lives are considered ideal for promoting health in that they are organised for more deeply binding reasons than health. Neighbourhoods, schools, workplaces and health care sites are characterised by frequent and sustained patterns of communication and interaction and therefore have the capacity to facilitate healthful choices (Mullen et al 1995). Partnerships between community residents and health professionals, and between community groups, are more readily established and maintained in the ordinary settings of their lives. Particular settings often reach populations differentiated by age, stage, socioeconomic status and other circumstances, and this makes it easier to deploy resources and evaluate outcomes appropriately as well as encourage community participation. In short, healthy settings provide the basis for nurturing human and social capital.

The advantages of settings as the site of health promotion are summarised as follows:

- They provide channels for delivering health promotion.
- They represent units of identity, such as at school or work.
- Diffusion of ideas occurs in, and is facilitated by, settings.
- They provide access to gatekeepers.
- Policies can be readily implemented in a particular structure.
- They provide access to specific populations.
- Funding categories for health promotion usually specify settings.
- They contain unique practice and/or training traditions.
- Professional identities are linked to settings. (Mullen et al 1995)

The settings approach is encapsulated in the Jakarta Declaration on Health Promotion into the 21st Century (WHO 1997). This declaration acknowledges the Ottawa Charter for Health Promotion and encourages integration of all five strategies of the Ottawa Charter into all settings where health is to be promoted. These settings include the physical, political and social environments. Community education and participation are seen as the core elements in achieving community health, and these rely on partnerships between governments, non-government organisations, and all public and private sectors of society (WHO 1997). The Jakarta Declaration is reproduced below.

Jakarta Declaration on Health Promotion into the 21st Century

1. Promote social responsibility for health

Decision makers must be firmly committed to social responsibility. Both the public and private sectors should promote health by pursuing policies and practices that:

- avoid harming the health of other individuals
- protect the environment and ensure sustainable use of resources
- restrict production and trade in inherently harmful goods and substances such as tobacco and armaments, as well as unhealthy marketing practices
- safeguard both the citizen in the marketplace and the individual in the workplace
- include equity-focused health impact assessments as an integral part of policy development.

2. Increase investments for health development

In many countries, current investment in health is inadequate and often ineffective. Increasing investment for health development requires a truly multisectoral approach, including additional resources to education, housing and the health sector. Greater investment for health, and reorientation of existing investments— both within and between countries—has the potential to significantly advance human development, health and quality of life.

Investments in health should reflect the needs of certain groups such as women, children, older people, indigenous, poor and marginalised populations.

3. Consolidate and expand partnerships for health

Health promotion requires partnerships for health and social development between the different sectors at all levels of governance and society. Existing partnerships need to be strengthened and the potential for new partnerships must be explored.

Partnerships offer mutual benefit for health through the sharing of expertise, skills and resources. Each partnership must be transparent and accountable and be based on agreed ethical principles, mutual understanding and respect. WHO guidelines should be adhered to.

4. Increase community capacity and empower the individual

Health promotion is carried out *by* and *with* people, not on or to people. It improves the ability of individuals to take action, and the capacity of groups, organisations or communities to influence the determinants of health.

Improving the capacity of communities for health promotion requires practical education, leadership training and access to resources. Empowering individuals demands more consistent, reliable access to the decision making process and the skills and knowledge essential to effect change.

Both traditional communication and the new information media support this process. Social, cultural and spiritual resources need to be harnessed in innovative ways.

5. Secure an infrastructure for health promotion

To secure an infrastructure for health promotion, new mechanisms of funding it locally, nationally and globally must be found. Incentives should be developed to influence the actions of governments, non-government organisations (NGOs) educational institutions and the private sector to make sure that resource mobilisation for health promotion is maximised.

'Settings for health' represent the organisational base of the infrastructure required for health promotion. New health challenges mean that new and diverse networks need to be created to achieve intersectoral collaboration. Such networks should provide mutual assistance within and between countries and facilitate exchange of information on which strategies are effective in which settings.

Training and practice of local leadership skills should be encouraged to support health promotion activities. Documentation of experiences in health promotion through research and project reporting should be enhanced to improve planning, implementation and evaluation.

All countries should develop the appropriate political, legal, educational, social and economic environments required to support health promotion.

The Jakarta Declaration represents the vanguard of health promotion for this millennium. The statement is firmly grounded in the principles of primary health care and social justice, with a clear focus on community empowerment. It is the culmination of a century of thinking about health promotion and includes a synthesis of conceptual approaches that revolve around maintaining the infrastructure and conditions within which people can make healthful choices, then building the community's capacity to make these choices. Importantly, it also directs those undertaking health promotion to adopt an evidence-based approach to both policy and practice (WHO 1998).

Contemporary health
promotion approaches

Throughout the twentieth century, the field of health promotion proliferated. Today, there is a move towards gathering qualitative research evidence on what works, and how various communities approach capacity building for a healthful future. Community empowerment and partnerships are part of the global rhetoric (Mechanic 1999; Tsai Roussos & Fawcett 2000). What is needed now is a more realistic approach to community health promotion than that afforded by global models. Whitelaw and colleagues (1997) decry such models on the basis that they may lead to systematising an approach that should be based on difference and uniqueness rather than similarity. Caution must also be taken in relation to empowerment strategies, some of which have tended to create marginalised subgroups within a community out of those not yet ready to participate in the community's development plans (Falk Rafael 1999).

A further challenge lies in developing a more comprehensive approach to health promotion than in the past.

Revisiting risk:
proximal and distal risk factors

Current notions of health risk distinguish between *proximal* risk factors, such as diet, cholesterol level, exercise and other lifestyle factors under the control of the individual, and *distal* factors such as socioeconomic status, employment and social support (Green 1999). Some researchers contend that modern epidemiology and cultural values have conspired to focus attention on proximal, individually based risk factors instead of social conditions (Link & Phelan 1995). Contemporary health promotion discourse broadens the concept of health risk to include not only individual and social risks to health, but also the interrelationships between the two. By considering proximal and distal factors simultaneously, we can piece together images of how people's lives evolve over time in the context of lifestyles and circumstances (Mirowsky 1998). These images over time can then be used to illuminate the myriad processes from pregnancy to ageing, and the way such factors as culture, unemployment, economic hardship, oppressive work conditions or geographical dislocations increase the risk of unhealthy pregnancies, child-rearing practices and disease and impairment in later life. This is a more comprehensive approach to health promotion than has been used in the past.

Despite the growing number of studies into the interrelationships among risk factors, mass media campaigns and group-based health education programs continue to badger people on the links between proximal factors such as smoking or eating a high-fat diet, and a particular negative health outcome (Livingston 1997). This information should be used where there is a window of opportunity, at the time a person is accessing health services or built into patterns of work, family life and recreation (Mechanic 1999). The intention of such health education messages should be to cultivate knowledge on the cumulative and interactive nature of risk factors, so that people are left to make choices based on *their* overall determination of risk and, in turn, decide what, and to what extent, contributing factors can and should be changed. For example, an individual would benefit from knowing that if they have asthma and live in a damp home or one with dust mites, encounter chemicals at work (for example, as a welder), and walk, jog or live in an area of considerable air pollution, smoking may be fatal.

At the societal level, knowing the particular interrelationships between the environment, workplace, social class, racism, sexism and poverty would help re-vision health policies from a single disease orientation and a focus on the individual, to ones that acknowledge the interdependence and reciprocal interactions between individual and societal determinants of health, and the multiple health outcomes that flow from these (East 1998; Hertzman 2001; Kunst, Geurts & Van den Berg 1995; Link & Phelan 1995; Livingston 1997; Wilkinson 1996). To be effective, we need 'a balanced portfolio of health education and health promotion directed at proximal risk factors under greater control of individuals and more distal risk conditions controlled by others' (Green 1999, p 81).

A comprehensive approach to health promotion is somewhat daunting, particularly when the easier-studied determinants of health (smoking and poverty) continue to attract greater attention from funding bodies and current policy makers (Cole et al 1999; Collins 1995). We know this segmented approach has not worked in the past: medical services do not create health; police and prisons have only a minor impact on crime; social workers have little effect on social problems; teachers have minimal capacity to overcome childhood traumas; and family therapists cannot prevent families from falling apart (Wilkinson 1996). Healthy social policies therefore cannot simply add expensive services; they must be aimed at identifying more fundamental changes that will achieve a balance between service provision and prevention. Healthy social policies and the initiatives that flow from them must aim to reduce material deprivation, invest in infrastructure, lower social gradients and enhance sustainability. This begins with providing uniformly accessible antenatal care, then early pre-school programs, school-based health services, adolescent counselling and mentoring services, family support, including stress management and nutrition support, job training for adults, lifestyle support during ageing and, at all stages of life, appropriate interventions for illness or injury (Tarlov 1996).

Report card
for the new millennium

As we engage with communities in this first decade of the twenty-first century, it may be useful to explore how well our health promotion strategies are working. First, let's look at the individual. Despite national and international goals and targets for healthy lifestyles, and widespread public information on high-risk behaviours, people continue to smoke, drink excessive amounts of alcohol, eat too much dietary fat and undertake too little exercise. Research indicates that many of these behaviours are interrelated. For example, there is strong evidence concerning the close association between the use of tobacco and alcohol, with cigarette smoking seen to be a forerunner to alcohol use (Ma, Betts & Hampl 2000). Drinking habits, in turn, have been found to alter individuals' food selections and nutrient intakes, which suggests that a comprehensive program targeting all these risk factors would be more effective than emphasising any single factor alone (Ma et al 2000).

If we examine the context that supports these risky behaviours, the most visible element would have to be the influence of the political industrial arena. Because the tobacco, alcohol and food industries all have an indisputable stake in keeping people smoking, drinking alcohol to excess and eating fatty foods, health promotion efforts must address these at the political and organisational levels (Morgan & Marsh 1998).

Cigarette smoking is the greatest challenge, as it is the most potent threat to health today, and one for which most countries have instigated at least some regulatory controls (Green, Nathan & Mercer 2001). Directing health promotion strategies towards the policy environment has resulted in widespread measures to regulate product labelling, the industry itself, community and workplace settings, and the individual. This approach ensures a comprehensive program in which:

- consumers are warned of the dangers of tobacco use and informed of the toxic constituents
- the price of tobacco is inflated through taxation
- tobacco advertising and promotion is banned or restricted
- people are prohibited from smoking in public places
- minors are prevented from purchasing tobacco
- levels of tar and nicotine are restricted or prohibited (Green et al 2001).

Such extensive legislation is required because the tobacco pandemic flows from 'a powerful industry that promotes and sells a deadly and addictive, albeit legal, product that [is] responsible for more than 4 million preventable deaths per year' (Green et al 2001, p 112). WHO reports that the figure will rise to 10 million tobacco-related deaths per year by 2030, 70 per cent of which will damage developing countries (Harlem Brundtland 2001).

There is, however, room for optimism. The International Union for Health Promotion and Education (IUHPE) recently reported to the European Union on the evidence of health promotion effectiveness, indicating that one of the most important areas where health promotion had made a difference was in tobacco control (McQueen 2001). The group found evidence of a powerful inverse relationship between price and use of tobacco, reinforcing strategies that have led to taxation-related price increases for tobacco products (McQueen 2001).

Health promotion planners in many countries have developed incremental programs to counter tobacco use, including efforts to reduce consumption through pricing. Australia, New Zealand and Singapore were early leaders in banning tobacco advertisements and sponsorships since the early 1970s. These countries, and Sweden and Hong Kong, continue to have the lowest rates of smoking in the world, demonstrating the effectiveness of government controls (WHO 2000). Globally, we are not doing too badly on this front. Increased taxation on tobacco products has halved tobacco consumption in Australia since 1960 (Chapman 1997). Singapore has one of the lowest rates of smoking in the world. Countries like Canada have had warning labels on cigarette packages for many years and Canada is now considered to have the most stringent anti-smoking policy regulations (Green et al 2001). Since the mid-1990s countries such as South Africa, Poland and Fiji have also developed comprehensive tobacco control policies that could serve as a model for others (Green et al 2001). And these successes are reinforced by a 1999 World Health Assembly resolution authorising an international Framework Convention on Tobacco Control (FCTC) that would address the tobacco crisis at a global level (Green et al 2001). This is ongoing, with the group continuing to meet regularly.

Research into what works in reducing smoking reveals that the broader policy approach may be the best direction to take. Studies investigating individual behaviours show that continual bombardment by the media urging people to quit smoking has minimal impact on many smokers. They know smoking is unhealthy for them and their children, yet it may be their only source of stress relief (Beeber 1996). The key to helping them to quit or remove their children from the smoke environment is understanding the diverse nature of personal motivation and people's inclination to set personal goals. Wechsler and colleagues' (1996) studies indicate that fewer than 20 per cent of people with a less-than-ideal behaviour pattern are prepared to change at any one time. Even when they are prepared to do so, only one in five who try to change their health-related behaviour succeeds the first time. Smokers take an average of three to four attempts before they successfully quit, with weight loss being the hardest change of all to make. Behaviour change is even more difficult for those with chronic diseases like diabetes. Making lifestyle changes while trying to live a normal and fulfilling life is, for these people, a constant balancing act (Susman & Helseth 1997).

As advocates for change we need to guide people away from unrealistic goals and help them understand the merits of a phased-in approach to change. However, at the same time, we need to seek best investments. The authors of the report on health promotion effectiveness to the European Union revealed the following evidence:

- Comprehensive approaches to health promotion using all five strategies of the Ottawa Charter are the most effective.
- Certain settings (schools, workplaces, cities and local communities) offer practice opportunities for effective health promotion.
- People, including those most affected by health issues, need to be at the heart of health promotion programs and decision-making.
- Real access to information and education, in an appropriate language and style, is vital.
- Health promotion is a key investment—an essential element of social and economic development (IUHPE, cited in McQueen 2001, p 265).

Another investment for the future lies in supporting research to build the evidence-base for health promotion. One of the areas where further evidence is needed concerns the effectiveness of collaborative partnerships (Tsai Roussos & Fawcett 2000). This should begin with accurate and sensitive indicators of community health needs, such as population-level data on alcohol-related vehicular crashes and vaccine-preventable diseases, and place-based information, such as morbidity and mortality indicators (eating habits, sports injuries, violence, illicit drug use) in specific urban neighbourhoods (Tsai Roussos

& Fawcett 2000). These authors suggest that case study research linking indicators of need with the effects of partnerships will provide meaningful data from which to promote health.

In an annual review of health promotion in urban environments, Freudenberg (2000) identified the following ten strategies that will continue to promote health in our communities:

- access to quality primary care
- increased health knowledge
- reduction in risky behaviours
- increased social support
- reducing stigma and marginalisation
- advocating health-promoting policies
- improving urban physical environments
- meeting basic needs
- creating supportive social environments
- reducing income inequality.

It is interesting to reflect on the past, to extract from it lessons for the future. The 'old' health promotion taught us much about individual behaviour and the usefulness of various approaches to health education. We can now use that information to plan 'new', sustainable, comprehensive, community-wide health promotion strategies from a model of partnerships that will, in the process, build community competence in the settings of people's lives (Goodman et al 1996; Shediac-Rizkallah & Bone 1998).

thinking critically

Health promotion

1   Identify four developmental phases that signalled a change in the way health promotion has been approached over the past century.

2   Using Green and Kreuter's health promotion model, devise a planned strategy for increasing physical activity among the ageing population.

3   Identify four important features of the healthy settings approach.

4   Compare and contrast the Ottawa Charter and the Jakarta Declaration.

5   Construct a health promotion plan for enhancing the health of migrant women in an urban environment.

6   Discuss the pros and cons of including social marketing in the health promotion plan above.

7   Describe a competent community.

REFERENCES

Beeber, S. (1996). Parental smoking and childhood asthma. *Journal of Pediatric Health Care*, 10(2): 58–62.

Chapman, S. (1997). Simon Chapman honoured by WHO for tobacco control. *In Touch*, 14(8): 1.

Cole, D., Eyles, J., Gibson, B. & Ross, N. (1999). Links between humans and ecosystems: the implications of framing for health promotion strategies. *Health Promotion International*, 14(1): 65–72.

Collins, T. (1995). Models of health: pervasive, persuasive and politically charged. *Health Promotion International*, 10(4): 317–24.

Cottrell, L. (1983). The competent community. In: W. Lyon (ed), *New Perspectives on the American Community*. Homewood, Ill: Dorsey Press.

East, L. (1998). The quality of social relationships as a public health issue: exploring the relationship between health and community in a disadvantaged neighbourhood. *Health and Social Care in the Community*, 6(3): 189–95.

Egger, G., Fitzgerald, W., Frape, G., Monaem, A., Rubinstein, P., Tyler, C. & Mackay, B. (1983). Results of a large scale media anti-smoking campaign in Australia: the North Coast Healthy Lifestyle Program. *British Medical Journal*, 287: 1125–87.

Emanuel, E. & Emanuel, O. (1996). What is accountability in health care? *Annals of Internal Medicine*, 124: 129–39.

Esler-McMurray, A. (1980). The body shop: marketing a healthy lifestyle. *The Canadian Nurse*, 76(4): 46–8.

Evans, R. & Stoddart, G. (1990). Producing health, consuming health care. *Social Science and Medicine*, 31(12): 1347–63.

Falk Rafael, A. (1999). The politics of health promotion: influences on public health promoting nursing practice in Ontario, Canada from Nightingale to the nineties. *Advances in Nursing Science*, 22(1): 23–41.

Freudenberg, N. (2000). Health promotion in the city: a review of current practice and future prospects in the United States. *Annual Review of Public Health*, 21: 473–503.

Goeppinger, J., Lassiter, P. & Wilcox, B. (1982). Community health is community competence. *Nursing Outlook*, 30: 464–7.

Goodman, R., Steckler, A., Hoover, S. & Schwartz (1993). A critique of contemporary health promotion approaches: Based on a qualitative review of six programs in Maine. *American Journal of Health Promotion*, 7(3): 208–20.

Goodman, R., Wandersman, A., Chinman, M., Imm, P. & Morrissey, E. (1996). An ecological assessment of community-based interventions for prevention and health promotion: approaches to measuring community coalitions. *American Journal of Community Psychology*, 24(1): 33–61.

Grace, V. (1991). The marketing of empowerment and the construction of the health consumer: a critique of health promotion. *International Journal of Health Services*, 21(2): 329–43.

Green, L. (1999). Health education's contributions to public health in the twentieth century: A glimpse through health promotion's rear-view mirror. *Annual Review of Public Health*, 20: 67–88.

Green, L. & Kreuter, M. (1991). *Health Promotion Planning: An Educational and Environmental Approach*. Mountain View, Ca: Mayfield.

Green, L., Glanz, K., Hochbaum, G., Kok, G., Kreuter, M., Lewis, M., Lorig, K., Morisky, D., Rimer, B. & Rosenstock, I. (1994). Can we build on, or must we replace, the theories and models in health education? *Health Education Research*, 9(3): 397–404.

Green, L., Nathan, R. & Mercer, S. (2001). The health of health promotion in public policy: drawing inspiration from the tobacco control movement. *Health Promotion Journal of Australia*, 12(2): 110–16.

Hancock, T. (1992). The healthy city: utopias and realities. In: J. Ashton (ed), *Healthy Cities*. Philadelphia: Milton Keynes, pp 22–9.

Harlem Brundtland, G. (2001). Statement by Dr Gro Harlem Brundtland, Director-General WHO, to the Fifth Global Conference on Health Promotion, Mexico City, 5 June 2000. *Health Promotion International*, 16(1): 95–8.

Harris, E. & Wills, J. (1997). Developing healthy local communities at local government level: lessons from the past decade. *Australian and New Zealand Journal of Public Health*, 21(4): 403–12.

Hertzman, C. (2001). Health and human society. *American Scientist*, 89(6): 538–44.

Iannantuono, A. & Eyles, J. (1997). Meanings in policy: a textual analysis of Canada's 'Achieving Health for All' document. *Social Science and Medicine*, 44(11): 1611–21.

Kickbusch, I. (1997). Health promoting environments: the next step. *Australian and New Zealand Journal of Public Health*, 21(4): 431–4.

Kotler, P. (1975). *Marketing for Non-profit Organisations*. Englewood Cliffs: Prentice-Hall.

Kreuter, M. (1992). PATCH: its origin, basic concepts, and links to contemporary public health policy. *Journal of Health Education*, 23(3): 135–9.

Kunst, A., Geurts, J. & Van den Berg, J. (1995). International variation in socioeconomic inequalities in self reported health. *Journal of Epidemiology and Community Health*, 49: 117–23.

Labonte, R. (1986). Social inequality and healthy public policy. *Health Promotion*, 1(3): 341–51.

—— (1994a). 'See me, hear me, touch me, feel me'. Lessons on environmental health information for bureaucratic activists. In: C. Chu & R. Simpson (eds), *Ecological Public Health: From Vision to Practice*. Brisbane: Institute of Applied Environmental Research, pp 269–76.

—— (1994b). Health promotion and empowerment: reflections on professional practice. *Health Education Quarterly*, 21(2): 253–68.

Lasater, T., Carleton, R. & LeFebre, R. (1988) The Pawtucket heart health program: utilizing community resources for primary prevention. *Rhode Island Medical Journal*, 71: 63–7.

Link, B. & Phelan, J. (1995). Social conditions as fundamental causes of disease. *Journal of Health and Social Behavior* (extra issue): 80–94.

Livingston, M. (1997) Update on health care in Canada: what's right, what's wrong, what's left. *Journal of Public Health Policy*, 19(3): 267–88.

Ma, J., Betts, N. & Hampl, J. (2000). Clustering of lifestyle behaviors: the relationship between cigarette smoking, alcohol consumption and dietary intake. *American Journal of Health Promotion*, 15(2): 107–17.

Maccoby, N. & Solomon, D. (1981). The Stanford community studies in heart disease prevention. In: R. Rice & W. Paisley (eds), *Public Communication Campaigns*. Beverley Hills: Sage.

McAlister, A. (1981). Anti-smoking campaigns: progress in developing effective communications. In: R. Rice & W. Paisley (eds), *Public Communication Campaigns*. Beverley Hills: Sage.

McMurray, A. (1993). *Community Health Nursing: Primary Health Care in Practice*, 2nd edn, Melbourne: Churchill-Livingstone.

McQueen, D. (2001). Strengthening the evidence base for health promotion. *Health Promotion International*, 16(3): 261–8.

Mechanic, D. (1999). Issues in promoting health. *Social Science and Medicine*, 48: 711–18.

Mirowsky, J. (1998). An informative sociology of health and well-being: Notes from the new editor. *Journal of Health and Social Behavior*, 39: 1–3.

Morgan, I. & Marsh, G. (1998). Historic and future health promotion contexts for nursing. *Image: Journal of Nursing Scholarship*, 30(4): 379–86.

Mullen, P., Forster, J., Gottlieb, N., Kreuter, M., Moon, R., O'Rourke, T. & Strecher, V. (1995). Settings as an important dimension in health eucation/promotion policy, programs and research. *Health Education Quarterly*, 22 (3): 329–45.

Nutbeam, D. & Catford, J. (1987). The Welsh heart program evaluation strategy: progress, plans and possibilities. *Health Promotion*, 2(1): 5–18.

Raeburn, J. & Rootman, I. (1998). *People-Centred Health Promotion*. New York: John Wiley & Sons.

Robertson, A. & Minkler, M. (1994). New health promotion movement: a critical examination. *Health Education Quarterly*, 21(3): 295–312.

Shediac-Rizkallah, M. & Bone, L. (1998). Planning for the sustainability of community-based health programs: conceptual frameworks and future directions for research, practice and policy. *Health Education Research*, 13(1): 87–108.

Sindall, C. (1992). Health promotion and community health in Australia: An overview of theory and practice. In: F. Baum, D. Fry & I. Lennie (eds), *Community Health Policy and Practice in Australia*, Sydney: Pluto Press Australia and Community Health Association, pp 277–95.

Susman, J. & Helseth, L. (1997). Reducing the complications of type II diabetes: a patient-centered approach. *American Family Physician*, 56: 471–8.

Tarlov, A. (1996). Social determinants of health: the sociobiological translation. In: D. Blane, E. Brunner & R. Wilkinson (eds), *Health and Social Organisation: Towards a Health Policy for the Twenty-first Century*, London: Routledge, pp 71–93.

Tsai Roussos, S. & Fawcett, S. (2000). A review of collaborative partnerships as a strategy for improving community health. *Annual Review of Public Health*, 21: 369–402.

Valanis, B. (1986). *Epidemiology in Nursing and Health Care*, Norwalk: Appleton-Century Crofts.

Wechsler, H., Lovine, S., Idelson, R., Schor, E. & Coakley, E. (1996). The physician's role in health promotion revisited—a survey of primary care practitioners. *New England Journal of Medicine*, 334(15): 996–8.

Whitelaw, S., McKeown, K. & Williams, J. (1997). Global health promotion models: enlightenment or entrapment? *Health Education Research*, 12(4): 479–90.

Wilkinson, R. (1996). *Unhealthy Societies: The Afflictions of Inequality*. London: Routledge.

World Health Organization (WHO) (1997). The Jakarta Declaration on Health Promotion into the 21st Century. Jakarta: WHO.

—— (1998). The fifty-first world health assembly, health promotion. Geneva: WHO.

—— (2000). The World Health Report 2000. Health systems: improving performance. Geneva: WHO.

World Health Organization-Health and Welfare Canada-CPHA (1986). Ottawa Charter for Health Promotion. *Canadian Journal of Public Health*, 77(12): 425–30.

Young, D., Haskell, W., Barr Taylor, C. & Fortmann, S. (1996). Effect of community health education on physical activity knowledge, attitudes and behavior. *American Journal of Epidemiology*, 144(3): 264–74.

Sustainable health
for the individual and family

Section

Introduction
to the Section

This section introduces the notion of health and wellness along a continuum of developmental stages. Chapter 5 examines children as a population group. Healthy childbirth and healthy children are the most important predictors of sustainable health in the community, and in civilisation as a whole. In creating and sustaining the health of children, we invest in the health of all people. This chapter is based on the contention that each community has a unique capacity for nurturing young people, regardless of constraints that may be related to environmental, economic, social, political and cultural factors. The role of the health advocate is to help community members analyse that capacity, and to investigate the health determinants and risk factors that must be addressed in order to sustain health and wellness.

The health status of adolescents in any community provides a barometer of a community's progress in generating health and wellness. At this most crucial stage, a large segment of the population is launched from childhood to adulthood, from dependence to independence. How adolescents negotiate this transition is the most important indicator of how health and wellness will be valued in their future adult lives. The impact of peer pressure and social structures are among the most important determinants of healthy lifestyle choices. The adolescent's choices, and the extent to which these are supported by others, often establish a pattern for life, for health or illness. Chapter 6 explores some of these choices and the risk factors that most deeply affect the health of adolescents, which may be predictive of the extent to which they will become healthy adults.

Healthy adulthood reflects the culmination of healthy lifestyle choices made by the individual, tempered by hereditary, social and environmental conditions. In the adult population the outcomes of health service provision are also visible, as by the time most people reach adulthood, they have encountered the health care system on at least one occasion. These encounters may be aimed at redressing a clinical problem, providing an opportunity for illness prevention in the future, or both. The way adults use the health care system is therefore of great importance to the pattern of living that will sustain or impede the quality of their lives as they approach ageing. In Chapter 7, the major risk factors and lifestyle determinants of healthy adulthood and the role of the health care system are discussed in a way that acknowledges the dual influence of the environment and its structures, and personal choices, on health.

Chapter 8 examines the features of healthy ageing. The burden of illness, injury and disability for those over age 65 is addressed in relation to ways of monitoring states of health for older citizens and decreasing their levels of risk for ill health. The health professional's role in assisting the elderly to expect, and then to achieve, health and wellness is paramount at this time of life, as older people rely more heavily than others on advice and guidance from those they encounter in a range of health services. A model for healthy ageing is presented as an example of self-determination in achieving a long and healthy life.

Chapter 9 provides an insight into the contemporary family, discussing the importance of the family as infrastructure for sustainable health. The influence of the family on all stages of development is addressed, from childhood to old age. The role of the family in health has traditionally been described in terms of structural rather than process issues. However, in a rapidly changing society it is essential to address the interaction between the two. In this new century, family structures present a kaleidoscope of configurations. Along with these new structures are evolving processes for securing and maintaining the health of family members and dealing with outside influences. Culturally determined roles are also being constantly reformed and reframed, as communications technology brings families from one community into contact with many others, creating a realm of new expectations. The impact of technology and changing family structures and processes is discussed in this chapter with respect to the role of the health advocate. It is based on the perspective that understanding is the key to helping others achieve health and wellness.

In Chapter 10, gender issues are discussed under the rubric of healthy men and healthy women. Too often, gender issues have tended to polarise health promotion activities toward either females or males, sometimes at the expense of the other. In discussing these issues within the same chapter, distinctions and areas of congruence are illuminated, with the result of greater understanding of the ways in which both women and men can capitalise on their unique strengths and overcome their respective areas of risk for illness, injury or disability. One of the most important elements in gendering health promotion is to ensure equity of access to education. This is outlined in the context of facilitating better health for women and men using the principles of primary health care.

Chapter 11 addresses Indigenous people's health and risk. International reports indicate little progress in redressing the disproportionate burden of illness, injury and disability among Indigenous people. Many factors constrain Indigenous people's capacity for health and wellness, some of which are being addressed in a more empowering way than others. Globalisation is addressed in relation to its potentially harmful effects on the health and development capacity of Indigenous people. The chapter ends with suggestions for redressing the culturally embedded inequities that limit the extent to which Indigenous health can be achieved.

CHAPTER 5

Healthy
children

ntroduction   One of the greatest indicators of health and wellness in a community is
the extent to which it nurtures healthy children, as they will become the healthy adult citizens
who can make a community vibrant. Any investment in healthy children is therefore an investment in the social and human capital of the community. In some communities, the health of
young people is hindered by an array of social determinants of health that compromise
healthy childhoods. In others, children are prepared for adulthood in a way that allows them
to use their social, physical, economic and environmental influences to greater advantage.
This chapter attempts to chart a course towards healthy adulthood by considering the major
threats and opportunities in child health, and the influence of the local, national and global
communities on the development of healthy children.

objectives **By the end of this chapter you will be able to:**

1 Identify the five most important influences on child health in contemporary society

2 Describe the major risk factors that negatively influence child health

3 Discuss family issues influencing child health and well-being

4 Explain two major opportunities to foster positive developmental outcomes in early childhood

5 Identify three community goals for sustaining child health

6 Explain how a primary health care approach to child health can empower the community.

The healthy
child

What makes children healthy? If we reflect back on Figure 3.2, it is evident that the same factors influencing the health of a community also influence the health of children. These include the world into which they are born, the national policy environment that encourages or discourages the expression of their culture, their genetic makeup and that of their parents, education and early preparation for employment, the family's area of residence and socioeconomic status (SES), their access to health care and their parents' inclination to access health services, the extent to which healthy behaviours are modelled in the family and community, and features of the physical environment.

Healthy children are those whose physical health and fitness is balanced with their social, emotional and spiritual lives, and who are guided toward developing to the highest level of health and wellness, given the constraints of their particular circumstances. At opposite ends of the scale, these circumstances either jeopardise health opportunities or provide optimal conditions for growth. Most children grow up in families whose circumstances lie somewhere between these two ends of the health continuum. The major influence on the health of a child begins before birth, with genetics.

Genetics

An individual's genetic make-up (genome) sets 'the main features and boundaries within which life is experienced' (AIHW 2000, p 138). It is also a blueprint for the way a human being interacts with his or her environment, including restorative responses to any damage done by environmental agents (AIHW 2000). Despite these 'best-laid plans', many children come into the world without the genetic endowment that would enable them to grow and develop into healthy and fit adults. As a result, some children spend at least a portion of their childhood with a degree of disablement. Some, especially those with intellectual disabilities, develop health problems in later life that are not uncommonly under-diagnosed, diagnosed late or inadequately managed (Durvasula & Beange 2001). Some children live their entire lives with chronic, life-limiting disease or with intermittent episodes of acute illness. On the other hand, many children who are born with disabilities develop into healthy adults and learn to manage their condition within a supportive environment. Sometimes a child with a disability draws family members closer together, but in other families the strain intensifies the child's experience of disablement and seriously compromises family stability.

There are those who believe the old adage that 'forewarned is forearmed' and that if expectant parents understand their chances of having a child with a disability, they will be better able to cope with the situation or to make a choice for alternative action. For this reason, genetic testing is now the norm among mothers considered at risk of having a child with a genetic illness. Testing varies depending on parental risk factors, local health care resources and personal choice. In places where there are sufficient health care resources, many pregnant women undergo amniocentesis, which involves withdrawing a sample of amniotic fluid from the mother's uterus and testing it for biochemical and chromosomal defects. This process and other genetic tests have become rapidly and markedly refined in the past decade because of the Human Genome Project (HGP).

The HGP was formally begun in the United States in 1990, with the intention of mapping the genes lying on twenty-three pairs of chromosomes in the human body, to obtain a single reference sequence of the three billion chemical bases that make up DNA (Dobson 2000; Williams & Lessick 1996). The project was completed in 2001 and, as a result, medical advice and treatment regarding genetics is more comprehensively informed than at any time in previous history. The major scientific outcome of the project is a genetic blueprint to match genes with their functions and to detect genetic variations (Dobson 2000). This will allow improved screening, diagnosis and predictive testing for genetic disorders, which provides us with a new set of possibilities (AIHW 2000; Andrews 1999). For expectant parents, for example, there is clearer information on the relative risk involved in giving birth to a child. For workers, the combination of genetic risk added to environmental exposure gives a more specific set of potential health outcomes. This type of information helps guide people in their choices as well as assisting clinical decision-making. Additional spin-offs to the project have included development of gene therapies, advancements in technologies for microtesting, and greater sophistication of analytical methods to link vast arrays of clinical and biomedical data (AIHW 2000).

One of the most important outcomes of the HGP project is that it has instigated widespread debate on a range of ethical, legal and social implications of the emerging information. The focus of much of this debate is on potential implications for families and society as a whole, to ensure that the new knowledge is managed in a socially responsible way for the benefit of future generations (Lee & Paxman 1997; Murphy & Risser 1999). It is also imperative that health care professionals guiding expectant parents maintain a current understanding of existing legislation as a basis for guiding families (Murphy & Risser 1999). To ensure a relatively consistent approach to the debate, scientists from the HGP will meet with members of WHO on an ongoing basis to ensure that measures will be taken to guard against inequities in the benefits of the research (Whyte 2000). Potential inequities could involve differential or limited access to scientific and clinical knowledge and information about alternative choices for a pregnancy, and to information related to the social issues involved in raising a disabled child (Shakespeare 1999). Similarly, predictive genetic testing may place increased pressure on the health care system for recurrent testing or gene therapy (Andrews 1999).

The widespread debate that has ensued from the HGP has had a negative social impact on some people, creating fear, for example, regarding the successful cloning of Dolly the sheep in Edinburgh, Scotland. Imagining an era of cloned human beings or 'designer babies', many people have registered opposition to this line of research. Others see the HGP as a forerunner to developing tissue for transplantation or tissue repair, which in itself has provoked wide discussion on both the merits and moral uncertainties surrounding such developments. Another view applauds the new technological advances that have flowed from the HGP, seeing the potential to allocate resources more appropriately with more accurate information on the causes and correlates of specific diseases.

Genetic testing of pregnant women is now commonplace, particularly for older mothers who may be at risk for having a child with a genetic defect. The tests are usually followed by providing information to parents on the statistical probability of them having a child with a genetic problem. For some parents, this presents a heart-rending dilemma in relation to continuing or discontinuing a pregnancy that is likely to result in a disabling condition for the child. Although the benefits of genetic testing include better reproductive planning, relief from uncertainty and, increasingly, the potential for gene therapy, some families prefer to forego the opportunity for testing, for personal reasons (Williams & Lessick 1996).

In some cases, concern over the future has led people away from testing. It is important that all health professionals advocating for families and children maintain a non-judgemental attitude towards families' decision(s), and provide educational support and information at each step of the decision-making process. This involves maintaining sufficient knowledge about all sides of the issues to provide appropriate guidance without coercion, and working toward preserving the family's autonomy in decision-making, whether the decisions involve testing, participating in genetic research, or managing the pregnancy (Lessick & Anderson 2000). The ultimate aim of professional guidance is the primary health care goal of family empowerment.

Healthy
pregnancy

Healthy pregnancy is a powerful beginning in reducing the global burden of illness, injury and disability (WHO-UNICEF-UNFPA-World Bank 1999). The World Bank estimates that 20 per cent of the global burden of disease among children under age five can be attributed to poor maternal health, nutrition, and quality of obstetric and newborn care (World Bank 1999). In the industrialised nations, a pregnant woman has a one in 1800 chance of dying from causes related to her pregnancy. In the developing countries, complications of pregnancy and childbirth are the leading cause of death among women of childbearing age, affecting one in 48 pregnancies (World Bank 1999). Since 1987, the World Bank and other international agencies have promoted the Safe Motherhood Initiative, which has sought to redress complications of pregnancy and childbirth. The Initiative's three areas of focus include prevention and management of unwanted pregnancy and unsafe abortion, skilled care during pregnancy, and access to referral care for any complications to ensure continuity of care across the health care continuum (WHO-UNICEF-UNFPA-World Bank 1999).

In the industrialised countries, a range of initiatives have also addressed the problems of pregnancy, including screening for risk factors and attempting to make childbirth safer, particularly when it occurs in emergency circumstances. Maine and Rosenfield (1999) contend that the most significant gains in reducing maternal mortality are a result of improvements in institutionally based medical interventions. They argue against the disproportionate amount of funding that has gone toward risk identification and antenatal care compared with emergency obstetric care. Their criticism revolves around the fact that identification of risk factors is not a predictor of which women will have complications during childbirth, and that it is the conditions of childbirth that should be improved (Maine & Rosenfield 1999). However, their position is at odds with an empowerment perspective, in that they seem to be emphasising the need for medical interventions. Chalmers and Mangiaterra (2001) agree with WHO and many others who argue that care for normal pregnancy and birth should be de-medicalised. Care for normal pregnancy and birth should be provided with only those medical interventions that are seen as essential (Chalmers & Mangiaterra 2001).

Maternal care is a challenge during both pregnancy and childbirth. A growing body of research indicates that healthy pregnancy is determined by the myriad of influences that creates or constrains health in any other circumstance. Pregnant women who have delayed childbirth until their own bodies have matured, who have completed at least a high school education, who have access to a healthy diet, who have adequate and culturally appropriate antenatal (preventative) care and adequate care at the time of childbirth, and whose life situation allows them to maintain harmony between physical, social and emotional health, have a greater chance of having a healthy infant than those who do not (Akukwe 2000; Hardy & Miller 2000; Guildea et al 2001).

Healthy pregnancy also has been found to be associated with healthy and balanced lifestyles, including regular exercise at least three times per week. Tobacco use during pregnancy has been identified as a lifestyle factor having a negative effect on the child. Research has linked mothers' tobacco smoking to impairment in the child's intellectual ability, language skills, behaviour problems (including hyperactivity) and delinquency and crime in adulthood (Brook, Brook & Whiteman 2000). These researchers found that maternal smoking had an adverse effect on the child's behaviour, especially in terms of negativity, which, they believed, could lead to future behaviour problems (Brook et al 2000). Other research has found that smoking, substance abuse, maternal age, attitudes about the pregnancy, stress, domestic violence and poverty are identified with poor birth outcomes, such as low birthweight and preterm delivery (Berger 2001; Hardy & Miller 2000). However, these risk factors must not be taken as a way of blaming the mother for the extent to which she has been able to maintain a healthy lifestyle, as there may be a number of other influences that affect birth outcomes or her opportunity to lead a healthy lifestyle. In any developing foetus, numerous factors interact to produce unpredictable effects. For example, lifestyle factors interact with biological or genetic factors to the extent where a child with the genetic predisposition for being tall may in fact be short in height because of poor intrauterine nutrition. Similarly, environmental factors such as toxic substances and family stress can also have a modifying effect on genetic expression, changing the outcomes of a set of genetic characteristics (Hardy & Miller 2000).

Antenatal care is another important element in successful pregnancy. Accessing preventative care and monitoring foetal development reduces the risk of infant malnourishment and mortality. It is also an opportunity for pregnant women to discuss their emotional concerns regarding pregnancy. In some cases, this means the difference between a calm, positive experience and one where anxiety interferes with the woman's adjustment and sometimes that of her partner. In many developing countries, women have little or no educational opportunities, and often have no access to the type of guidance necessary for both a healthy pregnancy and subsequent family planning.

The United Nations Family Planning Association and the World Bank, which sponsor substantial research in this area, underline the importance of education for women, indicating that educated women have smaller families and better spacing between children, and their children tend to be healthier and better educated. Women with six or more years of education have been found to have lower rates of infant, under-five and maternal mortality (UNFPA

2000; Akukwe 2000). Access to education also has an effect on women in industrialised countries. A comparison of American women with twelve years of education and those with fewer years of education found the less-educated women to have higher rates of delayed antenatal care, low birthweight infants and infant deaths (Akukwe 2000). The exact nature of the link between education and poverty remains a topic for further research, but the existing evidence points to poverty as one of the most important determinants of pregnancy outcomes.

Infant mortality
and risk

Infant mortality rates are a global benchmark for healthy pregnancies and, in some cases, for the health of the population. In some areas of the world, infant mortality has not changed much, even with the large amount of research into the direct causes of death. The Global Burden of Disease studies reveal a significant 17.5 per cent fewer deaths among children aged 0–4 years in 1999 than a decade earlier. However, 15 per cent of newborn children in Africa are expected to die before reaching their fifth birthday, compared with 3–8 per cent in the rest of the developing world (Ahmad, Lopez & Inoue 2000). In many of these cases, infant mortality is linked to social determinants, especially poverty and a lack of access to nutritious foods. The exception to this occurs where there is inadequate quality of clinical care to the extent of causing neonatal deaths from intrapartum asphyxia and prematurity (Guildea et al 2001).

In the OECD countries, such as the United States, Canada, the United Kingdom, Australia and New Zealand, the infant mortality rate is typically lower than in developing countries, where there is usually a lack of access to antenatal care (OECD 1999; Statistics Canada 2001). The infant mortality rate of Indigenous people is one exception to these norms. In Australia, for example, the infant mortality rate among Indigenous people is three to four times higher than that of the non-Indigenous population (AIHW 2000). The New Zealand difference between Indigenous and non-Indigenous infant mortality is not quite so marked, although the rate is approximately double for Maori and 25 per cent higher for Pacific Islanders (NZHIS 2001). The most significant factor for declining infant mortality is the development of technologies that keep very low birthweight (VLB) babies alive. However, many VLB babies still die in the first 24 hours after birth or during the neonatal period.

Many parents today are more aware than their predecessors of risk factors that are universally known to increase the risk of a VLB baby. The role of diet, especially one that contains iron and other vitamins, is well publicised by health and medical service providers in many countries. However, current research continues to unravel the links between dietary intakes of vitamins and minerals during pregnancy, and a variety of birth outcomes. For example, studies into the causes of infant morbidity in industrialised countries indicate that neural tube defects (anencephalus, spina bifida and encephalocele) are caused by folic acid deficiency. This has provided the impetus for government assistance with folic acid supplementation for pregnant women and those likely to become pregnant, with the result of a decrease in incidence and prevalence of these diseases (AIHW 2000). Another decline in infant and postneonatal mortality has occurred because of a worldwide reduction in deaths from SIDS, which has been attributed to a major campaign urging parents to place their infants in a supine or side-lying position while sleeping (AIHW 2000; Fukui et al 2000; Malloy & Freeman 2000; Mitchell et al 1997).

Social determinants
of child health risk

One of the most important social issues of our time is the profound effect of poverty on child health (Aber et al 1997; WHO 1999). The magnitude of the problem is staggering, considering the extreme impoverishment in poor regions such as sub-Saharan Africa. In some parts of Eastern Europe and the former Soviet Union alone, 50 million children live in poverty (Baker 2000). Child poverty has been found to be the most important predictor of ill health in childhood (Fancourt 1997; Montgomery, Kiely & Pappas 1996; Turrell et al 1999; Whitehead 1995; WHO 1999). Poverty has a far-reaching effect on children, beyond the childbirth experience. It has been found to be a strong predictor of prostitution, teenage pregnancy, HIV/AIDS, malnutrition and poor preconception health status in both developing and industrialised countries (Akukwe 2000).

Poverty shows an interactive effect with a number of other socially determined conditions of children's lives. A comparative analysis of eight industrialised countries confirmed that it is not only the overall rate of poverty but inequities related to the distribution of wealth that place children at risk of illness. The risk is higher in the United States, for example, than other countries, because of the large and ever-increasing gap between the rich and the poor. The United States has the extra burden of a large proportion of single-mother-headed families living in the lowest SES group, many of whom are also at risk because of the hazards of living in urban environments (Freudenberg 2000; Montgomery, Kiely & Pappas 1996).

As is the case for poor health outcomes in the general population, the gradient effect mentioned previously places low-SES families at higher risk than those at successively higher levels of income (Hertzman 2001a; Keating & Hertzman 1999). At the global and national levels, this is related to inequities in the distribution of wealth within a population, which in turn may be linked to diminished social opportunities, such as the chance to gain an education (Ratzan 2001). This may help explain why the level of child health, taken as a national set of indicators, is lower in the United States, for example, than in other countries, where the gap between rich and poor is not as wide (Keating

& Hertzman 1999). In that country, disparities affect women of colour disproportionately, as many are among those at the lower end of the scale, living in the types of neighbourhoods that place constraints on them being able to raise healthy children. These mothers typically face barriers against making changes or even seeking adequate health services, including inadequate or unsafe transportation systems and access to affordable health care (Robert 1998). Where the family does not have external assistance, few opportunities are presented for enrichment of the child's early educational experience, which perpetuates disadvantage. Researchers have found, for example, that children from high-SES families have three times as much speech directed to them in the first year of life than do low-SES children, a disparity that widens during later years when language acquisition speeds up (DiPietro 2000).

A comprehensive review of studies finding a link between SES, morbidity and mortality showed a number of threats to infant and child health as a result of being born into low-SES families (Turrell et al 1999). These findings were not reached in all studies reviewed by the researchers, but some evidence was found to support the following associations:

- Infants:
  - higher rates of low birthweight, including lower birthweight for gestational age
  - developmental delays
  - prolonged duration of acute illness, diarrhoea and/or vomiting
  - increased propensity to need resuscitation after birth
  - higher rates of pre-term delivery
  - less likelihood or early cessation of breastfeeding and heavier weight at nine and twelve months, possibly due to non-breastfeeding and/or early introduction of solid food
  - more medical visits and admissions to hospital
  - less attendance at antenatal visits, maternal and child health centres.
- Children:
  - lower survival rates for acute lymphoblastic leukaemia and lower survival time
  - higher incidence of drowning and near-drowning in bathtubs or swimming pools
  - higher mortality due to non-accidental injury and neglect
  - more chronic health problems, higher rates of bacterial pathogens and intestinal parasites
  - poorer dental health
  - higher than average illness symptoms, including more bronchitis in boys, and excessive colds
  - higher rates of general injury, pedestrian and bicycle injuries, including those requiring hospital admissions, and non-accidental head injuries
  - higher rates of physical abuse and neglect
  - higher blood lead concentrations
  - higher rates of developmental delay
  - tendency to be shorter, have a language or speech defect, score lower on memory and motor scales and scales of cognitive ability, and lower mean mental development index scores

- experience more behaviour disturbances and social problems, including temper tantrums, being solitary or withdrawn, aggressive, disruptive, attention-seeking or distressed, and have poor concentration spans
- more likely to smoke, have poor dental habits, and have higher sodium and fat content in their diet
- less likely to belong to a sporting club (Turrell et al 1999, pp 20–1).

Environmental conditions are involved in many of these findings, related to the housing and neighbourhoods that are affordable for low-SES families, which may place young children at risk (Freudenberg 2000). They often have poor air and water quality, toxic waste dumps and incinerators, less healthy housing, workplaces and recreational options, with potential exposure to toxins such as lead paint, asbestos and pest infestation (Robert 1998). The physical environment is also an important element in child health and illness in places like the African continent, where there are limited food supplies because of land degradation or displacement of people in search of employment (WHO 1999).

For some time now, researchers at the Canadian Institute for Advanced Research have been studying the social determinants of health in relation to neuroendocrine development, behaviour and the social elements of child rearing. Their findings indicate that the social partitioning or gradient effect is not simply due to inadequate food and shelter because of economic conditions (Hertzman 2001b). They suggest that the latent effects of early experiences are a vital element in explaining subsequent health outcomes. For example, children who do not mature out of the aggressive stage that typically occurs at 24–28 months, and who are raised in authoritarian or apathetic environments, are most at risk of offending as adolescents (Hertzman 2001b). Finding no evidence of late-onset aggression led the researchers to conclude that the best period of intervention to prevent delinquency is the period prior to entering school.

Advice from this group of researchers is that health promotion interventions should occur long before social stratification becomes apparent, during those critical periods in childhood when coping skills are developed (Hertzman 2001b; Mustard 1996, 1999). They see the window of opportunity as occurring from birth to approximately three years of age, when important dispositional and regulatory templates are formed that, in later life, influence the individual's coping abilities (Mustard 1999). These templates are so important as to set the stage for the extent to which people will have the propensity to addiction or any other areas of social or behavioural risk (Keating & Hertzman 1999). Hertzman (2001a, p 538) explains these 'biological pre-sets' in terms of 'biological promise or vulnerability'. The developing person experiences the promises or vulnerabilities as ongoing interactions with the intimate, civic and broader socioeconomic and physical environments. These interactions shape and set the individual's prospects for health through a pathway throughout the whole of life, in which health is determined through personal resources or resiliencies, injuries or vulnerabilities (Hertzman 2001a).

Because of these emotional and biological propensities, some believe the focus of health promotion should be on enriching early parenting, and resources deployed appropriately (Hardy & Miller 2000; Mustard 1999).

However, the broader socioeconomic environment must also be rearranged to support the interaction between the two sets of factors, and this can only be done through the creation and equitable distribution of wealth. This would see improvements to housing, water, air, nutrition, child spacing, working conditions and education, and promotion of the type of social environments that would cultivate prosperous, tolerant, democratic societies with strong civic communities (Hertzman 2001a). This sounds like the sensible way forward for health promotion, but it has attracted some criticism in relation to fundamental inequities. Criticisms mainly focus on the way the research findings could be used in government policies for health spending, to abdicate their responsibility for public expenditures on health and social services, leaving societies to fix their own environmental and social conditions (Poland et al 1998). It is an interesting argument, and an indication of the political nature of health promotion. Perhaps both sides could be argued, resulting in increased government spending on preventative services and industrial policies that would create such supportive environments as sustainable employment and a range of other equitable social conditions.

Confronting
risk

Immunisation

WHO claims that immunisation has been the greatest public health success of all time (WHO 1999). In the 1970s WHO established a goal to have universal immunisation of children against diptheria, pertussis, tetanus, tuberculosis, poliomyelitis and measles. Goals were also set to eradicate, through immunisation, smallpox (achieved in 1977), poliomyelitis (still under way) and, in the future, measles (Plotkin & Orstein 1999). In fact, ten major diseases can now be controlled by vaccination, including diptheria, tetanus, pertussis, polio, measles, tuberculosis, yellow fever, mumps, rubella and *Haemophilus influenzae* type b (Hib) infection (Burgess 1997). To date, between 80 and 90 per cent of the world's children are immunised against diptheria, tetanus, pertussis, polio, measles and tuberculosis (WHO 1999).

One of the most important decisions parents must make is related to having their children immunised, yet many fail to do so because of either a lack of understanding or misinformation about the risks involved. Immunisation involves giving the child a vaccine designed to stimulate production of specific *antibodies* that protect the child from developing a particular infectious disease. When the majority of children in a population are vaccinated against the disease, there is seen to be a high level of *herd immunity*; that is, the chances of the infectious agent being spread amongst others is markedly reduced (Burgess 1997). The public health goal—to maintain the best standard of health for the greatest number of people—requires that as many children as possible in the population be immunised.

Although immunisation is one of the most effective public health measures in the world, between two and three million preventable deaths still occur from six diseases: measles, whooping cough, tetanus, polio, tuberculosis and diptheria, with measles accounting for nearly one million deaths a year (Miller 1999). Eighty-four per cent of global deaths from measles occur in the African and Southeast Asian regions (Miller 1999). Total eradication of poliomyelitis and measles, as WHO intends, will not only benefit the community in terms of child health, but will save at least $1.5 billion annually in the cost of routine vaccination (Burgess 1997).

In the industrialised countries, such as North America, the United Kingdom, Australia and New Zealand, immunisation levels are maintained at approximately 90 per cent, with some regional variations. In some cases, particularly in the United States, where there is no universal medical coverage, the rates fluctuate, but in other countries (Australia, Canada, New Zealand, the United Kingdom) where such coverage exists, it is provided through the health services (AIHW 2000). In some cases, dips in the rate of immunisation have occurred because of public anti-immunisation concerns. Thompson (1997) recounts that in the 1970s in the United Kingdom and the 1980s in the United States, there were some suggestions from parents of children with neurological disabilities that their children's problems may have been caused by pertussis vaccination. A documentary in the United Kingdom claimed in a court case that 36 of these children had been brain-damaged over the previous 12 years and because the children had, in fact, been vaccinated, they were awarded damages.

Following this case, the Vaccine Injury Act was introduced in the United Kingdom in 1979 and the rate of vaccinations began to plummet. Almost immediately, a severe epidemic of whooping cough occurred, with 5000 children hospitalised, some for serious complications. A similar event occurred in the United States where, by 1984, 255 lawsuits had been filed against the drug companies manufacturing the vaccine. As a result, the cost of the vaccine rose considerably, representing a substantial economic burden on families with no national health care scheme. All but one of the companies manufacturing the vaccine withdrew from production, further inflating the cost. Meanwhile, extensive research studies were conducted to examine the association between pertussis vaccination and neurological illness. Although some association was demonstrated, it was calculated to be negligible in the population as a whole. For those children who did succumb to acute neurological disease, it was suggested that there may have been pre-existing underlying brain or metabolic abnormalities, but the results of the research have not proved this conclusively (Thompson 1997).

In the United States, where it is a prerequisite of entry to school that children be immunised, research studies have shown that where parents do not obtain the first scheduled immunisation, they tend to not start immunisation at all (Hanna et al 1994). In some cases, family mobility prevents the children from finishing a course of immunisation once they have begun. In other cases, parents have been unable to keep track of whether each child has had the full schedule. One answer, according to Canadian authorities, is to consider re-initiating immunisation for all children beginning school (or pre-school) where there is no available record that the child has had the full schedule of immunisations. Evidently, better surveillance is required and, perhaps more importantly, public campaigning in all countries to provide parents with accurate and rational information on the necessity for children to be immunised. This is particularly important in an era when so many children attend formal child care. The dilemma inherent in immunisation is that of coercion, which runs counter to the primary health care philosophy. Immunisation therefore presents health professionals with a challenge that must be met. The goal must always be to facilitate health, and one would expect that people will make healthful choices given accurate information, presented sensitively and with respect for difference.

Accidents and injuries

Childhood is the time when the major emphasis of most parents is on protecting their children from accidents and injuries. In many cases, accidents are caused by the perils existing in the environments within which young children grow, so the onus is on all of society to help keep children safe from harm.

UNICEF (2002) reports that injuries are the cause of death for 20 000 children in the world's wealthiest nations (OECD countries), even though the rates of injury-related deaths in these countries showed a decline of 50 per cent from 1970 to 1995. Sweden, the United Kingdom, Italy and the Netherlands have the lowest rate of child injuries, while the United States and Portugal register the highest rates, over twice that of the leading countries (UNICEF 2001). This is cause for concern, given the fact that, for every child death, many more live with varying degrees and duration of disability and trauma (UNICEF 2001).

Injuries affect very young children disproportionately, and researchers have found that the most common causes of deaths from injury include drowning, fire, falls, poisoning, and intentional injury (UNICEF 2002). One of the greatest hazards is that of accidental poisoning from things like fuels, solvents, cleaners and polishes, but many other household products can cause serious poisoning—even eucalyptus oil or alcoholic beverages (Wiseman 1995). Another domestic hazard relates to the risk of accidental injury from furniture. Young children slip through the crevices in beds, especially bunk beds, and they fall from chairs and sofas (CAPA 1997).

In the developing countries such as Africa, falls are a major cause of traumatic injury in young children, second only to infectious diseases as a cause of death (Africa News Service 2001; Mock 2001). The rate of child deaths in traffic accidents is also five times higher in Africa than in the European Union, despite the relatively low rate of vehicle ownership. Injury control in the African continent, as in many other developing nations, has not been a priority of governments, who tend to use their limited resources for other services, such as those related to infectious diseases (Mock 2001).

In the United States and Canada the highest risk of death from injury is from pedestrian and cycling accidents, and the figures are magnified to reflect the greater population density (UNICEF 2001; Canada Safety Council 2002). A Canadian survey indicated that half of all childhood injuries are serious, with approximately 736 000 students in grades 6 to 10 requiring at least one medical treatment annually for an injury (Ardern 2001). In Australia and

New Zealand, pedestrian and cycling accidents are also prevalent, but the most frequent cause of death by injury is childhood drowning (ABS 1999; AIHW 2000; Langley et al 2001). Some of these accidents occur because of the erratic behaviour of the 1–3 year age group. Their capabilities change at least daily, and parents often are stretched to the limit keeping up with them. However, other factors, such as SES, may put some families more at risk than others of having a drowning, or a serious submersion injury. Researchers have also found socioeconomic differences in injury rates among pedestrians and bicyclists from low-SES families, including a 20–30% higher injury risk (Hasselberg, Laflamme & Ringback Weitoft 2001). Although there has been speculation that lower-income families have a more relaxed attitude toward supervising children, often it is that they lack the knowledge and the means to make their children's environment safe (Peterson & Stern 1997).

For poorer families, substandard housing often creates a plethora of risk factors: balconies and windows without child safety catches, spaces in the home needing repair, unsafe electrical appliances, and crowded streets near high traffic areas with few alternative parks and play areas. Many childhood injuries are caused by the circumstances of poverty, including sole parent-headed households, low maternal education, low maternal age at birth, poor housing, large family size and parental drug or alcohol abuse (UNICEF 20002). Higher accident-proneness and frequency of medical attention have also been found among children from sole-parent households and stepfamilies (O'Conner et al 2001). Indigenous people are also more at risk than others, and perhaps this is related to SES. In Australia, for example, comparisons with non-Indigenous people show a 75 times greater risk of death by fire among Aboriginal children. Similarly, a comparison of Hispanic and non-Hispanic children in the United States shows more than three times the risk of injury-related mortality for Hispanic children (UNICEF 2002).

Climate and geography are also factors in childhood injuries. Warm climates see young children outdoors, in swimming pools or on the streets, and riding bicycles for longer periods of the year than in colder climates (Acton, Nixon & Clark 1997).

The most important preventative measure that can be taken by community health professionals is to teach parents about the need for close supervision of young children and explain how to take precautions within the home—for example, checking heaters, cooking equipment and electrical distribution, and ensuring that the child is not exposed to matches or lighters used for cigarette smoking. The community also has a responsibility for industrial safeguards—for example, ensuring adequate labelling of manufactured goods such as flammable clothing, nursery furniture and electrical appliances—and this is one area where collaboration with consumer organisations is extremely helpful.

Accident reduction strategies should include a concerted community effort. Bicycle helmet and car seat legislation should be combined with community awareness campaigns, strict regulatory codes for manufacturers, bicycle safety instruction in schools and environmental modifications such as safer road design and maintenance. Under the age of five, children's judgement cannot be relied upon, and so parental supervision is the most important element in maintaining child safety. After age five, children still need constant reinforcement and the best way for this to occur is through appropriate modelling by parents, teachers and other authority figures (Peterson & Stern 1997). There is also a need to entrench safety in leglisation, and this has instigated legal requirements in all states of Australia, New Zealand, the United States and all provinces of Canada for the mandatory wearing of seat belts and the use of car seats for all young children. Researchers in the United Kingdom claim only modest success in overcoming political inertia in that region, and are currently lobbying for creation of a dedicated agency for injury prevention, surveillance and control, and a program of research to inform work in this area (Stone, Jarvis & Pless 2001).

Safety instruction and guidance is an essential element of community health literacy, and this should be ongoing throughout children's development because as they grow, so does their exposure to danger. In the United States, the American Academy of Pediatrics has issued a statement of anticipatory guidance for families to prevent children falling from heights (Preboth 2001). However, this will only be useful if families who live in multi-storey buildings, most of whom are low-SES families, have both the capability and the resources to heed this advice (by, for example, installing window guards). Educational messages should also be directed at the children, in age-appropriate styles to accommodate the way different age groups conceptualise the information. If this approach is taken, there is a better chance that misunderstandings will not create anxieties that cause *increased* rather than decreased carelessness (Peterson & Stern 1997). Children's stories are usually most appropriate for teaching children about safety because the information can be embedded within recognisable events and thus will usually be better remembered.

To counter automobile accidents, the UNICEF report recommends that the problems be addressed through preventative measures such as laws on impaired driving, safer cars, reduced exposure and better emergency services (Canada Safety Council 2002). It is also important that parents and teachers have access to accurate information on the risks involved in childhood activities, as many fail to understand the severity of outcomes of casual, neighbourhood accidents, or to be aware of safety standards. A further area for vigilance, especially at school, is the psychological effect of injuries on children, which are often neglected given the seriousness of the physical injury (Stoddard & Saxe 2001). Health professionals and teachers can assist families in picking up symptoms of post-trauma problems and by lobbying for modifications to the environment that predispose its young residents to a greater incidence of accidents. This is particularly important in rural or remote areas, where mortality rates from accidents among children under age 15 are nearly double those of metropolitan dwellers (AIHW 2000).

All families, rich or poor, rural or urban, need access to adequate and appropriate accident prevention information. Educational information should be culturally sensitive, and directed at all cultural groups residing in the community. Presentations must be designed to provide information for informed decision-making, in order to promote community empowerment rather than coercion, and they should be accompanied by recommendations for environmental modifications that include intersectoral input. Comprehensive strategies to address child safety issues will attract a greater hearing among politicians if they include involvement from health, education, transport, the business community, the community council, consumer organisations, the police and any service clubs within a community, with a focus on ensuring safety and protection for all young people.

Diet and nutrition

From birth onwards, maintaining adequate nutrition is one of the most essential ingredients for healthy childhood. For at least the first six months of life, breast milk is the most ideally balanced diet for newborn infants, and provides immunity from many diseases for the infant. However, in many places, because of the pressure on women to return to work quickly, the number of breastfed children is declining. Campaigns to encourage women to breastfeed have been underway in most countries, but nowhere is the need so acute as in the developing countries, where infants not only are often deprived of the superior nutritious value of breast milk, but may also suffer from gastrointestinal illnesses acquired from contaminated bottle formulas and, in many cases, a lack of medication to treat these conditions (UNFPA 2000; WHO 1996).

Good nutrition is the basic ingredient for helping children grow strong, fit and healthy. This begins in the family home, and most parents attempt to establish healthy eating from a very early age where their resources are adequate. However, some families have neither the knowledge nor the resources to provide low-sugar, low-fat foods, and others become preoccupied with busy schedules, leaving children to make their own dietary decisions. Most communities allocate considerable resources to encouraging healthy diets in day care centres and in school health programs but are sometimes fighting a losing battle, with young children's constant exposure to television advertisements urging them to consume unhealthy diets. A group of researchers in New Zealand monitored the nutritional quality of food in television food advertisements targeted at children, in order to assess the potential impact of this on eating behaviour (Wilson, Quigley & Mansoor 1999). They found that if children ate only the advertised foods, they would consume a diet too high in fat, saturated fat, protein, free sugars and sodium, and these diets would be deficient in the fibre and minerals essential for good health (Wilson et al 1999).

Promoting good nutrition is now a crucial part of school health because of the large numbers of families where both parents must remain in full-time employment. In many places, the scope of school health services has expanded to ensure that healthy lifestyles are seen as integral to learning. Many education and health departments collaborate to devise programs aimed at good nutrition, physical education, guidance and counselling (Kolbe, Kann & Brener 2001). The cooperative nature of these programs is the key to their success, and most encourage family involvement, so it is not uncommon to see parent volunteers managing healthy canteens that once sold junk food, and acting as teacher aides and role models for healthy living. The trend towards community participation in school health programs provides a good example of primary health care in practice, using the setting as the focus for health promotion, and this is discussed further in Chapter 12.

Health, fitness and lifestyle

Besides a nutritious diet, children need to maintain a level of physical activity sufficient to promote cardiovascular fitness and the muscular capacity to complement bone growth through periods of rapid development. Levels of fitness among children in most industrialised nations are declining to alarming standards. To some extent, this can be attributed to ease of transportation, the growth of technology that has seen more children in sedentary play, and a lack of role modelling by parents, who are themselves tied to sedentary lifestyles. Declining activity in adolescence and adulthood has led to obesity in epidemic proportions, which has a profound impact on the future health of young people, as well as having significant financial costs (French, Story & Jeffery 2001). In Australia, a survey in one state indicated that only around 25 per cent of boys in Year 6 and 30 per cent of boys in Years 8 and 10 have adequate aerobic capacity (AIHW 2000). The proportion of Australian overweight or obese children is a serious problem placing many children at risk for obesity in later life (Booth et al 2001). Current rates of overweight children and adolescents between 2 and 17 years are approximately 21 per cent for boys and 23 per cent for girls, which is only marginally below the 25 per cent rate of obesity found in American children (AIHW 2000; French et al 2001). From a population perspective, this does not bode well for reversing the trend towards inactivity in adulthood, which currently sees more than one-third of the adult population inactive to the point of placing them at risk for cardiovascular disease (AIHW 2000).

One approach to teaching children about physical fitness is to refocus physical education from an emphasis on *how* the game is played to *why* it is necessary for health and well-being. This type of approach can also be used to educate young children about such risky behaviours as smoking and drug abuse. Quite often, programs addressing substance abuse are not introduced until the high school years, yet epidemiological studies reveal that some children begin smoking and/or drinking alcohol as early as Year 4, indicating, as some public health professionals believe, that we must begin to consider cigarette smoking as a paediatric disease (Bush & Iannotti 1993; Lee & Paxman 1997). As with physical fitness, children need explanations of the dangers of tobacco smoking, but they also need a plausible reason for alternative behaviour. Programs that emphasise the incompatibility of smoking and drug use with being fit and healthy (and thus capable of playing sport), tend to be better received than giving children heavy-handed directives that simply emphasise that risky behaviours are bad for them. However, this must be matched by initiatives that will create healthy environments to support healthy eating and exercise programs in conjunction with other healthy lifestyle behaviours.

Childhood asthma

Exercise and diet are especially important for children with asthma, one of the most neglected problems in community health (AIHW 2000; Bauman 1996). Asthmatic children typically have frequent airway obstructions caused by inflammation and excess mucous in the airway, and constriction of the bronchial passageway. Often the asthma attack is triggered by a respiratory illness, allergens or pollutants in the air (including tobacco smoke), food chemicals, emotional factors, exercise or changes in humidity and temperature (AIHW 2000; Beeber 1996). A high proportion of asthmatics are allergic to house dust mites, which are more prevalent in temperate, coastal climates (AIHW 2000). Parental smoking is considered an important factor in precipitating childhood asthma, or at least wheezing attacks, which are considered a surrogate measure of asthma (Cunningham et al 1996).

Worldwide rates of asthma are increasing dramatically, but for reasons unknown, Australia and New Zealand experience higher prevalence and morbidity and mortality than any other developed countries. Researchers have studied a range of causal factors such as antenatal smoking and parental smoking postnatally, heredity, respiratory infectious agents and air quality, but the only factors that seem peculiar to the Australasian region seem to be pollens, moulds and house dust mites (AIHW 2000; Bauman 1996). Interestingly, Australian Aboriginal children have a lower prevalence of asthma than their white counterparts, for unknown reasons, although environmental factors are suspected (Veale et al 1996).

It would appear that a number of interrelated risk factors have led to the increase in prevalence of childhood asthma. One of these is related to ozone. Ozone is a known air pollutant, but its exact role in either causing or triggering asthma is unknown. When air pollutants are slow to disperse because of atmospheric stagnation and high levels of ultraviolet radiation, ozone levels increase in the ambient air. However, in large cities with high pollution levels caused by industrial and automobile exhaust, oxidation of the ozone occurs, leaving the ambient air with a relatively greater concentration of nitrogen dioxide than ozone (Devereux et al 1996). This suggests that the web of causation includes not only a cluster of precipitating factors, but a further combination of environmental conditions favourable to the disease. Prevention and control of asthma presents a classic case for collaboration between health and environmental scientists and the need for wide dissemination of knowledge between and among different professions and sectors.

Childhood stress

Children today are exposed to a great many stressors. A review of the research on stress among children suffering injuries indicates that life stress may be associated with inattention and injury, particularly in showing a link with gender (being male), previous injury and injury requiring hospitalisation, injury following alcohol or drug use, stressful event scores (especially from having a relative ill or deceased), school failure or suspension, getting a summer job, and breaking up with a girlfriend or boyfriend (for older children) (Stoddard & Saxe 2001). The mechanisms involved in stress are somewhat unclear, and this lack of clarity may be preventing policy developments that would more adequately address early childhood trauma such as physical and sexual abuse (Shaw & Krause 2001).

Nowhere are the effects of post-traumatic stress more evident than in the child victims of war (Husain 1999). In many parts of the world, hundreds of thousands of young children are left to forage for food and water, deprived of access to immunisation and exposed to infectious diseases. Their physical states are doubly compromised by torture, trauma, rape and other abuses and the emotional stress of separation from family members and dislocation from their homes (Cliff & Noormahomed 1993). Their lives represent one of the most pressing global child health problems and one that must demand attention from all health policy makers, particularly when budgetary and immigration decisions are being considered in the international political arenas.

case study...

Refugee children in detention

Over the past few years, the world has seen an alarming erosion of the international commitment to provide humanitarian protection to people fleeing persecution (Silove, Steel & Mollica 2001). With five million people seeking asylum during 1980–99, the industrialised countries that have been their destinations have increasingly built or extended facilities to detain asylum seekers. In some countries, asylum seekers have made allegations of brutality, excessive discipline, physical constraint, inability to access health care, and constant threats of being repatriated to the repression of their home countries (Silove et al 2001).

Australia alone has a policy of detaining all individuals who enter the country without a valid visa, whether asylum seekers or not. Since June 2000 approximately 3500 asylum seekers, including 450 children, have been held in Australian detention facilities (Silove et al 2001). Having fled a range of difficult conditions in their homelands, many of these people have paid smugglers to sail them to Australia rather than wait to be 'processed' to determine their refugee status in their home country. Because they have jumped the immigration queue by paying the people smugglers to bring them across the ocean, there has been a backlash against them on the basis of the seeming

inequity in jumping the queue ahead of those who could not afford such a gambit.

The approach taken by the Australian government is called 'the Pacific Solution', and it involves cooperative agreements between Australia and small island nations in the South Pacific to house the refugees who cannot be accommodated in detention centres in Australia. They remain in detention centres, in Australia and elsewhere, until their status is resolved. The centres are less than optimal for people who have endured severe hardship in their home countries, some of whom also lost family members at sea during their escape.

The facilities are located in relatively isolated areas surrounded by barbed-wire fences, with limited access to social, health and legal services. In some cases there have been 'suicide attempts, acts of mass violence, breakouts, rioting, burning of facilities and sporadic hunger strikes' (Silove et al 2001, p 1436).

Health professionals working with the families have reported that the children among them have exhibited stress-related behaviours thought to be linked to confinement in severe heat with inadequate opportunities to play with others, or in trying to adjust to many traumatic changes during their short lives. Most have the added difficulty of living in a culture unfamiliar to them, without the benefit of a common language to at least communicate with others. A psychiatrist from Baghdad University, Faculty of Medicine, himself a detainee, has expressed concern about the psychological effects manifest among his fellow detainees. He describes detention as a daily 'mounting of stress and tension caused by the environment' (Sultan 2001, p 1438). He believes the residential, administrative and judicial factors converge to undermine his mental state and that of the others, several of whom manifest severe depressive illness. After extreme persecution at home, his shock at the human rights violations they have received in a Western country is palpable (Sultan 2001). Many asylum seekers worry about their children and their mothers, especially when they may be at increased risk of abuse and exploitation from being confined in mixed-sex detention facilities (Kisely et al 2002). Other concerns revolve around widespread use of anthelmintics and anti-malarials irrespective of infective status, and excessive administration of analgesics and tranquillisers (Kisely et al 2002).

The amount and type of publicity surrounding the detention of asylum seekers has been adversely affected by global events, such as the terrorism of 11 September in the United States. Many of the people in detention are visibly Muslim, which has fuelled discrimination and polarised the communities in which they are detained, to either the humanitarian side of their plight or to allegations of 'queue jumping'. The latter group believe they are among the wealthy in their home countries and it is unfair to offer them migration status over their poorer counterparts who may not have the financial resources to jump the queue. The situation is difficult to resolve in a way that would help the children.

Some residents of the communities closest to the detention centres have argued for releasing the detainees into existing communities until they can be 'processed', if only for the children's sake, but this has been rejected by the immigration department on the basis of inequity. This is thought to be a moot point, given the more than 10 000 'overstayers' from the United States and the United Kingdom who reside in the country illegally, with no threat of detention (Yencken & Porter 2001). The community's sense of cohesion has evaporated in the chasm between extremes of public opinion. On one side are human rights advocates attempting to counter allegations of bigotry and racism reinforced by the international press. On the other are those who believe the government's approach is adequate and fair, even though it has yet to be informed by a clearly articulated policy (Kisely et al 2002).

The Pacific Solution has caused conflict within the small island communities, where people are desperately in need of resources. Helping Australia deal with the refugee crisis will ultimately provide them with facilities that may improve quality of life for the long-term residents. However, it also has the potential to undermine community values, particularly in having had the development of their physical environment imposed on them by their wealthy neighbour. In addition to health concerns, choices will have to be made, arguments won, and lifestyles adjusted. It is a huge rippling effect in a global body of water. The situation is a classic example of the effects of environmental displacement, globalism, nationalism, civil strife, the moral elements involved in community health, social justice and the interdependence of people everywhere.

Child sexual abuse

One of the problems in addressing child sexual abuse at the community level is the lack of data defining the extent of the problem, and the knowledge that many incidents of abuse go unreported. It is possible that this problem cannot be estimated, as the effects on the child rebound throughout his or her lifetime. Evidence of the prevalence of child sexual abuse derives from two flawed sources: official reports and retrospective accounts, neither of which is accurate because of the secrecy and shame surrounding sexual abuse, the criminal sanctions against it, and the dependent age and status of the child (Fleming 1997; Nurcombe 2000). Research reports indicate a stable incidence over the past 40 to 50 years, although sexual abuse is more widely known in recent years (Nurcombe 2000). Risk factors for child sexual abuse are numerous, and most point to a cluster of factors that include being physically abused, having a mother who is mentally ill, and social isolation (Fleming, Mullen & Bammer 1997). Sexually abused children often come from low-SES families where there is a high frequency of other social and interpersonal problems. These can contribute to both the risks and the long-term deleterious effects of the abuse, including the risk of sexually transmitted diseases and psychiatric illness (Britton & Hansen 1997; Romans 1997).

Communities cannot respond effectively to child abuse without considering the overall needs of the child in the context of his or her life (Cloke 1997). Research studies worldwide have produced overwhelming evidence for social and interpersonal problems as the sequelae of abuse in childhood and some problems are exacerbated by the outcomes of disclosing the abuse (Nagel, Putnam & Noll 1997). All forms of abuse seem to have effects that last into adulthood, and where the abuse is sexual in nature there is usually a direct effect on sexual adjustment, the capacity for intimacy in adult life and, in some cases, perpetuation of a cycle of abuse (Romans 1997; Shah 1997). Many children live in a 'totality of abuse' where they are locked into a pattern of family violence (Tomison 2000). One of the most serious sources of abuse is the clergy. For whatever reasons, this type of abuse is currently garnering widespread public attention. From a community perspective, this is a positive turn of events, given that it will be more openly confronted and, hopefully, dealt with in a way that will prevent future abuse. However, solutions come at considerable emotional expense for many individuals, both men and women, who have been exploited by those in positions of trust and authority.

Other kinds of abuse also require response by the community, for the sake of child protection. The International Labour Organization (ILO) reports that there are approximately 250 million economically active children in the world between the ages of 5 and 14 (cited in ICN 1999). Ludicrously, many of these children are engaged in industries that produce medical and dental instruments for use in industrialised countries. In one city in Pakistan alone, 7700 child workers are employed as subcontractors in the manufacturing of these instruments (ICN 1999). This is not an isolated case, as child labour is rife in many countries, especially those producing garments for the markets of the industrialised world. This extends all the way from the more than one million children in Egypt who work in the fields to control the cotton leafworm, to Asian migrants assisting their parents as outworkers assembling various pieces of clothing (UN 2001). As with the children working with steel instruments, there are few provisions for safety surveillance or protection from exploitation, or measures taken to enhance their growth and development. To eradicate such practices requires widespread recognition that it is occurring. This must also be accompanied by urging consumers to make some changes at the point of sale level, followed by lobbying for policies that would control industries thriving on the blatant abuse of children.

In countries like China, children are also open to exploitation of a different kind. In some areas, wealthy childless couples are able to buy infants previously stolen from a family or coaxed from the mother for a pittance, which helps her feed the remaining family members. Some children born with disabilities, especially girl babies, are simply abandoned because of financial difficulties, (McLennan 2000). Beech (2001) reports that two-week-old girls are sold for $25, boys for $50. For poverty-stricken families this represents a more attractive option than growing chickens, which bring only $2 apiece. It is a reprehensible situation that tests the tolerance of human rights advocates and those attempting to assist such families.

Responding to the abused child requires cultural sensitivity as well as consideration of the vulnerability of youth (Powell 1997). Assessing children involves understanding the family's perspective, as different cultures have varying ideas of what may be considered maltreatment of a child, and what should be done about it (Powell 1997). The challenge lies in supporting the family and protecting the vulnerable. In all societies, the problem must be addressed with a focus on preventative strategies that are visible and comprehensive. These include early detection and response, childhood education, ongoing support for families, better informed treatment options and community education.

The family and parenting

As for adults, the patterns of illness, injury and disability in children show the effects of stressors in the social and cultural environment of contemporary family life (Turrell et al 1999). A holistic view of health dictates that our efforts to promote child health in the community must focus on children living in harmony with their physical, social and cultural environment. So the first place to address child health issues is within the family, where individual health and well-being are constituted.

The needs of infants and young children have not changed over the years. They still need physical care, love, nurturing, protection and a sense of belonging. But the context in which their needs are met has changed with every generation. It is easy to explain children's difficulties in terms of parent absence, especially as many couples work outside the family home. Some families are also transient, following jobs that may take them far from extended family support networks. However, other historical events have also conspired to change the way people parent these days.

At the turn of this century, most issues concerning parenthood were under the direction of medical doctors. In the 1920s it became common practice to consult nurses or paediatricians for all matters relating to child care. By the late 1930s, kindergarten and child guidance professionals were recognised as the new experts on child rearing. In the 1960s and 1970s, expert knowledge emerged through women's organisations such as those that addressed natural childbirth and/or breastfeeding. Today, the insidious professionalism of what was once exclusively the domain of the family has had the effect of placing considerable pressure on today's first-time parents to consult a guru at every turn. As a result, some have all but relinquished the right to make up their own minds about child care. Many young parents feel guilty at being forced to spend so little time with their children, and because of conflicting research reports about the effects of institutional child care for very young children, often feel anxious and depressed about their role as parents, usually with no older generation available to soothe their fears.

Today's urban lifestyles often leave young families feeling alone and lacking in meaningful relationships with others as they emerge daily from the work-place exhausted and in need of reassurance. In the past, families either inherited or selected their support networks, and had time to discuss issues related to child rearing. Now people live in isolation, either physical or emotional, and come to rely on health professionals as their source of guidance and support. And because they often lose the perspective of what is normal *for their child*, they accept the blame for any deviation from what are often unrealistic expectations. Exceptions to this scenario occur in many cultural groups, which still provide a strong support base for babies and their parents.

Increasingly, young mothers from these extended family networks are returning to the workforce and suffering the additional strain of falling through the cracks between the old culture and the new. So even in those groups with strong traditions of child care, there is a need to have members of the older generation understand what may be new parenting styles. A further frustration lies in the fact that today's new parents are caught between two competing social attitudes: one which reifies parenthood and thus scorns the quick return to work of the mother, and the other which considers paid work as the only legitimate occupation. This latter notion is reinforced by government policies, which usually offer disproportionate subsidisation of child care for working parents rather than those providing family support at home.

The role of the health professional in helping parents nurture their young revolves around the primary health care principle of empowerment. As family and child health advocates, we must act as a filter to ensure that our guidance gets through to them in their busy lives but does not sabotage family health competence (Dunst & Trivette 1996). Parents must be included as participants in decisions related to their children, and the advocate's role is to support their decisions and assist them to reveal and explore the full range of options and choices pertinent to decisions (Rushton, McEnhill & Armstrong 1996). At the policy level we need to uncover the hidden facets of family issues that would inform public policy debate, including caregiving within the family, sharing of care between the public and private sphere, and reassessment of models and resources for care. By keeping family issues on the public agenda there is a greater chance of creating healthy public policies and thus a family-friendly, and child-friendly, society.

Critical pathways
to child health

Perhaps the best investment in child health lies in the education of women. The pre-eminence of maternal education is validated in numerous studies demonstrating its significance to child survival (DiPietro 2000; WHO 1999), in developing competence for lifelong coping (Mustard 1999), and in breaking the cycle of poverty (UNFPA 2000). The direct association between poverty and health has been recognised for some time; recently, the complexities of this association have become clearer (Ratzan 2001). It is commonly understood that children can reduce a woman's financial potential by interrupting employment during the years of peak growth in earnings. When mothers with low earning potential become separated or divorced, they and their children often become poor. Distress from the combined economic and interpersonal crisis often interferes with the mother's work performance and the children's school performance. The quality of their lives is compromised by social stress, poor social networks, low self-esteem, high rates of depression, anxiety, insecurity and the loss of a sense of control (Wilkinson 1996). The longer the period of disruption and distress, the greater the probability that the mother and her children will fail to advance. Both may have residual problems with relationships, precipitating an inter-generational tendency toward family break-up. Combined with higher fertility among less-educated women, these break-ups drive a growing rate of cyclical poverty among women and children (Mirowsky 1998; Wilkinson 1996). Understanding the complexities of this cycle suggests that the pathway to health promotion extends from pre-conception advice on diet, smoking, exercise and self-esteem, to political decisions aimed at enhancing structural support for families at all stages from birth through maturation to death.

A second critical pathway overlaps the first, in that it should address the links between individual cognitive development and competence, and the aspects of society and the environment that either provide social buffering, social risk or social enhancement. Some of the major risk factors for poor health outcomes for children have been identified as difficult temperament, harsh parenting, abuse or neglect, parental mental illness or substance abuse, family conflict, low SES, and poor links with the community (AIHW 2000). A socioecological view of child health includes both proximal and distal factors, some of which may be found in neighbourhoods, religious groups and nationalities (Earls & Carlson 2001). There is a pressing need to better understand the residential composition of communities, including the larger societal forces that act to stratify groups by race, ethnicity and social class (Earls & Carlson 2001). This must also extend to understanding the constellation of factors, such as quality of housing, schools, parks and recreational areas, businesses and transportation networks, that allow us to appreciate children as agents in their daily activities and local habitats (Earls & Carlson 2001). Greater insight into the multiple relationships across the different settings of people's lives that combine to create health and illness would be a major step in achieving health for all the world's children (Schwartz, Susser & Susser 1999).

A major review of studies on child development indicates that individual differences in social and intellectual development arise through intrinsic and experience-dependent processes, which means that development across cognitive, socio-emotional, language and motor domains is highly interrelated (DiPietro 2000). This suggests that enrichment or deprivation in one domain can affect development in the others (DiPietro 2000). This body of research also challenges the notion of a 'critical period' or limited window of opportunity for intervention. DiPietro's analysis suggests that there is brain development throughout all periods of life. By confining our interventions to early childhood, we risk abandoning those who have been damaged in early life, as was inadvertently done when potential adoptive parents were discouraged from adopting American crack cocaine babies and Romanian orphans, both of whom had suffered early deprivation. Her analysis reveals a greater receptivity to changes over a longer period of development, even in adolescence, for children who have been placed in a supportive environment (DiPietro 2000).

A number of large-scale studies are currently under way around the world, to inform interventions in childhood. In 2000, President Clinton signed the Children's Health Act in the United States, which laid the groundwork for a major national study on the impact of the environment on child health, with study findings due in 2004 (US President's Taskforce on Environmental Health Risks and Safety Risks to Children 2000). Another national study, the National Longitudinal Survey of Children and Youth, began in Canada in 1994, to investigate whether early child outcomes of development predict later success, and the implications of this for investments in child health (Statistics Canada 1998). A further development in North America is the collaborative study between Americans and Canadians to compare mortality and income inequality among the ten Canadian provinces and fifty US states. To date, they have discovered that the United States has a level of mortality 30–60 per cent higher than in Canada, which has a more egalitarian income distribution (Hertzman 2001a). This demonstrates the importance of the distribution of wealth in nurturing health. A major study in Australia has also been conducted from the Western Australian Research Institute for Child Health, with follow-up studies focusing on the social factors that support the healthy development of children (Silburn et al 1996).

Converging data from child development research supports the contention that healthy children are more likely to develop from an environment of good early parental care that fosters positive coping responses (DiPietro 2000). It would appear that the best chance for healthy children lies in providing healthy relationships with children, where caregiving is contingent, responsive and characterised by warmth and security, with permission to explore their environment (DiPietro 2000). Hertzman (2001b) further suggests that children need to see themselves from very early in life as learners. He believes that when they are encouraged to develop the aptitudes they have, this will pull along learning in weaker areas. Parents should protect their children from undue stress while allowing them to develop coping skills in a safe, cohesive environment. By age four or five, the quality of community life begins to have an effect, and this is when the social ecology of child health is cultivated by such environmental features as neighbourhood design and housing policies that foster cohesion (Earls & Carlson 2001; Hertzman 2001a).

Goals for
child health

The major health issues for children's health in today's society include the following:

- safety/injury prevention
- immunisation
- healthy lifestyle—fitness/activity
- diet/nutrition
- mental/emotional health.

In order to achieve child health in any community, *all* known risk factors must be acknowledged and incorporated into a community's goals and targets for prevention, protection and health promotion. An intersectoral approach is essential and this is congruent with the strategies of the Ottawa Charter for Health Promotion (WHO-Health and Welfare Canada 1986). The five strategies for child health are discussed below.

Building healthy public policy

Healthy public policy for children involves ensuring that policies governing illness and injury surveillance, health and fitness promotion, family support systems and sustainable environments are all developed coherently, so that all influences on health are acknowledged by society. This includes developing and monitoring manufacturing safety standards, housing standards and legislation (such as that governing seat belts and bicycle helmets) that guide safe behaviour. Laws mandating the licensing of child care workers also fall into this category.

The issue of policies governing paid child care has generated widespread debate in a number of countries. At least 40 per cent of under-threes in Scandinavia are in child care, which receives public funding. A similar proportion attends child care in Canada, the United States and New Zealand but on the basis of self-funding (Sutherland 2001). In the United States, the United Kingdom, Japan, Australia and some European countries, the combination of statutory parental leave and low levels of public child care provision means that child care responsibilities are left to employers, with variable results. Many companies use child care as a benefit, to be used in attracting the best workers, which can simply worsen existing inequities (Sutherland 2001). For some middle wage earners, opting for voluntary part-time work allows a balance between work and home. The proportion of families accepting this mix of work and home child care in Japan, the United Kingdom and the Netherlands has now risen above 30 per cent of the female workforce, with the Netherlands also having the largest proportion of male voluntary part-time workers—13 per cent, compared to the average of 3–4 per cent elsewhere in Europe (Sutherland 2001).

Leaving the child care solution to parents causes many families to suffer prolonged reductions in income and a lack of opportunity for promotion once they revert to part-time work. The Nordic countries of Denmark, Finland, Iceland, Norway and Sweden have the most generous entitlements to parental leave for both parents, which is expected to encourage fathers to become more involved in child rearing (Sutherland 2001). Yet in highly competitive workplaces many fathers relinquish their right to this leave, particularly as disparities between male and female salaries persist. This is one area where industrial policies would make a difference to both parental attitudes and child rearing. Initiatives to help parents maintain a balance between work and parenting are important, as conflicts between the two have been identified as a major contributor to mental health problems, at least among North American adults (Hertzman 2001b).

Policies must respond to children's holistic needs for balance and potential. This means that physical education programs must be considered integral to education programs and not just an 'add-on' to learning. Similarly, programs that cultivate 'health literacy' must be supported (Kickbusch 2001; Ratzan 2001). Sporting activities and recreational facilities must be secured to offer opportunities for building strong bodies and spirited minds, and these must be considered as important to community development as economic ventures. Resources must also be allocated for parent education and parent support, particularly for working parents and separated parents, who need to be equally aware of and involved in sustaining the health of their children. Policy development for healthy children thus exemplifies the need for intersectoral collaboration at all levels. This includes communication and cooperative decision-making by agencies responsible for decisions related to family law, local education, health, sport and recreation departments, local councils, state and provincial governments, consumer groups and the environment.

In some cases, policies governing health targets need to be re-prioritised. For example, where opportunities for immunisation are inequitable, or where access to physical fitness or mental health initiatives for children are not available, the community may have to pressure for policy changes. Perhaps the most important policy decision governments must make acknowledges the importance of antenatal care in sustaining the health of the entire population. Such policies could be argued on the basis of research into the link between nutrient and vitamin requirements in utero, and subsequent states of health and illness in later life. Antenatal care that ensures adequate dietary intake and careful monitoring of growth patterns has the capacity to increase lifespan, enhance quality of life and reduce the cost of illness care for the population, making it the most important policy focus in public health.

Creating supportive environments

This strategy includes planning for child-friendly physical environments, developing school-based safety education programs and providing resources for positive parenting. Any attempt to reduce childhood accident rates must include community-wide initiatives such as introducing bicycle paths, protected play areas and safe playground equipment. The importance of the setting for health and safety must be recognised. Children spend a large proportion of their time in school settings, and there must be adequate resourcing within health budgets to ensure that schools are safe and healthy settings within which young children can not only learn, but thrive.

Supportive environments for child health also include those conducive to healthy pregnancy. Services that provide health surveillance and monitoring for pregnant women must be widely available, and this includes workplace-based resources. With the demise of child health nurses in many neighbourhoods, new parents must have access to alternative sources of information and support. Parenting resource centres are now being established in Canada on the advice of the research evidence garnered at the Canadian Institute for Advanced Research. Different provinces are trialling different approaches to evaluating child support at both the neighbourhood and community levels (Hertzman 2001a). In Australia, nurses and other health professionals working in the community are providing parenting classes and dietary advice at opportune times, whenever and wherever they encounter young families, but resources remain scarce. At all political levels, health professionals have an obligation, which many are accepting, to lobby governments to make child and parent issues a priority. This extends across urban and rural communities, and includes advocacy for information that is both culturally appropriate and family friendly.

Strengthening community action

In order to foster community empowerment, parents, grandparents, teachers and others need to be made aware of their community's strengths and resources as well as the areas of particular risk to young children. Health advocacy involves validating their ideas and informed choices by assisting them to implement health and safety initiatives at the local level. Grandparent-to-child programs have also been established in some areas, with overwhelming success. The underlying premise of these programs is surrogate caring. Many older people live at a distance from their grandchildren and, likewise, other children have a need for grandparenting but, for whatever reason, have no grandparent available to them. The result of bringing the two together is increased caring and a sense of intergenerational connectedness. Another advantage is that, for sole supporting working parents, an extra support person who is also older and mature can be invaluable in helping to care for the child(ren).

Parent-to-parent programs are another way of strengthening community action. These programs, which allow opportunities for sharing, often provide an outlet for new parents to express concerns and to share resources and strategies for parenting. In addition, they provide an opportunity to socialise with others in similar situations, and thus guard against the ill effects of the isolation that new parenting often brings. The health professional's role in such groups is a facilitative one, bringing people together to strengthen their combined resources and helping them compile a data base of resources for any additional services required.

Developing personal skills

It is up to health, education and community welfare groups to ensure that the community has appropriate educational opportunities for skills development for health carers, teachers, parents and the children themselves. This is fundamental to effective teamwork that focuses on the child, rather than the vested interests of the various people involved with helping children maintain health. Eliminating teacher in-service sessions is often excused on the basis of competing priorities; however, teachers need to be constantly updated on the changing needs of children and the latest findings relevant to their health. Similarly, child care workers need to have access to the most up-to-date information and the evolving research information that guides their practices. Developing and updating personal skills needs to be viewed in terms of the inextricable link between physical and emotional health in pregnant women, their children and the population in general. Care must therefore be taken in setting goals so that child health goals are seen in the context of developing healthy parents and healthy parenting.

Reorienting health services

In the past, public health services included a relatively equitable distribution of public health or child health nurses throughout the community to support and assist parents in maintaining the health of their children. In Australia and New Zealand, the rationalisation of services has created inequities in service provision, with some families enjoying neighbourhood centres for monitoring and guidance, while others, particularly those who live in rural areas or in the outer suburbs of large cities, have to rely on central hospital-based services and their local general practitioner (GP). It is interesting to hear of the reduction in child and family support programs in the same political context as the rhetoric about the 'family-friendly society', especially when there is research evidence to justify the expenditure. A set of research studies in Australia considered a number of risk factors associated with child abuse, concluding that the first several months of a child's life is the time of highest risk (Cazdow, Armstrong & Fraser 1999; Armstrong et al 1999, 2000; Fraser et al 2000). The researchers found that home-visiting interventions from as early as six weeks of age have a positive impact on maternal, infant, family and home environment (Armstrong et al 1999, 2000; Cazdow et al 1999; Fraser et al 2000).

The findings of this group of studies led the researchers to conclude that the immediate postnatal period presented 'an exciting window of opportunity to access high-risk families who may otherwise have become marginalized from traditional services' (Fraser et al 2000, p 1400). As Vimpani (2000, p 538) suggests, these data indicate that we need a 'revolution in thinking, similar to that which preceded taking young children out of the factories and mines of the nineteenth century and schooling them'. The evidence-base indicates that the future of society rests in having all young children equipped emotionally and cognitively for their place in society. This means ensuring that both acute and preventative care are provided, and that parents have access to parenting education that will assist them in providing anticipatory guidance and protection from the hazards of everyday life (Hardy & Miller 2000).

In many cases, no central resource centre exists for health professionals to follow through with their good intentions. Many also experience difficulties accessing information and/or support related to changing practices or culturally appropriate services. In the United Kingdom, where community health services are provided on a geographic basis, the situation is less critical. Health visitors and district nurses are responsible for a geographically determined segment of the population and they assume responsibility for most of the family's health needs in collaboration with a designated community GP. This ensures that childhood screening, surveillance, family counselling and referral of family members to other services is maintained. A similar service is provided by public health nurses in Canada. In the United States, where the system is dominated by a 'user pays' scheme, the cost of health care precludes this type of service for everyone, exacerbating existing inequities.

The issue for all involved in child health is to recognise that the organisation of services is changing rapidly in response to shrinking health care budgets. In the interest of access and equity, all health professionals must work more closely together to ensure that families don't fall through the cracks of service provision. This involves greater teamwork than ever before, and careful evaluation of services and health outcomes. Regardless of the type of service, all health encounters should be carefully documented, a task that is made less onerous by the widespread access to computers.

It is important to respond to the request of the Jakarta Declaration on Health Promotion (WHO 1997) to gather a systematic base of evidence on health issues and outcomes in a variety of contexts and with a focus on the environment. Many epidemiological investigations begin from a worker in the field noticing a cluster of certain types of illnesses, or observing the outcomes of a change in the health environment. This type of informal research is integral to the role of all health professionals and is absolutely essential to heighten awareness of the interplay between the environment, individual and group behaviour, and biological factors. Research findings must be used to inform and thus empower the community to become involved in decision-making related to health services.

thinking critically

Child health in the community

1   Identify five important influences on child health in today's society.

2   Identify four agencies or sectors responsible for some aspect of child safety in your community.

3   Compare and contrast the health and safety risks of schoolchildren in the following:
   ● a rural community where most children live on farms
   ● an inner-city neighbourhood with most families of low socioeconomic status
   ● a middle-class, ocean-side community
   ● a suburban community 15 km from a large metropolitan area.

4   Explain how health professionals can build health literacy among young people

5   Identify two goals for improving the health and safety of children in your community.

6   Describe three activities in a local school or recreational setting that illustrate primary health care in practice for young children. For each, explain the importance of the setting in promoting child health.

REFERENCES

Aber, J., Bennett, N., Conley, D. & Li, J. (1997). The effects of poverty on child health and development. *Annual Review of Public Health*, 18: 463–83.

Acton, C., Nixon, J. & Clark, R. (1997). Bicycle riding and maxillofacial trauma in young children. *Medical Journal of Australia*, 165(5): 249–51.

Africa News Service (2001). Shock figures on child injuries, Comtex, http://web3.infotrac.galegr.../purl=rcl. Retrieved 21 February 2002.

Ahmad, O., Lopez, A. & Inoue, M. (2000). The decline in child mortality: a reappraisal. *Bulletin of the World Health Organization*, 78(10): 1175–91.

Akukwe, C. (2000). Maternal and child health services in the twenty-first century: critical issues, challenges and opportunities. *Health Care for Women International*, 21: 641–53.

Andrews, L. (1999). Genetics, reproduction and the law (interview). Association of Trial Lawyers of America. *Trial*, 35(7): 20.

Ardern, C., Pickett, W., King, M. & Boyce, W. (2001). Injury in Canadian youth: a brief report from the health behavior in school-aged children survey. *Canadian Journal of Public Health*, 92(3): 201–3.

Armstrong, K., Fraser, J., Dadds, M. & Morris, J. (1999). A randomized, controlled trial of nurse home visiting to vulnerable families with newborns. *Journal of Paediatric Child Health*, 35: 237–44.

— (2000). Promoting secure attachment, maternal mood and child health in a vulnerable population: a randomized controlled trial. *Journal of Paediatric Child Health*, 36: 555–62.

Australian Bureau of Statistics (ABS) (1999). Children, Australia: A Social Report. Canberra: AGPS.

Australian Institute of Health and Welfare (AIHW) (2000). Australia's Health, 2000. Canberra: AGPS.

Baker, A. (2000). Number of children living in poverty. *Time*, 23 October, p 22.

Bauman, A. (1996). Asthma in Australia: dawning of a public health approach. *Australian and New Zealand Journal of Public Health*, 20(1): 7–8.

Beeber, S. (1996). Smoking and childhood asthma. *Journal of Pediatric Health Care*, 10(2): 58–62.

Beech, H. (2001). China's infant cash crop. *Time*, 29 January, pp 38–9.

Berger, C. (2001). Infant mortality: a reflection of the quality of health. *Health and Social Work*, 26(4): 277–83.

Booth, M., Wake, M., Armstrong, T., Chey, T., Hesketh, K. & Mathur, S. (2001). The epidemiology of over-weight and obesity among Australian children and adolescents, 1995–97. *Australian and New Zealand Journal of Public Health*, 25(2): 162–9.

Britton, H. & Hansen, K. (1997). Sexual abuse. *Clinical obstetrics and Gynecology*, 40 (1): 226–40.

Brook, J., Brook, D. & Whiteman, M. (2000). The influence of maternal smoking during pregnancy on the toddler's negativity. *Archives of Pediatrics & Adolescent Medicine*, 154(4): 381–92.

Burgess, M. (1997). Immunisation in the year 2020 and beyond. *Australian and New Zealand Journal of Public Health*, 21(2): 115–16.

Bush, P. & Iannotti, R. (1993). Alcohol, cigarette, and marijuana use among fourth-grade urban school-children in 1988/89 and 1990/91. *American Journal of Public Health*, 83(1): 111–15.

Canada Safety Council (2002). Child injury deaths—is progress stalled? Home page, http://www.safety-council.org/info/child/oecd.html. Retrieved 21 February 2002.

Cazdow, S., Armstrong, K. & Fraser, J. (1999). Stressed parents with infants: reassessing physical abuse risk factors. *Child Abuse & Neglect*, 23(9): 845–53.

Chalmers, B. & Mangiaterra, V. (2001). Appropriate perinatal technology: A WHO perspective. *Journal of Obstetrics and Gynecology Canada*, 23(7): 574–5.

Child Accident Prevention Foundation of Australia (CAFPA) (1997). *Kidsafe House*. Brisbane: CAPFA, Queensland Health.

Cliff, J. & Noormahomed, A. (1993). The impact of war on children's health in Mozambique. *Social Science and Medicine*, 36(7): 843–8.

Cloke, C. (1997). Save the children. *Nursing Times*, 93(14): 35–7.

Cunningham, J., O'Connor, G., Dockery, D. & Speizer, F. (1996). Environmental tobacco smoke, wheezing, and asthma in children in 24 communities. *American Journal of Critical Care Medicine*, 153: 218–24.

Devereux, G., Ayatollahi, T., Ward., R., Bromly, C., Bourke, S., Stenton, S. & Hendrick, D. (1996). Asthma, airways responsiveness and air pollution in two contrasting districts of northern England. *Thorax*, 51(2): 169–74.

DiPietro, J. (2000). Baby and the brain: advances in child development. *Annual Review of Public Health*, 21: 455–71.

Dobson, R. (2000). Working draft of the human genome completed. *Bulletin of the World Health Organization*, 78(9): 1168–9.

Dunst, C. & Trivette, C. (1996). Empowerment, effective helpgiving practices and family-centered care. *Pediatric Nursing*, 22(4): 334–43.

Durvasula, S. & Beange, H. (2001). Health inequalities in people with intellectual disability: strategies for improvement. *Health Promotion Journal of Australia*, 11(1): 27–31.

Earls, F. & Carlson, M. (2001). The social ecology of child health and well-being. *Annual Review of Public Health*, 22: 143–66.

Fancourt, R. (1997). Child health in times of social and economic change. *New Zealand Medical Journal*, 110: 95–7.

Fleming, J. (1997). Prevalence of childhood sexual abuse in a community sample of Australian women. *Medical Journal of Australia*, 166: 65–8.

Fleming, J., Mullen, P. & Bammer, G. (1997). A study of potential risk factors for sexual abuse in childhood. *Social Science and Medicine*, 21(1): 49–58.

Fraser, J., Armstrong, K., Morris, J. & Dadds, M. (2000). Home visiting intervention for vulnerable families with newborns: follow-up results of a randomized controlled trial. *Child Abuse & Neglect*, 24(11): 1399–1429.

French, S., Story, M. & Jeffery, R. (2001). Environmental influences on eating and physical activity. *Annual Review of Public Health*, 22: 309–35.

Freudenberg, N. (2000). Health promotion in the city: a review of the current practice and future prospects in the United States. *Annual Review of Public Health*, 21: 473–503.

Fukui, S., Sawaguchi, T., Nishida, H. & Horiuchi, T. (2000). Declining SIDS rate in Japan corresponds to reduction of risk factors. Paper presented to the SIDS International Conference, Auckland, 8 February.

Guildea, Z., Fone, D., Dunstan, F., Sibert, J. & Cartlidge, P. (2001). Social deprivation and the causes of stillbirth and infant mortality. *Archives of Disease in Childhood*, 84(4): 307–13.

Hanna, J., Wakefield, J., Doolan, C. & Messner, J. (1994). Childhood immunisation: factors associated with failure to complete the recommended schedule by two years of age. *Australian Journal of Public Health*, 18(1): 15–21.

Hardy, J. & Miller, T. (2000). Growing up healthy, wealthy, and wise. *Contemporary Pediatrics*, 17(2): 63–70.

Hasselberg, M., Laflamme, L., Ringback Weitoft, G. (2001). Socioeconomic differences in road traffic injuries during childhood and youth: a closer look at different kinds of road user. *Journal of Epidemiology and Community Health*. 55(12): 858–62.

Hertzman, C. (2001a). Health and human society. *American Scientist*, 89(6): 538–44.

—— (2001b). Determinants of health. Presentation to the Commission for Children and Young People (CCYP), Queensland Health. Royal Children's Hospital, Brisbane, 21 November.

Husain, S. (1999). Teachers as therapists: a program to help war traumatized children around the globe. *IACAPAP Bulletin*, August, http://www.iacapap.org/bulletins/nr10/article15.htm. Retrieved 21 February 2002.

International Council of Nurses (ICN) (1999). Press release: Safeguard Childhood. Geneva: ICN.

Keating, D. & Hertzman, C. (1999). Modernity's paradox. In: D. Keating & C. Hertzman (eds), Developmental Health and the Wealth of Nations: Social, Biological and Educational Dynamics. New York: Guildford Press, pp 1–20.

Kickbusch, I. (2001). Health literacy: addressing the health and education divide. *Health Promotion International*, 16(3): 289–97.

Kisely, S., Stevens, M., Hart, B. & Douglas, C. (2002). Health issues of asylum seekers and refugees. *Australia and New Zealand Journal of Public Health*, 26(1): 8–10.

Kolbe, L., Kann. L. & Brener, N. (2001). Overview and summary of findings: School health policies and programs study 2000. *Journal of School Health*, 71(7): 253–63.

Langley, J., Warner, M., Smith, G. & Wright, C. (2001). Drowning-related deaths in New Zealand, 1980–94. *Australian and New Zealand Journal of Public Health*, 25(5): 451–7.

Lee, P. & Paxman, D. (1997). Reinventing public health. *Annual Review of Public Health*. 18: 1–35.

Lessick, M. & Anderson, L. (2000). Genetic discoveries: challenges for nurses who care for children and their families. *Journal of the Society of Pediatric Nurses*, 5(1): 47–52.

Maine, D. & Rosenfield, A. (1999). The safe motherhood initiative: why has it stalled? *American Journal of Public Health*, 89(4): 480–2.

Malloy, M. & Freeman, D. (2000). Birth weight and gestational age-specific sudden infant death syndrome mortality: United States, 1991 versus 1995. *Pediatrics*, 105(6): 1227–39.

McLennan, L. (2000). Poverty the bar to a normal, smiling face. *The Australian*, 12–13 August, p 7.

Miller, M. (1999). Introducing a novel model to estimate national and global measles disease burden. *International Journal of Infectious Diseases*, 4: 14–20.

Mirowsky, J. (1998). An informative sociology of health and well-being: Notes from the new editor. *Journal of Health and Social Behavior*, 39: 1–3.

Mitchell, E., Tuohy, P., Brunt, J., Thompson, J., Clements, M., Stewart, A., Ford, R. & Taylor, B. (1997). Risk factors for sudden infant death syndrome following the prevention campaign in New Zealand: a prospective study. *Pediatrics*, 100(5): 835–96.

Mock, C. (2001). Beyond our borders: injury in the developing world. *Western Journal of Medicine*. 175(6): 372–4.

Montgomery, L., Kiely, J. & Pappas, G. (1996). The effects of poverty, race, and family structure on US children's health: data from the NHIS, 1978 through 1980 and 1989 through 1991. *American Journal of Public Health*, 86(10): 1401–5.

Murphy, M. & Risser, N. (1999). Pediatric genetic testing, *The Nurse Practitioner*, 24(6): 100–6.

Mustard, J.F. (1996). Health and social capital. In: D. Blane, E. Brunner & R. Wilkinson, eds, *Health and Social Organisation: Towards a Health Policy for the Twenty-first Century*. London: Routledge, pp 303–13.

—— (1999). Social Determinants of Health. Presentation to University of Queensland Centre for Primary Health Care. Brisbane, 5 August.

Nagel, D., Putnam, F. & Noll, J. (1997). Disclosure patterns of sexual abuse and psychological functioning at a 1-year follow-up. *Social Science and Medicine*, 21(2): 137–47.

New Zealand Health Information Service (NZHIS) (2001). Health Statistics. Auckland: NZHIS.

Nurcombe, B. (2000). Child sexual abuse 1: psychopathology. *Australian and New Zealand Journal of Psychiatry*, 34: 85–91.

O'Connor, T., Davies, L., Dunn, J. & Golding, J. (2000). Distribution of accidents, injuries, and illnesses by family type. *Pediatrics*, 106(5): 1130–5.

OECD (1999). OECD Health data 99: a comparative analysis of 29 countries. Paris: OECD.

Peterson, L. & Stern, B. (1997). Family processes and child risk for injury. *Behaviour Research and Therapy*, 35(3): 179–90.

Plotkin, S. & Orstein, W. (eds) (1999). *Vaccines*. Philadelphia: WB Saunders.

Poland, B., Coburn, D., Robertson, A. & Eakin, J. (1998). Wealth, equity and health care: a critique of a 'population health' perspective on the determinants of health. *Social Science and Medicine*, 46(7): 785–98.

Powell, C. (1997). Protecting children in the Accident and Emergency department. *Accident and Emergency Nursing*, 5: 76–80.

Preboth, M. (2001). AAP statement on falls in children. *American Academy of Family Physicians*, 64(8): 1468.

Ratzan, S. (2001). Health literacy: communication for the public good. *Health Promotion International*, 16: 207–14.

Robert, S. (1998). Community-level socioeconomic status effects on adult health. *Journal of Health and Social Behavior*, 39(March): 18–37.

Romans, S. (1997). Childhood sexual abuse: concerns and consequences. *Medical Journal of Australia*, 166: 59–60.

Rushton, C., McEnhill, M. & Armstrong, L. (1996). Establishing therapeutic boundaries as patient advocates. *Pediatric Nursing*, 22(3): 186–9.

Schwartz, S., Susser, E. & Susser, M. (1999). A future for epidemiology? *Annual Review of Public Health*, 20: 15–33.

Shah, R. (1997). It is easier to build strong children than to mend broken men. *Iowa Medicine*, March: 110–11.

Shakespeare, T. (1999). Manifesto for genetic justice. *Social Alternatives*, 18(1): 29–32.

Shaw, B. & Krause, N. (2001). The effects of childhood trauma on health in later life. *The Gerontologist*, 15 October, p 215.

Silove, D., Steel, Z. & Mollica, R. (2001). Detention of asylum seekers: assault on health, human rights, and social development. *The Lancet*, 357(9266): 1436–7.

Silburn, S., Zubrick, S., Garton, A. et al (1996). Western Australia Child Health Survey: family and community health. Perth: ABS & TVW Telethon Institute for Child Health Research.

Statistics Canada (1998). National longitudinal survey of children and youth, http://www/hrdc.gc.ca/arbb/conferences/nlscyconf/flyer-e.shtm. Retrieved 21 February 2002.

—— (2001). *Health Indicators*. Ottawa: Canadian Institute for Health Information.

Stoddard, F. & Saxe, G. (2001). Ten-year research review of physical injuries, *Journal of the American Academy of Child and Adolescent Psychiatry*, 40(10): 1128–60.

Stone, D., Jarvis, S. & Pless, B. (2001). The continuing global challenge of injury, *British Medical Journal*, 322(7302): 1557–8.

Sultan, A. (2001). Viewpoint on asylum seekers. *The Lancet*, 357(99266): 1437–8.

Sutherland, T. (2001). The world on a treadmill. *The Australian*, 10 September, p 11.

Thompson, S. (1997). Vaccination: protection at what price? *The Australian and New Zealand Journal of Public Health*, 21(1) suppl: 1–8.

Tomison, A. (2000). Issues in child abuse prevention: exploring family violence. *Australian Institute for Family Studies*, 13, Winter: 1–23.

Turrell, G., Oldenburg, B., McGuffog, I. & Dent, R. (1999). Socioeconomic determinants of health: towards a national research program and a policy and intervention agenda. Brisbane: Queensland University of Technology School of Public Health, Centre for Public Health Research, Ausinfo, Canberra.

UNICEF (2001). A league table of child deaths by injury in rich nations, Florence Italy, UNICEF, *Innocenti Report Card*, Issue 2, February 2001.

—— (2002). Press release: league table of child deaths from injury. UNICEF home page, http://www/unicef/org/newsline/01per10htm. Retrieved 21 February 2002.

United Nations (2001). Human Rights Watch Report. New York: UN.

United Nations Family Planning Association (UNFPA) (2000). The state of world population 2000, New York: UN.

US President's Task Force on Environmental Health Risks and Safety Risks to Children (2000). The Longitudinal Cohort Study (LCS), Washington: USDHSS.

Veale, A., Peat, J., Tovey, E., Salome, C., Thompson, J. et al (1996). Asthma and atopy in four rural Australian Aboriginal communities. *Medical Journal of Australia*, 165(4): 192–6.

Vimpani, G. (2000). Editorial: home visiting for vulnerable infants in Australia. *Journal of Paediatrics and Child Health*, 36: 537–9.

Whitehead, M. (1995). Tackling inequalities: a review of policy initiatives. In: M. Benezeval, K. Judge & M. Whitehead (eds), *Tackling Inequalities in Health*. London: King's Fund, pp 22–52.

Whyte, B. (2000). WHO defines priority actions to address developments in human genetics. *Bulletin of the World Health Organization*, 78(9): 1169–78.

Wilkinson, R. (1996). *Unhealthy Societies: The Afflictions of Inequality*. London: Routledge.

Williams, J. & Lessick, M. (1996). Genome research: Implications for children. *Pediatric Nursing*, 22(1): 40–7.

Wilson, N., Quigley, R. & Mansoor, O. (1999). Food ads on TV: a health hazard for children? *Australian and New Zealand Journal of Public Health*, 23(6): 647.

Wiseman, H. (1995). Accidental childhood poisoning. *Health Visitor*, 68(4): 163–4.

World Bank (1999). Safe Motherhood and The World Bank: Lessons from 10 years of Experience. Washington: The World Bank.

World Health Organization (WHO) (1996). *The World Health Report 1996: Fighting Disease, Fostering Development*. Geneva: WHO.

— (1997). The Jakarta Declaration on Health Promotion into the 21st Century. Jakarta: WHO.

— (1999). *World Health Report 1999. Making a Difference*. Geneva: WHO.

World Health Organization-Health and Welfare Canada-CPHA, (1986). Ottawa Charter for Health Promotion. *Canadian Journal of Public Health*, 77(12): 425–30.

World Health Organization-UNICEF-UNFPA-World Bank (1999). Joint Statement on Reduction of Maternal Mortality. New York: UN.

Yencken, D. & Porter, L. (2001). *A Just and Sustainable Australia*. Melbourne: The Australian Collaboration.

CHAPTER 6

Healthy
adolescents

Introduction   Adolescence is one of the most critical stages of a person's development, for it is in this crucial transition from childhood to adulthood that many risky behaviours are experimented with and, sometimes, adopted as lifestyle patterns. What distinguishes the adolescent who progresses through the tortuous path to healthy adulthood from others who fall victim to high-risk behaviours, such as smoking, over-eating, or abusing alcohol or other harmful substances, unsafe sexual activities and self-inflicted injury, remains elusive. The mix of risk factors and personal choices leading to the burden of illness, injury and disability in adolescence is an interesting area and one that has generated considerable research interest. This chapter explores some elements of healthy adolescence and determinants of risk in an attempt to illuminate the various elements that influence the transition to adulthood in the twenty-first century.

objectives   **By the end of this chapter you will be able to:**

1   Identify the two most important influences on healthy adolescence

2   Describe at least four factors that put adolescents at risk for illness, injury or disability

3   Explain the web of causation for adolescent suicide

4   Discuss family issues influencing adolescent health and well-being

5   Identify three goals for sustaining adolescent health in a community

6   Explain how a primary health care framework can be used in planning strategies for adolescent health

7   Describe the role of the media in reinforcing risky behaviours among adolescents.

The healthy
adolescent

When most people imagine healthy adolescents they usually think of physically fit young people engaged in some sort of social activity—at least that's what the media attempts to portray in magazines, movies and TV commercials. This is a picture of balance and potential, of happy, physically well people striving to reach their life goals. But in reality, many young people's lives contradict this image. Frustrated by societal expectations, information overload, forecasts of gloomy employment prospects and retracting family support, many teenagers suffer from anxiety, depression and poor physical health. Maintaining a 'mix' of emotional, social and physical well-being is therefore one of the greatest challenges of the adolescent period, and often it is the vigilant eye of the school nurse, teacher or sports coach that identifies signs of distress or of ill health. For many of these 'helping' professionals, understanding the dynamics of healthy adolescence is fundamental to providing assistance for those going through this important stage of life.

Adolescent health determinants
and risk factors

Adolescence is that period in a person's life where all energies are focused on preparing for adulthood. During the teenage years, sculpting out an adult identity seems to take precedence over any other issue (Erikson 1963). In the transition from child to adult, young people 'try on' a range of identities to try and develop a sense of themselves in relation to the world and other groups of people. Many find this difficult, particularly balancing these changes with maintaining relationships with family and friends. Some young people suffer from increased alienation and emotional distress during this period of rapid change, because of diminishing support from families, schools and the other institutions that, in the past, provided a scaffold for development (Bronfenbrenner 1986).

Some erosion of the adolescent's support system is linked to a climate of economic restraint and impending recession, creating pressures on societal institutions to do more with less (Drummond 1997; Gillis 2000). This often causes a gap in support services that would in some cases mean the difference between adopting a healthy pathway to adulthood and becoming sidetracked to an unhealthy lifestyle. To a great extent, the problems of young people are related to their expectations. The bombardment by media images of enchanted lifestyles that flow from consuming the right products, merging with images of excessive violence, leads many adolescents to become confused about which expectations are real and which are a fabrication. Compounding their concerns are the expectations of society and its various cultures and subcultures, which engulf and often overwhelm young people just at the time they are supposed to be gaining the freedom to be individuals.

Researchers have found that young people, especially young women, report high levels of symptoms such as respiratory complaints, headaches, stomach disorders, skin problems and concerns about weight as well as mental health problems such as nervousness, anxiety, sleep problems and depression (West & Sweeting 1996). These authors suggest that the findings of this body of research may represent only the tip of the iceberg. In a major review of psychosocial disorders among young people, young women were found to suffer from more mental health problems than males, but this may be attributed to their greater willingness to admit to psychological distress and seek help for it (D'Espaignet & Rickwood 1995; Rutter & Smith 1995).

Both male and female adolescents today find themselves in a social malaise, where their environment is pervaded by economic recession, unemployment, low-paid jobs and the sense of having no future (West & Sweeting 1996). Paradoxically, this sense of futility occurs within a context of information overload, so the young person is bombarded on the one hand by stimuli engendering action, and on the other by messages that say 'don't bother'.

Many react to the mixed messages by becoming anxious and depressed. Some go on to manifest suicidal behaviours, crime, alcohol and drug abuse, depression and eating disorders.

One view among those attempting to help guide adolescents to become healthy adults is that the problems of youth are complex and intractable. A more optimistic perspective sees gradual improvements in adolescent health over their counterparts of a couple of decades ago. However, the report card on adolescent health varies widely between countries. There is evidence in Australia and New Zealand, for example, that young people are generally in good health and see themselves that way (AIHW 2000; Statistics New Zealand 1998). But it is less than ideal in some categories. Both Australia and New Zealand have enjoyed some success in reducing one of the greatest causes of injury to adolescents, namely road traffic accidents (AIHW 2000). However, as in other industrialised countries, neuropsychiatric disorders and drug dependence are escalating and now constitute the largest proportion of the burden of illness, injury and disability among young people (AIHW 2000; Mathers, Vos & Stevenson 1999; WHO 1999, 2000b, 2001). The burden of illness in industrialised countries is, however, quite different from the situation in low- and middle-income countries, where the nature of adolescent life carries higher risks of contracting communicable diseases such as HIV/AIDS, or being involved in road traffic accidents, war and civil violence (WHO 1999, 2001). Youth in all countries are, however, at risk of mental illness.

Mental health issues

The most pressing mental health problems for adolescents in the twenty-first century are depression, youth suicide, health-damaging behaviours and the type of alienation that leads to substance abuse (AIHW 2000; Statistics NZ 1998; Lamarine 1995; Sawyer & Kosky 1996; WHO 1999, 2000b, 2001). In certain cases, adolescent distress is a sequel to childhood accidents and injuries, a form of post-traumatic stress syndrome (PTSD) (Stoddard & Saxe 2001). But to a greater extent, young people's emotional distress stems from relationship problems which, during adolescence, seem to invade all facets of their lives, especially for girls (Gillis 2000). This is magnified considerably for the 5–10 per cent of adolescents who are gay, lesbian or bisexual (Nelson 1997; WHO 2000a). A heterosexist society often leads to feelings of stigma and social isolation, which create an additional strain on the gay person's transition through adolescence. Many young gay people become victims of family or societal violence and fall prey to unhealthy lifestyles. As a result, they are over-represented in the statistics for depression, anxiety disorders, substance abuse, homelessness, sexually transmitted diseases and youth suicide (Nelson 1997; WHO 2000a).

Adolescents in general are at risk of responding to stress in ways that are less than helpful, particularly with the pressures of studying and/or balancing work and family relationships. Among the challenges for health professionals trying to help them is their hesitancy to use traditional health services and the 'inverse care law', which contends that those most at risk are less likely to seek or want advice (Jacobson & Wilkinson 1994). For boys especially, prevailing gender norms often prevent them from seeking help for personal stress and this may be compounded if, when they do seek assistance, the diagnoses and/or treatments also reflect gender biases among health professionals (WHO 2000a).

Youth homelessness

When interpersonal difficulties persist, adolescents sometimes run away from home. Some return several times; others fail to find a comfortable niche within which to grow and find a direction, and instead revert to a life on the streets. This group is now recognised in many countries as at risk for major health problems, particularly in large inner-city areas, where they are easy prey for exploitation into the world of drugs and prostitution (Freudenberg 2000).

Homeless youth are a serious problem, given that emotional instability, abuse and family conflict may have precipitated their departure from the home (National Crime Prevention 1999). Conditions on the street leave them at risk for a host of different illnesses, addictions, victimisation and further conflict or mental instability (Breakey 1997). The issue of homelessness raises the question of whether there have been any real public health gains for young people in the past few decades. At the turn of the last century, the problems of youth were related to infectious diseases, being unemployed and living in large, inner-city areas with poor hygiene, insufficient clothing and heating and a lack of nutritious food (Vimpani & Parry 1989). Today, many homeless youth live in exactly these conditions, with no chance of meeting the housing, income support, education and employment conditions necessary for good health (Breakey 1997). As adolescents their needs are often focused on peers, which often results in perpetuating the unhealthy behaviours of substance abuse or criminal acts aimed at self-protection. Their lives often become a revolving door of ill health, in which the stigma of homelessness results in them being subjected to moral, rather than public health, attention, much like the victims of HIV infection in the early days of that epidemic.

Gillis (2000) contends that there is a need to address how adolescents can be socially supported, and with what outcomes. However, the type of peer support received by many homeless youth is often less than helpful. Few role models exist among their peer group from whom they could derive either support or inspiration, which may lead to a worsening of the negative, self-destructive cycle of group despair. According to Mechanic (1999, p 714), groups can 'scapegoat and intimidate as well as support, can reinforce dysfunctional behaviors and can isolate individuals from other constructive and normalizing influences'. One of the most serious outcomes of being destitute to the extent of homelessness is suicide, the major problem of youth in the world today.

Adolescent suicide

A million people commit suicide every year, and 10–20 million attempt to end their lives (WHO 2001). Approximately one-fifth of these are among the world's adolescent population and many are among the 70 million in the world who also suffer from alcohol dependence (WHO 2001). WHO calculates the rate of suicide among young males, the group most at risk of suicide, at 24 per 100 000 of the population, approximately 3–4 times more at risk than females, who often attempt suicide but not as successfully as males (WHO 2001). In the United States a youth commits suicide every two hours. American suicide rates have increased steadily throughout the last two decades, but not to the extent of those in the South Pacific (NH&MRC 1999; Watkins 2002). In North America there has also been an alarming increase in suicidal behaviours among African American and Native American males, and children under age 14 (US DHHS 2001; Watkins 2002). The pattern for Canadian adolescents is similar to that seen in the United States, with a marked increase in suicides among adolescents throughout the past 30 years to where it is now the second-leading cause of death for this group, after motor vehicle accidents (Gillis 2000). Britain and other parts of Europe are also experiencing some increase in the incidence of suicides, but not at the rate of young people in Australia and New Zealand (NHS Health Advisory Service 1995).

In Australia and New Zealand, the rate of youth suicide and intentional injury is the highest of all industrialised countries and nearly twice the prevalence among young people in developing countries (WHO 1999). In New Zealand, the rate among young males was recorded in 1999 at 22.4 per 100 000 population, twice the rate for young females and only slightly lower than the Australian rate among young males (25.7 per 100 000) (NH&MRC 1999; NZ Ministry of Health 2001). In both countries, the rate of suicide among Indigenous people (Aboriginal, Maori and Pacific Islanders) is also steadily increasing (NH&MRC 2000; NZ Ministry of Health 2001).

Global rates of youth suicide indicate a growing public health problem among adolescents, and the problem has precipitated a move by WHO to make mental health issues its first priority (WHO 2001). The situation may be even more serious than the statistics indicate, given that suicide cases are often obscured by classifications identifying the cause of death as injuries, whether by motor vehicle accidents or drug overdoses. The extent of risk is also difficult to specify, particularly in relation to other risk factors such as alcohol and drug dependency. The problem is serious, irrespective of how it is defined. In Australia, for example, in the two decades from 1979, the rate of suicides among Australians rose by 40 per cent and the death rate for drug dependence among young people rose to five times the 1979 rate (AIHW 2000). One in five males and one in ten females were found to have some type of substance abuse disorder, either harmful use or dependence on drugs (AIHW 2000).

The constellation of risk factors for suicide can be categorised within the domains listed below, and are shown in the web of causation in Figure 6.1.

Domains of risk for adolescent suicide:

1 Social and economic disadvantage
  - low-SES family
  - family subject to economic adversity
2 Childhood and family adversity
  - marital dysfunction

- family instability
- impaired parenting, aggression modelled in the home, no sympathetic listener
- child abuse
- parental psychopathology
- lack of kinship networks
- lack of access to spiritual elders, traditional healers

3 Individual vulnerabilities
- genetic predisposition
- personality characteristics, particularly hopelessness, neuroticism, external locus of control
- gender and its interactions with other factors—male roles, norms, disinclination to seek help and guidance
- conflict surrounding sexual orientation
- physical disorders, malnutrition, illnesses
- behavioural disposition, tendency toward aggression vs denial, internalisation
- career identity conflicts

4 Mental disorders
- depression, bipolar mood disorders, schizophrenia
- substance dependence, abuse
- onset of mental disorders at a time of developmental stress

5 Exposure to stressors and adverse circumstances
- interpersonal problems, losses
- friends, relatives have committed or attempted suicide
- previous suicide attempts
- learned responses to stress creating co-factors of aggression, violence, substance abuse, unprotected sexual activity
- school problems, truancy
- other conflicts
- disruption of friendship networks
- disciplinary crisis
- geographic separation from sources of support (transitory work, migration)
- recent contact with legal system and/or police
- unemployment
- personal debt, including gambling problems
- transience

6 Contextual factors
- social, cultural factors that may encourage or discourage suicidal behaviours
- social, economic change creating income decline, overcrowding, less access to services
- timing and sequence of help-seeking
- prevailing macho culture
- lack of support services
- incarceration

- misdiagnosis and inappropriate guidance from health professionals, especially related to conduct disorders or behavioural problems
- access to immediate and irreversible means such as firearms, poisons.

(Beautrais, Joyce & Mulder 1997, 1999; Drummond 1997; NH&MRC 1999; NZ Ministry of Health 2001; Statistics NZ 1998; WHO 2000a, 2001)

Research into suicide and intentional injury is proliferating, particularly with the vast amount of evidence now accumulated on the magnitude of the problem. Most studies have found a correlation between suicide rates in the population and unemployment or financial hardship but this is a complex relationship, influenced by many individual, social and cultural factors (Beautrais, Joyce & Mulder 1999; Cantor & Slater 1997; Drummond 1997; NH&MRC 1999; WHO 2001). The distal or social factors of unemployment and low income appear to be associated with persistent stress, which may lead to a whole range of risky behaviours, including alcohol and drug abuse (Allison et al 1999).

Brent's (1995) review of the literature reveals that the most important set of risk factors for completed and attempted suicide in adolescents are mental disorders and substance abuse. He reports that over 90 per cent of all youthful suicide victims have suffered from at least one psychiatric disorder, and names this as *the* most important risk factor. The WHO analysis of factors concurs (WHO 2001). However, stressful life events such as low family cohesion, interpersonal conflict, interpersonal loss, personal and parental legal/disciplinary problems, physical/sexual abuse, a recent move and exposure to suicide, all may lead a young person to this extreme act, particularly if several of these factors are present (Brent 1995). Another group of researchers suggest that the two main issues that lead an adolescent to thoughts of suicide are family and school problems. They claim that extreme distress may be caused by the disparity between academic performance and the expectations of either the teenager or his or her family (Dukes & Lorch 1989). This 'aspirational model' is an area being researched in relation to other risk factors (Stephens 1996). Stephens explains that whole groups in society are becoming alienated because of growing polarisation between extreme affluence and frustrated aspiration. This arises when young people are fed unrelenting advertising for various consumer goods, at the same time as they are told to suffice with their own existing resources (Stephens 1996).

Concern over youth suicide is one of the things that has precipitated increased interest in the health issues of young people. Until the 1990s, when these rates skyrocketed, the needs of adolescents were either hidden or ignored by many health authorities. West and Sweeting (1996) attribute this to the traditional gap between paediatrics and adult medicine, the relatively low use of medical services among young people, and the use of broad bands for official statistics, especially mortality rates, which often obscure the adolescent period entirely. A further reason relates to societal impressions of the teenage years as a time of fitness and wellness. This notion is currently being dispelled by surveys of young people themselves and, unfortunately, actions that decry a healthy state of transition (Jacobson & Wilkinson 1994).

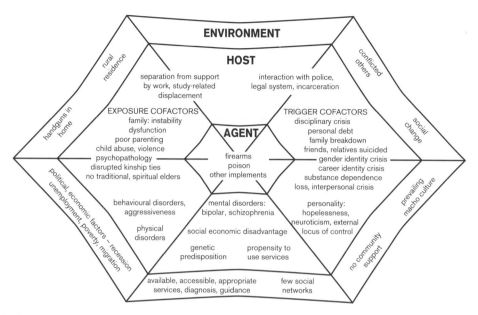

FIGURE 6.1 *The web of causation for adolescent suicide*

Eating disorders

Adolescents' images of themselves are embedded in the way they see their own bodies, leading some to excessive preoccupation with body image (Gillis 2000). The product of excessive social preoccupation with physical attractiveness in general, and thinness in particular, is often an eating disorder (Dixey 1996). The two most common eating disorders affecting adolescents are anorexia nervosa and bulimia. Anorexics avoid food to the point of emaciation, while bulimics tend to binge on large volumes of food and then purge their bodies by laxatives, self-induced vomiting, excessive exercise or a combination of these methods (Estok & Rudy 1996). The malnourishment caused by both these conditions puts young people at risk for dehydration, infections, cardiac problems, menstrual problems and, for those with bulimia, the additional problems of oesophageal irritation and dental erosion (Estok & Rudy 1996). An increase in the prevalence of eating disorders is becoming evident in all but the developing countries (Wakeling 1996). However, the incidence has recently shown an increase in second-generation migrants from developing nations and many non-Caucasian populations, indicating that eating disorders have become a world-wide public health problem (Nadaoka et al 1996; Wakeling 1996).

As with many of the problems of youth, researchers hold mixed views about what prompts a young person to become anorexic or bulimic. The spectrum of symptoms is generally conceded to result from a combination of emotional, physical, sociological and family factors, and it has recently been hypothesised that there may even be a genetic predisposition (Zerbe 1996). Population studies have concluded that the increased prevalence is connected with social changes in everyday life, such as the greater availability of food, and changes

147

in the role of women in society making them more preoccupied with their appearance (Nadaoka et al 1996).

Dieting is thought to potentiate disordered eating through cycles of dieting and regaining weight (Dixey 1996). Studies in the United Kingdom reveal that half of all British women are overweight, so the fact that 60 per cent are dieting is a good thing (Dixey 1996). The other side of this issue is, however, the link between dieting and eating disorders. The type of dieting may be less than helpful, as it is primarily middle-class women who diet to engage in conspicuous 'healthist' behaviours for purposes of 'differentiation and mutual affirmation' (Crawford, in Dixey 1996, p 52). These women may be serving as role models for their daughters.

Research in the United States reveals increased rates of eating disorders among young men, especially male homosexuals and those engaged in sports that emphasise thinness and appearance, such as dance, gymnastics, running or rowing. In some cases, addiction to activity also becomes part of the eating disorder syndrome (Zerbe 1996). Most studies, from various parts of the world, conclude that there is a strong relationship between eating disorders and depression and low self-esteem, especially when this is manifest in obsessive-compulsive traits. The only thing that seems certain is that the eating disorder seems to occur as the culmination of some type of emotional turmoil (Gotestam, Eriksen & Hagen 1995; Willcox & Sattler 1996; Zerbe 1996).

Many blame the media for women's preoccupation with thinness in that it is the main dictator of society's female norms (Tiggermann 1995). Some responsibility must also be apportioned to the beauty and fashion industry, and community groups in several countries have been lobbying to promote images of normal-sized women rather than the waif-like models currently projected in magazines and other media. The dangerous message in most of the fashion magazines is one of overvaluing appearance as a measure of personal worth (Zerbe 1996). This kind of thinking needs to be overturned from a very young age, particularly when younger children are constantly bombarded with images of ultra-thin models on TV. Unfortunately, the insidious influence of these images is not usually felt until there are severe symptoms and an entrenched, disordered body image that may take years to reverse. Health professionals must become aware of the influence of these images on the health and well-being of young people, and join consumer groups in lobbying for change. Their guidance must be based on recognised *patterns* of behaviour and an understanding of the outcomes of eating disorders. This information should also be provided to parents, sports coaches, teachers and all those involved with fostering healthy teenage development and progression into healthy adulthood.

Lifestyle
choices

Although family and social factors often influence the extent to which adolescents can achieve high levels of health and wellness, lifestyle choices play a large part in determining how they will negotiate the transition into healthy adulthood. Gillis (1994) reports that the contribution of lifestyle choices to subsequent morbidity and mortality is greater in adolescents than in any other age groups. The most important of these choices are related to alcohol and drug consumption, smoking, safe sexual practices, diet and activity patterns. In many cases, the pattern for one of these behaviours is linked to the others.

Studies show strong links between tobacco smoking, low income, low consumption of healthy foods and violence (Freudenberg 2000). Research carried out on a nationally representative sample in the United States identified a relationship between physical activity and several other health behaviours. The results of the study showed that little or no involvement in physical activity was associated with cigarette smoking, marijuana use, poor dietary habits, television viewing, failure to wear a seat belt and perception of low academic performance (Pate et al 1996). A national study in Canada also linked broad social determinants to tobacco and alcohol use and a low likelihood of physical activity (Allison et al 1999). Researchers conclude that investigations must be refocused from studying the risks related to one isolated behaviour to those that examine patterns of behaviour. From this work, environmental influences are emerging as the important determinants of health and of risk.

As mentioned in Chapter 4, life in the city seems to create its own cluster of risks, ranging from socioeconomic factors such as poverty, to the reinforcement of risky behaviours (Freudenberg 2000). French, Story and Jeffery (2001) reviewed the literature addressing environmental influences on eating and physical activity and identified a number of patterns preventing young people from being fit and well. They cite market research data showing that in the 1990s in the United States, for example, soft drink consumption increased more quickly than consumption of any other food group. As a result, adolescents consumed twice the amount of sugar of a normal diet, with the added sugars in soft drinks representing one-third of the total amount. The researchers attribute at least some of this excess to the increased availability of soft drink vending machines in schools and worksites (French, Story & Jeffery 2001).

A further trend throughout most industrialised countries is the increasing popularity of eating out frequently at fast-food restaurants. This has been especially noticeable as many women enter the workforce. Frequent fast-food restaurant use is associated with higher energy and fat intake and excess weight gain (French et al 2001). This is occurring at a time when portion sizes have been increased in pre-packaged, ready-to-eat products and at restaurants. One example comes from Coca Cola, which has increased its small bottles from 6 oz to 10 oz and replaced its 12 oz can with a 20 oz bottle. McDonalds markets 12 oz 'child-size' drinks that in the 1950s were considered 'king-size'. Adult 'small-size' are now 16 oz. Even bagels and muffins that used to be 2–3 oz are now 4–7 oz (French et al 2001).

One problem, according to the analysis, is that young people are increasingly underestimating their portion sizes and intake. A further problem lies in the fact that the foods most heavily advertised on TV are those that are over-consumed, including confectionaries, snacks, convenience foods, soft drinks and alcoholic beverages, with fruits and vegetables among the least-advertised foods. Pricing strategies have also played a part, with widespread reductions in the price of food. Interestingly, a study of 12 secondary schools and 12 work-sites revealed that when the price of nutritionally dense foods like fruit and vegetables was dropped, adolescents changed their purchasing behaviour to the lower-priced foods. This provides significant insight into what environmental factors could be modified to change adolescent eating behaviours (French et al 2001).

This review of the research also looked at physical activity in the United States, concluding that there has been little change in adolescents' physical activity during the past few decades. Americans spend six times more time watching television than exercising or doing sports and they are less likely to walk or use a bicycle for transportation than take an automobile. The research found no association between the density of free exercise facilities and exercise frequency, but there was a stable trend towards using parks, community recreation and walking/cycling trails where these were accessible (French et al 2001). Canadian data show that adolescents are more physically active than adults, but 'females participate less in physical activities, consider themselves less fit, and are less likely to be active by age 20 than males' (King & Cole, in Gillis 2000, p 249).

In Australia, no nationally accepted procedures have been developed to ascertain participation in sport and organised activity. However, a 1997 national survey indicated that around 60 per cent of the 18–29 year age group was involved in some type of activity (AIHW 2000). This is similar to the New Zealand figures, which show only slightly higher rates of exercise among male youths than among females (NZ Ministry of Health 2001).

Recreational drug use

The importance of studying patterns of adolescent behaviour is best illustrated in the case of drug and alcohol consumption. Behaviours begun in adolescence may provide a 'gateway' for continuation or progression to greater levels of substance abuse in adulthood. Drug abuse harms society and the community by reducing users' physical and mental health and productivity, by reducing family and social functioning and by increasing crime (Sindelar & Fiellin 2001). Young people with low self-esteem are at risk for abusing drugs and this can lead to family disruption, poor parenting, abandoned children, fear among community members, drug-related crime and a lack of neighbourhood cohesion (Sindelar & Fiellin 2001).

The personal cost of illicit drug use is enormous. Many people who use and/or abuse drugs in the early stages of adolescence fail to consider the long-ranging effects on health from such contagious diseases as hepatitis B and C, tuberculosis and HIV/AIDS. A further concern is that, despite wide and unresolved debate on the issue, experimentation with 'soft' substances such as alcohol and marijuana may lead to abuse of more lethal substances, or at least to a wider range of substances (Kandel 1975; Kandel, Yamaguchi & Chen 1992).

Toxic substances have a cumulative effect from adolescence to adulthood that is often poorly understood. In the absence of any clear dose–response data, *any* level of consumption of toxins such as nicotine and alcohol must be considered a compromise to adult health status. One illustration of this was revealed in the findings of a New Zealand study, where smoking cannabis five times a week was found to have a similar effect on respiratory disease as smoking a daily pack of cigarettes (Taylor et al 2001). This may be attributed to the different dynamics in cannabis smoking, where increased puff volume and inhalation time creates a more substantial 'burden' of inhaled material. The research team studied a birth cohort of nearly 1000 individuals at age 21 and found that even after six weeks of cannabis smoking, cannabis-dependent people had the same level of risk of developing chronic obstructive pulmonary disease as regular tobacco smokers. This is a significant finding, given the level of risk (15 per cent in tobacco smokers) and the steady increase in cannabis use in New Zealand over the last 10 years (Taylor et al 2001). The findings also point to an urgent need for ongoing research to address the constellation of effects from a wider range of illicit substances, and they indicate a need to address smoking among Maori youth, who are now twice as likely to smoke as they were a decade ago (Statistics NZ 1998).

Factors associated with substance abuse in adolescents have been studied in many different settings. The research reveals a higher rate of substance abuse among school dropouts than those who remain in school. This effect may be due to education, or the entire range of interactions with socioeconomic factors, given that the dropout rate is highest among the socially disadvantaged (Swaim et al 1997). Other interrelationships have been noted in relation to violence. Young people who frequent bars are more likely to be involved in risky behaviours, including violence (Parks & Quigley 2001). They may also be greater risk-takers in relation to alcohol and drugs because they have been victimised by family violence and/or maltreatment (Miller, Maguin & Downs 1997).

We cannot describe substance abuse as a single phenomenon, because of the wide variability in types and levels of abuse and abusers. The culture within which they consume their preferred substances also changes dramatically with time. Cocaine provides a case in point. In the 1980s many older adolescents and young adults who could afford cocaine began the habit of inhaling the substance through their nostrils. It was seen to be a drug they could manage while out for the evening, and began to be associated with dancing and other party situations. In the 1990s public health officials had to contend with a new type of cocaine addict: the injecting cocaine user, who tended to use the drug in private situations, as heroin has always been used. Informal reports revealed that the cocaine injector tends to become a bit 'crazy' when high, losing all sense of judgement, and this led to suspicions that cocaine, rather than heroin users, were the ones sharing needles, engaging in unprotected sex and thus spreading the HIV virus (Swaim et al 1997). A further outcome of this trend was the amount of violence it unleashed. Freudenberg (2000) reports that between 1985 and 1993, teenage homicide rates more than doubled as a result of crack addiction and the availability of guns. During this period, the drug trade became the largest employer of young people and caused widespread destruction in many of their lives. Current information indicates declining homicide rates throughout the United States and this may be a cause for at least cautious optimism (Freudenberg 2000).

Drugs in sport

One aspect of drug use that has thus far been poorly researched is the use of drugs in sport. Following such high-profile cases of abuse as Ben Johnson's positive drug test at the 1988 Olympics, and the accusations of drug use among the Chinese swimming team at the 1996 Olympics, the public has become much more aware of the pervasiveness of drugs in sport. One little-known fact is that some psychoactive drugs designed to enhance performance actually *decrease* performance because of adverse cardiovascular effects and impaired judgement (Schwenk 1997). A major problem is that of anabolic steroids. Steroids are becoming more prevalent with teenagers involved in sports despite tighter legislation, school-based education and drug testing in competitive events (Tanner, Miller & Alongi 1995). In two separate research studies conducted in the United States, it was found that 14–15 years tends to be the age when teenagers begin to use steroids. Both studies revealed that just over 1 per cent of females and 4–6 per cent of males take steroids to increase strength and/or improve muscle mass (DuRant et al 1993; Tanner et al 1995).

Young people other than elite athletes take steroids because they believe it makes them look attractive, which is a major influence on most adolescents. The hazards of steroid use need to be recognised not only for the physiological effect of the drugs, but because adolescent users of anabolic steroids are likely to use other drugs as well: marijuana, cocaine, cigarettes, smokeless tobacco, alcohol and mood-altering substances. Studies of these types of patterns of drug use also identify the added danger of sharing needles and the risk of HIV and other infections (D'Elio et al 1993; DuRant et al 1993). Any attempt at health education targeting adolescents must therefore take a comprehensive approach to encouraging healthy lifestyle change rather than singling out any one behaviour.

Tobacco smoking

Cigarette smoking is the largest preventable cause of death in the industrialised world (WHO 1999). If smoking patterns are not changed, about 500 million people who are alive today will eventually die from tobacco-related deaths (WHO 1999). After years of gathering and disseminating conclusive evidence on the health effects of smoking, and convincing many countries to establish tobacco control policies, WHO (1999) reports that smoking prevalence is decreasing in developed countries. Australia, Canada, Japan, New Zealand, the United Kingdom, the United States and most northern European countries have had the most significant declines in smoking. However, tobacco smoking is still rising dramatically in the developing world. On current patterns, smoking will kill 10 million people annually worldwide, more than from malaria, maternal and childhood conditions and tuberculosis combined, making it one of the most significant targets for health promotion (WHO 1999).

Nicotine is an addiction that takes hold almost exclusively during childhood and adolescence (WHO 1999). Around half to three-quarters of teenagers in OECD countries try smoking, and half quit immediately, with the rest becoming lifelong smokers. Half of the latter group will die from smoking (WHO 1999). Alarmingly, 70 000 12–17 year old Australians take up smoking each year, the highest rate of uptake being among 16–17 year olds: 28 per cent of boys and 32 per cent of girls. A further cause for concern is the coexistence of smoking and alcohol consumption behaviours in this age group. Australian researchers found that frequent use of tobacco and alcohol was also associated with more frequent marijuana use, particularly for frequent drinkers. Interestingly, their study also revealed that coffee use is already common in the early teens, and this is a pattern of drug taking that extends into the rest of people's lives, once they develop a caffeine habit. This research looked at patterns of smoking and alcohol use, and found that the consumption of both nicotine and alcohol becomes more common in the mid-teens, with marijuana use most common in older teens. This pattern is consistent with the notion of a sequential progression in the initiation of drug use across the teen years; that is, using one drug often leads to using another (Hibbert et al 1995).

Gender differences have also been evident in the research. Hibbert and colleagues' (1995) study found that, like other American and British studies of gender differences in smoking rates, females smoke at a higher rate than males and are more likely to smoke on a regular basis than young men. The authors cite several studies linking smoking to cervical cancer, early menopause, complications of oral contraceptive use, unfavourable outcomes of pregnancy and vulnerability to lung cancer, concluding that smoking among female adolescents remains a serious public health problem.

Smoking is a particular problem for countries like China, which contains one-fifth of the world's population and more than 30 per cent of the world's smokers (Zhu et al 1996). China now leads the world in tobacco production and the price is obvious, as more Chinese now die of lung cancer than any other cause. Based on the knowledge that the earlier a person begins to smoke, the more likely it is that they will become a regular smoker, a group of researchers conducted a large national study among Chinese elementary schoolchildren. Their findings revealed that most young people aged 10–12 begin to smoke as a result of peer pressure. As in other countries, there is a direct link between young people's smoking and low socioeconomic status, having parents, siblings or teachers who smoke, and not believing that smoking is harmful to health (Zhu et al 1996). Health promotion efforts in that country thus need to focus on young people's beliefs and the effect of role modelling on their behaviour, in order to prevent the current alarming rates of smoking-related mortality from further escalating. This will require a collaborative approach from all levels of society.

Sexual health

Another area of high risk for adolescents is sexual behaviour. The two most important reasons for concern about unsafe sexual health practices are teenage pregnancy and sexually transmitted diseases, as both have a profound effect on adolescents. Despite the risk of disease or pregnancy, many young people still report that their education in sex, sexuality and sexually transmitted disease is either nonexistent, inappropriate or acquired through their own sexual experience (Few, Hicken & Butterworth 1996). Researchers at the Alan Guttmacher Institute in the United States report that 30–50 per cent of teenagers have their first sex education course after grade 10, which, for many, is too late, as they have already been sexually active (Rodriquez & Moore 1996). Another view, however, is that regardless of the type or amount of education provided, adolescents may be at risk because messages or information are ignored or dismissed as not relevant to them. This may be linked to their stage of cognitive development in that without prior experience of a negative outcome they may be hesitant to take appropriate risk reduction steps.

This proposition was examined in the research conducted by Hewell and Andrews (1996), who studied contraceptive use among female adolescents who had experienced either an abortion or a negative pregnancy test. They found that 99 per cent of the post-abortion group and 50 per cent of those having a negative pregnancy test began to use reliable contraception immediately following; however, by the time of their follow-up clinic visit, those figures had dropped to 28 per cent and 6 per cent respectively. This led them to conclude, as had previous researchers, that risk-taking behaviours in adolescents are the result of short-term thinking and the propensity to not plan ahead or anticipate the consequences realistically (Fortenberry 1997; Hewell & Andrews 1996). For some reason, adolescents entertain the idea that they are magically protected from dangers that only happen to other people, a phenomenon some have called 'magical thinking' (Zigler & Stevenson-Finn 1987).

Teenage pregnancy

Globally, 14 million teenage girls give birth each year (Leete 2000). The teenage mother's developmental stage has profound effects on the outcomes of pregnancy. It is interesting that, despite the worldwide trend to greater use of contraception, and falling rates of teenage pregnancy in countries like Australia (to around 20 per cent), there remains a rise in the proportion of teenage pregnancies in the United Kingdom, Canada and the United States (AIHW 2000; Condon, Donovan & Corkindale 2001; Gillis 2000). The United Kingdom has one of the highest rates of teenage pregnancy in Western Europe, where half the pregnancies under age 16 and one-third among 16–19 year olds end in termination (Seamark & Gray 1997). The Canadian figures show a different outcome than that occurring in the United Kingdom, with 24 000 infants carried to term out of an annual 38 000 unwanted teenage pregnancies (Gillis 2000).

Pregnancy generates developmental change at any age, but in the adolescent it can create a developmental crisis as the young girl struggles to deal with two stages at once: adolescence and young adulthood (Rodriquez & Moore 1996). Idealised notions about pregnancy and parenthood are often guided by visions of love, affection, closeness and sharing, and this can contribute to both becoming pregnant and deciding to continue with the pregnancy (Condon, Donovan & Corkindale 2001). Deciding what to do about the pregnancy is extremely stressful, especially for those with the option of legalised abortion.

Where childbirth is the outcome, the strains of parenting can provide an enormous burden. This is the case for the majority of those who experience teenage pregnancy, as many of these girls come from socioeconomic conditions of relative deprivation, which is made more difficult by educational, economic and social difficulties (Gillis 2000; Irvine et al 1997; Jacobson & Wilkinson 1994).

Choosing between persevering with the pregnancy and having an abortion is one of the most difficult issues that confront young adolescent women, as this can pervade a young woman's life forever. In some cases, the abortion issue is expedited by social structures, such as those in Singapore, where abortion is legal. It is also mandatory for any teenager under age 16 to be counselled at the Institute of Health (Yang 1995). In many other countries, especially the United States, the anti-abortion, or 'pro-life' movement is publicly visible and, at times, wields a powerful influence on the pregnant adolescent's decision. Small wonder then, that teenage mothers tend to experience conflicts. These often lead to emotional outbursts, dramatic mood changes and acute depression, which, if the choice is made to continue with the pregnancy, can lead to child abuse (Zigler & Stevenson-Finn 1987). Other risks to the child occur because of the teenage mother's early stage of development. Because of their physiological immaturity, they tend to have a higher risk of complicated pregnancies, including hypertensive disorders and low birthweight babies (Cunningham & Boult 1996; Yang 1995). In many cases, teenage mothers also smoke and ingest alcohol and other substances, compounding the risk to the child and to themselves.

From a social perspective, teenage pregnancy has a devastating effect on many teenage girls. Even in some African communities, where teenage pregnancy is somewhat more culturally tolerated than in other areas, the result is as devastating as elsewhere, in terms of interrupting the young girl's education and thus cutting off at least some opportunities for employment and thus resources for parenting (Buga, Amoko & Ncayiyana 1996). At the societal level, supporting teenage mothers and their child(ren) is costly, and consumes funds that could otherwise be deployed elsewhere in the health and social system. This is a particular problem in the United States, where the rates of teenage pregnancy continue to be the highest of most developed nations (Hewell & Andrews 1996; Yang 1995). Rodriquez and Moore (1996) report that half of American teenage mothers go on welfare within a year, rising to 77 per cent within five years. At a cost of $9200 per single mother and child for the first year of support, this is substantially more costly than the $64 required to provide family planning for a sexually active teenager.

Sexually transmitted infections

The threat of sexually transmitted infections (STI) has always existed, but the HIV/AIDS epidemic has caused renewed alarm. The majority of deaths occurring in low- and middle-income countries can be attributed to HIV and tuberculosis, which sometimes coexist (WHO 1999). Approximately 21 million people have died from AIDS since the late 1970s and 36 million people are now living with the disease, most in middle- or low-income countries (WHO

1999). More than 70 per cent of the victims live or have died in sub-Saharan Africa (UNAIDS 1999).

In countries like Botswana, Swaziland, Lesotho and Zimbabwe, more than a quarter of the population is infected with AIDS (UNAIDS 1999). Like many other African countries where the deaths have all but halved life expectancy, nearly half the population of Zimbabwe is under the age of 18 (Schatz & Dzvimbo 2001). HIV/AIDS and the accompanying epidemic of tuberculosis have therefore become the worst perils of adolescence.

Contrary to early thinking on HIV/AIDS, the disease affects females at nearly the same rate as young males (UNAIDS 1999). The United Nations identifies a cluster of factors as poverty, discrimination, lack of education and opportunity, and the subordination of women, all of which converge to place young women at greater risk than males (Schatz & Dzvimbo 2001; UNAIDS 1999). Like young people in other countries, high school students are the recipients rather than the co-creators of cultural information on morality and personal development. Unfortunately, this has had little effect on behaviour since AIDS health education programs were instituted in 1993 (Schatz & Dzvimbo 2001).

The extent of this epidemic in the population is astounding, but the link between HIV infection and other STIs is also of grave concern. In the United States, approximately three million teenagers acquire STIs each year, which increases the risk of subsequent HIV infection (Coyle et al 1996; Wasserheit 1992). Chlamydia is particularly prevalent in persons aged 15–24. Because it is usually asymptomatic, many cases go undetected and untreated. It is important for young girls especially to understand the need for periodic testing for chlamydia and other STIs, as they can sometimes cause infertility. One indisputable fact is that using a condom prevents transmission of most of these infections. Yet despite one in four 16–19 year olds being sexually active, many teenagers are still not using condoms with any consistency (Coyle et al 1996; Hiltabiddle 1996; Yang 1995).

With the increased publicity about HIV and AIDS, condom use, at least among university students, has been reported at as high as 60 per cent in Australia, Scotland and France (Rodden et al 1996). However, there has been great variability in the research, with rates of condom use fluctuating according to such factors as age, education and ethnicity (Rodden et al 1996). The fact remains that, despite a worldwide increase in condom use, many young people continue to be at risk from a range of STDs, HIV/AIDS and pregnancy.

Countering risk:
healthy adolescence

Progressing through adolescence in the twenty-first century is fraught with dangers that flow from a myriad of factors, ranging from infectious diseases to media assaults on the sensibilities of daily life. Rather than tackle any one factor, the major objective for promoting health among adolescents should be to create healthy pathways to adulthood (Freudenberg 2000). Linking efforts in health, education, social services, juvenile justice, job training and youth development allows simultaneous consideration of proximal as well as distal factors, providing a comprehensive approach to strengthen the resilience of youth and their communities (Freudenberg 2000).

Predictive models targeting individual behaviours have failed to encourage behaviour change among adolescents (McKie et al 1993). The optimal approach to helping people change is to adopt a community approach, where analysis can be made of the social as well as personal determinants of health in the context of adolescent perceptions. This type of approach has been used to embed other health promotion interventions within the context of school, home, neighbourhood and community (Sawyer & Kosky 1996).

Programs to address risk must be cognisant of the environment, and the way the adolescent's social context interacts with his or her place in the world. This guides us toward examining the school as a context for change. Tresidder and colleagues (1997) studied the risky behaviours of a group of 16 year olds who had left school, compared with school attenders, and found higher rates of alcohol, cigarette and marijuana consumption, sexual abuse and drink-driving. They felt that these teenagers were missing the 'connectedness' to school that serves to protect adolescents against a range of 'acting out' behaviours, including drug use, higher risk of injury and risk of pregnancy (Resnick, Harris & Blum 1993). Young adolescents leaving school are a group at particular risk of ill health because they do not have the peer support or health surveillance offered in most school health services. Health education for this group should therefore target the neighbourhood and community.

One of the most successful American programs included five primary components: school organisation, curriculum and staff development, peer resources and school environment, parent education and school–community linkages (Coyle et al 1996). This is the approach suggested by the study of Zimbabwean young people (Schatz & Dzvimbo 2001). Without reinforcement and support in the family and neighbourhood, many programs are doomed to failure. The objective of adolescent programs is that they must harmonise the needs and aspirations of adolescents in a climate designed to foster both group and individual empowerment.

Goals for
adolescent health

The major health issues affecting adolescents include the following:

- physical health and well-being
- mental/emotional health and maturity
- healthy lifestyle
- minimisation of risky behaviours.

The place to begin improving adolescent health is at the societal level, encouraging all members of the community and society at large to recognise the major factors that place adolescents at risk for unhealthy choices. Gillis (2000) suggests that communities develop a web of protection that would guide young people away from dangerous choices towards mutually supportive networks that foster a sense of belonging. Once again, the strategies of the Ottawa Charter provide a framework for addressing the most salient issues for adolescent health.

Building healthy public policy

Policies to encourage healthy adolescence include those that address the need for teachers and other educators to be supported in their attempts to counsel young people. This is important because health promotion should be offered in the setting that is most conducive to change. For adolescents, this is primarily the school. Too often, teachers work in isolation, providing guidance and support to teenagers as an 'add-on' to their already overburdened work roles, with little recognition for their efforts. This can be addressed by all sectors of the community interested in cultivating a generation of young people. To address the problems of homelessness requires an intersectoral approach beginning with national industry policies that focus on education and employment geared toward both the needs and potential of youth.

Another area where public policy can help encourage healthy lifestyles among young people is in legislating for changes conducive to healthy choices. This includes such things as providing needle exchanges, condoms, reducing hotel hours, increasing the minimum age for the purchase of cigarettes, close monitoring of retail outlets selling harmful substances, and supporting media watch organisations. Healthy public policies should also address cultural issues in a way that is seen to be health promoting. This does not mean the introduction of sanctions against those who, in perpetuating cultural traditions, threaten the health of a community, but rather using the political and social mechanisms available to effect change.

The tobacco industry influences the politics of many countries with profits from sales of cigarettes, through denying the link between smoking and illness and through advertising. In the past few decades, they have benefited from the globalisation of trade, creating increases in the consumption of cigarettes in developing countries. The major policy goal to counter their influence is to create a 'fair information environment' (WHO 1999, p 72). WHO identifies the goals of tobacco control policies as:

- banning advertising and expanding public health information
- using taxes and regulations to reduce consumption
- building anti-smoking coalitions (WHO 1999; 2000c).

These strategies are already having a powerful effect in the industrialised countries, but much more needs to be done to ensure a global approach to this problem. The same steps identified at the global level can also be taken at the high school level, especially when various high schools are connected with others in the developing world. The 11th World Congress on Smoking and Tobacco issued a statement that a 10 per cent increase in cigarette prices generated by tax increases would see 42 million people quit smoking (WHO

2000c). This is recommended as a better policy direction and a better use of resources than policing legislation forbidding merchants to sell cigarettes to minors, a strategy that has yet to show any positive outcomes.

The drug problem is looming large on the horizon in developed countries, with many preventative programs failing to reach their goals. The issues surrounding illicit drug use should also be addressed at the policy level, beginning with in-depth exploration of heroin maintenance programs, drug courts and therapeutic communities (Sindelar & Fiellin 2001). The major obstacle in relation to drug treatment and rehabilitation has been the furore raised in the popular press over various programs. The role of a health professional includes being aware of the issues from all sides, and making sure politicians have a balanced view of what will create and sustain health for the whole community.

A further challenge lies in trying to ensure that community members are aware of all sides of various health issues. Some people resent being forced to wear bicycle safety helmets or being cut off from drinking at the bar when they have obviously had enough alcohol. Others believe that condoms and needle exchanges encourage sexual behaviour and drug taking. Some argue against government control on the basis that health and education departments may be making judgements concerning the well-being of their charges that are designed more for protection from litigation than the welfare of the young person. These community concerns need to be aired and discussed at all levels of the community. The most important issue for health professionals is to ensure that people have access to accurate information when making decisions about health and lifestyles so that the views of the vocal minority do not override opportunities for all community members to make informed choices.

Healthy policies must also be based on the priorities of the time. For example, policies have been slow to respond to the problems of homelessness, suicide and teenage pregnancy. However, some initiatives are exemplary. In Finland, for example, researchers have found that building healthy public policy and reorienting health services have had a marked effect on teenage pregnancies and abortions in that country (Kosunen & Rimpela 1996). A similar effect has been found in the Netherlands, where the rates of abortion have plummeted to the lowest in the Western world (Kosunen & Rimpela 1996). Likewise, Sweden's tobacco controls linked to global strategies have made Sweden the first and only country in the world to reach the WHO targets for smoking reduction (WHO 1999).

Creating supportive environments

An environment conducive to healthy adolescence is one in which adolescents feel safe to explore and to stretch their imagination for the future. Clearly, school is a major influence on whether or not teenagers feel free to question and to learn. Some opportunities must be provided in the formal education system for safe and guided discussion. This has been confirmed in studies of violence prevention programs at school, where confidentiality and adequate space and location were seen as the keys to successful intervention (Fiester et al 1996). To support young people, mechanisms can be put in place whereby teachers and parents can exchange ideas, clarify values and provide advice to adolescents that is consistent with family and societal expectations, yet allows freedom and creativity. Coyle and colleagues' (1996) model (*Safer Choices*), underlines the need for a comprehensive approach that is policy driven and yet empowering for adolescents and their parents. Tresidder and colleagues' (1997) findings on the importance of the school environment indicate a need to incorporate out-of-school support systems for young people who may fall through the cracks in health promotion campaigns because they are either out in the workforce or unemployed.

Strengthening community action

Community action to improve the health of adolescents should also involve fostering personal skills among parents, teachers, the business community and all others who provide support to young people. One study conducted in Canada found that parents' health-promoting lifestyles were significantly correlated with those of their adolescent daughters, providing support for the importance of parental modelling (Gillis 1994). This and other studies point to a need for parent support centres that shift the focus from paternalistic advice-giving to family-friendly suggestions for higher levels of health and wellness. African data support this, in showing positive results from programs aimed at single mothers and their daughters, who were both caught in the cycle of teenage pregnancy (Cunningham & Boult 1996).

The accessibility of services is as important as their substance. With both parents often working and with no available extended family support, there is a need for health information services in local neighbourhoods. At present, services to adolescents are provided through formal agencies such as school health services and family planning associations. Parents have little access to the information being given to their children unless the child chooses to initiate discussion with them. In many cases, there is not only a generation gap problem, but cultural conflicts as well, as migrant children quickly assimilate the values of their new culture without the involvement of their parents. Primary health care practice requires that access, equity, empowerment and cultural sensitivity be extended not only to the adolescent group, but to their parents and other relevant community members. Provision of accessible, coherent and culturally congruent family support centres would help achieve health goals for both groups and locate the source of information to where it can be most effective—at the heart of the community.

Developing personal skills

This strategy is perhaps the most important from the perspective of the adolescent. The teenage years are the pivotal point for the development of personal skills for adult survival. The most important element in developing personal skills is to educate adolescents on matters related to their health and to support them in changing. Many researchers have found that individual teaching can be most effective when it integrates functional knowledge (what must be done to improve health or prevent illness), motivational knowledge (how beliefs affect behaviour), outcome expectancy (belief in the effectiveness of preventative action) and self-efficacy (confidence that one can use skills effectively) (Becker 1974; Coyle et al 1996; Hiltabiddle 1996). Equally important, health teaching efforts need to be cognisant of the adolescent's egocentrism. As mentioned previously, most adolescents believe themselves to be utterly unique and often invulnerable. This may explain why, despite evidence of the dangers of certain behaviours, many still do not adopt healthy lifestyles (Hewell & Andrews 1996; Hiltabiddle 1996; Jacobson & Wilkinson 1994).

In addition to individual health education, one of the most effective means of changing behaviour is by peer modelling, whereby healthy, fit role models within their social sphere are used to convey health promotion messages. The two most important skills for healthy behaviours are social decision-making and problem-solving skills, both of which are components of health literacy (Elias & Kress 1994; Gillis 2000; Kickbusch 2001). These can best be learned in the context of examples, either in the classroom or within sports coaching or other venues in which teenagers interact. Through opportunities for problem solving and negotiating a range of views, young people learn to integrate social-cognitive, affective, behavioural and social relationship areas with critical thinking for both academic achievement and future healthful behaviours (Elias & Kress 1994). Such education sessions should also be culturally and linguistically appropriate, and focus on short-term effects of health behaviours rather than the longer-term goals of adults (Barg & Lowe 1996; Gillis 2000).

The dialogue for exchange should be not only appropriate for different ethnic groups, but also must respond to the unique culture of adolescence. Discussions should capitalise on the adolescent's desire for independent decision-making, allowing them to try on different styles (Gillis 2000). Education sessions, for example, should adopt a more democratic approach to sex education that would encourage discussion of adolescent perspectives on a range of lifestyle topics, including current culturally determined gender inequalities (Schatz & Dzvimbo 2001). Sessions should incorporate music, art and other artefacts of adolescent life so that they can readily identify with the context as well as the content. This is essentially an environmental approach in that it refocuses the emphasis of health teaching within a contextual frame of reference. It is also important to create a body of evidence as a basis for health planning, including some exploration of the value of both community and peer support networks in achievement of adolescent health goals (Gillis 2000).

Reorienting health services

One of the most important reactions of adolescents is alienation from societal institutions, including those that provide health care. School health centres are usually designed to be attractive to teenagers, and provide an invaluable teaching service. Drop-in centres and neighbourhood health clinics should also be designed for easy and confidential access, and these can be designed in collaboration with teenagers themselves (Goudie 1996). Hotlines for confidential guidance provide an invaluable service for those who hesitate to seek face-to-face information. In addition, there needs to be easy access to crisis care for those in need. Staff of emergency departments and psychiatric institutions may therefore need ongoing awareness training for dealing with the special needs of adolescents.

Places where young people congregate should also be the repository of information on health issues, especially to meet the needs of those who have left school or who have otherwise 'fallen out of the nest' (Tresidder 1996, p 229). In order to reach these adolescents, health education messages can be made available in shopping malls, computer game parlours, sports organisations and youth clubs. Radio and TV stations that attract a large teenage audience provide an opportunity to reinforce the messages of authority figures, or to have new ones developed by the adolescents themselves, that link the ideas of safe behaviour with popular culture.

One of the most consistent findings from studies of teenage preventative behaviours is their lack of knowledge on health issues. The latest findings of research studies must be made available to adolescents, their teachers, parents, school health nurses and all others who may find themselves in a position to offer guidance and support. Equally important is the need to have a truly collaborative approach to helping adolescents. Commitment to a partnership rather than a *provider* approach is necessary to ensure that the lines of communication remain open to all members of the health care team attempting to encourage positive health practices.

One of the most innovative approaches to promoting adolescent health is the harm reduction approach. In this approach, drug education, for example, focuses on preventing the potential harms related to drug use rather than trying to prevent the drug use itself (Duncan et al 1994). This major paradigm shift in drug education is based on the assumption that everyone in society uses some form of drugs, licit or illicit. The focus is on ensuring safety and survival. Instead of being castigated, drug users are taught safe methods of injecting, sniffing or using implements related to their behaviour. This approach also includes such structural supports as designated drivers, free taxis, coffee stops along highways, and changing social norms related to responsible drinking and responsible drink serving, needle exchange programs and free condoms.

The harm reduction approach is widely debated, gaining acceptance in some countries on the basis that people have always and will continue to engage in high-risk behaviours. The shift in thinking is that if health professionals can at least encourage those people and the general public to think about preventing the most serious outcomes, it may help to educate 'users'. Like drug courts as a designated way of dealing with young offenders, and heroin trials, this approach may also increase the availability of treatment services and change public perceptions in a way that will encourage treatment and instigate legal reform (Duncan et al 1994).

thinking critically

Adolescent health

1   Identify four high-risk behaviours of adolescents and corresponding risk-reduction strategies.

2   Discuss the contention that the context is the most important element of any health promotion program.

3   Identify three measures that can be taken to ensure cultural sensitivity in teaching adolescents about healthy sexuality.

4   Describe four health promotion resources available to adolescents in your community.

5   Describe three strategies for an adolescent smoking prevention program.

6   Develop an adolescent suicide prevention program for a local school.

7   Explain how health literacy can be used to promote adolescent health.

REFERENCES

Allison, K., Adlaf, E., Ialomiteanu, A. & Rehm, J. (1999). Predictors of health risk behaviors among young adults: analysis of the national population health survey. *Canadian Journal of Public Health*, 90(2): 85–9.

Australian Institute of Health and Welfare, (2000). *Australia's Health 2000*. Canberra: AGPS.

Barg, F. & Lowe, J. (1996). A culturally appropriate cancer education program for African-American adolescents in an urban middle school. *Journal of School Health*, 66(2): 50–4.

Beautrais, A., Joyce, P. & Mulder, R. (1997). Precipitating factors and life events in serious suicide attempts among youths aged 13 through 24 years. *Journal of the American Academy of Child and Adolescent Psychiatry*, 36(11): 1543–51.

—— (1999). Personality traits and cognitive styles as risk factors for serious suicide attempts among young people. *Suicide and Life Threatening Behaviour*, 29(1): 37–47.

Becker, M. (1974). *The Health Belief Model and Personal Health Behavior*. New Jersey: Charles B. Slack.

Breakey, W. (1997). Editorial: It's time for the public health community to declare war on homelessness. *American Journal of Public Health*, 87(2): 153–5.

Brent, D. (1995). Risk factors for adolescent suicide and suicidal behavior: mental and substance abuse disorders, family environmental factors, and life stress. *Suicide and Life Threatening Behavior*, 25, Suppl: 52–62.

Bronfenbrenner, U. (1986). Alienation and the four worlds of childhood. *Phi Delta Kappan*, 67: 430–6.

Buga, G., Amoko, D. & Ncayiyana (1996). Adolescent sexual behaviour, knowledge and attitudes to sexuality among school girls in Transkei, South Africa. *East African Medical Journal*, 73(2): 95–100.

Cantor, C. & Slater, P. (1997). A regional profile of suicide in Queensland. *Australian Journal of Public Health*, 21: 181–6.

Condon, J. Donovan, J. & Corkindale, C. (2001). Adolescents' attitude and beliefs about pregnancy and parenthood: results from a school-based intervention program. *International Journal of Adolescence and Youth*, 9: 245–56.

Coyle, K., Kirby, D., Parcel, G., Basen-Engquist, K., Banspach, S., Rugg, D. & Weil, M. (1996). Safer choices: a multicomponent school-based HIV/STD and pregnancy prevention program for adolescents. *Journal of School Health*, 66(3): 89–94.

Cunningham, P. & Boult, B. (1996). Black teenage pregnancy in South Africa: some considerations. *Adolescence*, 31(123): 691–700.

D'Elio, M., Mundt, D., Bush, P. & Iannotti, R. (1993). Healthful behaviors: do they protect African-American, urban preadolescents from abusable substance use? *American Journal of Health Promotion*, 7(5): 354–63.

D'Espaignet, E. & Rickwood, D. (1995). Trends in psychological distress among young Australian women aged 16–24: effects of age, occupation and final year examination. *Proceedings of the Third National Women's Health Conference*, Australian National University, Canberra, pp 310–14.

Dixey, R. (1996). Healthy eating in schools and 'eating disorders'—are 'healthy eating' messages part of the problem or part of the solution? *Nutrition and Health*, 11: 49–58.

Drummond, W. (1997). Adolescent at risk: causes of youth suicide in New Zealand. *Adolescence*, 32(128): 925–35.

Dukes, R. & Lorch, B. (1989). The effects of school, family, self-concept, and deviant behaviour on adolescent suicide ideation. *Journal of Adolescence*, 12: 239–51.

Duncan, D., Nicholson, T., Clifford, P., Hawkins, W. & Petosa, R. (1994). Harm reduction: an emerging new paradigm for drug education. *Journal of Drug Education*, 24(4): 281–90.

DuRant, R., Rickert, V., Ashworth, C., Newman, C. & Slavens, G. (1993). Use of multiple drugs among adolescents who use anabolic steroids. *New England Journal of Medicine*, 328(13): 922–6.

Elias, M. & Kress, J. (1994). Social decision-making and life skills development: a critical thinking approach to health promotion in the middle school. *Journal of School Health*, 64(2): 62–6.

Erikson, E. (1963). *Childhood and Society*, 2nd edn, New York: Norton.

Estok P. & Rudy, E. (1996). The relationship between eating disorders and running in women. *Research in Nursing and Health*, 19: 377–87.

Few, C., Hicken, I. & Butterworth, T. (1996). Alliances in school sex education: teachers' and school nurses' views. *Health Visitor*, 69(6): 220–3.

Fiester, L., Nathanson, S., Visser, L. & Martin, J. (1996). Lessons learned from three violence prevention projects. *Journal of School Health*, 66(9): 344–6.

Fortenberry, J. (1997). Health care seeking behaviors related to sexually transmitted diseases among adolescents. *American Journal of Public Health*, 87(3): 417–20.

Freudenberg, N. (2000). Health promotion in the city: a review of current practice and future prospects in the United States. *Annual Review of Public Health*, 21: 473–503.

French, S., Story, M. & Jeffery, R. (2001). Environmental influences on eating and physical activity. *Annual Review of Public Health*, 23: 309–35.

Gillis, A. (1994). Determinants of health-promoting lifestyles in adolescent females. *Canadian Journal of Nursing Research*, 26(2): 13–28.

—— (2000). Adolescent health promotion: an evolving opportunity for community health nurses. In: M. Stewart (ed), *Community Nursing: Promoting Canadians' Health*, 2nd edn, Toronto: WB Saunders, pp 241–82.

Gotestam, K., Eriksen, L. & Hagen, H. (1995). An epidemiological study of eating disorders in Norwegian psychiatric institutions. *International Journal of Eating Disorders*, 18(3): 263–8.

Goudie, H. (1996). Making health services more accessible to younger people. *Nursing Times*, 19(92): 45–6.

Hewell, S. & Andrews, J. (1996). Contraceptive use among female adolescents. *Clinical Nursing Research*, 5(3): 356–63.

Hibbert, M., Rosier, M., Carlin, J., Caust, J. & Bowes, G. (1995). Patterns of common drug use in teenagers. *Australian Journal of Public Health*, 19(4): 391–9.

Hiltabiddle, S. (1996). Adolescent condom use, the health belief model, and the prevention of sexually transmitted disease. *Journal of Obstetrics and Gynecological Nursing*, 25(1): 61–7.

Irvine, H., Bradley, T., Cupples, M. & Boohan, M. (1997). The implications of teenage pregnancy and motherhood for primary health care: unresolved issues. *British Journal of General Practice*, 47: 323–6.

Jacobson, L. & Wilkinson, C. (1994). Review of teenage health: time for a new direction. *British Journal of General Practice*, 44: 420–4.

Kandel, D. (1975). Stages of adolescent involvement in drug use. *Science*, 190: 912–14.

Kandel, D., Yamaguchi, K. & Chen, L. (1992). Stage of progression in drug involvement from adolescence to adulthood: further evidence for the gateway theory. *Journal of Studies in Alcohol*, 53: 447–57.

Kickbusch, I. (2001). Health literacy: addressing the health and education divide. *Health Promotion International*, 16(3): 289–97.

Kosunen, E. & Rimpela, M. (1996). Towards regional equality in family planning: teenage pregnancies and abortions in Finland from 1976 to 1993. *Acta Obstet Gynecol Scand*, 75: 540–7.

Lamarine, R. (1995). Child and adolescent depression. *Journal of School Health*, 65(9): 390–3.

Leete, R. (2000). Reproductive health, *OECD Observer*, 14 December, http://www.oecdobserver.org/news. Retrieved 20 February 2002.

Mathers, C., Vos, C. & Stevenson, C. (1999). *The Burden of Disease and Injury in Australia*. Canberra: AIHW.

McKie, L., Al-Bashir, M., Anagnostopoulou, T., Csepe, P., El-Asfahani, A., Fonseca, H., Funiak, S., Javetz, R. & Samsuridjal, S. (1993). Defining and assessing risky behaviours. *Journal of Advanced Nursing*, 18: 1911–16.

Mechanic, D. (1999). Issues in promoting health. *Social Science and Medicine*, 48: 711–18.

Miller, B., Maguin, E. & Downs, W. (1997). Alcohol, drugs, and violence in children's lives. Recent developments in alcoholism. *Alcoholism and Violence*, 13: 357–85.

Nadaoka, T., Oiji, A., Takahashi, S., Morioka, Y., Kashiwakura, M. & Totsuka, S. (1996). An epidemiological study of eating disorders in a northern area of Japan. *Acta Psychiatr Scand* 93: 305–10.

National Crime Prevention (1999). Living Rough: Preventing Crime and Victimisation Among Homeless Young People. Canberra: National Crime Prevention.

National Health and Medical Research Council (NH&MRC) (1999). National Youth Suicide Prevention Strategy—Setting the Evidence-based Research Agenda for Australia (A literature review). Department of Health and Aged Care, Canberra: AGPS.

NHS National Health Advisory Service (1995). Child and Adolescent Mental Health Services: Together We Stand. London: HMSO.

Nelson, J. (1997). Gay, lesbian, and bisexual adolescents: providing esteem-enhancing care to a battered population. *The Nurse Practitioner*, 22(20): 94–109.

New Zealand Ministry of Health Matu Hauora (2001). Suicide trends in New Zealand 1978–1998. Wellington: New Zealand Health Information Service.

Parks, K. & Quigley, B. (2001). Riskier lifestyle, aggression and public drinking. In: M. Martinez (ed), *Prevention and Control of Aggression and the Impact on Its Victims*. New York: Kluwer Academic/Plenum Press, pp 267–74.

Pate, R., Heath, G., Dowda, M. & Trost, S. (1996). Associations between physical activity and other health behaviors in a representative sample of US adolescents. *American Journal of Public Health*, 86(11): 1577–81.

Resnick, M., Harris, L. & Blum, R. (1993). The impact of caring and connectedness on adolescent health and well-being. *Journal of Paediatric Child Health*, 29, Suppl: 3–9.

Rodden, P., Crawford, J., Kippax, S. & French, J. (1996). Sexual practice and understandings of safe sex: assessing change among 18 to 19 year old Australian tertiary students 1988 to 1994. *The Australian and New Zealand Journal of Public Health*, 20(6): 643–9.

Rodriquez, C. & Moore, N. (1996). Perceptions of pregnant/parenting teens: reframing issues for an integrated approach to pregnancy problems. *Adolescence*, 30(119): 685–706.

Rutter, M. & Smith, D. (eds) (1995). *Psychosocial Disorders in Young People: Time Trends and Their Causes*. Chichester: John Wiley.

Sawyer, M. & Kosky, R. (1996). Mental health promotion for young people. A proposal for a tripartite approach. *Journal of Paediatric Child Health*, 32: 368–70.

Schatz, P. & Dzvimbo, K. (2001). The adolescent sexual world and AIDS prevention: a democratic approach to programme design in Zimbabwe. *Health Promotion International*, 16(2): 127–36.

Schwenk, T. (1997). Psychoactive drugs and athletic performance. *The Physician and Sportsmedicine*, 25(1): 32–46.

Seamark, C. & Pereira Gray, D. (1997). Like mother, like daughter: a general practice study of maternal influences on teenage pregnancy. *British Journal of General Practice*, 47: 175–6.

Sindelar, J. & Fiellin, D. (2001). Innovations in treatment for drug abuse: solutions to a public health problem. *Annual Review of Public Health*, 22: 249–72.

Statistics New Zealand (1998). New Zealand Now: Young New Zealanders. Wellington: Statistics New Zealand, Te Tari Tatau.

Stephens, C. (1996). Healthy cities or unhealthy islands? The health and social implications of urban inequality. *Environment and Urbanization*, 8(2): 9–30.

Stoddard, F. & Saxe, G. (2001). Ten-year research review of physical injuries. *Journal of the American Academy of Child and Adolescent Psychiatry*, 40(10): 1128–45.

Swaim, R., Beauvais, F., Chavez, E. & Oetting, E. (1997). The effect of school dropout rates on estimates of adolescent substance use among three racial/ethnic groups. *American Journal of Public Health*, 87(1): 51–5.

Tanner, S., Miller, D. & Alongi, C. (1995). Anabolic steroid use by adolescents: prevalence, motives and knowledge of risks. *Clinical Journal of Sports Medicine*, 5(2): 108–15.

Taylor, D., Poulton, R., Moffitt, T., Ramankutty, P. & Sears, M. (2001). The respiratory effects of cannabis dependence in young adults. *Addiction*, 95(11): 1669–77.

Tiggermann, M. (1995). The role of the media in adolescent women's drive for thinness. *Proceedings of the Third National Women's Health Conference*, Canberra: Australian National University, pp 164–7.

Tresidder, J. (1996). Perspectives on adolescent health in the 1990s. *The Australian and New Zealand Journal of Public Health*, 20(3): 229–30.

Tresidder, J., Macaskill, P., Bennett, D. & Nutbeam, D. (1997). Health risks and behaviour of out-of-school 16 year olds in New South Wales. *Australian and New Zealand Journal of Public Health*, 21(2): 168–74.

United Nations Programme on HIV/AIDS (UNAIDS) (1999). AIDS. Emerging issues and challenges for women, young people and infants. Geneva: UNAIDS Information Centre.

US Department of Health and Human Services (USDHHS) Centers for Disease Control (2001). Health, United States, 2001. Washington: DHHS.

Vimpani, G. & Parry, T. (eds) (1989). *Community Child Health in Australia*. Melbourne: Churchill Livingstone.

Wakeling, A. (1996). Epidemiology of anorexia nervosa. *Psychiatry Research*, 62: 3–9.

Wasserheit, J. (1992). Epidemiological synergy: interrelationship between human immunodeficiency virus infection and other sexually transmitted diseases. *Sexually Transmitted Diseases*, 19: 61–77.

Watkins, C. (2002). Suicide and the school: recognition and intervention for suicidal students in the school setting. Baltimore Services for Children, Adolescents, Adults and Families, www.baltimorepsych.com/Suicide.htm.

West, P. & Sweeting, H. (1996). Nae job, nae future: young people and health in a context of unemployment. *Health and Social Care in the Community*, 4(1): 50–62.

Willcox, M. & Sattler, D. (1996). The relationship between eating disorders and depression. *The Journal of Social Psychology*, 136(2): 269–71.

World Health Organization (WHO) (1999). *World Health Report 1999. Making a Difference*. Geneva: WHO.

—— (2000a). What about boys? A literature review on the health and development of adolescent boys. Geneva: Department of Child and Adolescent Health and Development, WHO.

—— (2000b). Child and adolescent health and development. Geneva: WHO.

—— (2000c). The health and economic consequences of Smoking. Geneva: WHO.

—— (2001). World Health Report 2001. Mental health. New understanding, new hope. Geneva: WHO.

Yang, M. (1995). Adolescent sexuality and its problems. *Annals of the Academy of Medicine*, 24(5): 736–40.

Zerbe, K. (1996). Anorexia nervosa and bulimia nervosa. *Postgraduate Medicine*, 99(1): 161–9.

Zhu, B., Liu, M., Shelton, D., Liu, S. & Giovino, G. (1996). Cigarette smoking and risk factors among elementary school students in Beijing. *American Journal of Public Health*, 86(3): 368–75.

Zigler, E. & Stevenson-Finn, M. (1987). *Children: Development and Social Issues*. Lexington, MA: Heath.

CHAPTER 7

Healthy
adults

ntroduction   By the time most people have reached adulthood they have usually experienced at least one illness or injury serious enough for them to seek medical help. For most adults these are acute episodes, resolved without major intervention or residual effects. For others, however, chronic, disabling conditions either cause premature mortality or compromise their quality of life. The difference between these two groups is related to many factors, including the same types of things that influence child and adolescent health. However, adults are the population group who make the majority of decisions regarding lifestyle, health service use and such other health determinants as education, employment, place of residence and family structure. Adult choices for health are better informed these days, since the mapping of the human genome and information that flows from the Global Burden of Disease studies. This chapter will take a look at adult risk and determinants of health in the context of this revolution in health information.

objectives   **By the end of this chapter you will be able to:**

1   Identify the usefulness of Global Burden of Disease (GBD) information for the adult population

2   Identify the major elements of the burden of illness, injury and disability among adults

3   Identify the main lifestyle factors affecting the burden of illness, injury and disability among adults

4   Explain how the environment affects the major lifestyle factors that in turn affect the health of adults

5   Discuss the implications of the Human Genome Project (HGP) for the health of the adult population

6   Explain the role of health care services in maintaining the health of adults

7   Explain how the health of adults can be improved using the strategies of the Ottawa Charter for Health Promotion.

The healthy
adult

Adulthood is the time of a person's life when the intersecting influences of biology, the environment and lifestyle are most apparent. By the time people have become adults, their innate predispositions have combined with their past and current lifestyles and a variety of life circumstances to set a pattern for the future. For most, the prospects for a long life free of the burden of illness and disability is good. However, for many people, especially older males, the quality of their lives will be compromised by sight, hearing, speech, mobility, emotional or mental conditions, or the need for medications (AIHW 1996a).

Health determinants
and risk factors

For more than a century, health researchers have been trying to explain relative states of health and illness in various population groups. During the 1990s, research carried out under the auspices of the Centers for Disease Control and Prevention in the United States analysed the relative weight of factors leading to morbidity and mortality in adults, and concluded that the tendency to die prematurely had not changed much since the 1970s. Mortality was due to four main factors: human biology (20%), environmental factors (20%), inadequate health care (10%) and unhealthy behaviour and lifestyles (50%) (AIHW 1996a; Lee & Paxman 1997; McGinnis & Foege 1993). Half of all deaths could be attributed to such risk factors as tobacco use, diet and activity patterns, alcohol, microbial and other toxic agents, firearms and motor vehicle injuries, sexual behaviour and illicit drug use (McGinnis & Foege 1993). The way lifestyle factors have become entrenched in causing the burden of disease has been further confirmed by the Global Burden of Disease (GBD) studies (Murray & Lopez 1997; WHO 1999, 2001b). WHO explains that global mortality is caused by the following risks:

- tobacco use (6%)
- hypertension (5.8%)
- inadequate water and sanitation (5.3%)
- risky sexual activity (2.2%)
- alcohol use (1.5%) (WHO 1999).

The implication of this information is that poor health is not necessarily our destiny. Health and ill health are determined through the many social elements of daily life that affect lifestyle choices. Lifestyle choices, in turn, are made in relation to occupation, education, the environment (including the policy environment), family structure, major life events and social networks. Inadequate water and sanitation cause disease, particularly for the poor. The addictions caused by unchecked tobacco company advertising exacerbate the effects of air pollution. Hopeless life circumstances thrust young people into prostitution with the attendant risks of violence and sexually transmitted diseases. The rapid growth in vehicular traffic throughout the world magnifies the risk of road trauma (WHO 1999). So, as health advocates, we need to consider the distal, structural issues, such as poverty, housing, educational and social support services and employment opportunities, and help create positive choices for the proximal risk factors that include unhealthy behaviours (AIHW 1996a; Lee & Paxman 1997; WHO 1999).

Individual and family lifestyle choices are also moderated by the availability of accessible, affordable and culturally appropriate services to treat and prevent illness and to sustain wellness. One of the greatest challenges, however, lies in determining the effectiveness of various services or programs (WHO 2000, 2001b). Because health and illness are also generated by a multitude of interactions between factors, it is particularly difficult for health planners to measure health outcomes as a direct response to certain interventions.

For example, the outcomes of government-sponsored anti-smoking or anti-pollution campaigns may not be fully realised for years. In the time lag between exposure to a program, and health outcomes, many things change, including people's behaviour.

Although there is a lack of precision in attributing health gains to particular services or activities, it remains important to undertake program planning and development from a data base of local knowledge and information that allows comparison with other places and other groups. We must therefore continue to measure morbidity and mortality rates, the extent to which people are exposed to health information, the ways in which they gain knowledge and skills to sustain their personal health, to access appropriate treatment for illness and injury and, ultimately, the ways they are able to achieve quality of life.

The burden of
illness, injury and disability
in the adult population

WHO reports that in the early decades of this century, we will face a double burden of disease (WHO 1999). The first is the emerging epidemics of non-communicable diseases and injuries that are becoming increasingly prevalent in all countries of the world. The second is the 'unfinished health agenda' of the last century's major infectious diseases (WHO 1999, p 14).

The communicable disease burden

The communicable disease burden is enormous, particularly for the poor. About half of the global poorest 20 per cent live in India, and a quarter in sub-Saharan Africa. Most of the remainder live in Bangladesh and Southeast Asia, China, the Middle East, Latin America and the Caribbean (Gwatkin, Guillot & Heuveline 1999). Together with under-nutrition and complications of childbirth, infectious diseases disproportionately affect those living in poverty. Maternal conditions, HIV/AIDS and tuberculosis are the three major causes of disease burden in developing countries (WHO 1999, 2001a). Seventeen million Africans have died of AIDS since the 1970s and, of the 40 million people worldwide living with AIDS, 28.1 million live in Africa (UNAIDS 2001).

Although HIV/AIDS was slower to emerge in Asia and the Pacific, it is now a major problem there, with more than 7.1 million people living with the disease (UNAIDS 2001). Fifteen thousand adults and children are now living with HIV/AIDS in Australia and New Zealand (UNAIDS 2001). The resurgence of tuberculosis (TB) in the Western Pacific is also attributed, to some extent, to the HIV/AIDS epidemic and is known to be responsible for 25 per cent of the global total of TB cases (WHO 1999). Sub-Saharan Africa has also experienced a 20 per cent rise in TB cases since 1997 (WHO 2001a).

One of the misconceptions about HIV/AIDS is that it is a disease of young people. This may be the case in sub-Saharan Africa, where few people afflicted with the disease live to grow old, but it is not always the case in developed countries. In the United States, 10 per cent of all AIDS cases reported to the Centers for Disease Control and Prevention (CDC) in the United States have involved individuals 50 years of age and older, 10 per cent of these being among persons over age 60 (Whipple & Walsh Scura 1996). Although proportionately fewer adults contract AIDS than other illnesses (coronary heart disease, cancer) or injuries, it is a major public health problem because of its lethal nature, and because it is preventable. The United Nations Programme on HIV/AIDS (UNAIDS 2001) reports evidence that HIV infection rates in North America, parts of Europe and Australia are rising due to unsafe sex and widespread injecting drug use, which is shifting the epidemic towards deprived communities.

A large proportion (71%) of all HIV infections worldwide are a result of heterosexual transmission. In the industrialised world, homosexual transmission is generally responsible for a much larger proportion (93 per cent and 88 per cent respectively), but the number of people infected through heterosexual intercourse is increasing (Choi & Catania 1996; Kault 1996; Li et al 1996; Zierler & Krieger 1997; UNAIDS 2001). In countries like China, the majority of cases (73%) occur as a result of IV drug use (Yu et al 1996).

Because of the myth of 'homosexual-only' transmission, people have been particularly slow to understand the escalating risk of women contracting the disease. The risk is especially acute in women of colour, but again this is a reflection of socioeconomic status. Studies of women in the United States, Zaire, Zimbabwe and South Africa illustrate the links between women being economically destitute and having to engage in sex for material sustenance (Zierler & Krieger 1997). In many parts of the industrialised world, women exchange sex for drugs, thus doubling the risk of contracting the disease. In the African countries this is sometimes at the request of their families for purchasing land or building materials, or to repay debts. At the same time, men's labour migrations at times of shrinking jobs become a source of infection as they seek sexual contact along their routes (Zierler & Kreiger 1997).

Men's sexual behaviour in the industrialised nations has also put women at risk. One US study of women living in inner-city, low-income housing developments found that approximately one-third were put at risk by the behaviour of their sexual partners, whether through sexual activity or their use of injected drugs (Sikkema et al 1996). In this study, women were found to have high levels of HIV-risk knowledge, but they did not fully understand how to use a condom, and held misconceptions about the physical appearance of most people with HIV infection. Many had also contracted other sexually transmitted diseases, which is a known co-factor for HIV infection (St Louis, Wasserheit & Gayle 1997). The authors concluded that health education programs must be designed to incorporate 'prevention messages and skills focused on partner relationships and the issues of power imbalance in traditional sexual relationships, social and economic dependence on a male partner, and the priorities of daily life for impoverished women' (Sikkema et al 1996, p 1127).

The non-communicable disease burden

Non-communicable diseases have overtaken communicable diseases as the leading cause of mortality worldwide (Gwatkin et al 1999). The main non-communicable disease burden in industrialised countries is caused by mental and behavioural disorders, which carries 12 per cent of the global burden of disease, a burden that is climbing steadily higher (WHO 2001b). The next-highest burden of disease can be attributed to cardiovascular disorders (10%). The third-highest is attributable to cancers, which cause 5 per cent of GBD in low- and middle-income countries and 15 per cent in high-income countries (WHO 1999).

One of the most remarkable findings of the GBD studies has been the extent of depression among both industrialised and developing countries. Major depression is now the leading cause of disability globally (WHO 2001b). Five of the ten leading causes of disability worldwide are mental disorders: depression, alcohol use, bipolar affective disorder, schizophrenia and obsessive-compulsive disorder (Andrews, Sanderson & Beard 1998; WHO 1999). Although most of these conditions are not causes of death, together they account for 28 per cent of all years lived with a disability (Menken, Munsat & Toole 2000). In the market economies of North America, the United Kingdom and Australia, harmful drug use is also one of the ten leading causes of disability (Andrews et al 1998).

Alcohol dependence is another area recognised as a major cause of disease burden, particularly for adult men. Globally, 70 million people suffer from alcohol dependence (WHO 2001b). Alcohol also plays a role in the burden of cardiovascular disease which, along with cerebrovascular disease (stroke), is among the most significant conditions worldwide (WHO 1999). Alcohol also plays a role in a large number of injuries, including road trauma, homicide, self-inflicted injuries, homicide and domestic violence (WHO 1999, 2001b).

The most prevalent form of cancer is lung cancer, most of which is attributable to tobacco smoking (WHO 1999). Smoking continues to be the norm throughout many European countries and in Asia, the latter of which has half the burden of cardiovascular disease in the world (Rodgers & MacMahon 1999).

Healthy
lifestyles

The GBD evidence has shown conclusively that the leading causes of today's burden of illness and poor quality of life are related to modern lifestyles. Risk factors such as smoking, alcohol consumption, physical inactivity, hypertension level, obesity, high blood cholesterol and inadequate fruit and vegetable consumption account for most of the burden of disease in Australia, where heart disease and stroke claim nearly 40 000 lives per year (AIHW 2001). Ten per cent of Australia's disease burden is attributable to tobacco smoking, followed by seven per cent attributable to physical inactivity (Mathers et al 2000).

Unhealthy lifestyles are a feature of many countries today, even those with healthy traditions. The Eastern Mediterranean Regional Office of WHO reports on the health status of that area, which is going through a major epidemiological transition. Population ageing, increasing urbanisation and changes in nutritional habits and lifestyle are creating a more hazardous lifestyle than in the past. Mediterranean people are eating higher fat content in their diets. Over 17 million people in that region have diabetes and a further 17 million have impaired glucose tolerance. People continue to smoke, and exercise little. Coronary heart disease is seen at younger ages than previously, and hypertension is known in 20 per cent of adults, which may be magnified when the amount of hidden hypertension is considered (WHO 1999).

Physical
activity

One of the most important targets for health promotion is physical activity. In today's society, more people than ever before lead a sedentary lifestyle. Technology has made daily physical activity unnecessary, and inadvertently condones the opposite in industrialised countries, where many jobs involve computer-based work. One-third of the adult population in Western countries choose to also spend their leisure time relaxing instead of in some type of physical activity (French, Story & Jeffery 2001; Guerzoni 1996). This is of great concern when the costs of exercise are compared with the costs of treating illness.

The research indicates the importance of physical activity as it plays a part in cardiovascular disease, colon, lung and breast cancer (AIHW 2000). Regular exercise, such as daily walking, is free, and the health gains are enormous in terms of keeping fit, burning off extra calories and coping with stress. Regular physical activity also appears to reduce depression and anxiety, improve mood and enhance people's ability to perform daily tasks throughout their life span (Lee & Paxman 1997). In the 1970s and 1980s many developed countries witnessed a 'healthy lifestyle' trend in which jogging was a central feature. Subsequent publicity about stress fractures and a more balanced view of exercise has seen the trend level off to where many former joggers have switched to walking. In Australia, approximately 50 per cent of adult males and 49 per cent of women are walking at a level considered beneficial to health (AIHW 2000). In the United States, figures range considerably, but the last reported data indicate small increases in the number of people engaging in activity to keep fit (French et al 2001).

Embarking on a program of physical activity such as a walking program may also act as a catalyst for other positive lifestyle practices. Some people tend to quit smoking, lose weight and have less stress once they begin a physical exercise program (Johnson, Boyle & Heller 1995). Research evidence has shown that combining moderate vigorous sporting activity and quitting cigarette smoking are independently associated with lower rates of death from all causes and from coronary heart disease in middle-aged and older men (Paffenbarger et al 1993).

Weight **control**

Weight control remains a problem for many people. In males, the body mass index (weight/height^2) gradually increased throughout the 1980s and 1990s throughout the Western world (Galuska et al 1996; Knuiman et al 1995). In North America, 50 per cent of adults in the United States and 30 per cent of Canadians are now considered obese (French et al 2001; Statistics Canada 2001). Australians are following this trend, with 43 per cent of women and 63 per cent of men considered obese (AIHW 2000). Preventative measures for coronary heart disease therefore need to be dramatic and should focus on both exercise and reducing dietary intake (Crowley, Dunt & Day 1995; Young et al 1996).

Weight control programs, especially for women of low SES, have had only modest successes (Jeffery & French 1996). Canadian surveys show that those with limited incomes are more inclined to participate in health-inhibiting than health-enhancing behaviours (Reutter 2000). The research shows that healthy eating patterns and participation in sport increases with income, whereas smoking decreases with income. These factors conspire to leave Canadians of low SES in poorer health (Reutter 2000).

Smoking

The GBD studies have shown smoking to be the greatest public health problem of our time, with 150 million deaths expected to occur because of tobacco smoking in the first quarter of this century (WHO 1999). Tobacco is a risk factor for some 25 diseases and accounts for approximately 15 per cent of deaths from all causes, including cardiovascular disease (coronary heart disease and stroke), cancers and obstructive pulmonary disease, in all age groups. This figure is closer to 50 per cent in those with a lifetime smoking history (AIHW 1996b; WHO 1997a).

Approximately one-third of these tobacco-related deaths could be avoided if half of current adult smokers quit. It is estimated that 1.15 billion people smoke tobacco today, 82 per cent of whom live in low- and middle-income countries. In these countries, rates of tobacco consumption have steadily increased, while declining dramatically in the United States and other developed countries (WHO 1999). Smoking-related diseases cost governments thousands of millions of dollars, with thousands of millions more lost because productive lives are cut short by tobacco use (WHO 1997). In addition, the data on passive smoking shows an increased risk of lung cancer, and some association with children's ailments such as SIDS, low birthweight, intrauterine growth development and respiratory disease (Haglund 1997; WHO 1999).

In the industrialised nations, the annual cost of smoking-related deaths is exorbitant. In Australia, for example, where 25 per cent of Australian men and 20 per cent of women aged 14 or over smoke, the cost of health care for smokers has been estimated at over $600 million. It is 10 times that amount ($68 billion) in the United States, where a quarter of the population smoke (AIHW 2000; Escobedo & Peddicord 1996). Smoking is also the leading cause of domestic fires in the high-income countries, entailing billions of dollars of property loss annually (WHO 1999). The rate of smoking is proportionally higher for Aboriginal people (Andrews, Oates & Naden 1997) and those of lower SES (Escobedo & Peddicord 1996; Reutter 2000), particularly those who live in urban environments (Freudenberg 2000).

In Europe, Asia and many developing countries, smoking presents an even greater public health problem than in other countries. The prevalence of smoking in India, for example, has been estimated at as much as 45–48 per cent among males. Indian women, who chew betel quid rather than smoking tobacco, are dying of oral cancer at a rate greater than that of breast cancer (Haglund 1997; Narayan et al 1996). In China, where more than a third of males smoke, it is predicted that by the year 2020 there will be 2–3 million deaths annually from tobacco-related disease (Haglund 1997; Zhu et al 1996).

We have only recently begun to understand the mechanisms of smoking-related illness, although it has been acknowledged for years that the carcinogens in cigarette smoke attack tissues in the larynx, oral cavity, oesophagus, lung and urinary bladder. This creates damage by generating free radicals, which place increased demand on the antioxidant systems that protect cells from damage (Margetts & Jackson 1993). Further exacerbating the problem is the fact that most smokers have lower intakes of the foods that provide protective antioxidant nutrients such as vitamin C (English, Najman & Bennett 1997).

There is now conclusive evidence of the links between smoking, inadequate diet and a hazardous intake of alcohol (Breslau et al 1996; English et al 1997). Once again, this points to the need for lifestyle modification programs to address risk factors and a lifestyle that may reinforce unhealthy patterns of living. WHO decrees that this cannot be accomplished without broad popular support at the local level, where national and international initiatives for tobacco control must begin. A concerted effort to counter smoking needs to include: widespread information on the links between smoking and health; advertising bans, taxes and regulations; smoking cessation programs; and building anti-tobacco control coalitions (WHO 1999).

Cancers

Tobacco smoking also has a role to play in cancers and respiratory illnesses, particularly lung cancer, which has the most significant burden of disease of all forms of cancer (WHO 1999). Some cancers share risk factors, but for most cancers, there are unique combinations of risk factors that vary according to age, gender and race (AIHW 2000). The most obvious of these are breast cancer, which occurs primarily in women, and prostate cancer, which occurs only in men. Estimates indicate that 30 per cent of cancers can be attributed to smoking, 30 per cent to dietary influences, two per cent to radiation exposure, 5–15 per cent to infectious agents, and the remainder to both modifiable and non-modifiable (genetic) risk factors (Trichopoulus et al, in AIHW 2000).

The most common cancer overall is prostate cancer, accounting for 23.5 per cent of all cancers in males (AIHW 2000). The incidence of cancer increases with age, especially for males, who have higher rates of cancer than females over age 55. However, during ages 30–54, females have nearly seven times the incidence of males, because of cancers of the cervix, uterus, ovary and breast (AIHW 2000). The major risk factors for breast cancer are increased age and family history. Other risk factors include previous history of breast cancer or benign breast disease, larger body size, and reproductive factors such as late age at first birth or not having had a child, early menstruation, late menopause, use of oral contraceptives at an early age, hormone replacement therapy, and exposure of breast tissue to ionising radiation (AIHW 2000). Current information suggests that a high-fat diet and consumption of alcohol may also play a role in breast cancer (AIHW 2000).

Melanoma is significant in Australia, as rates of this type of cancer are the highest in the world, with Australia having a 10-fold higher rate than England and Wales, and up to 150 times higher a rate than in some other countries. This type of cancer has been steadily increasing in Australia, especially in males over age 60 (AIHW 2000). The major risk factor for melanoma is UV radiation exposure, and the incidence is higher in those with fair hair, sun-sensitive skin, many moles, and high recreational exposure with frequent sunburns (AIHW 2000).

Survival rates from cancer have improved over the past two decades. The survival rate is an indication of the biology of the disease and host factors, the availability of health services and medical intervention. Because these factors are not always comparable, especially where health services differ, international comparisons are imprecise. However, the trend indicates an improvement in relative survival at five years for Australian women from 70 per cent in the 1970s to approximately 77 per cent in the late 1980–90s. This compares with 64–70 per cent in the United Kingdom, 69–80 per cent in Scandinavia, 73–75 per cent in Canada and 62–81 per cent in the United States (Taylor & Coates 1997).

Adult accidents
and injuries

Injuries are now known to be responsible for one out of every six years of disability, or 16 per cent of the global burden of disease (Krug, Sharma & Lozano 2000; WHO 1999). Most injuries are sustained from road trauma (17.5%), falls (12.2%), interpersonal violence (10.1%) and self-inflicted injuries (9.7%) (Krug et al 2000).

The mortality rate from injuries is not significant among adults in industrialised countries, although it is the leading cause of death among young people, most from suicide and motor vehicle accidents (AIHW 2000). Alcohol is a major factor in nearly 50 per cent of motor vehicle injuries. Over the past decade, Australia has had significant improvements in the rate of motor vehicle injuries due, in part, to improved public education programs, better law enforcement, stricter penalties, better roads and improvement in vehicle safety design. However, the opposite trend is seen in developing countries, where increased road traffic leads to higher risk of injury and resources are not adequate for road maintenance (WHO 1999).

Other injuries that occur among adults include occupational injuries or falls at home (from bicycles, horses, ladders or scaffolding etc), accidents related to using power tools, farm machinery and poisonings (AIHW 2000). However, the most contentious form of injury is that caused by violence, particularly violent crime, which is becoming an all too pervasive characteristic of society.

Violence is perpetrated not only by criminals but also by those in altered states of consciousness brought about by substance use. Many countries, most notably the United States, experienced a firearm and handgun-related epidemic of violence early in the 1990s (Gardiner, Norton & Alpers 1996), which is beginning to decline as we begin this century (Freudenberg 2000). However, because burglaries and other crimes against property are on the increase everywhere, many people have either armed themselves or are less hesitant than in the past to use force in protecting their property. Some attribute the propensity to strike back to television violence, but this is as yet unresolved. One side of the debate argues that there is no direct link between what is modelled on TV and what occurs in real life; but the opposing view is that young people are brought up to believe that violent retribution is a normal response in situations where a person is attacked or where efforts towards achieving some sort of goal are thwarted.

The issue of firearms use is one that should be of grave concern to public health professionals. In Australia and New Zealand the pro-gun lobby groups promote the notion that most incidents of firearm misuse are committed by either unlicensed owners with illegal weapons or the mentally ill. However, a study of all non-fatal firearm injuries in a three-year period in New Zealand revealed that a large number were perpetrated by licensed gun owners, including half of those involved in domestic disputes (Gardiner et al 1996).

The role of government in regulating weapons also continues to be a contentious issue. The worst episode of mass violence ever experienced in Australia occurred in 1996 in Tasmania, where 35 people were killed and 18 others were seriously injured by a deranged, lone gunman. The episode sparked an international debate on gun laws and provided the stimulus for the world's most comprehensive set of gun control regulations. Interestingly, health organisations, with few exceptions, were slow in registering their views, perhaps indicating that there is still a need to make social conditions a normal part of the health agenda (Peters 1996). In any event, it is imperative that further research be conducted on violence in the community, as much to dispel misconceptions about the conditions within which these events occur as to draw people's attention to the way violent lifestyles compromise community health.

Given current knowledge of the role of risk factors in maintaining the health of adults, efforts to help people change should focus on lifestyle factors (Mathers et al 2000). However, lobbying for structural changes such as government controls on regulating tobacco, firearms and alcohol are also important elements in discouraging harmful behaviours. Both must be integrated into any community health promotion program.

Promoting healthy lifestyles should begin from where people see themselves and their health status. Being healthy is a personal code, embedded in the cultural system to which people belong (Kleinman 1988). Lifestyle practices are influenced by the way people see themselves positioned within the culture, and within the larger scheme of the social world, and this influences their receptivity to health messages. The challenge is to ensure that health promotion initiatives tread a delicate balance between informed personal choice and a heavy-handed approach to public control. This balance can be achieved within initiatives that acknowledge aspects of the physical as well as the social environment.

Environmental
risk factors

Approximately 25–33 per cent of the global burden of disease can be attributed to environmental risk factors, the outcomes of which are greatest in countries of lower economic development (Smith, Corvalan & Kjellstrom 1999). Risk factors that jeopardise the health of adult populations arise from the effects of environmental influences, and the interaction of these with personal and sociocultural factors. Explicit assessment of this type of risk has been one of the most difficult tasks in public health (Calvert & Ewan 1995), but it is rapidly becoming an area of interest to health researchers throughout the world.

Environmental factors, especially air pollution, are known to play a role in respiratory conditions, including chronic obstructive pulmonary disease (COPD), asthma, emphysema and bronchitis (AIHW 2000; Freudenberg 2000; Lee & Paxman 1997). In developing countries, where around 50 per cent of people rely on coal or biomass in the form of wood, dung and crop residues for domestic energy, women and children are exposed daily to high levels of indoor air pollution (Bruce, Perez-Padilla & Albalak 2000). Estimates of the resultant risk of respiratory disease, cancers and other illnesses suggest that this is the cause of some 2 million excess deaths per year in developing countries (Bruce et al 2000). Most respiratory ailments occur as a result of some potent combination of hereditary, environmental and lifestyle factors. In many cases, occupational exposure either triggers or exacerbates a respiratory condition, especially where workplace dust is poorly controlled.

Studies of workplace pollutants and subsequent health and safety education have heightened awareness of the need for reduction in workplace air pollution, and this comes at a time when more people are also quitting smoking (Brown et al 1997). The research is guarded on the role of occupational exposures and asthmatic episodes, and some uncertainties remain about the relative contribution of occupational exposure as a risk factor for asthma. However, a body of evidence has identified significant relationships between employment as a sawmill worker, laboratory technician, spray painter, baker, plastics and rubber worker, welder or cleaner and the risk of developing the disease (Beach et al 1996; Kogevinas et al 1996; Siracusa et al 1995).

Today there is also greater public awareness of such environmental factors as global warming and changes in the ozone layer, atmospheric idiosyncrasies, transportation and consumption patterns, and systems of waste management (AIHW 2000; Calvert & Ewan 1995). Studies in the South Pacific identified the hole in the ozone layer over Antarctica as being responsible for at least some of the high rates of skin cancer in the southern hemisphere, and this has been widely publicised (AIHW 2000). Although many fair-skinned people can expect an increase in skin cancer from the previous effects of the high concentrations of UV rays, the ozone layer is predicted to recover within the next quarter century (AIHW 2000).

Much remains to be learned about the health effects of environmental pollutants, but studies on air pollution in all corners of the globe have now provided us with an inventory of chemicals defiling our air, primarily from automobile emissions and industrial waste. An estimated 130 000 premature deaths and 50–70 million incidents of respiratory illness occur annually in developing countries alone, because of air pollution (McMichael 2000). This knowledge is yet to have an impact on people's behaviour. In two of the most notorious cities for air pollution, Sao Paulo, Brazil, and Mexico City, the number of vehicles and the number of daily automobile trips are rapidly increasing, rather than decreasing (McMichael 2000).

The human health impact of global ecology, primarily climate change, is the subject of a relatively new body of research (Patz, Engelberg & Last 2000). The physical effects of climate extremes and significant weather events such as floods, fires, storms or drought include increased likelihood of heat and cold stress, exposure to trauma and, occasionally, post-traumatic stress disorder (PTSD), loss of shelter, famine, burns, cardiac and respiratory conditions and malnutrition (Patz et al 2000). These conditions are more likely to be worse for urban dwellers, where increased exposure to various chemicals, lead, traffic hazards and the 'urban heat island' amplification of heat waves occurs (Freudenberg 2000; McMichael 2000). From a global perspective, the environmental risks are acute, given the growth in urban migration from around 5–50 per cent over the past two centuries (McMichael 2000).

The weather also has an effect on air pollutant formation and transport, the flooding and release of toxic chemicals from disposal sites and, indirectly, can be a causative agent in several cancers. A further area of influence is the effect of climatic conditions on disease agents, vectors and their habitats, which may be affected by the geographic distribution (Patz et al 2000). Microbial contamination during floods may alter marine and freshwater ecology and affect the incidence and prevalence of such water-borne and food-borne diseases as malaria, dengue fever, encephalitis and viral infection, particularly in highland cities in low-latitude countries (McMichael 2000; Patz et al 2000). Cholera, food poisoning, shellfish poisoning, leptospirosis and diarrhoeal diseases may also be caused by weather-induced food and nutrient productivity and plant pathogens. Geographic displacement from extreme weather conditions can also cause human conflicts and a range of social and emotional effects from overcrowding or exposure to trauma (Patz et al 2000). Interestingly, Smith and colleagues (1999) suggest that information can also be toxic and therefore cause social and emotional illness. They use the examples of verbal abuse, racism or television violence, as toxic, environmental stressors.

Genetic
risk factors

To some extent, genetic factors are also environmental, given that they have been influenced by the environments of many years ago (Smith et al 1999). Since the Human Genome Project (HGP) there has been a clearer understanding of the influence of genetic factors on health, which is helping to inform the population as well as those making treatment decisions. As the research evidence accumulates on how nature and nurture interact at the cellular level, families and communities will have many decisions to make about their ecosystems and exposures, the risk/reward ratios of different activities, and even when to alter their genomes (Fielding, Lave & Starfield 2000). With genetic information, the basis for decisions regarding health may shift to how risks can be reduced through pharmacotherapy, changes in health habits, or avoiding or minimising certain exposures (Fielding et al 2000). For example, in the workplace, levels of exposure to toxic substances may be reset on the basis of variations in genetic risk (Fielding et al 2000). This type of change will have to be considered from a legal as well as a health perspective, particularly in relation to civil liberties. Provocative questions will be posed in many contexts. For example, will the person with an increased genetic predisposition to back injuries be precluded from employment where lifting is required? And will *all* information on risk, including all possible biotransformations arising from genetic interactions, be contained on *all* consumer goods (Fielding et al 2000)?

The HGP will have an enormous impact on the health of populations in the years to come. Wise choices in community health in the HGP era will depend on 'excellent science, compassionate values, effective communication, appreciation of diverse cultures and preferences, openness to new knowledge and alternative views, commitment to disease prevention and health promotion, and progress in closing the gaps between diagnosis and treatment and between diagnosis and prevention' (Omenn 2000, p 10).

The issues open to debate concern insurability, confidentiality and comparisons between risk information for the management of non-genetic as well as genetic conditions (Omenn 2000). The areas generally considered in promoting the health of adults include knowledge of risk and treatment preferences, which are typically based on information traditionally provided by health professionals at the time of diagnosis. With the virtual explosion of information technologies, these decisions will likely be made in future, with the help of a computer chip that will test large numbers of genes simultaneously in various disease states, and after treatment with a prescribed drug (Omenn 2000). One of the issues that must be considered is whether or not to resource population-based genetic testing for disease presence and susceptibility (Austin, Peyser & Khoury 2000). A more important question may be whether or not such testing creates inequities of access for some members of the population who could not afford it, and stigmatisation and discrimination for those who undergo such testing (Austin et al 2000).

This level of sophistication in knowledge development will help people anticipate where preventative action can be undertaken or where early intervention is required. This must be done with a watchful eye on the technologies and innovations that can be explained in a variety of ways. Futurists believe that the field of bioinformatics will continue to become highly refined so that genetic information can be translated into clinically relevant information for diagnosis and treatment (Austin et al 2000). New treatments, particularly pharmacological treatments and gene therapy, will have to be incorporated into the knowledge base for all medical practitioners. The new information will also require the health professional to be familiar with many and wide-ranging permutations of states of health. For those in public and community health, population-wide decisions will be based on new methods of epidemiological analysis, including new understandings of the transmission and pathogenesis of infectious diseases (Austin et al 2000). Statistical genetics is already an evolving speciality, investigating family studies and linkage analysis, and this field will continue to grow.

How to approach the role of advocate will be the greatest challenge for those working in communities. The large volume of information may be confusing for some people, swaying their decisions either toward or away from consent to treatment. One dilemma will therefore revolve around how to inform both consent and refusal (Omenn 2000). Health professionals will have to become reoriented toward the new research techniques as well as ways of supporting people who receive adverse news. This should ensure that the psychological effects of informing people of heightened risk receive appropriate attention and that all prevention and intervention is undertaken from an evidence-based practice orientation (Austin et al 2000). Most importantly, the findings of an expanding community health research agenda must be used with the principles of primary health care clearly in the foreground.

Countering risk:
healthy adulthood

The best prescription for adult health is community participation in intersectoral healthy lifestyle programs that combine strategies for overcoming proximal risk factors and those that effect the distal or structural alterations for risk minimisation or reduction. The most successful programs aimed at a comprehensive approach to health promotion have included community participation, media promotion, school-based health education, worksite health promotion, screening and referral of high-risk individuals, and education programs for health professionals (Crowley et al 1995).

The most important issues on the health promotion agenda for adults today are tobacco smoking, mental health and HIV/AIDS. To address these issues requires public awareness of the seriousness of each and information that will be both instructive and supportive. WHO has allocated a large resource base to providing information about the effects of tobacco smoke and how the problem can be addressed. The principles of control advocated by WHO include banning advertising, informing the public, increasing tobacco taxes and regulation of the places where people can smoke, deregulation of nicotine replacement products and supporting anti-tobacco coalitions (WHO 1999). WHO is also doing its part to ensure that the rate of HIV/AIDS infection is checked, particularly in Africa and Asia, and in bringing mental health issues to the world health agenda (WHO 1999, 2001). In addition, it has urged all people to become aware of the critical need for education throughout the world, to counter inequities and help communities build the capacity to overcome risks and optimise their strengths and resources.

---

case study...

Dis-ease in Burma

The following account illustrates the relationship between health and human rights. Dr Nancy Hudson-Rodd is a fellow Canadian who, as a nurse and social geographer, lives and teaches in Australia, primarily in development studies. Her views on the potential for health and development in Burma have been shaped by teaching Burmese students and visiting the country. She says, 'From Australia I try to understand how people's potential for good health can be achieved in an environment with many restrictions on human rights. I write here about the current social situation in Burma and delve into different, yet common perspectives of an elderly citizen and a comedian, both of whom I met in Mandalay.'

Military rule in Burma has created health hazards for the population through inadequate public expenditure on health and education, human rights violations, denying freedom of expression, and through waging civil war. The Burmese military rulers have also created health hazards for people of neighbouring countries, for as refugees and migrant workers flow out of Burma they spread HIV/AIDS, unaware of the risks. Treatable or preventable diseases and health conditions linked to poor socio-economic status are common. These include malaria, tuberculosis, leprosy, pneumonia, intestinal infections and malnutrition. Complications arising from lack of knowledge concerning reproductive health, and repressive laws, make illicit abortions one of the major causes of unnecessary death and suffering in young Burmese women. In concert with these socially, politically, economically, environmentally linked diseases are loss of life and injury related to civil strife, landmines, and infection with HIV/AIDS from use of unclean needles and unprotected sex. Financial resources are used to support armed conflict rather than health and education.

Burma's health care system ranks as the second most inefficient in the world (WHO 2000). The cost of health and medical care is beyond the reach of many people. A hysterectomy, for example, costs twice a working person's annual wage. Essential medicines are always in short supply and, for years, medicines have been sold on the black market or from privately operated pharmacies found in the streets close to the hospitals. The WHO review concluded that significant improvements would flow from shifting existing resources to preventative care and effective deployment of health professionals.

In Mandalay, I met an old woman who wanted to show me her X-rays, hospital records, and prescription for medication. I believe she has tuberculosis, and with no husband and no family she is unable to support herself and cannot afford the medications. She spoke of discouraging things: being aged, single, and ill in Burma. I expected a lighter note from the performing Moustache Brothers' Troupe of comedians, but this was not the case. Two members of the group have just been released from serving five years in a hard labour prison camp for having made jokes about the economic mis-management of Burma by the military at an Independence Day rally hosted by NLD Leader Aung San Suu Kyi in 1996. Now this troupe, which uses only traditional instruments and dance routines, is forbidden from performing. As was Aung San Suu Kyi until mid-2002, the Moustache Brothers' Troupe are under virtual house arrest, prevented from performing, even in the privacy of their own home. I reflect on the fact that, in a nation with no freedom of expression, the oral word is a tool to enhance empowerment of those already powerful, but not to express the needs and aspirations of those citizens of Burma who seek to laugh, live, create their own ideas, and achieve self or community development (personal communication, Nancy Hudson-Rodd, 2002).

Note: Dr Hudson-Rodd has produced a comprehensive discussion paper on Burma for Burma Action Ireland, at http://free.freespeech.org/bai/.

Goals for
adult health

Goals for adult health should be:

- to reduce the incidence of:
  - mental illnesses, particularly depression
  - cardiovascular disease and stroke
  - cancers
  - lung and respiratory diseases
  - accidents and injuries
  - infectious diseases, especially HIV/AIDS and tuberculosis

- and to create communities that are:
  - equitable
  - well informed
  - cohesive
  - vibrant
  - healthy
  - sustainable.

These goals can be achieved primarily through programs that educate people about the risk factors predisposing to illness, and those that facilitate healthy lifestyles in individuals and families, and through mechanisms that create healthy environments within which optimal lifestyles can be achieved. The Ottawa Charter guides the development of each of these strategies.

Building healthy public policy

The first element in healthy public policy making is to ensure representation by the local community. One Canadian study of policy planning at the local level suggests that ordinary citizens of a community should be the ones informing policy, given their knowledge of what works and what circumstances will promote participation and sustainability (Mittelmark 2001). Community health policies should be aimed at empowerment of deprived groups, providing support for coping and development (Mechanic 1999). This type of approach responds to the priority identified in the Jakarta Declaration on Health Promotion to conduct equity-focused health assessments (WHO 1997).

Some of the best policy developments have come from grass roots social movements such as road trauma activist groups, and the anti-gun and anti-tobacco lobbies. Parent groups have lobbied for years about drink-driving laws, penalties for vehicular manslaughter and safety measures. In Australia, government responses have been enormously effective, with marked reductions in the road toll from a comprehensive policy initiative to reduce the rates of road trauma. The policies include safety and law enforcement legislation, education programs and encouragement of safe practice, transport and land use planning, safety standards and engineering and evaluation of progress. A National Injury Prevention Advisory Council provides input into the policies to ensure policy makers are well informed on the basis of injury surveillance (NH&MRC 1999). Included are physical, economic and social aspects of the driving environment, and targets set for all concerned including automobile manufacturers, drivers, educators and the police (AIHW 2000). In the United Kingdom, where a similar program has been introduced, the rate of casualties has dropped significantly despite a growth in road traffic. Interestingly, drivers in that country are now almost three times as likely to be breath tested, but are less likely to fail the test than in the 1980s. This is reflected also in declining mortalilty rates (UK Department of Transport 1996).

Health promotion policies governing smoking have experienced a tortuous path. One of the difficulties with introducing anti-smoking policies has been an immensely powerful tobacco industry, which, until 1997, denied that cigarettes caused any illness, and successfully defended all lawsuits against them. This occurred despite confirmation in 1950 by the Royal College of Physicians in London, the United States Surgeon General and WHO that smoking causes lung cancer (Wynder & Muscat 1995). However, the industry, which maintains lobbyists in all states of the United States, succeeded in covering up its culpability in smoking-related mortality, perhaps because of government complacency encouraged by substantial revenues from tobacco tax. In 1997, a relatively small tobacco company, the Liggett group, created a worldwide controversy by openly admitting that research findings linking smoking and lung cancer had been suppressed for four decades by the tobacco industry.

What followed was an historic agreement between the United States government and the nation's largest companies to pay upwards of $500 billion to settle a number of damages claims by the victims and their families. The settlement was made on the proviso that once settled, the companies would receive immunity from further class-action lawsuits. Because of this judgement, in 1997, the government instituted control over nicotine, under the Food and Drug Administration (FDA) Act. The tobacco companies now have to stop selling cigarettes in vending machines and self-service displays, pay the medical bills of those with lawsuits pending, and fund an anti-smoking blitz intended to reduce youth smoking by 60 per cent in the next decade. If this proves successful, millions of young lives could be saved.

Several governments have attempted to control the tobacco industry by forcing it to reduce the amount of carcinogens in the cigarettes it produced. By 1993, health hazard labelling had been introduced by most of the large tobacco companies, and the amount of tar and nicotine in cigarettes drastically reduced (by almost a third). The latter development, however, has had a rebound effect on the health of some smokers. An unanticipated effect of the reduction in tar and nicotine is that smokers of low-yield cigarettes compensate for the low delivery of nicotine by inhaling the smoke more deeply and by smoking more intensely, causing a greater concentration of carcinogenic agents in their lungs. To make matters worse, this new, intense type of smoking is particularly noticeable among those employed in smoke-free environments. These are the smokers who slip outdoors as frequently as their job allows and puff deeply on their cigarettes to get the maximum effect in a short period of time, so they can hasten back to work.

WHO reports that regular and sustained tobacco taxes are the most successful policy initiative in reducing tobacco consumption (WHO 1999). They cite China as a best recent example of the potential health and revenue benefit of this type of approach. World Bank economists predict that a 10 per cent additional tax on tobacco would cut consumption by 5 per cent. These funds would generate an additional 4.5 per cent increase in revenue that would cover provision of basic health services for China's poorest 100 million inhabitants (Saxenian & McGreevey, in WHO 1999). This type of evaluation is helpful in terms of modelling the effect of tobacco smoking for future generations, so that both the intended and unintended outcomes can be part of the strategic planning processes for the future. A Canadian example also illustrates the need for ongoing evaluation. In 1994, a tobacco tax cut was introduced, much to the chagrin of the Canadian anti-smoking lobby. Research conducted by Statistics Canada revealed that almost immediately, the rate of decline in smoking was slowed (Hamilton et al 1997). This case demonstrates the need for vigilance in public policy development, and the need for all health promotion programs to be based on the growing body of information from all parts of the world.

Significant gains have also been made in environmental legislation in a number of countries, including the United States, Canada, Australia and New Zealand (Calvert & Ewan 1995; Smith et al 1999). These initiatives have seen better surveillance and monitoring of the environment, and more accurate diagnosis of environmentally determined illnesses. The environmental policy agenda is likely to expand at an unprecedented rate this century, given increased public awareness of the issues. Improving the physical environment requires interventions that focus on two dimensions: exposure to toxicities and rearrangement of the environment in a way that contributes to health (Freudenberg 2000; Smith et al 2000). The concentration of toxins such as lead, asbestos and various air and water pollutants must be monitored. Simultaneously, workplace and urban planning policies need to regulate exposures to these toxic substances. The physical design of cities, for example, needs to revolve around public safety, places for social interaction, access to physical exercise and the intangible aesthetic factors that may influence mental health (French et al 2001; Freudenberg 2000). Cities need to be made healthier, with widespread dissemination of the hazards of urban life, especially for migrants from rural communities, who are growing in numbers (McMichael 2000).

Creating supportive environments

As mentioned previously, nutrition and dietary habits play a large role in preventing illness. People of all socioeconomic strata are beginning to change their eating patterns, perhaps in response to the combination of health education campaigns and supportive environments (Dobson et al 1997). Supportive environments have also been effective in encouraging adults to take up a physical activity, as witnessed by the growth in the fitness industry (French et al 2001). Pricing strategies and accurate product labelling, especially where these are widely advertised, have also helped with healthy nutritional intake and reductions in tobacco smoking (French et al 2001; WHO 1999).

Given what we now know about the physical environment, people must be supported in their conservation efforts. For those who live in cities, there must be advocacy for recycling strategies, forms of transportation that reduce air pollution, and support for all environmental regulation (Freudenberg 2000). To enhance the social environment in a way that supports good health, community development must be undertaken in a way that enhances quality of life. Reducing graffiti, abandoned blocks containing hazards to children, and public drunkenness, and increasing safe spaces for interaction or recreation all have the capacity to promote social cohesion, which may reduce crime and violence (Freudenberg 2000). The research agenda on environmental issues must continue if communities are to participate fully in regulating the amount of degradation allowed to occur, and work towards sustaining their environments. Studies should address basic understanding of chemical actions, biomarkers of exposure, early effects, variations in susceptibility among the population, and the margin of exposure of different hazards that would compromise health and safety (Omenn 1996).

Many community-wide programs have also been established to prevent, and then provide support to those suffering from, injuries or illness. Intersectoral approaches to promoting safe neighbourhoods include input from city councils, schools, health professionals, transportation, urban planners, human rights experts, journalists and the public (Krug, Sharma & Lozano 2000). Despite the gains, many areas still require support structures. In developing countries, where the poorest populations are most at risk from household-related environmental disease, environmental pathways to better health must be developed in partnership with families and the community, and be aimed at sustainable modifications (Smith et al 1999). Where migration to urban environments is causing rapid transitions in lifestyle, as is occurring in Africa, people should be informed of the health risks and supported through the social and cultural changes (McMichael 2000).

One of the most important ways communities can be supported is in providing care for family carers. In the past, many people died from the major illnesses of adulthood, such as coronary heart disease, cancer and respiratory disease. Today, with technological advances prolonging their lives, people live with the disease for longer periods than in the past. Shrinking health budgets have shortened their hospital stay, resulting in a greater proportion of their rehabilitation time spent in the home and community. This places a burden of care on family members, who often forego paid employment to care for their ailing family members. Community support structures should provide both income and social support for these people, who often play a major role in keeping families together and promoting community cohesion.

Strengthening community action

The health problems of adulthood cannot be overcome without a supportive community infrastructure. Crime and violence in the community, the HIV/AIDS epidemic, carcinogens in the atmosphere, the plight of impoverished families, all must be seen as integral to the health of all community members. The role of the health professional is to ensure community-wide dissemination of current information on each of these topics, so that the community can make informed decisions about such things as crime and injury surveillance, providing support systems for the victims of illness, lobbying for environmental controls or assisting others less able to deal with their lives. Local people often have the most valuable information about environmental risks, including sources of exposure, behaviour patterns, cultural practices and local concerns that may be missed by external experts (Omenn 1996, 2000).

Examples of effective community action can be seen in a range of community programs to protect neighbourhoods from crime and injury. The 'Neighbourhood Watch' program is perhaps the best known. Its strengths are that it is recognisable and widespread, and all members of the community where it has been introduced are able to recognise a safe location should the need arise. Similarly, community action spawned the US movement, Mothers Against Drink Driving (MADD), which has successfully attracted thousands of members who have been able to lobby government bodies for a range of improvements to road safety and harsher penalties for those who drink and drive. Mothers of young Indigenous people who have turned to alcohol abuse and then to violence have also lobbied for alcohol controls. However, some inequities exist between rural and urban communities, which unwittingly disadvantage Indigenous people (Hancock et al 1996). The goal of popular movements and the role of health professionals in supporting these must be to ensure that all people receive support and the opportunity to participate in planning for the development of their community.

Developing personal skills

One of the classic examples of developing personal skills has been the worldwide movement to include adults in the move toward lifelong learning. In some countries this is called the University of the Third Age. In the International Year of the Volunteer (2000), many adults were valued in a wide variety of ways for offering their personal skills to others. A number of initiatives begun under the banner of volunteerism are expected to endure as examples of mature-age people taking on leadership roles in the community. Some of these projects include supporting access to the skills of older workers through mentorship schemes, and increasing the visibility of the over-55s in the workplace and in sporting endeavours.

Many non-government organisations draw heavily on the personal experiences of adults, particularly in relation to quitting smoking, obesity control and alcohol abuse rehabilitation programs. Others use adult skills for support programs for victims of heart disease, stroke, cancers or other disabling conditions. These initiatives show true partnership arrangements, where those with first-hand experience exemplify grass-roots modelling of healthy behaviours, even if they have not been instigated until later in life or until life events have precipitated lifestyle change. Using the experience and expertise of adults in the community ensures the bottom-up approach to health promotion and empowerment of local community members. Where the work is voluntary, there is also promotion of human rights and equality, which is a measure of a community's self-worth (Patterson 2001).

Reorienting health services

Health care today must focus on developing personal skills in the community, as well as the need to shift the way health services are designed and delivered. The quality of a health care system can be judged on the ways it assists people to enact their roles as both providers and consumers of health services. This includes how well or how badly the services address inequalities, how they respond to people's expectations, and to what extent dignity, personal rights and freedoms are respected (WHO 2000).

Health planning needs to explore the optimal mix of epidemiological and surveillance information, cost effectiveness and delivery mechanisms that will achieve the breadth and scope required. Rodgers and MacMahon (1999) suggest that health planning could help address the disproportionate number of deaths from cardiovascular disease in the developing world, which is approximately three times greater than in the industrialised world. They calculate that if there was population-wide hypertension screening and treatment, the world could avert about one million deaths per year in China alone (Rodgers & McMahon 1999). If these people were also convinced to quit smoking, the figures could predict even higher rates of disability years gained.

We also need to ensure the appropriate mix of individuals and groups to work towards health goals (St Louis, Wasserheit & Gayle 1997). Preventative services must be tailored to the needs of the population subgroup, whether rural, urban, Indigenous or non-Indigenous. Most importantly, health services, whether for care or prevention, must be coordinated, so that health departments do not become compartmentalised and thus lose sight of the context within which health can be created and sustained. Only by working in partnership with community-based organisations, employers, churches, service clubs and neighbourhoods, and by reorienting health services to the setting in which they will be most acceptable to people, will we achieve the level of health that the population of the twenty-first century deserves.

thinking critically

Adult health

1 Identify the three lifestyle issues most important to the health of adults.

2 Describe how you would plan a health promotion campaign to encourage greater physical activity among a group of 40–45 year old women.

3 Identify five important issues that must be addressed in a program to encourage sexual health among those at risk.

4 Design a set of strategies for reducing the rate of criminal violence in your community.

5 Explain the implications of the HGP for the population of your community.

6 Discuss the relevance of the burden of illness, injury and disability in the adult population to community health promotion strategies.

REFERENCES

Andrews, B., Oates, F. & Naden, P. (1997). Smoking among Aboriginal health workers: findings of a 1995 survey in Western New South Wales. *Australian and New Zealand Journal of Public Health*, 21(7): 789–91.

Andrews, G., Sanderson, K. & Beard, J. (1998). Burden of disease. Methods of calculating disability from mental disorder. *British Journal of Psychiatry*, 173: 123–31.

Austin, M., Peyser, P. & Khoury, M. (2000). The interface of genetics and public health: research and educational challenges. *Annual Review of Public Health*, 21: 81–99.

Australian Institute of Health and Welfare (AIHW) (1996a). *Australia's Health, 1996*. Canberra: AGPS.

—— (1996b). *Tobacco Use and its Health Impact in Australia*. Canberra: AGPS.

—— (2000). *Australia's Health 2000*. Canberra: AGPS.

—— (2001). *Heart, Stroke and Vascular Diseases, Australian Facts 2001*. Canberra: AIHW.

Beach, J., Dennis, J., Avery, A., Bromly, C., Ward, R. et al (1996). An epidemiologic investigation of asthma in welders. *American Journal of Respiratory Critical Care Medicine*, 154: 1394–400.

Breslau, N., Peterson, E., Schultz, L., Andreski, P. & Chilcoat, H. (1996). Are smokers with alcohol disorders less likely to quit? *American Journal of Public Health*, 86(7): 985–90.

Brown, A., Christie, D., Taylor, R, Seccombe, M. & Coates, M. (1997). The occurrence of cancer in a cohort of New South Wales coal miners. *Australian and New Zealand Journal of Public Health*, 21(1): 29–32.

Bruce, N., Perez-Padilla, R. & Albalak, R. (2000). Indoor air pollution in developing countries: a major environmental and public health challenge. *Bulletin of the World Health Organization*, 78(9): 1078–101.

Calvert, D. & Ewan, C. (1995). Risks to health, risk management and environmental health impact assessment. Editorial. *Australian Journal of Public Health*, 19(4): 325–6.

Choi, K. & Catania, J. (1996). Changes in multiple sexual partnerships, HIV testing, and condom use among US heterosexuals 18 to 49 years of age, 1990 and 1992. *American Journal of Public Health*, 86(4): 554–6.

Crowley, S., Dunt, D. & Day, N. (1995). Cost-effectiveness of alternative interventions for the prevention and treatment of coronary heart disease. *Australian Journal of Public Health*, 19(4): 336–46.

Dobson, A., Porteous, J., McElduff, P. & Alexander, H. (1997). Whose diet has changed? *Australian and New Zealand Journal of Public Health*, 21(2): 147–54.

English, R., Najman, J. & Bennett, S. (1997). Dietary intake of Australian smokers and nonsmokers. *Australian and New Zealand Journal of Public Health*, 21(2): 141–6.

Escobedo, L. & Peddicord, J. (1996). Smoking prevalence in US birth cohorts: the influence of gender and education. *American Journal of Public Health*, 86(2): 231–6.

Fielding, J., Lave, L. & Starfield, B. (2000). Preface. *Annual Review of Public Health*, 21: v–vi.

French, S., Story, M. & Jeffery, R. (2001). Environmental influences on eating and physical activity. *Annual Review of Public Health*, 22: 309–35.

Freudenberg, N. (2000). Health promotion in the city: a review of the current pratice and future prospects in the United States. *Annual Review of Public Health*, 21: 473–503.

Galuska, D., Serdula, M., Pamuk, E., Siegel, P & Byers, T. (1996). Trends in overweight among US adults from 1987 to 1993: a multistate telephone survey. *American Journal of Public Health*, 86(12): 1729–35.

Gardiner, J., Norton, R. & Alpers, P. (1996). Nonfatal firearm misuse: licence status of perpetrators and legality of the firearms. *Australian and New Zealand Journal of Public Health*, 20(5): 479–82.

Guerzoni, E. (1996). Getting physical. *Sport Health*, 14(4): 10–11.

Gwatkin, D., Guillot, M. & Heuveline, P. (1999). The burden of disease among the global poor. *The Lancet*, 354: 586–9.

Haglund, M. (1997). *The next wave of the tobacco epidemic: women*. Stockholm: National Institute of Public Health.

Hamilton, V., Levinton, C., St Pierre, Y. & Grimard, F. (1997). The effect of tobacco tax cuts on cigarette smoking in Canada. *Canadian Medical Association Journal*, 156: 187–91.

Hancock, L., Sanson-Fischer, R., Redman, S., Reid, A. & Tripoli, D. (1996). Knowledge of cancer risk reduction practices in rural towns in New South Wales. *Australian and New Zealand Journal of Public Health*, 20(5): 529–37.

Jeffery, R. & French, S. (1996). Socioeconomic status and weight control practices among 20 to 45 year old women. *American Journal of Public Health*, 86(7): 1005–10.

Johnson, N., Boyle, C. & Heller, R. (1995). Leisure-time physical activity and other health behaviours: are they related? *Australian Journal of Public Health*, 19(10): 69–75.

Kault, D. (1996). Assessing the national HIV/AIDS strategy evaluation. *Australian and New Zealand Journal of Public Health*, 20(4): 347–51.

Kleinman, A. (1988). *The Illness Narratives*. New York: Basic Books.

Knuiman, M., Jamrozik, K., Welborn, T., Bulsara, M., Divitni, M. & Whittall, D. (1995). Age and secular trends in risk factors for cardiovascular disease in Busselton. *Australian Journal of Public Health*, 19(4): 375–82.

Kokevinas, M., Anto, J., Soriano, J., Tobias, A., Burney, P. & the Spanish Group of the European Asthma Study (1996). The risk of asthma attributable to occupational exposures—a population-based study in Spain. *American Journal of Respiratory and Critical Care Medicine*, 154: 137–43.

Krug, E., Sharma, G. & Lozano, R. (2000). The global burden of injuries. *American Journal of Public Health*, 90(4): 523–6.

Lee, P. & Paxman, D. (1997). Reinventing public health. *Annual Review of Public Health*, 18: 1–35.

Li, Y., Gold, J., McDonald, A. & Kaldor, J. (1996). Demographic pattern of AIDS in Australia, 1991 to 1993. *Australian and New Zealand Journal of Public Health*, 20(4): 421–25.

Margetts, B. & Jackson, A. (1993). Interactions between people's diet and their smoking habits: the dietary and nutritional survey of British adults. *British Medical Journal*, 307: 1381–4.

Mathers, C., Vos, E., Stevenson, C. & Begg, S. (2000). The Australian Burden of Disease Study: measuring the loss of health from diseases, injuries and risk factors. *Medical Journal of Australia*, 172: 592–6.

McGinnis, J. & Foege, W. (1993). Actual causes of death in the United States. *Journal of the American Medical Association*, 269: 2207–12.

McMichael, A. (2000). The urban environment and health in a world of increasing globalization: issues for developing countries. *Bulletin of the World Health Organization*, 78(9): 1117–24.

Mechanic, D. (1999). Issues in promoting health. *Social Science and Medicine*, 48: 711–18.

Menken, M., Munsat, T. & Toole, J. (2000). The global burden of disease study: implications for neurology. *Archives of Neurology*, 57: 418–20.

Mittelmark, M. (2001). Promoting social responsibility for health: health impact assessment and healthy public policy at the community level. *Health Promotion International*, 16(3): 269–74.

Murray, C. & Lopez, A. (1997). Global mortality, disability, and the contribution of risk factors. Global Burden of Disease Study. *The Lancet*, 349 (10 May): 1347–52.

National Health & Medical Research Council (NH&MRC) (1999). Paradigm shift—injury. From problem to solution. New research directions. Canberra: NH&MRC.

Narayan, K., Chadha, S., Hanson, R., Tandon, R., Shekhawat, S., Fernandes, R. & Gopinath, N. (1996). Prevalence and patterns of smoking in urban India. *British Medical Journal*, 7046(312): 1576–9.

Omenn, G. (1996). Putting environmental risks in a public health context. *Public Health Reports*, 111: 514–16.

—— (2000). Public health genetics: an emerging interdisciplinary field for the post-genomic era. *Annual Review of Public Health*, 21: 1–13.

Paffenbarger, R., Hyde, R., Wing, A. & Lee, I. (1993). The association of changes in physical activity level and other lifestyle characteristics with mortality among men. *New England Journal of Medicine*, 328: 538–45.

Patterson, E. (ed) (2001). Disability Support Service Volunteers' Education Package. Gold Coast: Griffith University.

Patz, J., Engelberg, D. & Last, J. (2000). The effects of changing weather on public health. *Annual Review of Public Health*, 21: 271–307.

Peters, R. (1996). Australia's new gun laws: preventing the backslide. *Australian and New Zealand Journal of Public Health*, 20(4): 339–40.

Reutter, L. (2000). Socioeconomic determinants of health. In: M. Stewart (ed), *Community Nursing: Promoting Canadians' Health*, 2nd edn, Toronto: WB Saunders, pp 174–93.

Rodgers, A. & MacMahon, S. (1999). Blood pressure and the global burden of cardiovascular disease. *Clinical and Experimental Hypertension*, 21(5/6): 543–52.

Sikkema, K., Heckman, T., Kelly, J., Anderson, E., Winett, R., Soloman, L., Wagstaff, D., Roffman, R., Perry, M., Cargill, V., Crumble, D., Fuqua, R., Norman, A. & Mercer, M. (1996). HIV risk behaviors among women living in low-income, inner-city housing developments. *American Journal of Public Health*, 86(8): 1123–8.

Siracusa, A., Kennedy, S., DyBuncio, A., Lin, F., Marabini, A. & Chan-Yeung, M. (1995). Prevalence and predictors of asthma in working groups in British Columbia. *American Journal of Industrial Medicine*, 28: 411–23.

Smith, K., Corvalan, C. & Kjellstrom, T. (1999). How much global ill health is attributable to environmental factors? *Epidemiology*, 10(5): 573–84.

St Louis, M., Wasserheit, J. & Gayle, H. (1997). Editorial: Janus considers the HIV pandemic—harnessing recent advances to enhance AIDS prevention. *American Journal of Public Health*, 87(1): 10–11.

Statistics Canada (2001). Health indicators. Ottawa: Canadian Institute for Health Information.

Taylor, R. & Coates, M. (1997). Breast cancer five-year survival in New South Wales women, 1972 to 1991. *Australian and New Zealand Journal of Public Health*, 21(2): 199–205.

United Kingdom, Department of Transport (1996). Road Accidents in Great Britain 1995—The Casualty Report. London: HMSO.

United Nations Programme on HIV/AIDS (UNAIDS). AIDS Epidemic update. Geneva: UN/WHO.

Whipple, B. & Walsh Scura, K. (1996). The overlooked epidemic: HIV in older adults. *American Journal of Nursing*, 6(2): 6020–2.

World Health Organization (WHO) (1997a). Message from the Director-General of the WHO for World No-Tobacco Day 1997. Geneva: WHO.

—— (1997b). The Jakarta Charter for Health Promotion for the twenty-first century. Geneva: WHO.

—— (1999). The World Health Report 1999. Making a Difference. Geneva: WHO.

—— (2000). World Health Report 2000. Health systems. Improving Performance. Geneva: WHO.

—— (2001a). WHO Report 2001: Global Tuberculosis Control. Geneva: Communicable Diseases, WHO.

—— (2001b). World Health Report 2001. Mental Health. New Understandings, new hope. Geneva: WHO.

Wynder, E. & Muscat, J. (1995). The changing epidemiology of smoking and lung cancer histology. *Environmental Health Perspectives*, 103(8) Suppl: 143–8.

Young, D., Haskell, W., Taylor, C. & Fortmann, S. (1996). Effect of community health education on physical activity knowledge, activity and behavior. *American Journal of Epidemiology*, 144(3): 264–74.

Yu, E., Xie, Q., Zhang, K., Lu, P. & Chan, L. (1996). HIV infection and AIDS in China, 1985 through 1994. *American Journal of Public Health*, 86(8): 1116–22.

Zhu, B., Liu, M., Shelton, D., Liu, S. & Giovino, G. (1996). Cigarette smoking and risk factors among elementary school students in Beijing, *American Journal of Public Health*, 86(3): 368–75.

Zierler, S. & Krieger, N. (1997). Reframing women's risk: social inequalities and HIV infection. *Annual Review of Public Health*, 18: 401–36.

CHAPTER 8

Healthy
ageing

ntroduction   The terms 'ageing' and 'elderly' were once used as an indication that a person had begun the downhill journey to the end of life. Yet, today, as the world experiences a proliferation of medical and health-sustaining knowledge and technology, ageing has taken on a new connotation: that of unexplored possibilities. Many people over age 65 lead healthy and productive lives, some thriving in ways they could not during their middle years when their life circumstances prevented them from achieving a balance between work, recreation and family responsibilities.

Where once 65 was thought to be the beginning of the *older* stage of life, and thus a state of *decline* in health and wellness, today we do not consider a person older until they have reached at least a decade beyond that. Even then, the emphasis in health care has shifted from the 'damage control' approach of previous times, to advocating for health enhancement in the latter stage of life. This new way of thinking about older people is based on a contention that the so-called inevitable effects of ageing have been overestimated, while the modifying effects of diet, physical exercise, personal habits, coping styles, environment and psychosocial factors have been underestimated (Seedsman 1995). New technologies have also challenged perceptions of ageing, particularly since the introduction of gene therapy and other innovations that flow from the Human Genome Project. This chapter considers the social determinants of ageing, and the risks and enrichments confronted by societies with an ageing population. The burden of illness, injury and disability is addressed with a view to ensuring that ageing members of our society can be appropriately cared for by those of us who continue to benefit from their previous and current contributions to our human, social and economic capital.

objectives   **By the end of this chapter you will be able to:**

1   Describe the most important influences on health and wellness among the population over age 65

2   Discuss the concept of ageism and its implications for health care

3   Explain the importance of understanding the burden of illness, injury and disability among older persons

4   Explain the implications of understanding older persons' experiences of life and life transitions

5   Identify health promotion strategies for the ageing population using the Ottawa Charter for Health Promotion.

Healthy
older people

The most significant challenge for community health and development in the future will be caring for older people. They are the fastest-growing population group in all countries of the world, particularly the 'oldest old', those over 80 years of age (WHO 1999a). Europe continues to retain its reputation as the 'oldest old' part of the world, with an expectation that 25 per cent of the population will be over age 65 by the year 2020 (WHO 1999b). Even at the younger end of the scale, nearly one million people cross the 60-year-old threshold every month (ICN 2001). Worldwide, older persons constitute more than 580 million people and this is projected to increase to 1000 million by the year 2020 (WHO 1999a).

In all industrialised countries, demographers have identified a population 'bulge' of people over the age of 65, commonly referred to as 'population ageing'. The global population has aged because of sustained drops in fertility or birth rates, compounded by significant reductions in infant and adult mortality (Lloyd-Sherlock 2000; Randel, German & Ewing 2000). Australia,

New Zealand, Canada and the United States have a lower level of ageing (at around 12 per cent of the population) than many European countries (ABS 1999a; Craig 2000). Sweden has the highest proportion at 18 per cent, followed by Italy (17%), the United Kingdom and Greece (16%), Japan and a number of other European countries (15%) (ABS 1999a; Bergmark, Parker & Thorslund 2000; Castles 2000). One exception to this trend is Africa, where high rates of HIV/AIDS among younger groups have caused an uneven surge in demographic ageing. Compared to other countries, relatively few people in sub-Saharan Africa live to old age, resulting in a larger proportion of young people (Lloyd-Sherlock 2000).

Another aspect of population ageing shows differences according to gender. It is a well-known fact that women tend to live longer than men, but in the United States and some European countries, this is exaggerated by the high rate of violence and accidents among young males, which has left a disproportionately high number of females among older groups. Again, there are exceptions—in India, for example, where the relative socioeconomic disadvantage of women has had a negative effect on life expectancy, so that there are actually more older males than females (Lloyd-Sherlock 2000). The most remarkable fact about ageing in these countries is that by 2025, two-thirds of the world's older people will be in developing countries and most of them will be women (Randel et al 2000; WHO 1999b).

In order to promote health for older people, it is important to gain an understanding of the cumulative effects of risk factors and the burden of illness, injury and disability so that goals for health can be devised accordingly. Understanding the risks associated with ageing also assists health planning, given that older people utilise health care services to a proportionately greater extent than any other population group.

The burden of
illness, injury and disability
for older persons

The same conditions mentioned in Chapter 7 are those most commonly seen in the elderly, with cardiovascular and mental health disorders topping the overall list for most industrialised countries (WHO 2001). The burden of disability in countries like Australia increases with age, from approximately 4 per cent at age 0–4 to 84 per cent for those over age 85 (ABS 2000). Because of the past century's virtual explosion of health knowledge and technologies, many older people are now living longer, but with some type of disability. American projections reveal that women who reach their 65th birthday can expect to live another 19 years and men another 15.8 years (Belza & Wooding Baker 2000). This is similar to life expectancy in both Canada and Australia, where those aged 65 are expected to reach the age of 85 for females, and 81 for males (AIHW 2000; Statistics Canada 2001). The most common causes of mortality among older people are diseases of the circulatory system, malignant neoplasms and respiratory diseases (AIHW 2000).

By the time a person reaches age 65, the cumulative risk from unhealthy lifestyles is usually evident. Interactions between various risk factors that include the impact of low SES, hypertension, high blood pressure and/or cholesterol, inactivity, inappropriate diet, alcohol and/or other drug dependence and tobacco smoking conspire to thwart the process of healthy ageing. In the developing countries there is a double burden of illness, in that population ageing is also accompanied by persistent poverty (WHO 2001).

Although not all lifestyle factors are responsive to behaviour change, some older people *do* change their risky behaviours, especially where they have received a 'wake-up call' at the onset of a disease such as heart disease, diabetes or arthritis. To some extent, this differs according to gender. In Australia, for example, older men tend to participate in exercise to a greater degree than women. Many men and women continue to eat an unhealthy diet, which has led to a gradual increase in the proportion of people over 65 who are overweight (48 per cent of men and 43 per cent of women). However, this same age group reduced tobacco consumption throughout the latter part of the 1990s to 14 per cent among males and 9 per cent among females (ABS 1999b). This trend is also evident among older smokers in Canada, where only 12 per cent of those aged 65 and over now smoke (Craig 2000).

Among the population over age 65, the main disabling conditions are those that restrict physical activity, such as arthritis, circulatory and musculoskeletal conditions, and sensory problems (diseases of the eye or ear). Mental disability, including dementia and Alzheimer's disease, are the major causes of disability in the oldest old (over 80 years) (AIHW 2000; WHO 2001). More than half of both women and men have some type of disability after age 65, most involving a core activity restriction in bathing, dressing, eating, getting out of a chair or bed, walking, using public transportation or communicating with others (ABS 1999b). Approximately 60 per cent of these people have formal assistance with these difficulties, while more than 80 per cent are assisted by family members or friends (ABS 2000). This reflects a high proportion of people who continue to live in private dwellings after age 65 (91%). To some extent, this places a burden of care on their partners, who are also likely to be over age 65 (ABS 2000).

Carers spend varying amounts of time in the caring role, depending on a range of cultural and economic factors. In Japan, for example, where life expectancy is the highest in the world, it is customary to provide most care for ill or disabled family members in the home (Murashima et al 1999). In that country and many others, women account for more than half the family carers (ABS 1999c; Murashima et al 1999). This creates health risks for the carer, who often has disrupted sleep patterns, especially if they are caring for a person with mental health needs. In this case there is usually little opportunity to maintain social and emotional health. Caring also causes financial hardship for many families (ABS 1999c). However, most reports from carers express a willingness to provide care on the basis that it is a family responsibility, and this attitude is a reflection of social solidarity (ABS 1999c).

Healthy
ageing

Healthy ageing means having minimal disability and dysfunction, a manageable amount of stress, the support of family and friends, a feeling of being valued, and adequate resources to cope with the requirements of daily living. Although many people develop functional disabilities with increasing age, most have also developed ways of coping with illness or incapacity from the wisdom that comes from life experiences and personal resourcefulness. A lifetime of activity, both mental and physical, a balanced diet, a sense of humour, gainful employment and an environment conducive to healthy lifestyles seem to insulate people against the worst effects of cardiovascular diseases, cancers, mental illnesses and other life-limiting disabilities or dysfunction. This is greatly enhanced by living in a place where social support systems accommodate the long-term needs of the population, including provision for lifelong education, income security, retirement planning and a responsive health care system, and where environmental elements are conducive to health (AIHW 2000).

Hooyman and Kiyak (1999) use the concept of *environmental press* to explain the interface between an older person and his or her environment. Environmental press has a reciprocal relationship with personal competence, and varies according to the setting. In an institutional setting where an individual does not have to take responsibility for self-care, and where there are few resources and other people to stimulate the senses or challenge the mind, there is low environmental press. Living in a multigenerational household in which the older person plays a pivotal role generates high environmental press. According to the theory, individuals perform at their maximum level when the environmental press slightly exceeds the level at which they adapt; that is, where the environment challenges them to test their limits but does not overwhelm them. This is where the reciprocity comes in. Having a large number of people around or moving to a new environment increases the environmental demands, requiring the person to adapt in order to maintain personal competence. However, as with all of us, there are different thresholds of tolerance. It is logical to assume that the lower physical competence of those with multiple physical disabilities and chronic illnesses will limit the level of other demands with which he or she can cope (Hooyman & Kiyak 1999).

Socioeconomic factors
in healthy ageing

As with all other population groups, socioeconomic factors have a profound influence on older persons' health. The effects of low SES become acute as a person reaches that stage of disability that requires some type of care. This is a greater problem in some countries than others, depending on whether or not government policies direct funding for this type of assistance from the tax base

(McCallum 1999). In Japan, for example, ageing family members have been looked after from within a culture of extended families who maintain a high level of personal savings intended for this purpose. Japan has also maintained a high rate of employment of older workers, who receive government subsidies for remaining in the workforce (McCallum 1999). This is quite a different situation to that of many other industrialised countries, where older workers are victims of 'downsizing' or 'rightsizing' and now represent an increasingly large proportion of job seekers.

At a global level, the World Bank and the OECD Secretariat have raised alarms over the population ageing situation (OECD 1996; World Bank 1994). They propose that population ageing has been, and will continue to be, a drain on public expenditure through increased spending on pensions, health care and services for the elderly and, indirectly, by increasing levels of public indebtedness. Both agencies caution that this will make many countries vulnerable to intractable financial problems because of the spiral of increasing debt interest payments that will be incurred to fund services for the elderly (OECD 1996; World Bank 1994). Further reports from Europe have raised alarms because of the impending ageing of the post-war 'baby boomer' generation. From 2010 onwards, there will be a long period of decline in the working age population in most of the countries of the European Union (Europe Information Service 2001). This report suggests that from the year 2010, the dependency ratio— measured by the number of inactive to active workers in the population—will rise to a maximum of 1:40 in the year 2040, which for many countries will be financially untenable.

These international reports have sparked a moral panic, as population forecasts indicate increasing longevity in a large number of countries (Hargreaves 2000). Castles (2000) criticises the apocalyptic tone of much of the population ageing debate, suggesting that comparative data on health care expenditure among OECD countries show little correspondence between health care costs and population ageing, with the exception of financing pensions. His analysis of population ageing in relation to public spending over three decades suggests that government spending patterns have in the past been responsive to a wide range of factors. He contends that the financial obligations of any given country cannot revolve around population ageing, especially when most countries have been able to finance increases in pensions without incurring unreasonable public debt (Castles 2000). Vincent and Mudrovcic (2000) agree that there needs to be clearer articulation of the problems of an ageing population. Rather than describe population ageing as globally problematic, it would be more useful to examine ageing in the context of family and community structures that provide a wide range of support for their older members. To not do so would be ageist.

Ageism

Despite the fact that ageing is a normal part of life, many older persons are subjected to *ageism*. Ageism is a type of discrimination against older people on the basis of a number of misconceptions about their characteristics, attitudes and abilities. Some of the most common of these include believing that older people are inherently weak, have diminished physical and mental capabilities, are non-productive, resistant to change and dependent on others (Spradley & Allender 1996). Like younger people, the ageing population have physical, spiritual, psychological, social and cultural needs, but sometimes these are stereotyped as deficiencies. For example, an older person's irritability may be dismissed as something that occurs with ageing, when in fact it may be due to personality characteristics or a response to provocation, pain, disability or recent life events. Likewise, we all have moments of forgetfulness, but an older person's casual memory slip may be labelled as dementia or Alzheimer's disease, when it may be due to other factors such as motivation, the saliency of remembering, or personal interest (Wilkinson 1996).

Studies of ageism indicate that older people are discriminated against, even by older people themselves (Minichiello, Browne & Kendig 2000). Our service orientation in health care tends to focus more on illness care than support for older people to reach their potential. This reinforces social relations in which younger people are inclined to use patronising verbal and non-verbal communication (Minichiello et al 2000). To counter this type of stereotyping, the onus is on health professionals, family members and members of the general public to understand the important influence of a person's life biography and life events, on health. This 'life cycle' approach would help all members of society to understand life as realistically as it is experienced (Hudson-Rodd 2000).

Erickson's model of human life cycle stages contends that we all have certain characteristic 'crises' to resolve at various stages of development. In the context of his theoretical framework, the major life crisis of old age is the struggle between integrity and despair, the resolution of which is expected to produce wisdom. But this may be an over-generalisation of what actually occurs, because of wide variability among people's individual responses to the circumstances of their lives (Wilkinson 1996). Some older individuals experience entirely different life crises, and their responses may be anything but despair. Attitudes vary widely, and while some people do not consider themselves old at 80, others believe they have aged at 50.

Sometimes it is difficult to separate normal from pathological ageing because of variability in ethnicity, race and sociocultural affiliation. We know that heredity and lifestyle factors are important influences on a person's development throughout the lifespan, including the older years. A person's 'biological clock' for longevity is set at birth, even though it is influenced during life by lifestyle factors (smoking, diet, exercise), social factors and medical events. The way older people respond to their social, cultural and physical environment is highly individualistic and represents a composite of responses to stress, life events, behaviours and social support (Nilsson 1996).

Fortunately, there are a growing number of voices arguing for recognition of the 'normality' of ageing in the political, economic and policy arenas, as well as in health care (Borowski, Encel & Ozanne 1997; Randel et al 1999). Two distinct demographic trends are acknowledged by all sides of the debate: there will be a dramatic increase in the oldest old, and a 'boomer bulge'. However, the view that the larger numbers of old persons will lead to untenable service demands may not be quite so predictable, given the current general good health of those in their middle years. The higher rate of labour force participation among women baby boomers, and the consequent high rates of dual-income families have also put this group in a better financial position than previous generations (ABS 1999d). Combined with higher levels of private income and asset holdings, good health, availability of family and community supports, the situation sounds quite manageable if social values, attitudes and government policy are mindful of the needs of the older population (ABS 1999d).

What may eventuate from population ageing is a bimodal distribution of older people using the health system. One group can be expected to manifest a compression of morbidity related to the wearing out of organ systems at around age 100. The others may not live quite so long, but will remain generally healthy as their lifestyles help them cope with chronic illness and/or disabilities that would have been fatal years ago (Hooyman & Kiyak 1999). So, rather than blowing health costs out, perhaps the boomer generation will, in fact, have lower than expected health care expenditures and less reliance on long-term care services. This is also the opinion of Swedish analysts, who believe the elderly have been caught in the crossfire between population ageing and diminishing national resources (Bergmark et al 2000). In that country, which leads the world in the proportion of older people among the population, it is imperative to clarify the issues. The researchers argue that governments have not been as transparent as they should be in prioritising resource allocations. Instead, political processes are shaped through a complex 'pattern of manifest ambitions, tactical considerations, compromise and political horse-trading' (Bergmark et al 2000, p 315). They believe that the majority of pensioners are healthy and independent, with little need for medical or social services. Governments should value this, rewarding previous contributions to society made by older citizens. This would signal greater opportunity for distributive justice and add considerably to the social capital of any country (Bergmark et al 2000).

It is important to ensure that planning for an ageing future takes place in context. In the affluent countries, people are concerned about protecting inheritance of property, the adequacy of pensions and access to evolving health technologies. One of the positive outcomes of population ageing may be enhanced scientific, technological and economic developments that lead to more effective control of degenerative diseases and the ageing process (Horiuchi, in Hargreaves 2000). In developing countries, however, the ageing debate is quite different. It is about neglect, exclusion, vulnerability and poverty (Randel et al 1999). Randel and colleagues argue that we should analyse the potential, rather than the liability, of older people, especially given that they promote economic growth through national pension schemes, and are also more reliable than younger people in repaying credit.

Researchers are beginning to argue that appropriate health services for older people require intergenerational investment, in which age-based services and other social programs play an integral part (Borowski et al 1997; Hooyman & Kiyak 1999). This is based on the assumption that in any society, the relative hard times of one generation cannot be measured against the relative prosperity of another, so all generations need to identify how they can contribute to looking after the needs of the vulnerable. Otherwise one group will be at risk of erosion of citizenship, a peril that is rapidly closing in on the older generation (Borowski et al 1997). Intergenerational equity requires both horizontal and vertical alliances that would see young, old and middle-aged people seek mutually helpful health care solutions for a better future (Borowski et al 1997; Hooyman & Kiyak 1999; WHO 1999a).

Mental
illness

More than 400 million people worldwide suffer from some form of mental disorder (WHO 2001). The most prevalent among mental illnesses is depression, which is also reversible with treatment (Anderson 2001; Craig 2000; Rubenstein & Nahas 1998; WHO 2001). One of the outcomes of major depression in older people has been a variable but generally increased rate in suicides among the elderly. Although WHO has been trying to clarify which factors place older people most at risk of suicide, variability in surveillance has made this difficult, and in some cases the figures are masked by population-based data (Anderson 2001; WHO 2001). It may be that the real rates of suicide among the elderly have not increased, but with the lifting of taboos surrounding discussion of assisted death and suicide, there is now wider recognition of the problem.

Alzheimer's disease is one of the most devastating conditions of ageing, because it is both absolute and insidious. By the year 2020, some 80 million people will suffer from Alzheimer's in Africa, Asia and Latin America alone. The disease occurs most frequently in those over age 65 and its incidence doubles every five years with advancing age (WHO 2001). Along with other dementia states, Alzheimer's is the sixth leading cause of disease burden in Australia, accounting for 3.5 per cent of the burden of disease (AIHW 2000). Alzheimer's is a form of dementia in which a person is unable to rely on the past as a blueprint for the present or future, because they have forgotten everything learned in their earlier life. As the disease develops, the person loses the capacity for judgement and reasoning and, in some cases, is unaware that she or he is not functioning normally. In most cases, other family members have also been unaware that their elderly family member was having memory lapses, and so when the disease is diagnosed it is usually quite advanced. One of the most difficult challenges of Alzheimer's is the amount of stress placed on family caregivers, who often have to deal with intense agitation and anxiety on a daily basis. Consequently, many caregivers of family members with Alzheimer's are at risk of higher rates of depression than those found in the general population (Paveza, VandeWeerd & Bruschi 2000).

Another problem is that there are non-modifiable risk factors such as age and genetics among its causative agents, which make prevention difficult. Because of women's greater longevity they encounter a greater risk for Alzheimer's than men. Primary prevention of Alzheimer's is not possible at present, although there is some indication that gene therapies may be developed in future. Current health promotion strategies should therefore be directed at supporting the family caregivers and ensuring the safety and security of the person suffering from the disease. This includes maintaining function and security for sufferers, reorganising their routines to maximise function, minimising disturbances associated with the disease, such as agitation and depression, and promoting healthy lifestyles as much as possible (WHO 2001).

Medication
use

In the industrialised world, older people use health services more frequently than other age groups (WHO 2000; ABS 2000). Their use of services varies according to a range of factors, including SES, the health care system and its insurance arrangements, rurality, cultural norms, the extent to which they prefer to care for their own health needs, and their satisfaction with available services and service providers.

The most frequent reason for older persons accessing the health care system is related to medications. In Australia, orthodox medications are regularly used by persons aged 65 or more, with the most common usage (87.3%) recorded for those over age 75 (AIHW 2000). This is approximately similar to the situation in Canada, where 81 per cent of the non-institutionalised population over age 65 live with some form of chronic illness, many requiring medication (Craig 2000). For older people who do develop chronic illnesses, often the most difficult aspect of their condition is coping with medications. This may become an even greater problem in the future, as new pharmaceuticals are developed for gene therapy trials or, beyond this, to where pharmacological agents that avert or treat various chronic diseases gain acceptance among the medical community (Munro 2002).

Taking medications, especially where multiple drugs are required for one or a combination of conditions, is a particular source of distress among older people. For those with few problems, a medication regime may be relatively straightforward; however, as older people develop multiple problems or an exacerbation of an existing condition, they may find themselves referred to a number of health services, often for specialised diagnosis. In many cases, one drug is added to another, with one prescriber being unaware of the medications already being taken. This is as much a function of poor case management as the older person's inability to understand and explain his or her routine medication use. The result is *polypharmacy*, or multiple drug taking, which can have disastrous results, as the case opposite illustrates.

case study…

Polypharmacy

Mrs Griffin was 67 when she was diagnosed with diabetes mellitus. She had experienced several episodes of near-fainting, and each time it happened she would take a double dose of the arthritis medication that she had been taking for twenty years, and lie down until she felt better. Because she was also thirsty, she would also have a drink, and if it was late afternoon this would be a little nip of sherry, or a 'shandy' (beer and ginger ale). She also continued to take her thyroid medication, a 'silver compound' she got from the herbalist, sleeping pills at night, and some other tablets she had brought from the farm because her deceased husband used to take them to 'make his blood richer'. The day she was diagnosed with diabetes, she had had a more serious spell than previously, and fell unconscious. Her daughter took her to the emergency department of the local hospital, where she was assessed by an internist, prescribed an insulin regime and referred to the diabetes educator for guidance. Her GP was notified, but she decided not to visit him after her discharge from hospital, because all he ever did was take her blood pressure, tell her to go on a diet and send her the bill. Each time she took a trip back home to the bush she saw the country doctor, who gave her the same reassurance as always: she would 'live forever'. Besides, the diabetes educator would make sure she was okay.

About six months after her diagnosis, she felt she had accomplished a manageable balance of diet, exercise and the insulin tablets, so she went on a tropical vacation. While there, she was severely traumatised by a toxic insect bite. Within hours she had been admitted to hospital, where she suffered a mild stroke. She became severely depressed and never quite bounced back to normal after the stroke. She was put on anti-depressants for her mood states, an anti-hypertensive medication for her blood pressure, and returned home within one month. Three months later, she had a massive coronary and died on the way to the hospital. She had just had her 70th birthday. When the family sorted through her medications and contacted the GP, he was shocked to learn of the arsenal of medicines she had been taking on a regular basis, especially when he learned she had been taking them in combination with alcohol and caffeine substances.

No one had thought to check to make sure she had discarded the old pills for the new ones or that she was aware of the interaction between her prescriptions, over-the-counter medications and alcohol. No one medical practitioner had coordinated her medication regime or examined the potential for synergistic reactions. For the past two years, her preoccupation had been with the diabetes. No one could provide any meaningful explanation for why her body just 'packed up'.

The case above is not extraordinary. Many older people consume multiple medications without understanding their function, the sequence in which they should be taken, the compound effects, or the toxicity and side effects of each. So recognition of the problem has been the first important step towards more careful monitoring of polypharmacy among the older age groups in the community. The next step is wider public dissemination of medication information so that families and community members can be made aware of the dangers of self-medication and take steps to more closely monitor the effects of drugs taken in combination with each other.

Gender issues
and ageing

Some patterns of health and illness are related to gender. To understand ageing it is important to separate out the differences as experienced by men and women (Hudson-Rodd 2001). At all stages of the life cycle, men and women have different rates and types of illness, but this is most marked in later life. Women live longer but are more likely than men to experience chronic ill health. They also report more recent and minor illnesses and have a higher prevalence of severe disability. The prevalence of disability is higher for older men than women, and men are more likely to report cancers, diseases of the nervous system and sense organs, and respiratory and digestive diseases than women, who are more likely to report circulatory system and genito-urinary disease. Men over age 65 are more likely to be overweight, to smoke and to drink at a higher level of risk than women (ABS 1999b; AIHW 2000; Moser 1997; WHO 1999a). Women over age 65 are more likely to experience the stress of caregiving, sometimes for both children and grandchildren as well as their partners. In some countries, including several Southeast Asian countries, women have experienced a lifetime of poor health, low education, low work-force participation, poor access to nutritious food, and other effects of discrimination that accumulate throughout the life cycle (Hudson-Rodd 2001). Some, but not all, experience clinical sequelae.

Many men also suffer from clinical outcomes of lifestyle and life circumstances. For example, many men with prostate cancer die *with*, rather than *from*, the disease and, for a variety of reasons, have not experienced symptoms. Similarly, menopause and the period just preceding it (perimenopause) are the most misunderstood life transitions for older women. Either or both stages may be accompanied by vasomotor symptoms such as hot flushes and sweats but, contrary to common understanding, this does not necessarily result in decreased health status, increased use of health services or increased levels of depression (McKinlay 1992).

One of the health risks that occurs beyond age 40, and accelerates in the years following menopause is osteoporosis, and this disease affects almost four times as many females as males (AIHW 2000). It is a condition where there is loss of bone mass that subsequently weakens the bones, increasing the risk of back pain and fractures. Although heredity plays a part in the development of the disease, most of the factors contributing to the condition are modifiable with healthy lifestyle practices, such as maintaining a diet high in calcium, regular, weight-bearing exercise and reducing alcohol and caffeine intakes (Rubinstein & Nahas 1998).

Osteoporosis is also influenced by hormonal factors, specifically the amount of oestrogen in a person's bloodstream. During the time of menopause the decline in oestrogen accelerates the loss of bone mass; however, this may also occur in younger women. Young women who have 'turned off' menstruation through anorexia, long-distance running or other excessive exercise for periods longer than six months, or those whose body fat mass drops below 15 per cent of their normal weight, may begin to lose bone mass (Beard & Curtis 1997). The best way to prevent loss of bone mass and conditions such as osteoporosis is to adopt a healthy diet rich in calcium from an early age. And one of the best ways to combat the symptoms of oestrogen loss is to engage in regular, weight-bearing exercise, seven days a week if possible, regardless of age.

At the onset of menopause, many women also begin oestrogen hormone replacement therapy (HRT) to guard against further bone loss or any of the other effects of declining oestrogen levels, including sleeplessness, irritability or weight gain. However, the cost-benefit of HRT is inconclusive and remains a matter for debate. The issues revolve around information from clinical trials showing a greater likelihood of some types of malignancies in some women who have taken HRT. However, it is not known what combination of factors actually causes the malignancies in question and what weighting can be given to HRT in precipitating the disease. In short, the jury is still out, and with further clarification emerging from genetic studies one could reasonably expect a growing body of evidence to help resolve the issues sometime during the next decade.

Physical
activity

As this century gets under way, fit, active older people are a visible and proliferating group among active communities. Not only are older people noticeably present among community fitness and recreation groups, but the extent of participation has changed to where many of those over age 65 can be seen in a wider range of physical fitness activities than in the past.

This new emphasis on healthy lifestyles for older people is a result of a combination of factors, including increased life expectancy, technological innovations designed to make exercise more manageable for older people, and greater information about the potential of exercise in maintaining health. Technology has not only provided medical practitioners with the means to treat illness efficiently and effectively, but it has enhanced the capacity of the population to be self-determined in maintaining health and positive lifestyle practices. Many retired persons access the internet, for example, to receive not only health-related information, but information on social and recreational groups that encourage a range of active pursuits.

Community attitudes towards health and healthy lifestyles have also encouraged older people to feel comfortable participating in outdoor activities, joining their younger counterparts in sporting and recreational ventures that would have been unattractive to their forebears. To some extent this is also culturally determined. Studies in countries where physical fitness is highly valued report greater participation in physical activities. For example, Canadian data reveal that, contrary to the expectations of health professionals, 84 per cent of the elderly report doing something to maintain or enhance their health, including lifestyle changes, staying active, maintaining relationships and attending to health-promoting practices (Craig 2000). Similarly, in the United States it is the group over age 55 who report the greatest walking frequency (Freudenberg, 2000).

Australia and New Zealand are also physically active nations. Studies in Australia report that participation in sport and physical activity has increased from around 27 per cent in 1996–97 to 30 per cent in 1999, with those aged 60–75 having higher rates of participation than 45–59 year olds (AIHW 2000). Discrepancies between Australian-born residents and migrants from other countries such as Europe, Asia, the Middle East and North Africa indicate a cultural divide, with migrants increasing their physical activity according to longer residency in Australia (AIHW 2000). This attests to the influence of a supportive environment on healthy lifestyle practices.

Consumer trends have further normalised physical activity for the over-65s, perhaps in recognition that many older people have disposable income for travel, leisure activities, sportswear, reading materials, software and a range of consumer goods tailored to their special needs.

Professional knowledge about physical training for older people is currently experiencing a period of unprecedented growth. Formerly, it was believed that loss of strength was inevitable with ageing, but recent research shows that resistance training not only improves strength but also improves functional ability, thereby decreasing the risk of falls.

Falls are the most common source of injury in the population of older people, and although they may be caused by a range of factors including poor vision, foot disorders, depression, acute illness, dementia, over-medication, alcohol use and environmental hazards, many occur simply because of a lack of muscle strength (AIHW 2000; Edwards 2000). Exercise specialists concur that strength training can help build back the muscle mass diminished due to the loss of testosterone and growth hormone that occurs with ageing. Unless joint pain or musculoskeletal conditions contravene, resistance training may be beneficial for both males and females in older age, provided their program is undertaken with a preliminary medical assessment and conducted under the supervision of specialist exercise trainers (Munnings 1993; Pollock 1992).

Fitness and
personal attitudes

Positive attitudes towards physical activity have had many advantages. Researchers have identified the benefits of regular physical exercise in the elderly as increased cardiovascular function, lower morbidity and mortality from cardiovascular disease, less body fat, better lipid profile, slowed progression of osteoporosis, better balance and coordination, better functional capacity, better nutrition and sleep and, in many cases, reduction of anxiety, depression and other psychological disorders (Finucane et al 1997; Rubinstein & Nahas 1998). Further benefits have been shown in improved cognitive as well as physiological function, and in providing opportunities for socialisation (Williams & Lord 1997; Yaffe et al 2001).

As with all age groups, individual differences determine the extent to which older people will choose one or another type of activity. One type of exercise rapidly becoming popular among older as well as middle-aged people is the Chinese martial art, Tai Chi. Besides improving balance by teaching people to rotate the body slowly and walk with a narrower stance, Tai Chi helps people recognise the limits of their stability. It provides a slow, rhythmic sense of movement that has been shown, in the few research studies conducted to date, to avert falls in older people (Wolf, Coogler & Xu 1997).

A healthy lifestyle can be described as a unique pattern of living adopted by an individual in terms of his or her 'interaction with self, the social and material world and the values, orientations and strategies that are utilised for coping with change' (Seedsman 1995, p 40). A healthy lifestyle thus reflects the overall fitness orientation and accomplishments of an individual. Being fit encompasses not only the traditional notions of cardiovascular and respiratory fitness, muscle strength, endurance, flexibility and body composition, but relaxation, enhanced emotional well-being and a positive self-image. A fitness *attitude* is thus as essential as a well-exercised body. It is sustained during ageing by investing in life and the idea that life, to its final stages, is an adventure (Seedsman 1995).

Sexuality
and ageing

Sexual activity is a natural part of life, and sexual patterns established as a young person often remain throughout life (Steinke 1997). Sexual relationships provide love, intimacy, closeness and physical pleasure, which enhance a person's quality of life (Sanders 1999). Declining frequency of sexual activity is reported in all studies on sexuality and ageing, but this may be due to factors such as lack of an available partner, negative stereotypes about ageing, illness, a lifestyle that has become too routine or boredom (Sanders 1999). For many older people, maintaining sexuality and sexual activity can help to counter other elements that compromise quality of life. As a person's middle adulthood roles of worker, spouse or parent decline, he or she may feel a sense of renewal by resuming or intensifying sexual activity. This can also create a sense of validation for an older person who is feeling somewhat marginalised because of the loss of these roles. For some, the greater sense of intimacy provides a buffer against other stresses associated with ageing, including personal and social losses, and so, despite decreasing frequency, many people continue to experience sexual satisfaction.

To date, research into sexuality as well as other emotional and social elements of ageing has focused on traditional measurement techniques, rather than the quality-of-life issues so important to older people. This has tended to diminish the psychosocial side of ageing and fails to capture the holistic way people age, as well as various aspects of life quality, including their experiences, expressions of sexuality or unmet needs (Steinke 1997). A further problem with measuring needs is that the lives of older people tend to be examined through the narrow lens of a political economy, which focuses on inevitable performance deficits rather than regenerative strategies. The research on burden of illness is a prime example. Although it has been helpful in some ways, in others, the search for formulaic approaches has worked against a health promotion agenda for older people, particularly with language such as the disability-adjusted life year (DALY). Thinking of health in terms of DALYs reflects an overt bias away from the aged towards more 'socially productive' cohorts (Paalman et al 1998). Research on topics such as psychosocial health, particularly sexuality, must be conducted according to methods of analysis that illuminate the linkages between biological and behavioural factors, and that capture the realities of older persons' situations rather than those that impose 'all-or-none' scaling techniques (Kennedy & Minkler 1998).

Widowhood
and loneliness

A person's coping strategies are developed over many years of dealing with life's stressors; however, some situations have a profound effect on emotional status, particularly if they are unexpected. One such situation is widowhood, which is becoming an important part of the ageing research agenda. Widowhood is a key life event, which varies on an individual basis and results in differential effects on the well-being, self-concept and morale of older people (Bennett 1997; Pinquart & Sorensen 2001; Zettel, Rook & Morgan 2001). Older people have usually had some exposure to death, through losing friends or other family members, but the loss of a spouse is often the most difficult to deal with. A study of widows in the United States and Germany found the increasing burden of financial distress to be a major stressor for many widows (Hungerford 2001).

Most older women who are widowed have usually held traditional family roles, and for this reason may find themselves deprived of their self-identity and social context once their partner is gone. Some become fearful of their own death, particularly if the death of their spouse was sudden (Straub & Roberts 2001). In many cases, their physical and mental health deteriorates, as they have no one to shop for, cook for and share meals with (Bennett & Vidal-Hall 2000). Older widows may also be unprepared for making financial decisions, obtaining necessary services and socialising as a single person, particularly if they have been highly dependent on their spouse throughout married life (Carr et al 2000). The health of older men also tends to decline with widowhood.

Some men find it almost impossible to perform routine household tasks and develop social networks that were formerly organised by their wives. In these cases, widowhood is more isolating for them than for their female counterparts (Davidson 2000; Gallagher, Thompson & Peterson 1982).

The loneliness that ensues from losing a partner can either precipitate illness or aggravate pre-existing disorders in both men and women (Fees, Martin & Poon 1999; Rosenbloom & Whittington 1993). Often the interaction of ageing and loneliness has a multiplier effect, particularly for men (Rokach 2000). Some develop an increasingly poor self-image and an inability to cope with further losses or to concentrate on the present. Activity patterns shift, and many experience an almost constant restlessness and dissatisfaction with life (Donaldson & Watson 1996). The process of grieving may lead to depression and in some cases the person's interest in health, lifestyle and fitness declines. The most noticeable symptom of this is usually neglect of their nutritional intake, resulting in 'failure to thrive', a condition characterised by malnutrition, weight loss and depression (Newbern & Krowchuk 1994; Rosenbloom & Whittington 1993). Over time, some older people experience a positive shift into a new life phase (Cohen et al 2001; Feldman, Byles & Beaumont 2000; Pignatti et al 2000). However, others live with protracted periods of anger and discouragement, particularly if they live with disabilities and have few social support networks (Dykstra 2000; Schieman 1999). These feelings are seldom alleviated by the move into residential care which, because of the stress of further disruption, may actually exacerbate loneliness (Dykstra 2000; Tijhuis et al 1999).

Meeting
social needs

Adaptation to loss is a complex process that requires four major tasks: accepting the finality of the loss, experiencing the pain of grief, adjusting to the environment from which the deceased is missing, and withdrawing their emotional attachment to their partner. This is a very difficult process, and is almost impossible without some form of social support (Morgan 1994). It is important for communities to assist people in this stage of transition, by establishing personal and social networks where none exist. Some researchers have found that the process of adapting to ageing is highly dependent on friendship networks (Stevens 2001). The presence of a confidante can have a buffering effect on the stress of bereavement. This may be especially difficult for older men who have relied on their spouse for social support and find themselves in later life impoverished by a lack of friends or a social network (Stewart 2000).

Social isolation is one of the most pervasive conditions of ageing. There is a two-way relationship between isolation and health, in that ill health can both cause, and be caused by, being isolated from others (Age Concern England 2000). Sometimes this is because of limits to mobility; in other cases it may be due to family fragmentation, reduced public transport or poverty. For those who enjoy good physical and mental health, social networks may simply shift over time, but for those who are incapacitated by chronic illness or disability, being cut off from former affiliations can have a devastating effect. Religion and various forms of spirituality often act as an antidote to isolation, particularly as people age.

Religion
and health

In an era where traditional religious worship is falling out of favour with younger generations, and where the behaviour of spiritual leaders has been called into question, places of worship continue to be attended by large numbers of older people. The relationship between religion and health is the subject of a growing body of interest among health researchers, all of whom conclude that religion has a significant, positive effect on health (Chatters 2000; Levin 1994). These effects are evident in studies of self-limiting acute conditions, fatal, chronic diseases and illnesses with lengthy, brief or absent latency periods between exposure, diagnosis and mortality (Levin 1994). Religion is beneficial to physical health and promotes a sense of personal well-being and adjustment to life (Chatters 2000). Religious affiliation and the sense of belonging engendered by the church tend to buffer the adverse effect of stress, anger and other emotions associated with bereavement and other losses (Chatters 2000; Levin 1994). However, some aspects of the relationship between religion and health remain ambiguous. For some people, religion seems to enhance peacefulness, self-confidence and sense of purpose, while others are beset by guilt, self-doubt, shame and low-self-esteem; these responses may be a result of the interaction between personal belief systems and those that flow from the religious affiliation (Levin 1994). Recent research suggests that, for the majority, religion enhances self-esteem and personal competence (Chatters 2000).

Religion may be instrumental in shaping behaviours that determine risk-taking or health maintenance, which may include dietary restrictions, prohibition against alcohol or tobacco, or promoting healthy patterns of activity. Spiritual beliefs may also help to reduce the stressors of life by promoting the values of moderation and conformity (Chatters 2000). Religious involvement tends to influence internalised norms for behaviour, fear of sanctions for violations of behavioural norms and positive emulation of valued community members (Ellison & Levin 1998). This is evident in contemporary religious practice and discourse, which seem to be more responsive to the needs of those living stressful lives. For example, religious leaders now speak of reconciliation rather than the 'fire and brimstone' admonishments of the past. In religious terms, the word 'reconciliation' is used to introduce spiritual compatibility, or consistency in thoughts and deeds. This helps shape interpersonal behaviours that promote warmth, friendliness, love, compassion, harmony, tolerance and forgiveness (Chatters 2000).

Religious rituals may also promote a sense of self-worth, competence and connection with others, all of which are fundamental to health (Chatters 2000). Collective worship promotes a sense of community, in helping people feel they are not alone, even when life circumstances seem to leave them feeling abandoned. This type of communal activity, warmed by positive interpersonal behaviours, can be a source of solace to older people, especially in a world that may seem fast-paced and unrecognisable. Many therefore turn to religion in their older years, to work through life's transitions in a community of people who are spiritually similar, comfortable and caring. One of the transitions that often acts as a stimulus to return to religion is retirement.

Retirement

Many people fail to begin planning for their retirement until it is imminent, and find themselves having to sustain a living for up to a third of their lives, whereas in the past, the time between retirement and the end of life was considerably shorter. Throughout those years, the cost of living escalates and often, older retirees find they have inadequate financial resources. This can lead to a desperate need for revised financial planning in their 70s and 80s, which can leave some people vulnerable to exploitation by a range of financial advisors.

The link between SES and health is unequivocal. Older persons living in socioeconomic disadvantage tend to have higher rates of mortality and to have a greater burden of illness, injury and disability (AIHW 2000). Although this relationship extends across all age groups, the elderly may be placed at greater risk from inadequate financial resources, if they have existing illnesses that require expensive treatments, or if they are trying to ensure adequate preparation in case of a future need for some type of institutionalised care. Older women are often financially disadvantaged, especially if they have not planned for surviving their spouse. Their economic worries can be unremitting and irreversible, especially if resources are not forthcoming from family members. The best prevention is retirement planning; however, for many older people, this retrospective insight is less than helpful.

Seedsman (1995) suggests that retirement should be a time of optimism. At this time in a person's life, the pervasive element should be re-socialisation, where a life-enhancing lifestyle is substituted for old, debilitating habits. The features of this are:

- constructive social relationships
- a meaningful level of social integration
- positive self-regulation to stressful aspects of the environment
- effective functioning in accordance with genetic, physiological, psychological and physical capacities
- regular involvement in a series of intrinsically motivated behaviours that are pleasurable and satisfying, including, where possible, a balanced physical activity program for a minimum of three days per week (Seedsman 1995, p 41).

One of the greatest concerns of people after retirement is dislocation from their space, which is usually the family home or a place that has made them feel secure, following the departure of other family members.

Relocation

Many older people experience multiple relocations, from their own home to the residence of a family member, and sometimes back and forth between the homes of family members. They may also experience relocations between residential facilities, health care institutions and their usual residence. Each of these moves adds stress to their lives, especially if they have been forced by illness or family circumstances to leave a home in which they had spent a substantial portion of their lives. For some, the stress is exacerbated by the unpredictability of the move, because of its location or duration, or because it signals that the family has become scattered and there may be no one to take care of them (HelpAge International 2001). Relocation stress is influenced by several factors: the person's characteristics prior to the move, their attitude towards moving, their preparation for the move, their physical and cognitive status, and the extent to which they feel they have control over the move.

At some point, most people experience a loss of *place* in both the material and emotional sense. For the older person, this is usually quite painful, as the connection between people and place becomes more entrenched with time. Some people go through a period of grieving for their home in a way that surprises others, including family members, with its intensity. Besides losing the material comforts of their house, they have also lost the symbolic meaning of their sanctuary. Their home may contain the history of establishing and sustaining the family, the sense of satisfaction that comes from providing a protective environment for loved ones, the possessions and personal touches that make the family's mark on the home, and the peculiar way the home has acted as an enclosure for their most significant moments and memories. Dislocation from the family home because of financial peril causes extraordinary stress for some people, particularly with concerns about becoming homeless or dependent on institutionalised care in the future, or leaving their children financially liable following their death.

Goals for
healthy ageing

Healthy and successful ageing must provide:

- physical and emotional health
- adequate financial and health care resources to sustain the latter stages of life
- a balance between independent living and social support
- a place in which to feel safe and comfortable in living a dignified life.

Once again, the strategies of the Ottawa Charter for Health Promotion provide a guide to implementing these health goals.

Building healthy public policy

At a global level, the health and quality of life of many older people are subjected to the decisions of others. The most important policy initiative, then, must be to create greater participatory networks in which older persons are encouraged to plan for their own health needs. Acknowledging the links between SES and health, WHO has directed policy makers throughout the world to address health service infrastructure needs of all people, including the elderly, especially those living in poverty (WHO 2000).

At the national level, health policies should first ensure that basic needs can be met. This includes policies governing safe food and water, clean air and safe accommodation. One of the most important policy decisions affecting the health of the ageing population relates to housing and other types of accommodation for the elderly. Many older people move from home to hospital, to a hostel or palliative care environment and back to home. For some, these multiple transitions have distressing effects, particularly if financial support for accommodation is inadequate (HelpAge International 2001). Governments in many countries have experimented with a variety of funding arrangements for aged care, and none have fully met the needs of all people. Imbalances in services and the way they are funded have placed many older people at risk of chronic illness. This will place an undetermined burden on society in the future, as larger numbers require care that is effective in restoring their health to a level that can be accommodated in community living. One initiative that is the subject of a lobby by the International Labour Organization concerns universal state-funded financial security, such as pensions that would take the onus away from the individual (HelpAge International 2001). However, this has met with opposition from agencies such as the World Bank, which contends that people should save for their old age (HelpAge International 2001). This is a debatable option from the perspective of primary health care, and one that should be given greater public attention.

The International Year of Older Persons in 1999 provided the impetus for many countries to develop national strategies to care for their ageing population. The National Strategy for an Ageing Australia identified key areas for health promotion and preventing illness and disability, including measures to maintain physical and mental health, adequate nutrition, physical activity, preventing falls and other injury, early detection of sensory loss, managing incontinence and evaluating alcohol and other drug use (Bishop 1999). Since that time, there has been considerable progress in implementing a wide range of local initiatives, each of which responds to the national strategy.

Other countries have targeted fundamental problems that have interfered with the quality of older persons' lives. For example, in Japan the contribution of the elderly to society has traditionally been revered. However, that country, like most others, is confronting the challenges of an ageing population, an ageing workforce, and changing gender roles. As of 2000, Japan devised a system of long-term care insurance to respond to the burden placed on family members by an ageing population whose culture (and, therefore, personal preference) dictated that they be cared for at home. This is expected to assist women in entering or re-entering the paid labour force, to provide effective home and community-based care for those in need, and to preserve the cultural elements that value older citizens, including the industrial policies that reward older workers with financial remunerations (McCallum 1999). As McCallum suggests, this is a way of renovating the 'fittings' of society to make communities work better. It is also remarkable that the changes were effected through collaborative planning mechanisms that involved government and industry bodies and families.

Creating supportive environments

By the year 2020 most people will live in urban environments, including most of the population of developing countries (Freudenberg 2000). In some cases, this will be helpful for older people who wish to be surrounded by family and friends. Urban settings also tend to provide a greater number of resources to older people, such as day care centres and neighbourhood self-help groups, but they are also a source of stress and financial hardship for many older citizens. Cities come with their own hazards and protective influences. It will be important in a future where population ageing is a certainty, to ensure that allowances are made for physical facilities conducive to exercise but with safeguards for the elderly. To promote healthy lifestyles will also require the support of government, manufacturers, employers, retailers, schools and the media (Age Concern England 2000).

International Longevity Centres (ILCs) have been established through HelpAge International, a UK-based cooperative for global action on ageing. The ILCs now extend to the United States, Korea, Japan, France, the Dominican Republic and the United Kingdom to empower those who will manage change during the worldwide revolution in longevity through networking, research, policy development and intersectoral partnerships (Randel et al 1999). This level of support provides an example for the rest of the world to lend their voices to political and community support for ageing populations.

One of the most important groups in desperate need of supportive environments is the migrant population victimised by civil strife. Throughout the past century, many older people died not from old age but because of relocations caused by civil war, conflicts and natural disasters. This mandates preserving both the social and natural environments as places where all members of the global community can age in safety and health.

Another group at risk of unhealthy ageing is the rural community. The shrinking of the rural sector has caused many older rural people considerable stress. Away from their familiar space and sense of independence, many experience the crowding and financial stress of the cities for the first time during their retirement. Rural people are known for self-reliance and independence, yet often have little access to the means to live empowered lives, especially when they suffer from dementia or other mental illnesses. As with urban dwellers, poverty among older people leads to decreased social activity and voluntary participation, and this extends also to family caregivers who may have few resources and thus little respite from their role (Godfrey 1996).

---

case study...

Death on the beach

I live on one of the world's loveliest beaches. Each morning, from around 5 am, the fit, older members of my community come out to play. People who visit from Sydney or Melbourne often remark that they have never seen such fit older people, and I believe that is because they are constantly shaped and nurtured by this environment, with its expectation that regardless of how a person looks, or how slowly they move, or whether they swim or not, the beach is the place to be each morning at sunrise.

One morning not too long ago, as I walked along, I was greeted by one of the regulars. A former tennis player who keeps fit in her 70s, she joins a group of older people every morning at one of the picnic tables under the trees, where one couple brings a pot of tea, rain or shine, to share with the 'oldies'. Everyone in the community knows the group, especially the couple who bring the tea, and a year ago, they were honoured with a Friendship Award for their hospitality. My acquaintance, who I ran into

this particular day, usually stops by to have a sip and to say hello to whoever else has stopped by that day. (I go to work!) On the morning I saw her, she said, 'Hear about old Tom?' to which I replied that I had not. 'Well,' she said, 'yesterday about five minutes after sunrise, old Tom looked up, then slumped down over his cup of tea, dead.' 'My God,' was my first reply. 'How terrible!' 'What?' she countered. 'Are you kidding? On this beach, on a magnificent morning, surrounded by these people as the sun came up, sipping a cup of tea! He's the third one to go in that group this year, and the other two died on the sand. How can you think that's not a great thing?'

Her words chastised me for some time. How dare we make assumptions about older people's lives, or even their preferences? Perhaps he planned it that way, perhaps not, but he was there, living life to the fullest every day into his 80s, and is now fondly remembered around the teapot on that beach.

Strengthening community action

The United Nations has set down the following principles for supporting older persons:

1 independence
2 participation
3 care
4 self-fulfilment
5 dignity (HelpAge International 2001).

Each of our communities must seek ways of weaving these principles into community action, beginning with the fundamental elements of daily life and working towards empowerment and self-enhancement for older people. Poverty among the ageing population must be addressed at the community as well as the policy level. Self-help groups and mutual assistance schemes should in some cases be initiated by health and social welfare personnel, as these are the people most likely to become aware of community strengths as well as needs. This approach has also worked well in Canada for the prevention of falls among the non-institutionalised elderly (Edwards 2000). Community partnerships that include seniors with local knowledge of the hazards can be helpful in identifying where risks of falling occur and what types of interventions would be helpful (Edwards 2000).

Community action can also be supported by encouraging volunteer activities within the ageing population, including widow-to-widow support groups, those that focus on specific conditions or those that simply provide a comfortable place to pursue ongoing education (Ramsey 1992). Health professionals at the Center on Ageing at the University of Victoria in Canada report that many older people express a willingness to give time to one or more voluntary organisations, and these people should be encouraged and supported. If people participate in self-help, mutual aid and other voluntary groups, the research and practice interests of both lay and professional groups could expand the constituency advocating for more public involvement in the planning and delivery of a number of health and social services (Prince & Chappell 1994).

As communities age, the emotional and social needs of older people should not be overlooked. This means not overlooking their potential by excluding them from educational opportunities or the development of new relationships. One writer suggests that we must try to uncover their meaning *in* life, as distinct from the meaning *of* life, in that the former has a deeper, more personal, experiential and reflective connotation. Meaning in life is a 'common human quest for a map, known or felt, that guides decisions and action, that gives coherence to life, that weaves past, present and future together in continuity, that shapes patterns of behaviour in relation to the common and uncommon challenges of life' (Simmons, cited in Moore, Metcalf & Schow 2000, p 27). The first challenge lies in creating communities of dialogue that will sustain the quest in substantial and supportive ways (Moore et al 2000). The most significant way this can be achieved is by ensuring our elders have a 'caring connectedness' with others, and this is not always the case in youth-worshipping societies (Moore et al 2000, p 27).

One way to promote connectedness within the ageing community is to reinforce the value of religious institutions where this is appropriate to community members. Relocation to a different environment may cause many older people enormous stress if they are unable to retrieve the familiarity of the church, temple or synagogue and those who provide religious support. Our role as health advocates should include assessing older community members' needs for communication and worship with church members. This may involve arranging transportation, social networks of lay people with similar religious affiliations, or visits by members of the church, especially for those who are incapacitated and cannot meet what they may see as the obligations of their faith.

When the emphasis in daily life is always on the young, older persons' needs become invisible. Media images give the impression that old is the opposite of lively and fun and perpetuate the idea that 'morbidity' means morbidly dull (Barron McBride 2000). To overcome this stereotype, community action should engender the inherent dignity that accompanies age, but should also focus on new possibilities and the potential for change.

Developing personal skills

One of the most difficult challenges in health promotion for the older population is to change entrenched attitudes. Many older people, when confronted with a serious illness, will change their lifestyle habits. Studies have shown that even those over age 70 can benefit from better diets, appropriate levels of exercise and more mental stimulation than most receive at that age (Age Concern England 2000). However, personal behaviours also play a part, and it is sometimes more difficult to change personal habits among some people who have not yet experienced serious consequences of their behaviours. This has been the case in smoking cessation programs (Wakefield et al 1996). The implications for developing personal skills are clear. People need to be provided with both personal information (such as the results of lung function tests) and the structural support for change.

Older people often need to balance control of a chronic illness such as diabetes or heart disease with trying to live a normal and fulfilling life. Some older people try to give up smoking or to lose weight numerous times before they are successful, and go through several stages ranging from discouragement to commitment, just as occurs in younger people. However, they often have fewer activities to distract them when they are trying to make major lifestyle changes, and also have a longer history of the behaviour(s) than young people. We need to support unsuccessful, as well as successful, attempts and try to understand the difficulties inherent in trying to unlearn, then relearn, ways of behaving. Most importantly, it is crucial that older people are treated as unique human beings. For some, massage, therapeutic touch and alternative therapies provide a remedy to counter unhealthy lifestyles. Others respond to a more cognitive, rational approach and can be convinced to reframe the negative lifestyle practice as a threat to their longevity or to the quality of their life. The most successful persuasive techniques capitalise on both the unique and shared characteristics of people attempting to change, and place at least equal emphasis on community infrastructure that would support the change.

In many cases, older people can provide insights into how infrastructure and services should be developed. In the spirit of partnerships, they should be included in the research agenda that provides the evidence base for change. There is a need for in-depth research studies that would help dispel the sweeping generalisations that have focused on *in*competence, rather than *competence* in the elderly. In any investigation, older people should be included at each stage of the research process. As planning participants, they can help guide questions toward issues of relevance to them. This type of approach helps counter ageist stereotypes, as my colleagues and I discovered in our study of community perceptions of health and well-being. Our findings revealed that the same issues that concerned the very young were most important to older families—namely nutrition and exercise and ensuring a sustainable environment for the next generations (McMurray et al 1998). In a separate study, we also found that mental and physical health are inextricably linked. We followed a group of elderly people discharged from hospital following total hip replacement surgery to ascertain at what stage they reported positive levels of quality of life. The findings indicated that the surgery provoked immediate and highly positive emotional quality of life, because their incapacity had caused social isolation as well as the physical symptoms they had previously experienced (McMurray et al 2002).

Reorienting health services

Deploying health service resources to healthy ageing is a wise investment in community health (Sims et al 2000). Health promotion programs for older people need to be tailored to their particular community and to the self-identified sociocultural preferences of those who are being cared for. Given the great diversity between different age groups beyond 65, between cultures and between those with different levels of health and wellness, it is important to assess their individual needs before assigning them to one or another type of care. However, mandatory systems of formal assessment at each transition can also create gate-keeping dependencies (McCallum 1999). It is important to ensure the flow of information between institutions, families and all agencies working with older people to ensure that the burden of assessment does not add to the burden of care or the burden of illness.

One of the most important initiatives to prevent illness in the population of older people is provision for community screening for the major causes of illness, injury and disability (Rubinstein & Nahas 1998). Screening clinics should be accessible to older people, especially those who have existing disabling conditions such as sensory loss and/or mental health problems. (Rubinstein & Nahas 1997). It is also important to maintain accurate information on how the elderly are maintaining a healthy lifestyle, and this requires a base of research evidence. Research that garners older people's perceptions and focuses on culturally embedded health needs helps to inform health promotion programs and strategies that can be tailored to individual and group needs. This type of approach provides a better basis for health planning than relying on the assumptions of health professionals (Askham 1996).

It is interesting in this genomic era to think of how biology has come to dominate the research and policy agendas. The Human Genome Project has shifted the emphasis in health care from managing chronic conditions to 'quick fix' genetic engineering but no corresponding body of evidence is available to inform the processes of successful ageing. McCallum and Gieselhart (1996) caution that the world needs a balance between this type of research and a more social gerontological focus that would capture the lifestyle issues so important for older people in managing chronic conditions. Although there is a dearth of information on the variable and interactive effects of history, age, gender, race, lifestyle, socioeconomic status and education, the historical and lifestyle agenda is not seen to be quite as worthy of research support as studies that provide singular certainties, such as those being conducted in this 'Golden Age of Biomedical Research' (McCallum & Gieselhart 1996). And when such research *is* funded, the findings tend to reveal unequivocally that healthy lifestyle programs for older people have a strong and positive effect on fitness, notwithstanding the visible pleasure they engender (Ward 1994). It is therefore disappointing to see research funding following the opposite path, drawing conclusions about non-compliance from studies on *unhealthy* lifestyles, which once again places the emphasis on individual behaviours rather than the contexts that dominate people's lives.

A further topic for investigation concerns the environments within which people age. The effectiveness of healthy lifestyle promotion programs is dependent upon the physical environment within which it is received. Those programs devised for nursing home residents are often aimed at the older old, and would be inappropriate for those who live in relatively independent living situations in retirement villages or mobile home parks. Similarly, those who live alone or with families in private homes may have different needs from communal-living seniors. Their needs should be investigated in relation to the environment and the range of contextual features that promote positive health practices and quality of life.

In this era of economic restraint, increasing emphasis has been placed on community and home care, which increases the burden on family caregivers. These people need ongoing support and education that provides a base of information on rehabilitation strategies as well as the intervention technologies planned for their family member. They also have a significant need for respite care to prevent situations where they are overcome by the stress of caregiving. Caring for our ageing population requires careful deliberation on the 'mix' that constitutes optimal conditions for health enhancement. This includes access and equity in service provision, empowerment for the older person and his or her family, and a physical and social environment within which health can be achieved until the end of life within a milieu of encouragement and caring.

It also involves embracing the way older people's history is able to help shape the world. At a broad, social level, we appear to have overlooked the significance of history in mapping the future. Our contemporary social world revolves around the notion that economics, rather than history, will lead to solutions. Saul (1997, p 120) urges us 'to reassert our sense of belonging to a civilization rather than to an imaginary economic dialectic with inevitable conclusions'. Historical connections, he says, are much more important to civilisation. Few would disagree, particularly those who live in a society with a subterranean stream of grief for the past, in a world where even the economic might and power of the United States failed to offer protection against the type of terrorism witnessed in September 2001. The following excerpt from the poem 'The paradox of our time' (anon) encapsulates the sentiments of that day:

The paradox of our time in history is that we have taller buildings, but shorter tempers,
Wider freeways, but narrower viewpoints.

We spend more, but have less.
We buy more, but enjoy it less.
We have bigger houses and smaller families,
More conveniences but less time;
We have more degrees, but less sense,
More knowledge, but less judgement,
More experts, yet more problems,
More medicine but less wellness.

The poem goes on to outline the contrasts between today and the 'good old days' of the past, urging us in the last verses to hug each other more, to 'Give time to speak, give time to share the precious thoughts in your mind'. It is good advice, in recognition that the generations of the past continue to have much to contribute to the future.

thinking critically

Healthy ageing

1   Identify four significant influences on healthy ageing.

2   Describe three factors in the environment of older people that put older people at risk for illness, injury or disability.

3   Discuss the relationship between healthy communities and healthy ageing.

4   Describe three support services that could be developed to assist healthy ageing, and that are based on primary health care principles.

5   Devise a set of strategies to promote healthy ageing in your community using the Ottawa Charter for Health Promotion as a guide.

REFERENCES

Age Concern England (2000). The debate of the age. London: Author.

Askham, J. (1996). Ageing in black and ethnic minorities: a challenge to service provision. *British Journal of Hospital Medicine*, 56(11): 602–4.

Australian Bureau of Statistics (ABS) (1999a), Australia's Older Population: Past, Present and Future. Canberra: ABS.

—— (1999b). Australian Social Trends 1999, Health, Health Status, Health of Older People. Canberra: ABS.

—— (1999c). Income and Welfare. Caring in Australia, Canberra: ABS.

—— (1999d). Australian Social Trends—Population Projections, Our Ageing Population. Canberra: AGPS.

—— (2000). Income and Welfare. Support for Older People. Canberra: Year Book Australia, AGPS.

Australian Institute for Health and Welfare (AIHW) (2000). Australia's Health, 2000. Canberra: AGPS.

Barron McBride, A. (2000). Nursing and gerontology. *Journal of Gerontological Nursing*, July: 18–27.

Beard, M. & Curtis, L. (1997). *Menopause and the Years Ahead*. Fisher Books.

Belza, B. & Wooding Baker, M. (2000). Maintaining health in well older adults, *Journal of Gerontological Nursing*, July: 8–17.

Bennett, K. (1997). A longitudinal study of well-being in widowed women. *International Journal of Geriatric Psychiatry*, 12: 61–6.

Bennett, K & Vidal-Hall, S. (2000). Narratives of death: a qualitative study of widowhood in later life. *Ageing and Society*, 20(4): 413–29.

Bergmark, A., Parker, M. & Thorslund, M. (2000). Priorities in care and services for elderly people: a path without guidelines. *Journal of Medical Ethics*, 26(5): 312–23.

Bishop, B. (1999). The National Strategy for an Ageing Australia: Healthy Ageing Discussion Paper. Canberra: Ausinfo.

Borowski, A., Encel, S. & Ozanne, E. (1997). *Ageing and Social Policy in Australia*. Melbourne: Cambridge University Press.

Carlin, G. (2001). The Paradox of Our Time.

Carr, D., House, J., Kessler, R., Nesse, R., Sonnega, J. & Wortman, C. (2000). Marital quality and psychological adjustment to widowhood among older adults: a longitudinal analysis. *The Journals of Gerontology*, Series B: S197.

Castles, F. (2000). Population ageing and the public purse: Australia in comparative perspective. *Australian Journal of Social Issues*, 35(4): 301–16.

Chatters, L. (2000). Religion and health: Public health research and practice, *Annual Review of Public Health*, 21: 335–67.

Cohen, A., Maaravi, Y., Hammerman-Rozenberg, R. & Stessman, J. (2001). More alone but not more lonely at age 78. *The Gerontologist*, 41(15): 196.

Craig, D. (2000). Health promotion with older adults. In: M. Stewart (ed), *Community Nursing*, 2nd edn, Toronto: WB Saunders, pp 283–95.

Donaldson, J. & Watson, R. (1996). Loneliness in elderly people: an important area for nursing research. *Journal of Advanced Nursing*, 24: 952–9.

Dykstra, P. (2000). Changes in older adult loneliness: results from a six-year longitudinal study. *The Gerontologist*, 15 Oct: 233.

Edwards, N. (2000). Prevention of falls among seniors in the community. In: M. Stewart (ed), *Community Nursing: Promoting Canadians' Health*, 2nd edn, Toronto: WB Saunders, pp 296–316.

Ellison, C. & Levin, J. (1998). The religion-health connection: evidence, theory and future directions. *Health Education Behaviour*, 25: 700–20.

Europe Information Service (2001). Demography: Eurostat Confirms Ageing Population. *European Report*, 21 February, p 229.

Fees, B., Martin, P. & Poon, L. (1999). A model of loneliness in older adults, *The Journals of Gerontology*, Series B, 54(4): 231–40.

Feldman, S., Byles, J. & Beaumont, R. (2000). Is anybody listening? The experiences of widowhood for older Australian women. *Journal of Women & Ageing*, Summer/Fall: 155–76.

Finucane, P., Giles, L., Withers, R., Silagy, C., Sedgwick, A., Hamdorf, P., Halbert, J., Cobiac, L., Clark, M. & Andrews, G. (1997). Exercise profile and subsequent mortality in an elderly Australian population. *Australian and New Zealand Journal of Public Health*, 21(2): 155–8.

Freudenberg, N. (2000). Health promotion in the city. A review of the current practice and future prospects in the United States. *Annual Review of Public Health*, 21: 473–503.

Gallagher, D., Thompson, L. & Peterson, J. (1982). Psychosocial factors affecting adaptation to bereavement in the elderly. *International Journal of Aging and Human Development*, 11(2): 79–96.

Gilbert, K. (1996). 'We've had the same loss, why don't we have the same grief?' Loss and differential grief in families. *Death Studies*, 20: 269–83.

Godfrey, S. (1996). Identified gaps in the services to rural carers of frail/demented people. *Geriaction*, 14(1): 26–31.

Hargreaves, S. (2000). Burden of ageing population may be greater than anticipated. *The Lancet*, 355(9221): 2146.

HelpAge International (2001). The ageing and development report: poverty, independence and the world's older people. London: Earthscan.

Hooyman, N. & Kiyak, H. (1999). *Social Gerontology: A Multidisciplinary Perspective*, 5th edn, Boston: Allyn & Bacon.

Hudson-Rodd, N. (2001). Women's lives: social development implications of the demographic change in the Asia Pacific region. *Journal of Social Work Research and Evaluation*, 2(1): 73–81.

Hungerford, T. (2001). The economic consequences of widowhood on elderly women in the United States and Germany. *The Gerontologist*, 41(1): 103–10.

International Council of Nurses (ICN) (2001). ICN on healthy ageing: a public health and nursing challenge. http://www.icn.ch.

Kennedy, J. & Minkler, M. (1998). Disability theory and public policy: implications for critical gerontology. *International Journal of Health Services*, 28: 757–76.

Levin, J. (1994). Religion and health: is there an association, is it valid, and is it causal? *Social Science and Medicine*, 38(11): 1475–82.

Lloyd-Sherlock, P. (2000). Population ageing in developed and developing regions: implications for health policy. *Social Science and Medicine*, 51: 887–95.

McCallum, J. (1999). Enjoy healthy ageing in Australia and Japan. Seminar Presentation, Office of Ageing, Department of Families, Youth and Community Care. Brisbane: Japanese Consulate, 15 September.

McCallum, J. & Geiselhart, K. (1996). *Australia's New Aged*. Sydney: Allen & Unwin.

McKinlay, J. (1992). Advantages and limitations of the survey approach: understanding older people. In: J. Daly, I. McDonald & E. Willis (eds), *Researching Health Care: Design, Dilemmas, Disciplines*. London: Routledge, pp 114–37.

McMurray, A., Hudson-Rodd, N., Al-Khudairi, S. & Roydhouse, R. (1998). Family health and health services utilisation in Belmont, WA. A community case study. *Australian and New Zealand Journal of Public Health*, 22(1): 107–14.

McMurray, A., Grant, S. & Griffiths, S. (2002). Health-related quality of life in older persons discharged from hospital following total hip replacement. *Journal of Advanced Nursing* (in press).

Marinaro, D. (1997). Your turn. *Journal of Gerontological Nursing*, Oct: 52–5.

Minichiello, V., Browne, J. & Kendig, H. (2000). Perceptions and consequences of ageism: views of older people. In: *Ageing and Society*. London: Cambridge University Press, pp 253–78.

Moore, S., Metcalf, B. & Schow, E. (2000). Aging and meaning in life: examining the concept. *Geriatric Nursing*, 21(1): 27–9.

Morgan, J. (1994). Bereavement in older adults. *Journal of Mental Health Counselling*, 16: 318–26.

Moser, D. (1997). Correcting misconceptions about women and heart disease. *American Journal of Nursing*, 97(4): 26–9.

Munnings, F. (1993). Strength training: not only for the young. *The Physician and Sportsmedicine*, 21(4): 132–40.

Munro. C. (2002). Human genome project: implications for nursing practice. In: L. Young & V. Hayes (eds), *Transforming Health Promotion Practice: Concepts, Issues and Applications*. Philadelphia: FA Davis, pp 207–13.

Murashima, S., Hatono, Y., Whyte, N. & Asahara, K. (1999). Public health nursing in Japan: new opportunities for health promotion. *Public Health Nursing*, 16(2): 133–9.

Newbern, V. & Krowchuk, H. (1994). Failure to thrive in elderly people: a conceptual analysis. *Journal of Advanced Nursing*, 19: 840–9.

Nilsson, P. (1996). Premature ageing: the link between psychosocial risk factors and disease. *Medical Hypotheses*, 47: 39–42.

OECD (1996). Ageing in OECD countries: A critical policy challenge. *Social Policy Studies*, 20. Paris: OECD.

Paalman, M., Bkedam, H., Hawken, L. & Nykeim, D. (1998). A critical review of policy setting in the health sector: the methodology of the 1993 World Development Report. *Health Policy and Planning*, 13(1): 13–31.

Paveza, G., VandeWeerd, C. & Brischi, D. (2000). Impaired caregiving: the impact of self-esteem, burden of care and coping style on depression outcomes in caregivers of community-residing Alzheimer's patients. *The Gerontologist*, 15 Oct: 278.

Pignatti, F., Castelletti, F., Metitieri, T., Zanetti, E., Marre, A., Bianchetti, A., Rozzini, R. & Trabucchi, M. (2000). Living alone and mortality in an oldest old population living at home. *The Gerontologist*, 15 Oct: 365.

Pinquart, M. & Sorensen, S. (2001). Gender differences in self-concept and psychological well-being in old age: a meta-analysis. *Journals of Gerontology*, Series B, 56(4): 195–213.

Pollock, C. (1992). Breaking the risk of falls: an exercise benefit for older patients. *The Physician and Sportsmedicine*, 20(11): 149–56.

Prince, M. & Chappell, N. (1994). Voluntary Action by Seniors in Canada. Final Report. University of Victoria, Center on Aging.

Ramsey, P. (1992). Characteristics, processes and effectiveness of community support groups. A review of the literature. *Family Community Health*, 15(3): 38–45.

Randel, J., German, T. & Ewing, D. (eds) (2000). The Ageing and Development Report 1999: Poverty, Independence and the World's Older People. London: Earthscan Publications.

Rokach, A. (2000). Loneliness and the life cycle. *Psychological Reports*, 86(2): 629–43.

Rosenbloom, C. & Whittington, F. (1993). The effects of bereavement on eating behaviors and nutrient intakes in elderly widowed persons. *Journal of Gerontology: Social Sciences*, 48(4): 5223–9.

Rubinstein, L. & Nahas, R. (1998). Primary and secondary prevention strategies in the older adult. *Geriatric Nursing*, 19(1): 11–17.

Sanders, S. (1999). Midlife sexuality: the need to integrate biological, psychological, and social perspectives. New York: SIECUS Report.

Saul, J.R., (1997). *The Unconscious Civilization*. New York: The Free Press.

Schieman, S. (1999). Age and anger. *Journal of Health and Social Behavior*, 40(3): 273–90.

Seedsman, T. (1995). Ageing and the fitness factor: a need for clarification of the issues. *Australian Journal of Leisure and Recreation*, 5(1): 39–43.

Sims, J., Kerse, N., Naccarella, L. & Long, H. (2000). Health promotion and older people: the role of the general practitioner in Australia in promoting healthy ageing. *Australian and New Zealand Journal of Public Health*, 24(4): 356–9.

Spradley, B. & Allender, J. (1996). *Community Health Nursing: Concepts and Practice*, 4th edn, Philadelphia: Lippincott.

Statistics Canada (2001). Health indicators. Ottawa: Canadian Institute for Health Information.

Steinke, E. (1997). Sexuality in ageing: implications for nursing facility staff. *Journal of Continuing Education in Nursing*, 28(20): 59–63.

Stevens, N. (2001). Combating loneliness: a friendship enrichment programme for older women. *Ageing and Society*, 21(2): 183.

Stewart, M. (2000). Social support, coping, and self-care. In: M. Stewart (ed), *Community Nursing: Promoting Canadians' Health*, 2nd edn, Toronto: WB Saunders.

Straub, S. & Roberts, J. (2001). Fear of death in widows: effects of age at widowhood and suddenness of death. *Journal of Death and Dying (Farmindale)*, 43(1): 25–42.

Tijhuis, M., De John-Gierveld, J., Feskens, E. & Kromhout, D. (1999). Changes in and factors related to loneliness in older men. The Zutphen Elderly Study. *Age and Ageing*, 28(5): 491–6.

Vincent, J. & Mudrovcic, Z. (2000). Ageing populations in the north and south of Europe. *International Journal of Sociology*, 41(4): 371.

Wakefield, M., Kent, P., Roberts, L., & Owen, N. (1996). Smoking behaviours and beliefs of older Australians. *Australian and New Zealand Journal of Public Health*, 20(6): 603–6.

Ward, J. (1994). Exercise and the older person. *Australian Family Physician*, 23(4): 642–5, 648–9.

Wilkinson, J. (1996). Psychology 5: implications of the ageing process for nursing practice. *British Journal of Nursing*, 5(18): 1109–13.

Williams, P. & Lord, S. (1997). Effects of group exercise on cognitive functioning and mood in older women. *Australian and New Zealand Journal of Public Health*, 21(1): 45–52.

World Bank (1994). *Averting the Old Age Crisis*. New York: Oxford University Press.

World Health Organization (1999a). World health day will focus on ageing, *Bulletin of the WHO*, 77(3): 293.

—— (1999b). The World Health Report 1999. Geneva: WHO.

—— (2000). The World Health Report 2000. Health systems. Improving performance. Geneva: WHO.

—— (2001). The World Health Report 2001. Mental health: new understandings, new hope. Geneva: WHO.

Wolf, S., Coogler, C. & Xu, T (1997). Exploring the basis for Tai Chi Chuan as a therapeutic exercise approach. *Archives of Physical Medical Rehabilitation*, 78(8): 886–92.

Yaffe, K., Barnes, D., Nevitt, M., Lui, L & Covinsky, K. (2001). A prospective study of physical activity and cognitive decline in elderly women. *Archives of Internal Medicine*, 161(14): 1703–8.

Zettel, L., Rook, K. & Morgan, D. (2001). Substitution and compensation in the social networks of widowed women. *The Gerontologist*, 15 Oct (41): 39–40.

CHAPTER 9

Healthy
families

Introduction   Few people would challenge the notion that the family is the singularly most important influence on the health of a society. Although genetics, personal health and the accessibility of health and support services play a part in health and illness, it is the basic patterning of behaviours, attitudes, beliefs and values within the family that primarily determines whether and to what extent people make choices for healthy lifestyles. In this respect, the family is where health literacy, or health competence, is developed and nurtured.

Families come in many different forms, some of which dictate the way family members interact with one another. These differences can vitalise the community in ways that cultivate understanding and tolerance, or they can cast a shadow over the community because of harmful contextual factors, individual circumstances or patterns of interrelating. Regardless of its constitution, or how functional or dysfunctional it is, the family enacts a role as gatekeeper between people and all their environments, particularly the social environment. The 'fit' between the family and elements of these environments is an indication of the community's social cohesion. As health professionals engaged in community health promotion, it is essential that we understand the way families are changing and being changed by contemporary life. Towards that end, this chapter examines the family in the context of today's social changes in order to better understand their role in community health and, in turn, our role in supporting and maintaining this.

objectives   **By the end of this chapter you will be able to:**

1   Describe the roles and functions of families in society

2   Identify four significant ways in which families influence health and wellness

3   Explain the three most common factors that place families at risk for illness, injury or disability

4   Describe three modifiable elements of the environment that could help promote family health

5   Identify three community goals for sustaining family health

6   Develop a planning framework for promoting family and community cohesion.

Defining
the family

When we think of family, some of us think of the protective envelope that provides a refuge from the stresses and strains of the outside world. Others have the opposite reaction. To them, family is a combat zone, a kind of repository for the collective problems of both the inside and outside worlds. Most of us, though, hold a view of family that lies somewhere between these two extremes. The family is the filter, or mediating structure, that functions as a gatekeeper between us as individuals, and the society in which we live. It is a conduit through which society transmits to individuals its social and cultural norms, roles and responsibilities. The family also acts as a communicative structure from within, in that it provides a structure for bonding together individual attitudes, opinions and needs. These, in turn, can be used to inform societal policies and processes that vitalise communities.

The concept of family has come to mean many things to people, and to date there is no one accepted definition or standard form. The clergy often describe the family as exemplifying the morality of a society (Goode 1996). Sociologists tend to see families as primary agencies for socialisation, social control and transmission of cultural values, while psychologists see families as primary units for child rearing and the development of personality (Goode 1996). Economists tend to view the family as a unit of consumption. Before the age of industrialisation, the family represented the basic unit of both production and consumption, so it was often described as the cornerstone or major building block of society (Siena Group 1998). Today, the family is considered a pivot point for transitions, rather than a static entity (Siena Group 1998). This slightly different perspective captures the way families interact as a core dynamic centre in vital and active societies (Siena Group 1998). The mutual social and psychological support provided within these interactions is the key to developing both healthy individuals and a healthy society (Sweeting & West 1995; Wright & Leahey 1994).

Structural–functional definitions

The family can be defined according to its structures and relationships. Families can be seen as systems of people related by blood ties, marriage, legal adoption or residence, or by bonds of reciprocal affection and mutual responsibility (Wright & Leahy 1987, 1994). Structural–functional theorists describe the family as a social system whose major goal is to maximise the congruency between the family and society. Friedman (1986) identifies four related structural dimensions that interact to weave this family goal within the family's functioning: role structure, value systems, communication processes and power relations.

Role structure

Family roles and positions within the group are characterised by more or less homogeneous and predictable behaviours, which, of course, change with different circumstances and with changing societal expectations. In the *intact* or *nuclear* family, which is becoming less prevalent in today's society, husband and wife undertake various marital roles, such as parenting, recreation, housekeeping, kinship, and sexual and therapeutic roles (Friedman 1986). These roles are described as traditional in that, historically, the roles were determined by gender and organised around more than one generation (Ganong 1995). The extent to which these roles are maintained in today's society depends on whether they are flexible and responsive to the marriage structure, which may, in turn, depend on cultural expectations or individual preferences. For example, a young couple may decide at marriage that they will both contribute to the family's economic situation and/or share household work, or child care responsibilities. They may agree on simultaneous career development, or sequential opportunities, which would see each parent take turns being absent from the workplace for varying periods of time, perhaps during the time they are caring for young children. Similarly, children's roles or those of extended family may be pre-determined by the family's cultural or individual expectations. In some cases, the modern family is temporarily reconstituted by the inclusion of one or more non-familial members who enact a family role—for example, as a carer. In this respect, family structure and family roles are determined by decisions from within the family.

Family values

The rules or norms within which a family behaves are largely dependent on the family's shared values. Family values consist of ideas, attitudes and beliefs that are sometimes culturally determined but also rely on the family's history or resilience to life events. Family values include such things as the importance placed on material wealth, work, education, achievement in intellectual and recreational pursuits, equality, child-rearing practices, tolerance of others and social consciousness. A major function of families is to ensure that all members recognise these values, even if some are challenged and transformed over time. In many cases, there is a generational modification of values that evolves from interactions both within and outside the family (Friedman 1986). This is most often evident in migrant families who, in the process of acculturating to their new environment, adopt successively more of the new country's values with each generation. Similarly, adolescents typically go through a period of challenging family values. Some of the new values they assume are an attempt at asserting their independence, and are short-lived; however, it is reasonable to expect that most young people will establish their own family system with at least some transformation or modification of the value system of their family of origin.

Family communication

In the process of communicating with one another, families learn to recognise both the shared and individual characteristics of each member. One of the most important functions of family communication is to help each member with the process of *individuation*; that is, to develop a sense of self (Friedman 1986). Healthy communication patterns also help each family member learn about others and learn to make personal choices, and this helps each person to develop personal self-esteem and mutual respect. This is accomplished by: creating opportunities to express one's feelings, thoughts and concerns; active encouragement of spontaneity and authenticity; honest, constructive resolution of conflicts; and clear, consistent, unambiguous styles of communicating that convey affection, support and acceptance (Friedman 1986).

Family power structure

In families without mutual respect, there is often a chaotic style of communication where one family member dominates, controlling the actions of others. Healthy power structures are those with a more egalitarian structure, where there are flexible structures for sharing power among family members. In this style of relating, family members complement rather than subordinate each other. Individual members understand their respective roles in the family hierarchy and the extent to which they have authority over family decisions. This requires clear, predictable understanding of family role expectations and a commitment to sharing authority.

In addition to these structural dimensions and patterns, family health is generated by fulfilment of the following core functions:

- *Affection*   A caring, affectionate family environment provides the conditions within which family members can learn to trust one another and others outside the family.
- *Security and acceptance*   Having basic physical and emotional needs nurtured within the family instils a sense of safety and security that will promote the ability to be accepting of other community members.
- *Identity and a sense of worth*   Reflecting on family interactions allows family members to develop a sense of who they are and how their unique characteristics are linked to those of others.
- *Affiliation and companionship*   Throughout the lifespan the family creates a sense of belonging among members, which establishes a template for bonding together and with others.
- *Socialisation*   The family transmits a cultural and social identity that will embody the family's history and values and thus contribute to the community's collective identity, particularly in multicultural communities. This, in turn, influences community cohesion.
- *Controls*   Within the family all members come to recognise the rules and boundaries that provide realistic standards for public behaviour (Duvall & Miller 1985).

Developmental definitions

Developmental theorists suggest that families, and their members, go through various stages, each of which is to some extent quantitatively and qualitatively different from adjacent stages. These individual and family development trajectories are unique, and based on personal experiences or particular ways of having dealt with stressors in the past (Gottleib & Feeley 2000). Family theorists contend that the following stages and their correspondent tasks are designed to meet the family's biological requirements, cultural imperatives, and shared aspirations and values (Gottleib & Feeley 2000):

- the beginning stage of marriage, where the task is to relate harmoniously to the kin network and plan the family
- the stage of parenthood, where the young family is established as a stable unit
- the stage of raising pre-school children, where the need for protection and space, integration and socialisation predominates
- the children-at-school stage, where school achievement is promoted while the adults attempt to maintain a satisfying marital relationship
- families with teenagers, where the family attempts to integrate and communicate its values, lifestyles, and moral and ethical standards

- launching-centre families, where the children begin to leave home and the role of parents shifts to encouraging independence. As the older children marry, new adult family members are welcomed into the family.
- the post-parenting stage, where the parents attempt to maintain a sense of physical and psychological well-being through a healthy environment, sustaining satisfying relationships with children and ageing parents, and re-strengthening the marital relationship
- retired families, where the partners attempt to maintain comfortable living arrangements, maintain intergenerational family ties and, sometimes, learn to cope with the loss of a partner (Duvall 1977).

The family stages described above represent a set of family developmental norms. This is a starting point for today's families, which follow a more flexible line of development than their forebears, with less predictability, more transitions and different configurations than traditional families. Today, because of death or marital separation, more families live in transient family groupings where the family straddles one or several stages at once. Some families also experience the blending of two families, with some or all of the members of both becoming part of the core family for indeterminate lengths of time. When family members are separated or divorced there are new transitions, such as establishing various boundaries, dealing with children's access to parents, consolidating new relationships, reconstituting the family unit and planning for step-parenting.

In addition to marital separation, many families today experience older children leaving home and returning several times, depending on financial circumstances. Developmental theories are also challenged by the conventions of culture, which often determine whether or not the family includes members of three and four generations. So, although it is useful to consider various developmentally related family tasks, a categorisation truer to today's families may be simply: single or married adults living as a couple, with or without children; married adults living with young, teenage or adult children; people living alone; and intergenerational families comprising any of the above.

Family systems

Another approach to studying families is within the rubric of family systems theory. Systems theory describes the family as a conglomerate of parts (such as subsystems of children) that interact with the whole and, in turn, with aspects of the environment. However, once again, in this era of rapidly changing societal expectations, many families have fewer subsystems than in the past. Viewing the family as a set of systems and subsystems fails to capture the power relations that exist in families, whether these arise out of gender relationships or parent–child relationships (Wellard 1997). So today, we have no consensual notion of what constitutes family. Instead, the boundaries for describing families are varied and flexible, and we are left with a more-or-less accepted view that the family is whoever the family says it is.

Contemporary
families

Although there is probably no such a thing as a *typical* family in today's society, the social changes of the last century have brought about a profound effect on most families throughout the world. Declining birth rates, delayed marriage and childbearing, divorce, patterns of cohabitation, and the return of women to the paid workforce, have brought dramatic changes to family composition and child care arrangements. The stereotypical nuclear family of old, which consisted of two parents and their children, has ceased to be the norm. International trends in industrialised countries project that couple families without children will increase over the next 25 years, becoming the most common family type by the year 2016. This is associated with the decline in fertility, the trend toward one-parent-headed households and the ageing of the baby boomers, whose children will have left home (ABS 1999a). There will also be dramatic increases in the number of people living alone, again because of population ageing and the drastic decline in second marriages, and because of divorce or choosing to delay or reject marriage (ABS 1999a). For these reasons, industrialised societies show a distinct trend towards waiting until after age 30 to marry, or deciding against marriage altogether. In Australia, for example, 29 per cent of males and 23 per cent of females are expected to never marry (ABS 1999a). This is about average, with the United States having the highest marriage rate and Sweden the lowest (ABS 1999a). Another consistent trend is toward cohabitation, which has become the norm for those contemplating marriage (ABS 2000).

Divorce patterns have had a dramatic effect on the family in contemporary life, the most notable of which is that many of today's adults are expected to live alone for more years than as part of a couple (ABS 2000). Since the surge in divorce in North America in the 1980s, rates of divorce in both the United States and Canada have been declining. However, the US rate of divorce remains high (49%), but below divorce rates in Russia (65%), Sweden (64%), Finland (56%) and the United Kingdom (53%) (US Census Bureau 2000). In New Zealand, 47 per cent of marriages end in divorce, with 46 per cent in Australia having the same outcome (US Bureau of Census 2000). Chile has the lowest rate of divorce, followed by Italy and Turkey (ABS 1999a).

It is commonly thought that the increase in the proportion of single-parent households is a direct reflection of these divorce rates, but history shows that although these are increasing from what they were two decades ago, the proportion of single-parent households is similar to 100 years ago, when many women died in childbirth, resulting in a large number of father-headed families. This trend fluctuated during the two world wars of the last century. Today, single-parent households are primarily headed by the mother and, in most cases, this is because of child custody being awarded to the mother. The other reason for this trend is that many single women of childbearing age are now making a conscious choice to have children outside marriage (Hartley 1995; AIHW 2000).

These changes have also had an impact on child-rearing practices and, in turn, on the role of women. With 61 per cent of Australian women in the paid workforce, which is only slightly higher than most other industrialised countries, approximately half to three-quarters of all families with young children use some combination of formal and informal child care services. Most involve family carers, particularly grandmothers, some of whom are themselves engaged in at least part-time employment of their own or who also care for an older family member (ABS 1998; Castiglia 1994). These people are now referred to as 'sandwich carers', in that they maintain double-sided caregiving responsibilities.

Another major change in today's families has been brought about by declining fertility rates, which has changed mothering from being *all* of a woman's life to being only *part* of a woman's life. In industrialised nations such as Korea and Japan, birth rates are among the lowest in the world. Fertility rates are currently rising to replacement levels in the United States and Scandinavian countries, whereas in countries like Australia and some Western European countries, they have dropped below the replacement level (ABS 1999b; AIHW 2000). In countries like Thailand, Indonesia and China, birth rates are declining sharply, while in other parts of Southeast Asia (Papua New Guinea, Malaysia and Vietnam) fertility rates are the highest in the world (ABS 1999b).

An overly simplistic explanation for these variable fertility rates revolves around the negative relationship between women's status and childbearing. Women of low status or low education have traditionally been expected to have high rates of childbearing. However, bearing children today may be more appropriately related to a constellation of factors such as government support for child care, gender relations and family and community support. Paradoxically, in Sweden, where women have attained a high level of equality, generous social support from both government and family sources has allowed *all* women to balance career and family responsibilities. Swedish women have responded to this level of support by continuing to have children regardless of status.

Many believe the decline in fertility among women in industrialised nations is related to the effects of stress, from trying to combine paid work outside the home with caring for children. Despite the gains made in the last century, women have not achieved equality in the division of household labour or the workplace. This is an era where everyone is working longer hours, often under stressful conditions, in competitive environments, with minimal job security and shrinking finances (Yencken & Porter 2001). Added to this is the high cost of formal child care, which makes having more than one or two children almost impossible for women of childbearing age, especially if they are upwardly mobile and trying to maintain their place in the system. Many young women who delay childbirth see their work colleagues burning out because of these pressures and some make a deliberate choice to avoid having children. This decision is more readily available in this era than in previous times, when there were considerable societal pressures to have children. Young people today, married or not, cohabiting continuously or only occasionally, with one or more member(s) of the same or different genders, have been generally absolved from this type of societal pressure and vindicated by the media, to exercise free choice in determining the way *their* family will be shaped.

Healthy
families

Any prescription for healthy families, whether structural, functional, developmental or benchmarked against current norms, represents an ideal. In reality, families comprise individuals with their human frailties who are confronted with conditions of life that evoke less-than-ideal responses. To promote family health, it is important to recognise some of the risk factors that influence family health.

Risk factors and
determinants of family health

The interaction between health and socioeconomic factors has been discussed previously, and for families, low SES exerts its impact in a number of ways. These include: preventing adequate health practices and health care for family members, or access to family social support mechanisms; disempowering the family in decision-making; and creating stressors associated with occupational, educational and other family factors (Reutter 2000). Where the family also has a physically and/or mentally ill family member, the risk is multiplied to an extraordinarily high level.

Families and illness

In many families, at least one member has a chronic illness and must be cared for at home. The caregiving family is becoming more prevalent in today's society because of the larger proportion of older people among the population, many of whom have some form of debilitating illness. The economic difficulties experienced by many families are also challenged by parallel problems in the health care industry, which is increasingly required to do more with less. As a consequence, we live in an era of 'drive-through' health care, where the cost of caring for people in hospital has proved prohibitive for all but the most critically ill. This, coupled with recognition of the risk of *nosocomial* or hospital-induced infections, has led to the conclusion that hospitals are generally neither cost-effective nor conducive to successful rehabilitation. So the trend is increasingly towards home and community care, where family members provide ongoing rehabilitation and frequently manage illnesses of considerable acuity.

The move towards home care has had a profound impact on families around the world. Nearly 60 per cent of the oldest old (over age 80) with a severe or profound handicap live in households, cared for by relatives or others, with or without formal assistance. In Australia 3.5 million people, representing 20 per cent of the population, have some type of illness or disability, and the majority of these are cared for at home (ABS 1998). This is similar to the situation in many other countries, where irrespective of cultural traditions, family financial conditions see them regularly providing care for ill or disabled family members (ABS 1998; McKeever 1994; Mistiaen et al 1997).

One of the most challenging aspects of caring for a family member with a chronic illness is ensuring that the person's condition is maintained without the occurrence of a crisis. This is often an onerous task in that the family member with epilepsy, diabetes, asthma or a cardiac condition may be prone to intermittent, acute episodes of their illness. Although health professionals attempt to provide sufficient information and support to family caregivers, research studies have revealed that they often overestimate family members' health-related knowledge, underestimate the ill person's functional status, have poor understanding of the family's cultural needs and are sometimes insensitive to the family's intergenerational needs (Castiglia 1994; Jackson 1994; Morrow-Howell et al 1996; Reiley et al 1996). As a result, family members may be left to deal with medical crises, symptom management and other maintenance issues with less than adequate professional back-up, relying primarily on their own judgement, wisdom and resourcefulness. This is more pronounced for families living in rural areas, where back-up resources are extremely scarce (AIHW 1998). Because of this, rural families have been forced to become resourceful in finding ways to rely on family members, friends and religious associates for support, rather than the health care system (Hunsucker, Frank & Flannery 1999). The problem becomes magnified many times over for rural, migrant families, who have little time, many occupational hazards and virtually no culturally sensitive resources to assist them (Sandhaus 1998).

Caring for a chronically ill person in any circumstance is a stressful undertaking and, although the effects may differ in different families, caregiver stress has been known to cause physical and/or emotional illness in the caregiver(s) (Turner-Henson, Holaday & Swan 1992). Over time, many also experience gradually diminishing levels of support from others whose intentions may have been long-term, but who simply become victims to ongoing stress (Stewart 2000). Many caregivers also forego predictability and long-term planning for their own lives as they become trapped in a situation where they are unable to make career changes, relocate or implement retirement plans (Fink 1995). The stress of caring for a chronically ill person also places considerable strain on family harmony and social functioning, in some cases precipitating abuse of the ill or elderly (Fink 1995). Research has shown that the heavy burdens and constraints of caring for chronically ill children, for example, may significantly affect parenting behaviours as well as limiting opportunities for family interaction (Turner-Henson et al 1992).

An additional pressure that may be created by family caregiving is a sense of social isolation. In some cases, the family may become isolated either by the desire of the ill person to remain out of public view, or by the altruistic desire to manage the situation as well as possible (Sanders 1995). At times, caregivers get caught up in a cycle of caring without respite, becoming exhausted to the point of emotional breakdown. Whether this occurs because of a lack of available resources, a situation that prevents accessing help, or an unwillingness to seek assistance, it is a dysfunctional state for both the caregiver and the rest of the family. All families need cooperation and support from others, mutual caring and a sense of control, especially those who are called upon to assist with such an important task as managing another's illness. The challenge for health advocates is to recognise the bi-directional impact of family caregiving and to help families in this situation become empowered to develop the resources and support mechanisms required for the health of all members (Sanders 1995).

Family violence

One of the greatest risks to the health and well-being of families is violence among family members, especially parents. Within the family, children first experience physical aggression in the form of being 'spanked' or struck, presumably as a morally correct way of stopping undesirable behaviour (Strauss 2001). This type of corporal punishment acts as a 'cradle of violence' (Strauss 2001, p 187). If a child experiences this type of corporal punishment and also sees physical striking modelled by his or her parents, this sends a powerful message to the child that physically abusive behaviour is acceptable. A large body of research has shown that witnessing violence between parents is associated with serious psychological and social problems later in life and the tendency to hit other children, physically assault a spouse or non-family member, suffer from depression, commit a major crime and engage in masochistic sexual arousal (Strauss 2001). This body of evidence is so strong that it has led the American Academy of Pediatrics and the Canadian Pediatric Association to unequivocally warn parents against corporal punishment (Strauss 2001).

There are many widely held views about what constitutes abusive behaviour within families, including deprivation, emotional blackmail and a range of ways in which one family member wields power over another. The prevalence of these types of psychological violence is unknown, partly because of difficulties associated with surveillance of the behaviour and the unreliability of self-reports. However, there are data on the prevalence of intimate partner violence, which has shown a decline since the 1970s. The reasons for the decline are speculative, but researchers explain it on the basis of a groundswell of public opinion supporting gender equality, women's expanding options in the workplace that allow them to escape difficult marital situations, and a decrease in male approval of serious abusive behaviour (Strauss 2001). American studies also show an expansion of women's refuges, which means that the need for some type of intervention in family violence is at least being acknowledged. The declining prevalence of physical abuse of children also provides room for optimism and support for public information campaigns (Strauss 2001). This type of information is also filtering through to a growing body of information about separation and divorce, to assist parents in accessing support for all family members during what is often a protracted process of adjustment.

Separation and divorce

Despite changing family structures, many couples continue to marry or cohabit in the expectation that they will become a family unit, regardless of whether or not they intend to have children. However, as we have come to realise, this situation does not always endure. In the not-too-distant past, divorcing families were stigmatised on the basis of not conforming to societal expectations. In some cases, it seemed healthier for all family members to disengage themselves from a highly conflicted environment. However, divorced women, especially, were seen in a less favourable light than, for example, widows. The children of divorce were also somewhat stigmatised and any child behaviour that failed to conform to normal expectations was blamed on the fact that the child had come from a 'broken home'. Researchers of the 1970s tended to also blame the disruptive carry-over effects of divorce for the social and academic performance of children in school (Eastman 1989).

Early studies on the effect of divorce on children pointed toward children's resilience and allayed the fears of many separating parents that their actions would have adverse effects on their children (Hetherington 1999). Wallerstein's work in the United States initially supported this somewhat liberal view, but after 25 years of following the lives of 131 children through to their own adulthood, she and her colleagues realised that the major impact of divorce comes in adulthood, when these children are struggling to form their own adult relationships (Wallerstein, Lewis & Blakeslee 2000). On the basis of the earlier research into children's adjustment, many parents contemplating divorce believed that divorce was better for the children than living in a conflicted family (Wallerstein et al 2000). However, this may have been due to a lack of studies comparing children's adjustment in high-conflict divorced and non-divorced families (Hetherington 1999). Today, the evidence shows that, although children tend to be resilient, they still experience distress, apprehension, confusion and anger in response to marital conflict and divorce (Hetherington 1999; Wallerstein et al 2000). Children *do* suffer enormously from separation and divorce, as they do in any situation of high conflict.

Paul Amato, another researcher in this area, has conducted studies in the United States and in Australia, concluding that children's perceptions of family conflict are also important to their adjustment in adult life. If children have not perceived the family as conflicted, they tend to have a more difficult time adjusting. Those who have clearly seen that divorce alleviates the conflict tend to have less psychological distress later in life, higher life satisfaction, marital happiness and positive social relationships (Amato, Loomis & Booth 1995). These researchers argue, like Hetherington (1999) and Wallerstein et al (2000) that the long-term consequences of divorce are complex. Some children will be resilient and well adjusted, but others may experience negative and pervasive effects (Amato 1999). The fashionable rhetoric tends to argue that it is 'family process rather than family structure that is important in children's adjustment' (Hetherington 1999, p 114). However, Hetherington (1999) cautions all parties to divorce that successful coping and adaptation can be maximised if the divorce is harmonious and minimises stress, and if the residential parent is able to sustain authoritative parenting and not inflict a 'parent' role on the child (Hetherington 1999).

The focus of contemporary research into divorcing families is not so much on laying blame, as on emphasising the importance of parental support networks, which are seen as fundamental to healthy social and cognitive development in children (Melson, Ladd & Hsu 1993; Wallerstein & Blakeslee 1990; Wallerstein et al 2000). This signals a more balanced view of both adult and child behaviour with respect to divorce than in previous times. It also indicates societal acknowledgement that family separation may be due to any one or a combination of factors, including cultural factors and the environment. Consequently, societal attitudes are shifting toward acknowledging *variability* rather than *conformity* in families' behaviours, attitudes, beliefs and values, and this can be expected to continue over time.

Attitudes toward parenting from outside, as well as inside, the family home are also changing. In the past, the conflicts between separating parents often interfered with positive parenting. Many of these were related to custody of children. With an increasing body of research into post-divorce parenting, the child-rearing role of both parents is acknowledged, regardless of residence (McMurray 1997). New legislation in many countries has seen the language of separation and divorce changed to reflect the fact that *custody* of children is no longer the most important issue. Instead, the emphasis is on allowing all children *access* to parents, rather than the other way around. This elevates the role of the non-residential parent to a more equal status than previously, when the emphasis was on survival of the single-parent-headed household. Today it is expected that both parents create opportunities to contribute to their children's development not only financially, but emotionally and socially as well.

In many countries, new approaches to divorce laws have followed the lead set by the British Family Law Act of 1992, which mandated a parenting plan to be devised at the time of divorce. This ensures that the rights of the child(ren) supersede the rights of either parent. Parenting plans represent one of the most important initiatives in helping families adjust to divorce. They are designed to document both parents' negotiated goals and intentions to ensure safety, physical and emotional care, and education and legal responsibilities throughout childhood. Development of a parenting plan also helps to separate the processes of resolving money and property disputes from those involving the children. It is expected that humanising the approach to planning for the children's wellbeing after separation in this way will help to counter the effect of emotionally intense legal negotiations that often interfere with rational decision-making.

Although many people survive the emotional trauma of marital separation, it is one of the most stressful events in any person's life, and one that continues for varying periods of time. The risks to health are most evident in the period immediately following separation, particularly where no support system is available. The most enduring effect of separation and divorce is related to economic status and the interactive effects between poverty and health. For at least the initial years following marital separation, both sides of the family are worse off financially. Women who become the head of a separated household tend to be affected most and thus have become entrenched in what some have called the *feminisation of poverty*. This term refers to the large number of women who have become poverty-stricken by the circumstances of their lives, including divorce. A report on childhood in Norway describes this as the *pauperisation of motherhood*, placing the emphasis on outcomes for the mother (Frones, Jensen & Solberg, cited in Edgar 1992). The poverty of mothers raising children alone has been documented throughout the world, and is not only an issue for the women themselves but, as many researchers have discovered, the most significant predictor of child outcomes (Keating & Hertzman 1999; UNFPA 2000).

Demographic, economic
and social trends

Geographic mobility for both the family and its adult members is typical of today's family. In general, families tend to change location many more times in their lifetime than in the past. This may be due to unemployment and increased migration, as migrants tend to move several times in the first few years after arriving in a country (ABS 2000). The experience of multiple relocations, particularly in the context of migration, presents a stressful risk to family stability. In many cases, young families make the transition to both parenthood and a new country at the same time. This increases the complexity of the transition, which has an effect on subsequent patterns of family development. Sometimes the transition is made easier by migrating to a place where there is an enclave of people sharing the same ethnic identity, but this is not always the case. Adaptation to the new environment may also be affected by economic capacity and pre-migration experiences, especially if these have been traumatic. The United Nations estimates that there are currently about 125 million international migrants and 15 million refugees fleeing wars, civil strife, famine and environmental destruction (UNFPA 2000). These families are usually seeking a better life free from trauma, combat, physical injury from war, torture, rape, famine and separation from family members, as well as the loss of familiar social roles and kinship systems (Foss 1996; UNFPA 2000).

One of the most important elements in healthy immigration is the quality of the marital relationship, particularly in the first stage when the new couple has little knowledge of the available resources. The post-migration environment is also an important element in helping such families work through their adjustment. Essential elements in this process include the presence or absence of cultural and religious traditions, accessible educational and health care resources, social support and a political environment in their resettlement country that is amenable to peace and stability (Foss 1996).

Changing economic trends have also had a profound effect on the social milieu of families. In the past, children left home when they became adults, but today's financial uncertainties see more children leaving and returning several times, depending on education and employment opportunities. This creates multiple transitions and multiple adjustments for all family members as well as a sense of unpredictability for the parents, who may be looking forward to their own transition to the post-parenting stage without the financial hardship or social constraints of children. Resource constraints have also increased the proportion of young, dual-income, child-rearing families. With both parents employed, the responsibility for parenting shifts from the exclusive domain of the family to social institutions such as child care centres and schools. As a result, there is increased reliance on the advice of outside experts and little opportunity to parent intuitively. This has had a considerable impact on parenting styles.

Many new parents attempt to squeeze copious amounts of information into the immediate period following the birth of their child before parental leave expires, causing a steep learning curve characterised by anxiety and fearfulness. During this period they are also bombarded by consumerism, which creates media images of 'the good mother' designed to manipulate the mother's position as the chief family buyer (Rieger 1991). Such media manipulation tends to disempower young couples with a false sense of free choice, and this is worse where the family is isolated from friends or family who would help create a balance between consumer pressure and sensible decision-making.

Rural
families

In Chapter 1, the interdependent relationship between place and health was introduced and Chapter 2 explored this association in the context of urban lifestyles. A number of elements of rural communities also have important implications for the health of families.

Examination of the burden of illness, injury and disability reveals inequalities in the health status of rural families compared to urban dwellers, as evidenced in higher levels of mortality and illness according to the distance from metropolitan centres (AIHW 1998, 2000). The reasons for this include less access to health services, generally lower employment and SES, exposure to harsh environments and occupational hazards (AIHW 2000). Many Indigenous people are also rural dwellers and exhibit consistently lower levels of health (AIHW 2000). The relative weight of these factors is, however, difficult to determine, as unemployment and low SES are often linked to risk-taking behaviours, such as smoking and heavy use of alcohol, and these are not always dependent on the family environment. Cultural influences on behaviour can also interact with the social isolation of living in rural and remote areas to influence family health or ill health.

People who live in rural communities have distinct sociocultural, occupational and ecological characteristics (AIHW 1998; Hunsucker et al 1999). Rural sociocultural issues include a value system that prefers the relative autonomy of rural life to the complex interdependencies of urban life. Most rural people have a visible affinity for the land. Those who farm the land or provide services for agricultural communities tend to see their lives as interwoven with features of the land and its life-sustaining capacity. Rural life is closely integrated with rural work, so rural people tend to assess their health and quality of life in relation to work role and work activities (Long & Weinert 1989). For many families, a good life is a good house, good husbandry, hard work and blessed rain (at the right time!).

Many rural families believe their hard-working lifestyle to be healthier than that of urban dwellers, although they do report considerable stress (Humphreys 2000). Farmers, especially, tend to show a high level of acceptance of injury and disease, preferring to be seen as 'hardy' rather than as succumbing to a sick role (Strasser, Harvey & Burley 1994). From an ecological perspective, rural places are not always as hardy as the perceptions of their residents. Many rural areas revolve around single industries, such as farming or mining. As the industry declines, the outflow of resources occurs at great cost to the rural population. The decline in opportunities for productive work leads to a decline in financial resources and a concomitant decline in young role models for the next generation. This often causes people to lose optimism and become dispirited.

To those unfamiliar with rural life, the image of rural peace and serenity can be misleading. Although rural places do not suffer from the crowding and pollution of large cities, they do hold many risks to family health and safety. Rates of unintended injuries are higher in rural and remote areas, particularly for males and, with only minimal health services, injuries are often fatal (Hunsucker et al 1999; Long & Weinert 1989). Mortality from motor vehicle traffic deaths is also higher for rural people because they must travel greater distances for services, on roads of lower standard, in older automobiles, and often by a driver under the influence of alcohol (AIHW 1998).

With the economic downturn experienced over the past two decades, many rural families in both developing and industrialised countries have been forced into the cities to look for work or as refugees from civil unrest (WHO 2000). This displacement has caused severe emotional and financial distress as many experience a downward *social drift* (LeClair & Innes 1997). They find themselves in areas of low SES and then are exposed to a new set of social problems, such as disenchantment, poverty, inequality, and lack of access to housing and education. Many end up suffering from the stresses familiar to other disadvantaged urban families (Freudenberg 2000).

Rural or urban, the family unit is today diverse and dynamic in its composition, perceptions and performance. What it means to belong to a family is defined in many ways, depending on the meanings held by family members, and the ways they are bound together. In this respect, the 'family' has become a metaphor for belonging in general, as we describe our closest group memberships as 'like a family' (Curthoys 1999). But the family is both the most fragile and the toughest of all human institutions, the place where we hold our deepest tensions, fears and hatreds, and sometimes violence, madness and despair (Curthoys 1999). For some families, having a wider range of choices has enhanced the quality of members' lives, while in others the result has been dissatisfaction and disharmony. Industrialisation has played havoc with family expectations in the developed world. In the developing world, death, disease and civil strife are re-shaping the family. In industrialised countries, politicians dictate family structures and processes through policies that either enhance or mitigate against various notions of 'family', whose only certainty is change.

In the face of such unremitting change, families will need the support of societal structures and policies, and the commitment and guidance of all health professionals to ensure sustainability throughout the precariousness of this century.

Goals for
healthy families

The goals for healthy families are aimed at providing:

- physical, emotional and cultural support for all families
- access to the means for economic sustainability
- a common bond from which to relate to the outside world
- a sense of place, heritage and continuity.

Strategies for assisting families in meeting health goals must be linked to the wider social and cultural context of their lives.

Building healthy public policy

An ecological view of families must balance the public and private responsibilities for family health and safety to ensure that the family's rights to a life free from injury and ill health are paramount. Policies governing the environment must be shaped in a way that allows family members to adopt healthy behaviours and then be supported in their enactment. These policies include pricing mechanisms for alcohol and tobacco, regulations regarding seat belts, gun registration, environmental waste disposal and a host of other things that will create healthful conditions within which families can flourish, whether they live in urban or rural environments (Green, Nathan & Mercer 2001).

Policies that govern community services for families must be seen as a social investment rather than a public expense, and integral to the economic processes of a nation (Cass 1994a). This mandates a reconsideration of family assistance practices that stigmatise families when they are required to demonstrate their inadequacy before any public assistance is provided. Public policies must also respond to the difficulties of separated families, the effect of long work hours on families struggling to survive, and the second shift that occurs once they return home. The need for respite is essential for young working mothers who come home to the responsibilities of child care, and for family caregivers, who often need encouragement to seek respite care. Industrial relations policies that help rather than hinder families are an essential part of healthy community life. Workplace practices and family benefits in the workplace must therefore be seen as more than a fringe benefit, to where they become an instrumental part of working life. Then policies can be developed to support effective choices in integrating employment and family care combinations (Cass 1994b).

The term 'family-friendly policy' has become increasingly distorted with political usage. A family-friendly policy is designed in collaboration with families who will be not only recipients but co-creators of strategies that enhance health and well-being. Yet, all too often, governments devise their family-friendly policies on the basis of economic gains and without genuine collaboration with those who would enrich the policies with practical wisdom. Social service agencies, for example, are often the repository of a wealth of information, yet they are often relegated to the implementation stage rather than participating in the policy development process. At a wider level, policies that seal the fate of families in our globalised societies require the input of those with a broad perspective on what constitutes human rights and social conscience.

The status of refugees is a classic case where families are being imperilled by unhealthy policies. Detaining those who have sought asylum from global conflict, for example, without preserving family integrity, contradicts the human rights principles of actively engaging with people to encourage participation in decision-making and self-help (Silove, Steel & Mollica 2001). It also reflects a lack of consciousness of the plight of the global community and an unwillingness to develop common notions of what it means to be 'humanist' (Saul 1997).

One of the most important elements of supportive family policies is the extent to which they are inclusive. The way a family is defined sets boundaries for inclusion and exclusion when funding allocations are made. For example, government programs that fund programs for ageing families on the basis of such criteria as age and frailty fail to recognise that in doing so, they may sever a vital relationship between ageing family members. Government policies must therefore be developed in consultation with the community and the families who reside there. The basis for defining the family must be what people regard as their family, and public policy must be responsive to them (Bateman 1997). The special needs of migrant families, those with extended family households, Indigenous people and those whose family of definition is based on sexual preference must also be addressed within a family-friendly context.

Urie Bronfenbrenner (1982, p 112), who has written extensively about the need for a family ecology, sums up the public responsibility in creating and sustaining human development through caring for our young:

> *The involvement of one or more adults in care and joint activity in support of child rearing requires public policies and practices that provide opportunity, status, resources, encouragement, example, stability, and above all, time for parenthood, primarily by parents, but also by other adults in the child's environment, both within and outside the home.*

Policies must also be responsive to the vital need to create employment for successive generations of young people. This is particularly acute with an ageing society who will require care and economic support for many years to come. A generation unemployed can develop neither the skills nor the experience to provide infrastructure for an ageing society unless there are job-creation programs. This is a complex issue, particularly in a society where the national capacity to employ young people is prohibited by schemes that ensure that their wages achieve parity with older workers. Such a system leads to higher wages for a few, but fewer jobs for the majority. Our family-friendly policies must therefore revolve around the ways in which political decisions, finances, child care, family relationships, school, workplace training, domestic violence, aged care and other issues affect families' ability to create and sustain health (Hartley & McDonald 1994).

Creating supportive environments

One of the most important elements of helping families is to convey a sense of non-judgemental support. Often the language we use to describe single mothers or divorcees or those who have chosen single parenthood is less than supportive. In some cases our expressions are actually discriminatory as we refer to 'single-parent families', where the family actually has two parents but is headed by one adult residing in the home. In this case, the term 'separated family' or 'one-parent household' may be more appropriate and less dismissive of the parent who lives outside the family home. Similarly, our language needs to reflect various forms of families, including gay and lesbian couples with or without children.

Non-judgemental support is also required in the way we respond to people's need to balance the conventions of their culture with the circumstances of their lives. For example, in some communities it is unacceptable to be divorced, yet violence against women is tolerated. This presents a conflict for health professionals advocating for equality in marriage and the family, when the inclination may be to encourage a wife to leave her husband. We can all assist families by becoming knowledgeable about other cultures and developing mutually supportive systems with cultural sensitivity. This means shifting our own values to acknowledge different families' sense of history, heritage and rituals (Campbell 2001) and developing strategies for incorporating this knowledge into our plans for assisting them.

Strengthening community action

Advocacy means acknowledging family competence and preferences. The key to strengthening community action is family empowerment. As health professionals, our role is to allow families to own their *own* problems rather than telling them what to do, and provide the information and guidance that will assist with self-management and self-empowerment. We must therefore ensure that families are aware of the influences in society that affect their functioning and development. Our role is to filter health-related information, conveying the results of our research to them without engineering their strategies for change. This is particularly important in this information age, when the sheer volume of information is bewildering to many people.

Consolidation of family issues is crucial for the development of society. We must do our part in helping bring about widespread change to the allocation of health resources to support families in all their geographic, cultural, social and developmental configurations. This is a highly political undertaking and counter to historical views of family advocacy, which assumed that families needed only to have their social welfare needs met. The communications media has awakened us to the large number of hidden facets of family issues and sparked a debate over the public versus private nature of the family. Relationships between men and women, the rights and responsibilities of parents and children, and issues of sexuality are often highly contested areas of family life (Hartley, 1995). Yet the collective morality of communities is increasingly on the public agenda. If we can break this down into manageable 'reality bites' for families, they will be better prepared to modify self-imposed risks and/or improve their own environments. To be of real assistance to families, we should keep issues of concern to them at the centre of public focus.

Developing personal skills

We have a duty of care to help educate all family members, and this can be done in many ways. Societal attention should be drawn to the relationship between the education of women and the subsequent health of the family, and the relationship between environmental issues and the family's health agenda. The challenge is to balance resources and responsibility for community support with fostering individual responsibility and individual choice, so that family members gain mastery over their lives. We can also help families to understand the interconnections linking their members. When the family is seen as a foundation of community development, the relational aspects of family life are validated, effectively negating the notion that the family is little more than a holding environment.

As advocates for health and well-being in the family, we can enable that process through respect, understanding and therapeutic engagement with the family in ways that allow them to access our knowledge and our nurturing. This can occur within the context of a mobilising episode of caregiving, or in the ongoing dialogue we maintain as members of society. At times, this means that we must learn to engage families through a social rather than professional perspective, an approach that requires self-understanding and a transformation of consciousness (Gibson 1991). This type of engagement is a form of volunteerism, which is in itself a measure of social capital. A social approach will also help us to appreciate the plight of family caregivers, who often enter into therapeutic relationships with family members with inadequate support. It is our responsibility as health professionals to ensure that they are not disadvantaged by becoming unwitting 'guinea pigs' in our economic rationalising of health care. Our models of integrated (home and community) care must take their needs into consideration and recognise the need for resources to support family caregiving in all its forms.

Reorienting health services

We have a responsibility to connect the needs of families entrusted to our care with the wider global agenda. So, once again, we must think global and act local. Developing collective social consciousness helps all participants contribute to the equitable rationalisation of resources, especially in light of major demographic changes to fertility rates, ageing, migration, wars and employment patterns. However, regional needs must also be identified and become part of the local as well as larger health agenda.

For health professionals the most important aspects of family care are relational. Influencing the context within which families interact requires knowledge of local issues and the supports available for family support (Robinson 1996). Many of us can become therapeutically engaged with the family by assisting family empowerment in a multitude of ways: in our high-tech, high-touch care, in our nurturing of young people and their parents, in our understanding of society and the way in which social forces help and hinder the family's attempts to define itself to achieve health, well-being and happiness. Of course, this demands research, reflection and an attitude of tolerance. Family research must address the impact of public policies, the interface of families and the legal, religious and health care system, the impact of societal events such as economic downturns, natural disasters, wars, and changes in cultural values and attitudes (Ganong 1995).

Our research should respond to the challenges of evolving family forms. At this time in history, at least some research efforts should be directed towards the divorcing family, investigating ways of assisting people undergoing marital separation to understand their situation and to explore ways of redressing any negative influences on individual family members. We should also reorient our research strategies from focusing on problems to examining the distinguishing features of remarriages and stepfamilies, particularly with respect to cultivating effective, rather than ineffective, functioning (Ganong 1995).

thinking critically

Family health

1 Identify three major ways in which the family influences the health of society.

2 Identify five characteristics of contemporary families and how each of these influences the health of a community.

3 Describe four risk factors for family health and wellness.

4 Conduct an analysis of a family you know using one of the theoretical orientations provided in this chapter.

5 Examine one social policy with which you are familiar in terms of its historical precedents, responsiveness to family health needs and impact on family health.

6 Describe three strategies for encouraging empowerment in separated or divorced families.

REFERENCES

Amato, P. (1999). Children of divorced parents as young adults. In: E.M. Hetherington (ed), *Coping with Divorce, Single Parenting, and Remarriage*. New Jersey: Lawrence Erlbaum Associates, pp 147–63.

Amato, P., Loomis, L.S. & Booth, A. (1995). Parental divorce, marital conflict, and offspring well-being in early adulthood. *Social Forces*, 73: 895–916.

Australian Bureau of Statistics (1998). Income and Welfare, Caring in Australia. Canberra: ABS.

—— (1999a). Household and Family Projections, Canberra: AGPS.

—— (1999b). Australian Social Trends 1999, International Comparisons—Population. Canberra: ABS.

—— (2000). Marriages and Divorces, Australia. Canberra: ABS.

Australian Institute of Health and Welfare (1998). Health in rural and remote Australia, Canberra: AGPS.

—— (2000). Australia's Health 2000. Canberra: AGPS.

Bateman, G. (1997). Defining families for policy making. Paper presented at the Australian Institute for Family Studies Conference, Melbourne, 15 May.

Bronfenbrenner, U. (1982). Children and families: the silent revolution. *Australian Journal of Sex, Marriage and Family*, 3(3): 111–23.

Campbell, D. (2001). Global perspectives on wife beating and health care. In: M. Martinez (ed), *Prevention and Control of Aggression and the Impact on Its Victims*. New York: Kluwer Academic/Plenum Publishers, pp 215–27.

Cass, B. (1994a). Connecting the public and the private: a lasting legacy of the International Year of the Family in Australia. Perth: Edith Cowan University Public Lecture.

—— (1994b). Integrating private and social responsibilities: better partnerships between families, governments and communities. *Family Matters*, 37: 20–7.

Castiglia, P. (1994). Grandparenting: benefits and problems. *Journal of Pediatric Health Care*, 8: 79–91.

Curthoys, A. (1999). Family fortress. Chronicles of the Future. *The Australian*, 13 November, Sydney.

Duvall, E. (1977). *Marriage and Family Relationships*, 5th edn, Philadelphia: Lippincott.

Duvall, E. & Miller, B. (1985). *Marriage and Family Development*, 6th edn, New York: Harper & Row.

Eastman, M. (1989). *Family: The Vital Factor*. Melbourne: Collins Dove.

Edgar, D. (1992). Childhood in its social context. *Family Matters*, 33: 32–5.

Fink, S. (1995). The influence of family resources and family demands on the strains and wellbeing of caregiving families. *Nursing Research*, 44(3): 139–46.

Foss, G. (1996). A conceptual model for studying parenting behaviors in immigrant populations. *Advances in Nursing Science*, 19(2): 74–87.

Freudenberg, N. (2000). Health promotion in the city. A review of the current practice and future prospects in the United States. *Annual Review of Public Health*, 21: 473–503.

Friedman, M. (1986). *Family Nursing: Theory and Assessment*, 2nd edn, Norwalk, Conn: Appleton-Lange.

Ganong, L. (1995). Current trends and issues in family nursing research. *Journal of Family Nursing*, 1(2): 171–206.

Gibson, C. (1991). A concept analysis of empowerment. *Journal of Advanced Nursing*, 16: 354–61.

Goode, J. (1996). Comparing family systems in Europe and Asia: are there different sets of rules? *Population and Development Review*, 22(1): 1–20.

Gottleib, L. & Feeley, N. (2000). Nursing intervention studies: issues related to change and timing. In: M. Stewart (ed), *Community Nursing: Promoting Canadians' Health*, 2nd edn, Toronto: WB Saunders, pp 523–41.

Green, L., Nathan, R. & Mercer, S. (2001). The health of health promotion in public policy: Drawing inspiration from the tobacco control movement, *Health Promotion Journal of Australia*, 12(2): 110–16.

Hartley, R. (ed) (1995). *Families and Cultural Diversity in Australia*. Sydney: Allen & Unwin.

Hartley, R. & McDonald, P. (1994). The many faces of families. *Family Matters*, 37: 7–12.

Hetherington, E. M. (1999). Should we stay together for the sake of the children? In: E.M. Hetherington (ed), *Coping with Divorce, Single Parenting, and Remarriage*, New Jersey: Lawrence Erlbaum Associates, pp 93–116.

Humphreys, J. (2000). Rural families and rural health. *Journal of Family Studies*, 6(2): 167–81.

Hunsucker, S., Frank, D. & Flannery, J. (1999). Meeting the needs of rural families during critical illness: The APN's role. *Dimensions of Critical Care Nursing*, 18(3): 24–33.

Jackson, M. (1994). Discharge planning: issues and challenges for gerontological nursing: a critique of the literature. *Journal of Advanced Nursing*, 19: 492–502.

Keating, D. & Hertzman, C. (1999). *Developmental Health and the Wealth of Nations*. New York: The Guilford Press.

LeClair, J. & Innes, F. (1997). Urban ecological structure and perceived child and adolescent psychological disorder. *Social Science and Medicine*, 44(11): 1649–59.

Long, K. & Weinert, C. (1989). Rural nursing: Developing the theory base, *Scholarly Inquiry for Nursing Practice*, 3: 113–27.

McKeever, P. (1994). Between women: nurses and family caregivers. *Canadian Journal of Nursing Research*, 26(4): 15–21.

McMurray, A. (1997). Violence against ex-wives: anger and advocacy. *Health Care for Women International*, 18: 543–6.

Melson, G., Ladd, G. & Hsu, H. (1993). Maternal support networks, maternal cognitions, and young children's social and cognitive development. *Child Development*, 64: 1401–17.

Mistiaen, P., Duijnhouwer, E., Wijkel, D., de Bont, M. & Veeger, A. (1997). The problems of elderly people at home one week after discharge from an acute care setting. *Journal of Advanced Nursing*, 25: 1233–40.

Morrow-Howell, N., Chadiha, L., Proctor, E., Hourd-Bryant, M. & Dore, P. (1996). Racial differences in discharge planning. *Health and Social Work*, 21(2): 131–9.

Reiley, P., Iessoni, L., Phillips, R., Davis, R., Tuchin, L. & Calkins, D. (1996). Discharge planning: comparison of patients' and nurses' perceptions of patients following hospital discharge. *Image: Journal of Nursing Scholarship*, 28(2): 143–7.

Reutter, L. (2000). Socioeconomic determinants of health. In: M. Stewart (ed), *Community Nursing. Promoting Canadians' Health*, 2nd edn, Toronto: WB Saunders, pp 174–93.

Rieger, K. (1991). Effects of child care on young children: Forty years of research. Melbourne: Australian Institute of Family Studies.

Robinson, C. (1996). Health care relationships revisited. *Journal of Family Nursing*, 2(2): 152–73.

Sanders, M. (ed). (1995). *Healthy Families, Healthy Nation*. Brisbane: Australian Academic Press.

Sandhaus, S. (1998). Migrant health: a harvest of poverty. *American Journal of Nursing*, 98(9): 52, 54.

Saul, J. (1997). *The Unconscious Civilization*. New York: The Free Press.

Siena Group (1998). Family statistics country papers. Sydney: Siena Group.

Silove, D., Steel, Z. & Mollica, R. (2001). Detention of asylum seekers: assault on health, human rights, and social development. *The Lancet*, (357)9266: 1436.

Stewart, M. (2000). Social support, coping, and self-care as public participation mechanisms. In: M. Stewart (ed), *Community Nursing: Promoting Canadians' Health*, 2nd edn, Toronto: WB Saunders, pp 83–104.

Strasser, R., Harvey, D. & Burley, M. (1994).The health service needs of small rural communities. *Australian Journal of Rural Health*, 2(2): 7–13.

Strauss, M. (2001). Physical aggression in the family. In: M. Martinez (ed), *Prevention and Control of Aggression and the Impact on its Victims*. New York: Kluwer Academic/Plenum Publishers, pp 181–200.

Sweeting, H. & West, P. (1995). Family life and health in adolescence: a role for culture in the health inequalities debate? *Social Science and Medicine*, 40(2): 163–75.

Turner-Henson, A., Holaday, B. & Swan, J. (1992). When parenting becomes care giving: caring for the chronically ill child. *Family Community Health*, 15(2): 19–30.

United Nations Family Planning Association (UNFPA) (2000). The state of world population 2000, New York: United Nations.

US Bureau of Census (2000). National Center for Health Statistics, Washington: US Department of Commerce.

Wallerstein, J. & Blakeslee, S. (1990). *Second Chances: Men, Women and Children a Decade after Divorce*. New York: Tickner & Fields.

Wallerstein, J., Lewis, J. & Blakeslee, S. (2000). *The Unexpected Legacy of Divorce: A 25-year Landmark Study*. New York: Hyperion.

Wellard, S. (1997). Constructions of family nursing: a critical exploration. *Contemporary Nursing*, 6(2): 78–84.

Wright, L. & Leahey, M. (1987). *Families and Chronic Illness*. Pittsburgh: Springhouse Corp.

—— (1994). *Nurses and Families: A Guide to Family Assessment and Intervention*, 2nd edn, Philadelphia: FA Davis.

World Health Organization (2000). The World Health Report 2000. Health systems. Improving performance. Geneva: WHO.

Yencken, D. & Porter, L. (2001). *A Just and Sustainable Australia*. Melbourne: The Australian Council of Social Service.

CHAPTER 10

Health and gender:
healthy women, healthy men

Introduction Gender relations have an enormous impact on health. Gender-based health studies have shown a wide range of differences between men's and women's health status, treatments and vulnerabilities, primarily due to inequalities in society, inequities in health care and culturally embedded norms for health behaviour. Inequalities that exist in the economic, political, environmental and sociocultural aspects of our society hold back individual growth, community development and the evolution of society, to the disadvantage of both women and men (UNFPA 2000). Inequalities between women and men persist even in societies where equity and affirmative action policies exist and, to some extent, these inequalities are related to differential access to and control over resources, education, workplace issues, credit, technology, transportation, services and decision-making processes (UNFPA 2000).

Gender issues must be seen in terms of both women's and men's issues. The influence of gender on health extends to differential opportunities, constraints and the impact of change as they affect women and men's health and health behaviour. Without this understanding and a will to redress inequities, men and women will be unable to participate in partnerships to build strong families and viable societies. Gender equity and in-depth understanding of how health is interpreted in terms of gender are essential for maintaining human rights, development priorities and the future health of nations (UNFPA 2000). This chapter examines women's health and men's health from the perspective of primary health care principles in order to illustrate the linkages between gendered social relations and the creation and sustainability of health.

objectives **By the end of this chapter you will be able to:**

1 Describe the social construction of health, illness, injury and disability according to gender relations

2 Explain the central issues related to gender equality in health

3 Identify the most important influences on the maintenance of men's health and women's health

4 Identify three societal factors that compromise the health of women and men, respectively

5 Develop a community strategy for improving the health of women and the health of men.

Inequities in the burden of
illness, injury and disability

One of the most important principles of primary health care is access to health; not just health services, but the range of social conditions that assist individuals and their families to achieve, and then sustain, the level of health to which they aspire. Because the world has been socially constructed in a way that discriminates against women, this has been difficult for many women and their families to achieve. Social inequalities contribute to women's burden of illness, injury and disabilities to a greater extent than to those of men. This occurs because of unequal access to information, technology, benefits and resources, and because of socially and culturally entrenched attitudes that define women's role in society in reductionist, reproductive terms, and exclude them from full participation in policy-making and governance (Birn 1999; ICN 2000a). Men's health status also shows inequalities, in their lower expected lifespan, for example, and in the rate of earlier mortality from certain illnesses; however, these have been explained on the basis of behavioural norms that govern men's help-seeking and risk, rather than social inequities (WHO 2001).

Inequalities between women and men are a detriment to global health. The developing world is facing a crisis in population growth in those countries where there are already scarce resources and no hope for ecological sustainability in the future. Many women in developing countries would choose to limit their family size, given the opportunity, but decisions about family planning continue to be subjugated to culturally determined population control measures and their ignorance of how this could be changed (UNFPA 2000). As a result, male-dominated policies govern their personal health, the social environments within which their children will be raised and the development of their communities. Policies governing reproduction are the most significant way to redress the imminent population explosion in the places where it is of greatest concern. If there was universal access to family planning in the world, and women could choose the number of children they wanted, the fertility rates in those countries would fall by one-third (UNFPA 2000). It would also help to alleviate the poverty that keeps women from enhancing their health and the health of their family members.

Women
and work

At a societal level, women labour at the heart of many communities to ensure economic, cultural and social viability (WHO 1997). Yet cultural values, societal norms and values, and religious beliefs place lower value on the contributions, work, ideas and lives of women and girls. Women's work in developing countries places them at risk of respiratory ailments and other physical conditions because of unsanitary air and water, exposure to agricultural pesticides, and the strain of carrying wood and water for the family (WHO 2000a). In industrialised countries, home and community environments are also unsafe, exposing many women to toxic environments, crowding and violence (USOWH 2001). Yet women remain absent from decision-making or policy development that would redress working conditions. Globalisation, privatisation and trade liberalisation affect them unevenly and, in most countries, there is a lack of political will to include their participation in changing these practices (WHO 2000b).

Inequities also face women in the industrialised workforce, where women are often relegated to lower-status and lower-paying jobs, sometimes because of child-care or family care obligations. In some cases, this leaves them with little time to attend to their own health needs, and with fewer opportunities for self-improvement. This situation is worse for migrant women, who experience higher rates of work-related illnesses and injuries and a greater incidence of poor mental and emotional health (Meleis et al 1996; Spurlock 1995; Young 1996). They are more likely to live in poverty, have a greater frequency and severity of illness and be marginalised in health care by the lack of minority health care providers (USNWH 2001). Migrant women tend to work in dangerous, dirty and low-status occupations, suffering from the role strain of dual careers in paid and unpaid work with the additional stress of migration to unfamiliar surroundings. Many have moved away from the support of extended families. These women are also less likely than others to undertake training that would help overcome the language problems and other difficulties they experience in dealing with housing, transport, child care, health care and education services for their children (Yencken & Porter 2001).

Women in the higher levels of the workforce also are placed at risk for ill health by the compound stress of dual roles. Even those who attain management positions are in many cases still expected to undertake the majority of household tasks once they return home. Despite the fact that participation in paid economic activity is generally beneficial to women, for many the added responsibility of work at home (the 'second shift') is a health hazard. Scandinavian researchers have found a definite difference between the sexes in relation to the 'unwinding' period at the end of a day's work, concluding that, despite having made gains in reducing workplace inequities, women suffer from greater stress than men once they return home in the evening (Bergman, Carlsson & Wright 1996; Elstad 1996). This may also explain why marriage seems to have a more positive health effect on men than women (Oakley 1994). And it may be related to the fact that in marriage, men are usually nurtured and supported by their wives in terms of diet, health care and other healthy lifestyle factors, whereas the reverse is not often the case.

Women's health
and health risks

Gender differences that increase the risk of illness and injury for women are evident at the system, organ, tissue, cellular and subcellular levels (Gilbert 2000). These differences are manifest in women's drug responses, addiction, chronic disease state, susceptibility to infection, and vulnerability to mental and social problems (Gilbert 2000). Women's higher level of body fat is believed to alter their reaction to drugs (Gilbert 2000; USOWH 2001). Their reactions to alcohol also differ, not only in the speed of intoxication, but in that they have a higher incidence of liver disease from consuming less alcohol for shorter periods of time than men (Gilbert 2000). Older women also lose more bone mass than men and are more susceptible to lung cancer, even if they smoke the same amount of tobacco as men (Gilbert 2000).

Women throughout the world have a much higher prevalence of lung cancer than men (WHO 1999a; USOWH 2001). Their rate of lung cancer is rising because the large number of young women who began smoking early in life are now part of the 'baby boomer' generation, reaching the high-risk stage of life for lung and other cancers. Women are also disproportionately affected by smoking if they also use contraceptives, the combined effect increasing their risk for cardiovascular disease. Smoking has also been associated with cervical dysplasia and cancer, ectopic pregnancy, spontaneous abortion and maternal complications such as placenta previa and abruptio placentae. Pregnant women who smoke have twice the risk of infant mortality from all causes, including sudden infant death syndrome (Kendrick & Merritt 1996). Because they live longer, many women also suffer chronic disabling conditions such as diabetes, osteoporosis, osteoarthritis, obesity, urinary incontinence, Alzheimer's disease, fibromyalgia and chronic fatigue syndrome, all of which have a long trajectory of increasing impairment (USOWH 2001; WHO 1999a, 2000b).

Mortality rates also differ between men and women. Female infanticide, inadequate food and medical care, physical abuse, genital mutilation, forced sex and early childbirth takes the lives of many young girls in the developing world (UNFPA 2000). Even in industrialised countries, there are enormous disparities in health between men and women. Although heart disease is more prevalent in men, more women die from heart disease, to some extent, because they develop it later in life than men. These women have almost twice the likelihood of suffering a second heart attack and stroke than men, even though high levels of high-density lipoprotein (HDL) have a greater protective effect in women than in men (Gilbert 2000; USOWH 2001). Some differences are also found in the way women's diseases are manifest, which is thought to be mediated by differences in the mechanism of antibody formation (Gilbert 2000).

Women's
health care

Women are also made vulnerable to ill health by discriminatory practices in the health care system. Women receive diagnoses and treatment based on what works for men and research that has traditionally excluded women (ICN 2000a; USOWH 2001). In developing countries, girls and boys have unequal access to treatment and immunisation, which in many cases denies girls prevention from illness (UNFPA 2000).

Health care providers also treat women differently to men. They receive less thorough evaluations for similar complaints, their symptoms are frequently minimised, they are given fewer interventions for the same diagnoses, more frequent prescriptions for certain types of medications, and less explanation in response to questions (USOWH 2001). In some countries, health services and health workers do not conform to human rights, and to ethical, professional and gender-sensitive standards in the delivery of women's health services, nor do they ensure responsible, voluntary and informed consent (UN 2000).

One of the most noticeable effects of gender differences in health and health care lies in the evidence base for practice. Historically, medical researchers have considered cardiovascular disease a disease of males and thus have systematically excluded females from their studies. Yet cardiovascular disease causes more deaths in women than all types of cancers combined (USOWH 2001). In some cases, biomedical researchers have intentionally excluded women or selected only male data for analysis on the basis of either sample size or the desire for homogeneous or 'cleaner' results, uncontaminated by hormonal fluctuations. Still others have excluded female subjects to guard against causing harm to a developing or potentially developing foetus (Narrigan, Zones & Worcester 1997).

As a result of this type of bias, many diagnostic tests for cardiovascular disease have been developed from the results of male-only studies, which calls into question their sensitivity to female patients. Certain cardiac scans have been accepted as the norm, and yet they may be inaccurate for females because of the need to scan through breast tissue, or because of distortions related to women's biochemistry. Another difference is related to treatment. Women hospitalised for cardiac disease tend to have fewer diagnostic procedures while hospitalised and it is unknown whether this relates to a greater valuing of males, the willingness of women to make lifestyle changes (obviating the need for dramatic interventions) or the dilution of medical concerns about women because of their frequency of contact with the health care system (Beery 1995). In the United States, the system of costing various health care procedures has also shown gender bias in the comparatively low valuing of procedures conducted on women (Harer 1996).

The exclusion of women from research, diagnosis and treatment protocols is problematic for several reasons. One is that there are few studies of the ways women's symptoms differ from men's, but preliminary data suggest there may be serious differences. For example, some women present with shortness of breath or epigastric pain when they are having acute myocardial infarction, yet the (male) norm of chest pain is the basis for diagnosis (Beery 1995; Gilbert 2000). This could potentially distort the epidemiological understanding, risk factor identification, intervention and treatment of at least cardiovascular disease (Flitcraft 1996). It also has an implication for calculating the burden of other diseases and future trends in identifying health needs for women. In the case of the DALY framework some 'gender filters' and ultimately 'culture filters' should be incorporated into health care planning mechanisms to ensure that calculations of resource allocations based on health risk do not disadvantage women and exclude their importance to personal and family health (Sundby 1999).

Health
and beauty

One area of increasing concern to women's health advocates is the influence of the beauty industry in perpetuating unhealthy stereotypes of women. Images of women create societal attitudes that disempower females by setting unrealistic standards for behaviour or appearance. These images are directed at women in all forms of media and marketing. It is blatant consumerism, but insidious in light of the research that indicates distinct advantages in conforming to the ideal appearance. People who are considered beautiful or handsome are more likely to be seen as good, and more desirable as friends or partners, and they tend to gain better jobs than others. Those considered unattractive receive less attention as infants, are evaluated more harshly in school and earn less than their attractive counterparts (Zones 1997). This has a much more powerful impact on women than men, whose personal appearance is not governed by the strict norms seen in all forms of public media.

One of the biggest problems with societal expectation of attractiveness is the pervasive effect of the media on young women's perceptions of themselves and on their self-esteem. Naomi Wolf (1991) drew attention to the way these perceptions are politically and economically entrenched in our society in her exposé of the beauty industry. She argued that the focus on and demand for beauty has become more intense as women have achieved success. The 'Beauty Myth', that is, the belief in an objective quality called *beauty*, keeps male dominance intact by perpetuating women's insecurity about their appearance. Women are deceived by advertising and peer pressure to believe that beauty, as elusive as it may be, defines womanhood and whether or not a woman will be desired by men. The beauty myth has important implications for empowerment and consequently women's health, because when young women are continually questioning the adequacy of their appearance, they are distracted from more worthwhile and confidence-building pursuits (Zones 1997).

Reproductive and
sexual disempowerment

Women in developing countries have different psychological costs from inequality, although they share the outcomes of low self-esteem and high rates of depression with their sisters in the developing world (Mathers, Vos & Stevenson 1999; UNFPA 2000; WHO 2000a). For these women, a lethal combination of cultural, social, economic and personal factors often leaves them subjected to ongoing violence, rape, genital mutilation, forced pregnancy, sterilisation or abortion or other types of abuse in their daily lives. An African woman faces a 1 in 16 chance of dying from pregnancy-related causes. Worldwide, 99 per cent of all cases of women's mortality at childbirth occurs in developing countries (UNFPA 2000). What this illustrates is that women continue to be trapped within oppressive circumstances when it comes to reproductive health, even though the magnitude of the problem may be different. The United Nations reports that 'if women had the power to make decisions about sexual activity and its consequences, they could avoid many of the 80 million unwanted pregnancies per year, 20 million unsafe abortions, 500 000 maternal deaths, and many times that number of infections and injuries' (UNFPA 2000, p 2).

Powerful sociocultural norms, often reinforced by religious and judicial sanctions, exert societal control over when women should give birth, when they should not, and to whom the fruits of their womb belong (Varkevisser 1995). For many women, the fact that they have little control over their reproductive choices is a cause of extraordinary stress, matched only by the danger and emotional conflicts surrounding the act itself. In China, where there is abortion on demand because of the family limitation policy, abortion is part of the politics of survival, a fact of life to which Chinese women must accommodate (Rigdon, 1996). However, this is quite different in other countries, where abortion is frowned upon. As a result, unsafe abortions result in complications that cause approximately 40 per cent of maternal deaths worldwide, many of which occur among the poor and illiterate of Asian, African and Latin American countries and the Caribbean (Timpson 1996; Varkevisser 1995).

HIV/AIDS and other reproductive tract infections are a further problem for young women in developing countries. Women are more vulnerable to infection than males because anatomical differences sometimes make diagnosis difficult. Women can also be asymptomatic or have subtle symptoms that fail to alert them to the infection. Because of their subservience to men in countries like sub-Saharan Africa, they are unable to negotiate condom use or any other sexual controls. As a result, HIV-positive women outnumber males by 2 million in that region and many are dying from AIDS (UNFPA 2000). Women's experiences related to HIV/AIDS illustrate that they can be disenfranchised by oppression and discrimination on the basis of gender, race, sexuality and socioeconomic status. Being female, poor and a member of a racial minority can be stigmatising itself, but when AIDS is involved, there is an additional stigma related to the assumption of promiscuity, better tolerated in males than females (Bunting 1996; UNFPA 2000).

As HIV/AIDS has become increasingly prevalent among women, sexual inequality in diagnosis and treatment has become life-threatening. In societies where a man is considered to have exclusive rights to his wife's womb, a woman cannot refuse to have sexual intercourse with her husband, even if he has been unfaithful to her. Neither can she demand that he take precautions. Women with sole responsibility for child care do not see leaving their husbands as an option, particularly where his promiscuity is related to male labour migration caused by the family's economic condition. So most remain in a cycle of abject disempowerment for the sake of status, honour, love or the children (Varkevisser 1995; Zierler & Krieger 1997).

Violence
against women

Violence against women is a growing risk to women's health that is closely interlinked with women's roles in the family and society. It includes all intentional behaviours causing harm to women: dowry burnings, violence against domestic workers, against wives by mothers-in-law, female genital mutilation, abortions of female foetuses, intentional food deprivation to female infants, and assault by intimates (Campbell 2001). Female genital mutilation continues in 28 African countries, in parts of Asia, and in immigrant groups in industrialised countries. In most cases, this is conducted in unsanitary conditions without anaesthetic, causing haemorrhage, infection, urinary retention, blood poisoning, difficulty in childbirth, infertility and mental health problems among its victims

(UNFPA 2000). Wife *beating* is an act of physical aggression, condoned (often ambiguously) by certain cultures, whereas wife *battering* is understood as repeated physical and/or sexual assault within the context of coercive control, which is not usually sanctioned in any society (Campbell 2001). The latter has also been called couple violence or patriarchal terrorism (Campbell 2001).

One of the worst forms of violence against women is rape, whether it is a quiet, personal act of violence or whether it is political violence, perpetrated against women in times of war, to brutalise the enemy. Rape on this level, which is usually sanctioned by political leaders, has devastating consequences beyond the woman, to the entire community. Families suffer enormously, particularly where there are cultural sanctions against accepting women victims of rape back into the fold. This situation also creates a chasm between families trying to develop a sense of community during post-war reconstruction (Flitcraft 1996).

Rape is a major cause of injury to women, one from which many women never psychologically recover, even after their bodies heal. It is a crime that is rapidly increasing in prevalence in so-called civilised societies, and increasing in visibility in the developing countries. It is estimated that over 12 million adult women in the United States have been victims of at least one forcible rape, the legacy of which is often rape-related post-traumatic stress disorder (Schafran 1996).

By far the most pervasive form of violence against women is that perpetrated by an intimate spouse or partner. Domestic violence or domestic abuse, which is now the leading cause of injuries among women, consists of a pattern of coercive control typically designed to isolate the victim. It may be physical, sexual and/or psychological in nature and, sadly, this type of behaviour usually becomes a pattern from one generation to the next (Grisso et al 1996; Robbe et al 1996).

Violence against women is such a threat to health that it was recognised as a human rights violation by the UN in 1993, and defined as a serious public health problem by the WHO in 1996 (Campbell 2001). It is also becoming a matter of concern to the general public. The women's movement of the past 25 years has helped to heighten awareness of the prevalence and problems of domestic abuse, with general agreement that it is related to issues of power and control. Where women have greater equality, rates of battering are lowest (Campbell 2001). A simplistic view of family violence views the problem as men simply abusing their power, and women colluding in their own victimisation by not leaving. This perspective casts men as tyrants and women as masochists, which obscures the many complexities of family interactions within which the violence occurs (Goldner et al 1990). Many acts of violence are also perpetrated by wives and girlfriends against husbands or boyfriends, and the literature contains heated arguments about gender symmetry in spousal violence (Morse 1995; Sorenson, Upchurch & Shen 1996). Mutual violence, where both partners engage in assaults against the other, is also a problem, but irrespective of who strikes whom, the danger for women lies in the fact that men strike harder, so women are more often the victim of injury (Campbell 2001; Morse 1995; Strauss 2001).

The continuum of violence against women ranges from workplace harassment to mortal acts of personal violence. Sexual harassment can be verbal, physical and visual or written and can range from a disparaging remark to rape. In the United States, even a work environment that creates a climate hostile to women can be considered sexual harassment. The problem is related to workplace politics, in that the woman being harassed is typically at the mercy of a workplace superior and thus risks advancement in her work once the act is reported. Many refrain from reporting acts of sexual harassment on the basis that, like women in rape cases, they will be the ones under suspicion and charged with demonstrating that they did not provoke the incident. Harassment of any kind is more often perpetrated against women of colour, single mothers, working-class women, older women, lesbians, feminists and those with disabilities (Britton 1997).

One of the greatest frustrations in dealing with victims of violence is the lack of trust between health care professionals and the person needing assistance. Health care workers have been known to treat victims of abuse with little sensitivity, especially those who have been in the system previously. Often the woman's injuries are classified according to standard medical terminology, which often obscures the cause (Richardson & Feder 1996). Many nurses, doctors, police officers or ambulance attendants simply fail to understand why a woman who has been repeatedly abused doesn't just up and leave. Yet the problems with leaving are many and complex. In most cases, abused women are caught between maintaining their spousal attachment, economic survival, and their partner and children's well-being on one side, and their own physical and emotional well-being on the other (Campbell 1992; Vazquez 1996). For rural women, leaving is even more difficult, as they often suffer from geographical isolation and lack of resources (Dimmitt 1995).

As health professionals our first challenge is to understand and then lend non-judgemental support to all victims of violence. At a societal level, however, we must use the principles of primary health care to raise awareness of equity and empowerment issues. Our role as advocates includes becoming actively engaged in changing the social and cultural institutions that have given rise to notions of masculine entitlement and all those influences that shape society's attitudes towards women (Goodman et al 1993). This involves working with both women and men to eliminate all forms of violence and the disempowerment that leads to violence.

The greatest barrier to women's empowerment is the extent to which their lives are financially impoverished. Women make up 70 per cent of those living in the world in absolute poverty (ICN 2000a). Many women in the developing countries live their entire lives in hunger, malnutrition, overwork and sexual violence with no access to opportunities for relaxation, respite, health care or the opportunity for exercise that would build physical strength or healthy bone growth. Even in old age, in some countries, traditional widowhood practices pose the threat of abuse (WHO 2000a). The stage of widowhood is often doubly unhappy for women where it is preceded by a period of caregiving to the deceased spouse, especially if a woman has also lived with the pressures of caring for other family members (ABS 1999; USOWH 2001; WHO 2000a). Old age for this group is often a reflection of a lifetime of deprivation and the cumulative effects of environmental hazards or social disenfranchisement (WHO 2000a). Many older women suffer from physical and mental illness related to inadequate opportunities to lead a healthy lifestyle, or depression that flows from social isolation (Havens & Hall 2000; Rokach 2000).

Educating
women

Educating girls is the single most powerful way to promote equitable personal opportunities and pathways for community development. Women who have had access to formal education tend to marry at a later age than uneducated women, have smaller families, use family planning methods, make better use of antenatal and delivery care, seek medical care sooner for themselves and their family members, have higher standards of care and nutrition and therefore a higher probability of survival, and raise daughters to be more educated so that they can continue this progression (ICN 2000a; UNESCO 2000; UNFPA 2000). For these reasons, gender equity in educational opportunity has come to the attention of those involved in community development. As the new century began, Kofi Annan, secretary general of the UN, declared a ten-year Girls' Education Initiative, which he expects will have immediate benefit for family planning, nutrition, health, economic productivity, and social and political participation (UNESCO 2000). The initiative will be promoted on the basis of gender equality and sensitivity in all educational elements to try and eradicate illiteracy among girls.

Throughout the past two decades, women's health has attracted the attention and assistance of the international donor community. Most assistance has primarily revolved around fertility and reproductive health, without tackling the fundamental elements of gender equality (Birn 1999). Yet reproductive health has been shown to be inextricably linked with education. Women carry a special group of risks associated with reproduction, which are determined by social norms that prevail over women's literacy and education. Knowledgeable women are better able to understand the risks of pregnancy and childbirth and take steps to prevent these. In the past several years, attempts have been made to respond to women's need for education, especially in developing countries, to help them gain basic knowledge such as the need for sanitary practices in maintaining households and the link between unclean drinking water and their children's health (Curtis 1999). It is now widely accepted that education leads mothers to early, enhanced child-rearing practices. This nurtures the 'biological embedding' in their children, whereby children develop neuroimmune responses and pathways that help them become more resilient in the face of life stressors (Hertzman 1999).

Developing education and skills in young people of both genders has a flow-on effect to sustainable community development, especially if this is accompanied by equitable workplace policies. The UN explains that 'giving women farmers in Kenya the same support as men would increase their yields by more than 20 per cent. Similarly, raising Latin American women's wages to men's levels would increase national output by 5 per cent' (UNFPA 2000, p 6). This is the economic significance of education and skills development. But equally important is the contribution of women's education to the human and social potential of any society.

Hertzman (1999) explains the link between education, equity and health, contending that educational inequities can also be shown to have a remarkable effect, even on the competence of people in industrialised societies. He compared numeracy and literacy between the least well educated segments of Sweden, Canada and the United States populations. Sweden is one of the most egalitarian OECD countries, with high income equality, high life expectancy and a shallow socioeconomic gradient in health status. As mentioned in Chapter 2, the gradient effect represents the stepwise difference in health status between those of increasingly higher SES. The United States has low income equality, low life expectancy and a *steep* socioeconomic gradient (a wider gap between rich and poor), while Canada falls in between the two. The level of literacy and numeracy competence even among the *least* educated in Sweden is vastly better than in Canada and the United States, demonstrating the impact of equitable social conditions, including educational practices, on health, as measured in this case by life expectancy (Hertzman 1999).

Of the 10 million children not attending school in developing countries, 60 per cent are girls (UNESCO 2000). The United Nations urges its member states to lobby for the education of girls (UN 2000). It will take lifelong commitment by the governments of these nations, and the support of others, to understand the implications of keeping girls out of school. As health professionals we can assist this process by unravelling the links between empowerment, education, self-determinism and health for the benefit of society.

Men's health
and risk

Like women, men have numerous risks to health, most of which arise from gender roles, risky behaviours and lifestyles, responses to stress and a hesitancy to take action to protect their health or to prevent illness (ICN 2000b). Despite having most of the social determinants of health in their favour, men have higher mortality rates for all 15 leading causes of death (Meryn & Jadad 2001). Around the world, men's life expectancy is also consistently lower than that of women. Like women, the two most common causes of death for men are cardiovascular disease and cancers, but their burden of injury is much greater (AIHW 2000; Schmeiser-Rieder et al 1999). Researchers studying coronary heart disease (CHD) have found differential patterns of the illness according to geographical location. However, differences in gender ratios of smoking, obesity, hypertension, high plasma total and low high-density lipoprotein (HDL) were found to explain only 40 per cent of the variation in mortality in a comparison across 24 countries (Weidner 2000). This led the researchers to conclude that 'male anatomy is not destiny' (Weidner 2000, p 291).

Clearly, men's behaviour patterns place them at higher risk of illness, injury and disability. WHO (2001) reports that about 50 per cent of the variation in human life span is attributable to survival attributes that are fixed by the age of 30, but only one-half to one-third of this effect can be linked to genetic factors. With age, the effect of hereditary factors decreases, indicating a stronger behavioural element in causing illness. Men are known to be greater risk-takers than women, and more likely to engage in health-damaging risks such as over-indulging in alcohol consumption, smoking, dangerous driving and unsafe sexual practices (WHO 1999a). In the United States, for example, it is estimated that half of all deaths among men each year could be prevented through improvements in personal health practices (Courtenay 2001).

Men also respond differently than women to stress. Some react to the pressures of their lives with aggressive acts, which has been used to explain the disproportionately high rate of suicides among males, but this may also be a function of the social acceptability of men using the more lethal means of suicide, which include firearms and hangings. Other men react to stress by ignoring or denying its presence, and this is one plausible explanation for men's propensity to disregard bodily changes or symptoms of illness. Behaviours such as increasing alcohol, tobacco or food consumption in response to stressful events also predisposes them to workplace injuries (Brown 2001; Schmeiser-Rieder et al 1999). These responses to stress may be less adaptive physiologically, behaviourally and emotionally, which contributes to the burden of risk for CHD (Weidner 2000).

Men also respond to depression differently than women. Although they report more depression than women, they tend to cope with it less effectively, using strategies such as denial, distraction and increased alcohol consumption, rather than accepting depression as a disorder to be treated and a cause for ongoing vigilance, as it is perceived by women (Weidner 2000). In addition, men are more likely than women to be tended by their spouse or partner during illness (Schmeiser-Rieder 1999; WHO 2001). They are more than twice as likely as women to name spouses or partners as their source of social support, and are more seriously affected by the loss of a partner through separation, divorce or being widowed (Tijhuis et al 1999; Weidner 2000). This emphasises the different way that men and women perceive relationships with others, with women placing a higher value on the interpersonal support they receive from their social networks, while men tend to view social networks in relation to leisure activities (Schmeiser-Rieder et al 1999; Tijhuis et al 1999). Older men seem to suffer more from being isolated and having less social support than women, but the burden of their illness also affects the health of women, as their carers (WHO 2001).

Perceptions of health and personal expectations also differ between men and women. Women place greater emphasis on nutrition, rest, relaxation and feeling well. They consider health in terms of not being ill or needing medical attention. Men, on the other hand, see their bodies as machines and view exercise, strength and being fit as more important than nutrition and rest (ICN 2000b). It is interesting that men generally report feeling better than women, except in Finland, Ireland, Iceland and New Zealand, with American, Canadian and French men topping the 'feelgood factor' list (OECD 2001). This may, however, be related to health services. Men use health services infrequently and often delay seeking help until it is too late, whereas women's greater usage of services may reflect different expectations for health (ICN 2000b). People's idea of good health tends to become more demanding as health care improves, so this may reflect a self-perpetuating cycle (OECD 2001).

Besides being infrequent users of all health services, male patients visiting a medical practitioner tend to take longer to unravel some of their medical and personal issues. This may result in men being poorly served by the standard consultation time allocated by most general practitioners (Huggins 1995). Men often find it difficult to admit the existence of mental health problems, tending to fear the type of emotional intimacy required to discuss mental health, and are hesitant to ask for help (Huggins 1995). Men are also hesitant to complain about health care or health services and so the health care system has been slow to respond to their unique needs (Fletcher 1995).

Men's health and the way they approach health care is therefore constructed around societal notions of masculinity, which focus on strength and sexual function rather than a holistic understanding of the male condition. These masculine 'ideals' are, for many men, central to perceptions of self (WHO 2001). Societal views also perpetuate increased tolerance of men's behaviours that are not always conducive to good health. For example, societal tolerance of men's sexual indiscretions increases the risk of sexually transmitted diseases (STD), including HIV/AIDS (ICN 2000b). This is partly responsible for the rapid worldwide increase in STD infections among men, which accounts for a growing burden of disease for men aged 15–59. As for women, communicable diseases, including STD infections, are worse in Africa, where men in this age group have a 47.7 per cent probability of dying, compared to the world average of 22.5 per cent (Ogah 2001). Sexually transmitted diseases are also thought to precipitate male infertility and impotence, although these relationships have yet to be adequately studied (UNFPA 2000).

Societal pressures affect men at multiple levels of society. For example, livelihood dynamics in old age in agrarian societies are influenced by gender. Cultural norms dictate notions of inappropriateness in regard to work, diminishing men's resources and opportunities sooner than women's (WHO 2001). Political determinants also affect men's health to a greater extent than women's health, particularly for men ageing in a male-dominated era. As the family breadwinner, men tend to be more concerned than women with policies governing economic development, social security and insurance (Ogah 2001; WHO 2001). European men have shown interesting effects from political events. One example is the disproportionately higher mortality among Russian men in response to the social and economic disruption in the Russian Federation, with its decline in state paternalism (McKee & Sckolnikov 2001; WHO 2001). In contrast, men in Asia and Africa tend to be overly concerned with the international business community. The tobacco industry in Asia is a double-edged sword, given that it holds the health of Asian men to ransom, at the same time as it is valued as a vital component of the economy (Tan 2001). Likewise, in Africa, big business fans the flames of war by arms sales and trade in minerals. On that continent, 600 000 people, most of them men, are killed annually in conflicts (Ogah 2001).

Men's health is undoubtedly a product of culturally prescribed meanings about their roles and norms. American research demonstrates the linkages between beliefs and health outcomes. In the United States, mortality rates from CHD and the prevalence of serious health problems are highest in the South. This may be attributed to geocultural factors such as climate or agricultural practices, or they may be linked to Southern men's views about manhood, given that they hold the most traditional views of any group in the United States (Courtenay 2001). Similarly, the difference in life expectancy between African American men and other American men exceeds the difference in life expectancy between women and men in the United States. These differences warrant further investigation, particularly in relation to unravelling the relative risk of lifestyle factors (Courtenay 2001).

Research attention should also be directed to the increasing vulnerability of men undergoing remarkable societal changes. The intense competition and longer work hours that characterise many Asian nations trying to quell recession is taking its toll on both men's and women's health. Men are suffering from the effects of working in stressful jobs, in a climate of increased urbanisation with its concomitant problems. This is occurring at a time when, in Taiwan, Hong Kong, Singapore and Korea, more than 50 per cent of women are entering the workforce (Tan 2001). Yet the majority of fathers in these countries enact an authoritative role as the family breadwinner, playing with their children infrequently, with only one in five providing moral and spiritual direction (Leong 2002). Neither men nor women are coping well with the changes in Asian society, as men try to adjust to the changing role of their partners and spouses who were once their primary source of support, and women adjust to the increased workload with continuing expectations that they will fulfil this role.

Men's values
and health risks

One of Australia's early activists for men's issues has drawn attention to the emotional impoverishment of men and the need for them to engage in more self-caring and self-valuing (Biddulph 1995). He contends that many of men's health risks—violence, accidents, heart attacks, lung cancer and addictive behaviours—are sub-suicidal actions taken out of a deep sense of misery and a lack of meaning or purpose. He attributes these, to some extent, to a lack of fathering. In the burgeoning number of families where there is no father to provide role modelling and male bonding, young males are often left to construct their masculine roles from television, from stereotypes, and from the equally inept pretences of their peer group (Biddulph 1995). This is a problem for both young boys and girls, given the pace of life in most industrialised countries today, but it is a sentiment that needs to be expressed to men, to validate their important role in the family.

The lack of fathers in the home represents a crisis of parenthood. Family trends see many more men than in the past attempting to share child-rearing responsibilities but being poorly equipped from their own childhood socialisation for this important task. Paradoxically, one of the social conditions that jeopardises health, namely male unemployment, has increased the number of fathers now involved in child care. This may lead to renewed interest in men's contribution to parenting. In addition, for a small number of divorcing couples, the children remain in their father's home and the mother becomes the visiting or 'access' parent. However, this is still far from the norm, and for most divorcing fathers, moving away from the children has a profound impact on their parenting role.

Fathers who live outside the home confront an enormous number of obstacles in their attempt to remain involved with the children's upbringing. These men, usually non-residential fathers, are beset by the financial constraints that both partners to a divorce encounter, yet, due to societal expectations, they are still expected to be the family financier. Because of this, many feel disempowered by their inability either to adequately provide for their children or to establish a new relationship (McMurray & Blackmore 1993).

The men's
movement

Throughout the 1990s there has been a growing awareness of the specific health needs, experiences and concerns of men (Baker 2001). This was initially sparked by concerns over societal-level change, and the impact of socialisation practices on men's health (ICN 2000b). It has resulted in the formation of men's groups in a number of countries, designed to help men discuss some of the social and emotional issues that affect their lives. Early initiatives have now been more widely publicised and have connected men in a network committed to rearranging the social and cultural determinants of their lives in a way that fosters better health and well-being. In the United States, a national men's health week was established in 1994. Australia has been described as having done more for men's health as a mainstream issue than any other country, having conducted two national men's health conferences and a range of government-funded initiatives, including several state policy initiatives and a draft national policy (Baker 2001). England, Wales and Switzerland began men's health initiatives throughout 2000–01, and in 2001 the first World Congress on Men's Health was held in Vienna, during which the European Men's Health Initiative and the International Society for Men's Health was established (Baker 2001).

Men's future health rests in recasting masculinity in a way that allows them the freedom to develop a balance in their lives. For those of us in the health system it requires a new gender agenda, directed towards therapeutic justice for all people that eliminates gender deficits and disadvantages (Baker & Banks 2001; Meryn & Rieder 2001). Part of this agenda will be to direct research interest toward the areas of men's need that are under-researched, including relative disadvantage from socially determined health risks (Courtenay 2001).

There is also need for a stronger focus on the health of ageing males, including the possibility of effective hormone replacement therapies that would mediate their health risks (Kalache 2001; WHO 2001). Men should also be encouraged to change their health behaviours, perhaps by applying their management skills to the management of their health and the health of their environments (WHO 2001).

The potential for change in men's health is expected to follow the successes of the women's health movement. In the space of only two decades, women's health moved from public lobbying by women in the United States, to the formation of Offices of Women's Health and women's research agendas, to national policies and political platforms throughout the world (Birn 1999; Gilbert 2000). Beginning in 1979 with the UN's recognition of gender discrimination against women, the Convention on the Elimination of All Forms of Discrimination Against Women (CEDAW) was ratified by 161 countries in 1998. This was followed by a series of UN-sponsored declarations and statements that urged human rights and women's universal access to reproductive health (ICN 2000a). In 1995, the World Conference for Women held in Beijing mandated that religion, culture and traditions would no longer be reasons for depriving women from exercising their human rights, and this was reaffirmed at the 23rd special session of the UN General Assembly in 2000 (UNFPA 2000). Women's health has come a long way since the beginning of the 1980s, and it is expected that sometime during this next decade, the men's health movement will also enjoy health and health care relatively free from gender bias.

The problems of gender bias in our society are more than a war between the sexes. The women's movement was a battle against male oppressors, who have historically retained power through politics, economics and their prominence in society (Kalache & Lunenfeld 2001). The men's health movement has no such opponent or oppressor except complacency. The campaign for men's health should therefore revolve around forming a new culture where men will value self-care rather than see themselves as 'indestructible machines' (Kalache & Lunenfeld 2001, p 7).

Goals relevant to
gender issues in health

To address issues of gender in health, the following goals are important:

- Public awareness of requirements for gender equality
- Equal access to education for women and men that promotes health literacy and is sensitive to gender equality
- Gender equality in power and decision-making
- Ending all forms of discrimination and violation of the rights of girls
- Incorporating gender concerns into longstanding debates on areas other than health care (gun control, crime prevention)
- Heightening awareness of linkages between human rights and health care
- Promoting family safety and security

- Global, national and local involvement in all deliberations that affect gender relations
- Heightening public awareness of the effects of armed conflict, trade liberalisation and globalisation on women and men
- Developing equitable economic structures, policies and access to resources to advance the elimination of gender bias (UN 2000).

Building healthy public policy

One of the major recommendations of the many groups and conferences now being held on men's health is that governments must confront the issue of poverty and its effect on health. States need to ensure food security, support female-headed households, recognise the needs of migrants, ensure access to financial services for both males and females, create gender sensitivity in economic policy making, and examine the relationship between unremunerated work and poverty (International Nursing Review 1996). Male unemployment is a major issue for both men and women and should be dealt with sensitively and comprehensively from an economic as well as a social standpoint.

Overcoming poverty must also address the inequities surfacing in the area of international aid programs. International development projects all affect community life, but especially the daily lives of women. Sometimes these effects are not understood by those granting aid, yet they must be addressed within the life of any given project. For example, one project that provided piped water in Zambia resulted in a reduction in the time taken to fetch and carry water, but this left women with more time for other work, and thus *increased*, rather than *decreased*, their workload (Manderson & Mark 1997). Many economic development programs create a plethora of health hazards for local people who are so destitute that they will accept work that puts them at risk of exposure to chemical pesticides and other industrial hazards. This is particularly the case for women in developing countries, many of whom also relinquish the property they are given due to social and cultural pressure, and this defeats the intention of empowering their lives (Cox 1997).

In the industrialised nations, one obstacle to healthy public policies and practices for both women's and men's health has been the preoccupation with biological factors, particularly in relation to reproductive illnesses, at the expense of wellness and illness prevention. With shrinking budgets, few resources are left for critical social investments that promote health, such as education, job training, environmental safety and housing (Ruzek, Olesen & Clarke 1997).

Another obstacle to achieving women's health has been the contradictions purveyed by some aspects of feminism. The focus of feminist teaching is 'woman-centredness', and this has sometimes obscured the fact that women are a heterogeneous population who engage in a wide array of complex interactions with their communities in ways that are not always predictable. In the early days of the feminist movement, women's health issues were argued from a monolithic focus on gender, and women were urged to unite in voicing their concerns on the basis of gender uniqueness. However, as the movement was joined by women of many ethnic origins and varied perspectives, the base of examination was broadened from sex differences in health and health-seeking behaviour to the interactions between such things as race, class and cultural experiences. This more closely reflects today's quest by women to address the issues that will assist them in securing equitable conditions for health for themselves, their families and communities.

Policies for men's health must also place emphasis on the social conditions affecting health and well-being. Our policies for community health should address vulnerabilities at every level: roles in separated families, employment, overcrowding, homelessness and urban deterioration, migration patterns, rapid technological developments and the resource requirements of a rapidly ageing population and the rising costs of health care (Ruzek et al 1997; WHO 1999b, 2000b, 2001).

It is important that gender discrepancies in medical research, diagnosis and treatment be addressed. Research into differential conditions and responses for males and females is likely to gather momentum as the number of women's health advocates in the competition for research funds increases, and as the findings from their research creates a greater public awareness of historical omissions in the research agenda. Gender balance in the research agenda would help dispel the notion that women's health issues are related predominantly to gynaecology and child care. Similarly, a more balanced agenda would incorporate more than physical health problems in researching men's health, so that the relative causes of ill health across populations would become visible and attract preventative attention (Courtenay 2001). Researching the social conditions peculiar to both genders, the economic disparities in health that create advantages or disadvantages for families, and factors related to understanding environmental issues are crucial for the development of healthy public policies.

Research resources should be directed towards illuminating issues related to the education of women, and preserving the physical and social environment that will enhance women's economic status and allow them to better support their families within safe living and working conditions. Women everywhere have welcomed the surge in interest in, and research funding for, breast cancer research, for example, but we must guard against the 'novel technologies' approach of most medically dominated funding bodies, and this applies equally to research on male cancers (Narrigan et al 1997). Priorities for funding research studies should also include environmental and behavioural factors and the ways in which women's and men's social and culturally embedded meanings and issues of access lead to preventive behaviour, especially during ageing (WHO 2000). Medical researchers should be encouraged to extend the traditional methods of research to those offered by social scientists to examine people's *actual* experiences of health and illness, their preferences in health care and views of appropriate treatment interventions, and their roles as both carer and recipient of care.

Government policies must address the decriminalisation of abortion issue and the right to choose family planning strategies. In addition, women should be protected by law from such unhealthy cultural practices as female genital mutilation, infanticide and dowry-related violence (Campbell 2001). Other forms of violence can be overcome through a combination of community efforts and government initiatives. One of the most important measures that can be taken to reduce conflict-related violence is to encourage all governments to examine excessive military spending, even in the context of growing terrorism, and to balance spending with that intended to protect, assist and train refugees and displaced persons. Culturally appropriate shelters, health care, legal aid and other necessary services should be provided for all victims of violence.

Family-friendly policies should be designed to eliminate or reduce family violence and should be accompanied by corresponding legal initiatives based on a body of evidence revealing insights into gender-based violence. Woman-friendly policies must include job protection and training programs that promote women's self-reliance, facilitate their access to resources and create flexible work environments. Male-friendly policies must address workplace illness and injury, unemployment and men's lifestyle issues.

Creating supportive environments

Within our society, many things influence the health of women and the health of men, and most of these (social, cultural, demographic and environmental factors) are the same influences mentioned in conjunction with the creation of health for all people. The most powerful influence specific to women's health is equal opportunity, which encompasses the primary health care principles of equity, access, cultural sensitivity and empowerment. Women in all communities will only achieve and sustain health where they have the opportunity to do so, and this will only be possible where a society's institutionalised policies and processes provide access to health information and health care, equal consideration and provision of culturally appropriate health resources, the means to design and administer those resources by women themselves, and acknowledgement that all members of the community, women's families, their children and their important others, help create and sustain health.

Supportive environments for men must begin at birth, with the way we raise our male children. In the absence of fathers in the home, there should be more community programs instituted to provide male role models for young boys. The social environment within which young males are nurtured must allow them to balance traditional notions of masculinity with their need for emotional support. In turn, those parents attempting to raise children and provide for their emotional growth should be provided for. In today's society there remains little time for parents to share their concerns. For separated families this is particularly acute, as there is little respite from the duties of child care. Community-based information and support centres for parents can help provide a climate of concern so that individuals do not get swallowed up in the task of parenting, and have resources for personal growth. One of the most important vehicles for changing existing stereotypes and allowing both women and men a sense of possibilities is the mass media. By becoming involved with the local media we can ensure that culturally appropriate human rights information is disseminated and that non-stereotyped, balanced and diverse images of women and men are portrayed as models for the next generations.

Strengthening community action

Many social conditions that perpetuate gender bias can be addressed through balanced education programs for the young. However, these programs that target individual interventions must be adequately backed up by focusing on the community and societal conditions that undermine familial competence and encourage violence or other forms of human rights violations. Both age and gender discrimination must be eliminated in the workplace and emphasis placed on lifelong skills development (WHO 2000). In the community, people should be encouraged to develop person-to-person support in times of crisis and mechanisms for sharing problems and solutions. This involves healthy neighbourhood initiatives that promote social cohesion and intergenerational solidarity (WHO 2000). High-risk neighbourhoods can be the setting for activities such as parent groups, job retraining and collective action designed to empower community residents to deal with stress and risk factors, provide education, social support and tangible resources for family life to allow positive family interactions (Bowers Andrews 1994).

Developing personal skills

Government interventions and community action can provide the scaffolding for the empowerment of individuals, although healthy choices are a matter of personal knowledge and skills. Women need to be encouraged to overcome the vulnerability that results from being brought up to depend on males for social and personal esteem, and men need to recognise the need for a balanced lifestyle and a new awareness of the role of women, especially in traditional societies. Young people of both sexes need to understand the importance of intimacy and closeness, but from a perspective of equal power and decision-making in relationships.

Young women need to see how reproductive health and overall health both reflect and affect each other (Magrane & McIntyre-Seltman 1996). Women of all ages need to be encouraged to learn how decisions are made so that they can participate in securing their preferred future. This requires literacy programs, and for those communities where high rates of illiteracy exist, health information must be provided through radio and television, workshops and seminars, drama and community festivals, posters and leaflets (M'Jamtu-sie 1996).

To counter domestic abuse, person-centred and problem-focused interventions are essential. These entail programs to help people, especially young couples, develop personal coping and self-esteem by nurturing them through ways of accepting ownership for critical life functions. These programs are based on the belief that all people must be able to speak for themselves, that empowerment is the entitlement of all people, and that respect for personal dignity is integral to health, not just an 'add-on'. As health professionals, we must advocate for symbolic empowerment of people at the policy level, and demonstrate practical examples of empowering others by relinquishing control over health-related decisions that could easily be assumed by community members.

Reorienting health services

The notion of health risk must balance individual choices with institutionalised hazards. Both women and men are often the target of pervasive advertising by the food, alcohol and tobacco industries, and many women, especially, live in violent circumstances or work in circumstances of economic or sexual exploitation. So risk reduction must begin with the contextual issues that govern women's and men's individual behaviour. This is often problematic in a society dominated by individualist thinking, where efforts to impose 'passive controls'—such as gun control regulations, advertising restrictions and severe penalties for drink driving—are often rejected (Ruzek 1997). However, society must also provide both women and men with the individual resources to modify their behaviour. Lack of assertiveness is a risk factor for many things that compromise women's health: sexual harassment, economic exploitation, rape and domestic abuse. The system response to this requires an emphasis on empowerment skills such as assertiveness training, personal defence, stress management and other skills that help women gain control over things within their personal realm of influence and control (Ruzek 1997). These, in turn, should be balanced with services for men that respond to their emotional and expressive needs as well as physical needs.

One of the ways our health care of women can be improved relates to victims of violence. We have done little to overcome the revolving door syndrome for victims of domestic abuse. One way of dealing with this is to de-pathologise victims' responses by re-examining our treatment of such women. Often we tend to engage in subtle victim blaming when a woman is admitted into care on repeated occasions. By reframing the incident in terms of normal responses to abnormal events we may see a slightly different perspective on her condition, such as a victim of a long-term post-traumatic stress syndrome, rather than as someone who has attracted spousal abuse (Browne 1993).

Another way of addressing inequities in health services for migrant women in particular is to ensure cultural sensitivity in services for women. Many women migrants find the services of their host country ethnocentric and alienating. Given that it is the woman in many of these families who must choose health services for all family members, particular attention must be paid to removing communication barriers. This involves provision of language services in health service agencies, bilingual and bicultural health workers and NESB women's participation in health planning, data collection and service evaluation (Alcorso & Schofield 1992). Specialist services that sometimes separate women's services from children's services should also be reconsidered. Many women from developing countries find it impossible to navigate the maze of specialised services and need a place to receive health information and treatment that can simultaneously address their and their children's needs for a range of health concerns (AbuZahr, Vlassoff & Kumar 1996).

It is also important for all health professionals to be attuned to the needs of some women not to be attended by a male. Most health care services are male-centred, and many women from cultures unfamiliar to the service providers find they must explain their cultural context, their cultural perspective regarding health care, and the role of women within that culture before they can secure culturally appropriate services (Taylor & Dower 1997). Many hesitate to demand such services and thus are left with inadequate treatment. This is not quite as much of an issue for males, as in many countries female physicians are the norm. However, the special needs of migrant women must be addressed from a base of culturally appropriate information.

The challenge of women's health and, indeed, men's health, is to conceptualise their respective health issues from an *inclusive* rather than *exclusive* perspective. This type of approach will mobilise social forces for caring, curing and concern in a direction that will contribute to women's health and men's health as individuals and, within social relations, as members of communities (Ruzek et al 1997).

---

case study...

The Philippine POPCOM experience

The Philippine Population Commission (POPCOM) undertook to reorient population policies and programs to make population workers more gender-responsive. Their strategies included forming a critical mass of various community groups to demand policy shifts, encouraging women, development and environmental non-governmental (NGO) organisations to identify allies in government and international organisations, to engage in regular dialogues between health care workers and the government's central planning agency, and to use the media to promote their initiatives within the community.

The program was based on the recognition that there was differential access to and control over resources, credit, technology, training and services, with disparities evident in labour force and political participation rates. An historical emphasis on fertility and family planning needed to be broadened to include concerns about family formation, the status of women, maternal and child health, child survival, morbidity and mortality, population distribution and urbanisation, internal and international migration and population structure.

The group formed an interagency advisory committee, which conducted a survey revealing that POPCOM board members, staff and popu-

lation officers were generally not aware of the concept of gender or its implication for development. Most people held the assumption that population growth was a major concern as a threat to the environment, and a major cause of poverty and resource depletion. Once the level of awareness was understood, POPCOM began a gender-sensitising program, wherein policy and training groups were developed. The policy framework was designed to guide selected projects in key regions of the country to test certain approaches and mechanisms in promoting gender and reproductive health policies and programs. This included assessing the premarriage counselling program, integrating gender and reproductive health and rights in training, analysing community information projects from a gender perspective, mobilising youth councils to advocate for gender and reproductive health and rights, and mainstreaming gender and reproductive health concerns in the family welfare industry program. The overall objective of these initiatives was to serve as the basis for legislative reforms.

The program confronts the state machinery that governs gender issues. Far from the 'add women and stir approach', which grafts women onto all policies and programs, it is committed to questioning the basic assumptions upon which the ideology of family planning rests. It challenges the status quo by addressing gender relations within the household, across classes, and within the wider economic, political, environmental and sociocultural spheres, questioning the ways that existing values and norms entrench gender bias into the governance of the system. The group's thorough approach to their task has yielded a set of principles around which all future policies will revolve. These include autonomy, self-determination, equity, social justice, pluralism, participation, responsibility and accountability. The overarching goal is to enable men and women to live self-determined, productive, satisfying and fulfilled lives. To accomplish this it is acknowledged that both women and men must be able to exercise their capacities to achieve and sustain knowledge and skills to deal with issues that potentially compromise the quality of their lives (Danguilan & Verzosa 1996).

thinking critically

Health and gender

1 Explain four reasons why gender issues are important to community health.

2 Identify three health risks of females and three health risks of males related to gender issues.

3 Discuss three political, cultural or social issues related to reproductive health from the perspective of gender equity.

4 What five strategies would you recommend for an HIV/AIDS health education program for young males and females?

5 Devise one public policy and three strategies for implementation of a gender-related community health problem.

REFERENCES

AbuZahr, C., Vlassoff, C. & Kumar, A. (1996). Quality health care for women: a global challenge. *Health Care for Women International*, 17: 449–67.

Alcorso, C. & Schofield, T. (1992). Redirecting the agenda. The National NESB Women's Health Strategy. *Migration Action*, April: 15–19.

Australian Bureau of Statistics (1999). Income and Welfare. Caring in Australia. Canberra: AGPS.

Australian Institute of Health and Welfare (2000). Australia's Health 2000. Canberra: AGPS.

Baker, P. (2001). The international men's health movement. *British Medical Journal*, 323(7320): 1014–15.

Baker, P. & Banks, I. (2001). Men's health in Europe. In: Proceedings, 1st World Congress on Men's Health, Vienna, 2–4 November.

Beery, T. (1995). Diagnosis and treatment of cardiac disease. *Heart and Lung*, 24(6): 427–35.

Bergman, B., Carlsson, S. & Wright, I. (1996). Women's work experiences and health in a male-dominated industry. *Journal of Occupational and Environmental Medicine*, 38(7): 663–72.

Biddulph, S. (1995). Healthy masculinity starts in boyhood. *Australian Family Physician*, 24(11): 2047–52.

Birn, A. (1999). Skirting the issue: women and international health in historical perspective. *American Journal of Public Health*, 89(3): 399–407.

Bowers Andrews, A. (1994). Developing community systems for the primary prevention of family violence. *Family Community Health*, 16(4): 1–9.

Britton, B. (1997). Sexual harassment. In: S. Ruzek, V. Olesen & A. Clarke (eds), *Women's Health: Complexities and Differences*. Columbus: Ohio State University Press, pp 510–19.

Brown, A. J. (2001). Men's health in Australia. In: Proceedings, 1st World Congress on Men's Health, Vienna, 2–4 November.

Browne, A. (1993). Violence against women by male partners. *American Psychologist*, 48(10): 1077–87.

Bunting, S. (1996). Sources of stigma associated with women with HIV. *Advances in Nursing Science*, 19(2): 64–73.

Campbell, J. (1992). Ways of teaching, learning and knowing about violence against women. *Nursing and Health Care*, 13(9): 464–70.

—— (2001). Global perspectives on wife beating and health care. In: M. Martinez (ed), *Prevention and Control of Aggression and the Impact on Its Victims*, New York: Kluwer Academic/Plenum Publishers, pp 215–27.

Courtenay, W. (2001). Men's health in the USA. In: Proceedings, 1st World Congress on Men's Health, Vienna, 2–4 November.

Cox, C. (1997). Medical education, women's status, and medical issues' effect on women's health in the Caribbean. *Health Care for Women International*, 18: 383–93.

Curtis, L. (1999). Literacy and women's health. *International Journal of Humanities and Peace*, 15(1): 69–71.

Danguilan, M. & Verzosa, E. (1996). Making women and men matter: the Philippine POPCOM experience. *Health Care for Women International*, 17: 487–503.

Dimmitt, J. (1995). Self-concept and woman abuse: a rural and cultural perspective. *Issues in Mental Health Nursing*, 16: 567–81.

Elstad, J. (1996). Inequalities in health related to women's marital, parental, and employment status—a comparison between the early 70's and the late 80's, Norway. *Social Science and Medicine*, 41(1): 75–89.

Fletcher, R. (1995). An outbreak of men's health—the history of a welcome epidemic. Proceedings from the National Men's Health Conference, Canberra: AGPS, pp 26–31.

Flitcraft, A. (1996). Synergy: violence prevention, intervention, and women's health. *Journal of American Medical Women's Association*, 51(3): 75–6.

Gilbert, M. (2000). We *have* come a long way: women's health at the turn of the millenium. *The Permanente Journal*, 4(3): 76–83.

Goldner, V., Penn, P., Sheinberg, M. & Walker, G. (1990). Love and violence: gender paradoxes in volatile attachments. *Family Process*, 29(4): 343–64.

Goodman, L., Koss, M., Fitzgerald, L., Felipe Russo, N. & Puryear Keita, G. (1993). Male violence against women. *American Psychologist*, 48(10): 1054–8.

Grisso, J., Schwarz, D., Miles, C. & Holmes, J. (1996). Injuries among inner-city minority women: a population-based longitudinal study. *American Journal of Public Health*, 86(1): 67–70.

Harer, W. (1996). Gender bias in health care services valuations. *Obstetrics and Gynecology*, 87(3): 453–4.

Havens, B. & Hall, M. (2000). The relationships among isolation, loneliness, and the health of older women. *The Gerontologist*, 15 Oct 15: 220.

Hertzman, C. (1999). Population health and human development. In: D. Keating & C. Hertzman, (eds), *Developmental Health and the Wealth of Nations*. New York: The Guilford Press, pp 21–40.

Huggins, A. (1995). The Australian male: illness, injury and death by socialisation. Curtin University, Men's Health Teaching and Research Unit.

International Council of Nurses (ICN) (2000a). ICN on women's health. Nursing Matters fact sheet. Geneva: ICN.

—— (2000b). ICN on men's health. Nursing Matters fact sheet. Geneva: ICN.

International Nursing Review (1996). Women's health: how it scored in Beijing. *International Nursing Review*, 43(2): 59–63.

Kalache, A. (2001). Men's health, north–south prospects. In: Proceedings, 1st World Congress on Men's Health, Vienna: 2–4 November.

Kalache, A. & Lunenfeld, B. (2001). Health and the ageing male, Foreward, in Men, Ageing and Health, Geneva: WHO, pp 7–8.

Kendrick, J. & Merritt, R. (1996). Women and smoking: an update for the 1990's. *American Journal of Obstetrics and Gynecology*, 175: 528–35.

Leong, P. (2002). Daddy will provide, but no, he won't play. *The Sunday Times*, Singapore, 17 March, p 31.

Magrane, D. & McIntyre-Seltman, K. (1996). Women's health care issues for medical students: an educational proposal. *Women's Health Issues*, 6(4): 183–91.

Manderson, L. & Mark, T. (1997). Empowering women: participatory approaches in women's health and development projects. *Health Care for Women International*, 18: 17–30.

Mathers, C., Vos, T. & Stevenson, C. (1999). The burden of disease and injury in Australia. Canberra: AIHW.

McKee, M. & Sckolnikov, V. (2001). Men's health in Central and Eastern Europe as reflected by the toll of premature death. In: Proceedings, 1st World Congress on Men's Health, Vienna, 2–4 November.

McMurray, A. & Blackmore, A. (1993). Influences on parent–child relationships in non-custodial fathers. *Australian Journal of Marriage and Family*, 14(3): 151–9.

Meleis, A., Douglas, M., Eribes, C., Shih, F. & Messias, D. (1996). Employed Mexican women as mothers and partners: valued, empowered and overloaded. *Journal of Advanced Nursing*, 23: 82–90.

Meryn, S. & Jadad, A. (2001).The future of men and their health: are men in danger of extinction? (Editorial). *British Medical Journal*, 323(7320): 1013–14.

Meryn, S. & Rieder, A. (2001). The future of men. In: Proceedings, 1st World Congress on Men's Health, Vienna, 2–4 November.

M'Jamtu-sie, N. (1996). Health information for the grass roots. *World Health Forum*, 17: 277–82.

Morse, B. (1995). Beyond the conflict tactics scale: assessing gender differences in partner violence. *Violence and Victims*, 10(4): 251–72.

Narrigan, D., Zones, J. & Worcester, N. (1997). Research to improve women's health: an agenda for equity. In: S. Ruzek, V. Olesen & A. Clarke (eds), *Women's Health: Complexities and Differences*. Ohio State University Press, Columbus, pp 551–9.

Oakley, A. (1994). Who cares for health? Social relations, gender, and the public health. *Journal of Epidemiology and Public Health*, 48: 427–34.

OECD (2001). The 'feelgood' factor. OECD Observer. http://www.oecdobserver.org/news.

Ogah, G. (2001). Men's health in Africa. In: Proceedings, 1st World Congress on Men's Health, Vienna, 2–4 November.

Richardson, J. & Feder, G. (1996). Domestic violence: a hidden problem for general practice. *British Journal of General Practice*, April: 239–42.

Rigdon, S. (1996). Abortion law and practice in China: an overview with comparisons to the United States. *Social Science and Medicine*, 42(4): 543–60.

Robbe, M., March, L., Vinen, J., Horner, D. & Roberts, G. (1996). Prevalence of domestic violence among patients attending a hospital emergency department. *Australian and New Zealand Journal of Public Health*, 20(4): 364–68.

Rokach, A. (2000). Loneliness and the life cycle. *Psychological Reports*, 86(2): 629–43.

Ruzek, S. (1997). Women, personal health behavior and health promotion. In: S. Ruzek, V. Olesen & A. Clarke (eds), *Women's Health: Complexities and Differences*. Columbus: Ohio State University Press, pp 118–53.

Ruzek, S., Olesen, V. & Clarke, A. (1997). *Women's Health: Complexities and Differences*. Columbus: Ohio State University Press.

—— (1996). Topics for our times: rape is a major public health issue. *American Journal of Public Health*, 86(1): 15–16.

Schmeiser-Rieder, A., Kiefer, I., Panuschka, C., Hartl, H., Leitner, B., Schmeiser, M., Csitkovics, M., Schmidl, H. & Kunze, M. (1999). Men's Health Report, Vienna, 1999 and The Aging Male, http://www.HealthandAge.com.

Sorenson, S., Upchurch, D. & Shen, H. (1996). Violence and injury in marital arguments: risk patterns and gender differences. *American Journal of Public Health*, 86(1): 35–40.

Spurlock, J. (1995). Multiple roles of women and role strains. *Health Care for Women International*, 16: 501–8.

Strauss, M. (2001). Physical aggression in the family. In: M. Martinez (ed), *Prevention and Control of Aggression and the Impact on Its Victims*. New York: Kluwer Academic/Plenum Publishers, pp 181–200.

Sundby, J. (1999). Are women disfavoured in the estimation of Disability Adjusted Life Years and the Global Burden of Disease? *Scandinavian Journal of Public Health*, 27: 279–85.

Tan, H. (2001). Men's health in Asia. In: Proceedings, 1st World Congress on Men's Health, Vienna, 2–4 November.

Taylor, D. & Dower, C. (1997). Toward a women-centered health care system: women's experiences, women's voices, women's needs. *Health Care for Women International*, 18: 407–22.

Timpson, J. (1996). Abortion: the antithesis of womanhood? *Journal of Advanced Nursing*, 23: 776–85.

Tijhuis, M., De Jong-Gierveld, J., Feskens, E. & Kromhout, D. (1999). Changes in and factors related to loneliness in older men. The Zutphen Elderly Study. *Age and Ageing*, 28: 491–5.

UNESCO (2000). Women and girls: education, not discrimination. *OECD Observer*, 14 December, http://www.oecdobservier.org.

United Nations (2000). Report of the Ad Hoc Committee of the Whole of the twenty-third special session of the General Assembly. New York: UN.

United Nations Family Planning Association (UNFPA) (2000). The state of world population 2000. New York: UN.

US Office on Women's Health (USOWH) (2001). Women's health issues: an overview. Washington: US Department of Health and Human Services.

Varkevisser, C. (1995). Women's health in a changing world. *Tropical and Geographical Medicine*, 47(5): 186–92.

Vazquez, C. (1996). Spousal abuse and violence against women: the significance of understanding attachment. *Annals of the New York Academy of Science*, 789: 119–28.

Weidner, G. (2000). Why do men get more heart disease than women? An international perspective. *Journal of American College Health*, 48(6): 291–6.

Wolf, N. (1991). *The Beauty Myth: How Images of Beauty Are Used Against Women*. New York: William Morrow.

World Health Organization (WHO) (1997). Gender and Health: A Technical Paper. Geneva: WHO.

—— (1999a), The World Health Report 1999. Geneva: WHO.

—— (1999b). Ageing: Exploding the Myths. Geneva: WHO.

—— (2000a). Women, Ageing and Health. Geneva: WHO.

—— (2000b). Women 2000: gender equality, development and peace for the twenty-first century. Special session, General Assembly. Geneva: WHO.

—— (2001). Men, Ageing and Health. Geneva: WHO.

Yencken, D. & Porter, L. (2001). *A Just and Sustainable Australia*. Melbourne: The Australian Collaboration.

Young, R. (1996). The household context for women's health care decisions: impacts of UK policy changes. *Social Science and Medicine*, 42(6): 949–63.

Zierler, S. & Krieger, N. (1997). Reframing women's risk: social inequalities and HIV infection. *Annual Review of Public Health*, 18: 401–36.

Zones, J. (1997). Beauty myths and realities and their impact on women's health. In: S. Ruzek, V. Olesen & A. Clarke (eds), *Women's Health: Complexities and Differences*. Columbus: Ohio State University Press, pp 249–75.

CHAPTER 11

Healthy
Indigenous people

ntroduction The health of Indigenous people throughout the world is in a critical condition. Health professionals in all corners of the globe have joined with social policy makers and Aboriginal groups to try to get to the fundamental problems that create a consistently higher burden of illness, injury and disability among Indigenous people, with only marginal success in some places, and gross failure in others. It is crucial that the issues surrounding Indigenous ill health be discussed, but in a solution-focused rather than problem-focused manner, because in this era of rapid globalisation, the problems of Indigenous lifestyles and health are almost certain to worsen. People in many cultural groups fear that their cultural traditions will be invalidated by cross-border or multinational decisions that take little account of local needs and local voices. These problems may be magnified many times over for Indigenous people, given their disadvantaged starting point for negotiating retention of their culture.

Understanding culture must lie at the heart of assisting any group to achieve its goals. Within the cultural blueprint can be found the accumulated base of inherited ideas, beliefs, values, knowledge and traditions that bind people together. Although there are also variations within cultures, group beliefs and traditions determine people's views about health-related issues. Cultural norms often prescribe diet and eating habits, child-rearing practices, reactions to pain, stress and death, a sense of past, present and future, and responses to health care services and practitioners. For Indigenous people, all of these choices are embedded within a spiritual connection with the land.

The culture of Indigenous people is of particular concern to those of us advocating for community health and development. For many years they have experienced considerably poorer health status than other groups in society and, at a time when the non-Indigenous people of the world are enjoying increasingly better health, this is untenable. This chapter addresses the influences of historical, social, economic and situational factors that have prevented Aboriginal people from achieving good health. The discussion is aimed first at unravelling the problems of Indigenous ill-health in relation to non-Indigenous health, and then seeking solutions at a personal, family and cultural level that will begin to redress barriers to health and wellness and encourage the sustainability of Indigenous cultures.

objectives   **By the end of this chapter you will be able to:**

1   Explain the influence of historical factors on the health of Indigenous people

2   Explain the link between health and social justice for Indigenous people

3   Identify three risk factors for the burden of illness, injury and disability among Indigenous people

4   Discuss the implications of globalisation for Indigenous people of the world

5   Explain the importance of cultural knowledge in developing health promotion strategies

6   Devise a three-step strategy for working with Indigenous families to improve the health of their children.

Understanding
culture

Cultural groups are bound together by many things: art, customs, habits, language, roles, rules, shared meanings about the world and a sense of history. Culture is usually tacit in people's behaviours, an unconscious predisposition rather than a deliberate attempt to be distinctive. From an ecological perspective, culture prescribes the way people tend to interact with the environment and, in turn, the way their social organisation and cultural values are influenced by that environment (Eckermann et al 1992). Because this is a dynamic process, cultures change, adapting somewhat as they interact with their own environment and that of others. In some cases, this is of mutual benefit. For example, in multicultural societies, people of different cultures learn from one another, often enjoying each other's foods and ways of cooking, lifestyles and folkways such as festivals and celebrations. In some cases where two cultures attempt to interact within the same environment, there is the potential for culture conflict, particularly if one group has power over the other. Culture conflict can cause disharmony in the community, when members of the conflicting groups close ranks and withdraw from each other rather than cooperating to build a system of mutual community support. Without mutual support mechanisms, there is little chance of the community meeting its common goals or achieving health and a quality lifestyle for its residents.

Multiculturalism is a term that is sometimes used as a panacea for intolerance. Truly multicultural societies institutionalise understanding and tolerance of one another's cultural beliefs and practices in the context of daily living, and in planning for a future in which all cultures will be sustained. Not many societies achieve this level of multiculturalism, but it is seen to be an aspiration worthy of just and civil societies. Canada is the only country in the world to have a national multiculturalism law, which was devised as an attempt to legitimise the need for harmony among Aboriginal and non-Aboriginal groups and those who migrated to Canada from other countries (Kulig 2000). Although some have criticised the state of multiculturalism in Canada on the basis that mandating tolerance does not create real understanding, establishing the legal framework has been an important step in creating awareness of the need to understand and embrace diversity for the benefit of all society (Kulig 2000).

Aboriginal culture
and health

The term *Aboriginal* refers to the initial, or earliest, inhabitants of a place. They may also be described as *First Nations,* or *Indigenous*, people. However, membership in an Aboriginal group does not imply a monolithic society, for, like other cultures, Aboriginal people have diverse subcultures. Aboriginal groups live in a spectrum of ecological zones, speak many different languages, and have varying religious and healing practices, diets, family traditions, community and economic structures (Reid & Trompf 1991). But despite diversity in affiliations and lifestyles, most Aboriginal people have in common a history of colonisation that has left them disempowered in relation to other population groups. The history of Australia, New Zealand, Canada and the United States reveals a belief by their white European conquerors in their superiority over the native people. In most cases, this view was so extreme that the early explorers dismissed the very presence of Aboriginal people as irrelevant, because they failed to use the land in a way that would be expected in a civilised country. The colonisers thus declared the respective countries *Terra Nullius*—a land belonging to nobody (ACAR 1994; Eckermann et al 1992).

As the white colonialists developed the land, predictably, conflicts ensued between the European and native people. In Australia, once the presence of Indigenous people was acknowledged, the newcomers considered them treacherous, barbarous, lazy or mentally inferior. As a result, laws were passed which considered Aborigines wards of the government and therefore without proper citizenship (Eckermann et al 1992). This situation effectively created an institutionalised form of racism which resulted in mass undermining of the Aboriginal people's social organisation. Geographic groupings were dispersed, Aboriginal women were captured and alcohol was introduced to their culture. Their religious and spiritual beliefs were undermined by religious missionaries. Because they no longer had the right to use the land they had previously inhabited, their food supply was disrupted. The new landlords then upset the balance of nature through over-grazing and the destruction of grasslands and forest, with its edible seeds, roots and fauna (Eckermann et al 1992). The social, economic, political and physical environments embraced by their culture were thereby almost completely subjugated by the dominant white colonialists in what has been called 'pacification by force' (Bushy & van Holst Pellekaan 1995, p 223).

In those early days of white colonialism, institutionalised racism was supplanted with scientific racism, which contended that Aboriginal people were so low on the human scale that they deserved only subhuman treatment. No recognition was given for 'their powers of observation, memory, concepts and calculation of distance, knowledge of the natural world and athletic competence, because these abilities were used for different skills in a life style governed by different priorities' (Bushy & van Holst Pellekaan 1995). Few attempts were made to either understand or preserve Aboriginal culture. Instead these First Nations were exterminated by disease and war, dehumanised through alcoholism, sexual abuse and economic exploitation, and then blamed for being demoralised and living in squalour—a classic case of what we now call 'victim blaming' (Eckermann et al 1992).

Over time, and as a sense of social consciousness developed among colonial governments, eventually the European people began to work towards protecting the Aborigines. Attempts were made to assimilate them into white culture. This saw many young children removed from their parents so that they could be sent to white schools to gain what was considered to be 'appropriate' educational preparation. Children who were light-skinned were primary targets for removal, conceivably to protect them from abuse by their family members and other Aboriginal people who rejected them as being neither black nor white. These and other children removed from their families sometimes by stealth and force, *for their own good*, became the 'stolen generations'. They grew up in white missions and schools presuming that no such family existed.

As the civil rights movement gained momentum in the developed world, the injustice of this practice was recognised and attempts were made to make amends. In 1997, an Australian government inquiry into the stolen generations concluded that the forcible removal of Indigenous children was racially discriminatory, falling within the international legal definition of genocide (Yencken & Porter 2001). Despite a decade of working towards reconciliation between Aboriginal and non-Aboriginal people, no official apology has been forthcoming. In its absence, health professionals have joined with many other members of society to offer personal apologies to Indigenous people in the context of promoting self-determination and empowerment. This has been one step forward in achieving social justice.

Today, the goal of empowerment and self-determination for Aboriginal people has gradually become accepted by the majority of the non-Aboriginal population, but how this will be translated into better health has not yet been articulated. Two major questions remain, both relating to the future health of Aboriginal populations. How can the residual effects of past discriminatory practices be redressed? And how can Aboriginal health be improved? The first step in addressing these issues is to examine the existing baseline to see where to begin.

The burden of
illness, injury and disability
among Indigenous people

For many of the world's 300 million Indigenous people, life expectancy at birth is 10–20 years less than the rest of the population; infant mortality is 1.5–3 times greater than the national average, and a large proportion suffer from malnutrition and communicable diseases (WHO 1999). In many regions of the world, the health of Indigenous people is also threatened by damage to their habitat and resource base (Harlem Brundtland 1999). Certain Arctic populations are among the most exposed to environmental contaminants. Inhabitants of the Bikini Islands cannot eat their traditional foods because of radioactive contamination. Large-scale tourism, logging, mining, building dams and agri-business have disrupted many Indigenous people's lives and livelihoods. The world's oldest rainforest has been degraded, along with the lives of 3 million Dayak people of Indonesia (Harlem Brundtland 1999).

Indigenous people's burden of illness, injury and disability is so disparate from that of non-Indigenous people that WHO convened a meeting with Indigenous representatives from many countries in 1999, to develop The Geneva Declaration on the Health and Survival of Indigenous Peoples (WHO 1999). The objective of the declaration was for Indigenous people throughout the world to reaffirm their right of self-determination and to remind states of their responsibilities and obligations under international law to help address these. Their statement placed responsibility for Indigenous ill health on colonial negation of their way of life and world vision, the destruction of their habitat, the decrease of biodiversity, imposition of sub-standard living and working conditions, dispossession of traditional lands and the relocation and transfer of populations (WHO 1999).

The state of health for Indigenous people shows a consistent pattern of lower life expectancy in the Americas (North and South America), New Zealand (Aotearoa) and Australia, with Aboriginal Australians having the lowest of all these nations by at least 10 years (Kunitz 2000; Yencken & Porter 2001). This means that Australia is the only industrialised country in the world to have a section of its population face a shrinking life expectancy (Yencken & Porter 2001). The major causes of their early deaths are injury, coronary heart disease (CHD), diabetes and homicide, with males in the rural and remote areas suffering higher rates of injury than females (AIHW 2000).

Compared to the non-Indigenous population, Australian Indigenous people face a death rate 2.5 times higher. Infant mortality is three times higher, deaths among females from diabetes are 17 times higher and from cervical cancer eight times higher. Death from respiratory disease is six times higher and from injury three times higher. The prevalence of diabetes is 2–4 times higher and blindness is 10 times higher than that of non-Indigenous people (Yencken & Porter 2001). For the past three decades, Australians have experienced declining rates of mortality from heart disease, but Aboriginal and Torres Strait Islander people continue to die from CHD at a rate 50 per cent higher than non-Indigenous Australians (AIHW 1998; Ring 2001). Their overall rate of illness has been estimated at 3–4 times that of the non-Aboriginal population (Anderson 2001).

In New Zealand, the life expectancy among Maoris is about seven years less than that of non-Maoris, but the gap is closing. However, certain age groups continue to be at higher risk of illness and injury relative to the non-Maori population, including those under age one, where Maori children die at twice the rate of non-Maori, and women aged 45–64, whose rates of illness are nearly twice those of non-Maori (Statistics NZ 2001; Raeburn & Rootman 1998). For women in this age group, this rate of disease is similar to that of American Indian women, who have the highest age-adjusted rates for diabetes, cirrhosis and chronic liver disease (USNWLC 2001). It is also similar to the state of Indigenous chronic illness in Australia and Canada, where the risk of death from diabetes for Indigenous people is twice as great for men, and four times as great for women, as the risk for the non-Indigenous population (Daniel et al 1999; Ring 2001).

Maori women also have approximately a two-fold higher risk of breast cancer than non-Maori women (McCredie et al 1999). This is not the case for American Indian women, although these women have a high rate of accidents—twice the rate of the white population of women aged 25–44 (USNWLC 2001). Mortality from injuries in New Zealand show that it is Maori males aged 15–24 who have the highest mortality from injuries—up to three times the rate of their female counterparts, primarily from motor vehicle accidents (Statistics NZ 2001).

In summary, the life expectancy, mortality rates and burden of illness and injury for Indigenous people in the United States and Canada is only marginally better than the Maori, but considerably better than for Australian Aboriginal people (Bullen & Beaglehole 1997). For the period 1990–94, Australian Indigenous all-causes mortality rate was 1.9 times the Maori rate, 2.4 times the US rate and 3 times the all-Australia rate (Anderson 2001). Irrespective of certain improvements in injury rates and mortality in all countries except Australia, the risk factors for ill health persist. In fact, increases in chronic disease among Indigenous people in the industrialised countries are similar to those occurring in developing countries (Anand et al 2001).

The Indigenous state of chronic ill health can be traced to the persistence of risk factors. A recent Canadian study of risk factors for CHD among Aboriginal Canadians from the Six Nations Reservation revealed significantly higher rates of proximal risk factors such as smoking, glucose intolerance, obesity and other risk factors associated with CHD among this group compared with a similar group of people from European origin. These risks were also occurring alongside significant rates of unemployment and low household income relative to non-Indigenous Canadians (Anand et al 2001). The researchers concluded that addressing risk must include consideration of both proximal and distal, or societal, factors. Others concur, explaining that each type of risk compounds the other. Political, economic and social subjugations lead to unhealthy behaviours which, in turn, lead to further subjugation or disempowerment (Daniel et al 1999; Ring 2001).

The cycle of risk
for Indigenous ill-health

The cycle of risk clouds the future, not only for Indigenous people, but also for their non-Indigenous compatriots. Many Indigenous people live in poverty, some of which is a result of dispossession or destruction of their land (Harlem Brundtland 1999; Kunitz 2000; USNWLC 2001; Yencken & Porter 2001). For those who can afford housing, home maintenance is a problem, often because of a lack of basic infrastructure and municipal services (Yencken & Porter 2001). Sub-standard housing and inadequate diet and lifestyle predispose them to crowding, a lack of material well-being and ill health, for which few receive treatment. This is complicated in many cases by isolation, which leaves them without access to essential services, including health care (Yencken & Porter 2001). In some cases there are cultural barriers to health care, or exclusion from some types of care, because of a lack of understanding or compassion for tribal traditions or cultural sensitivities. This occurs in many Indigenous communities throughout the world, and has a strong impact on older women (Browne & Fiske 2001; Cunningham 2002; Hirini et al 1999; USNWLC 2001). For young people, isolation disadvantages their educational and employment opportunities, and they become recipients of welfare. This adds to feelings of dispossession at a time when the young are struggling with the developmental issues of roles, family relationships, peer relationships, codes of behaviour and, as mentioned in Chapter 6, living in a consumer culture that creates frustrated aspirations (Stephens 1996).

The persistent stress of unemployment and the absence of a sense of purpose leads some young people to risky behaviours such as violence, or tobacco and substance abuse (Allison et al 1999). Many lack the family cohesion to counter these behaviours, sometimes because there are few elders left, and they become victims of prejudice and discriminatory attitudes. Reactions to discrimination, idleness, frustration, peer pressure and the lack of intergenerational connectedness leads to social disintegration and cultural exclusion. This drives them further into the group that reinforces destructive behaviours, and some intensify their reactions by committing crimes or subjecting others to acts of aggression, for which they may be incarcerated, especially in states with mandatory sentencing laws. Incarceration leads to hopelessness, which leads many, especially if they have become severely mentally disturbed, to end their lives in custody, a situation that occurs with alarming frequency. This cycle is illustrated in Figure 11.1.

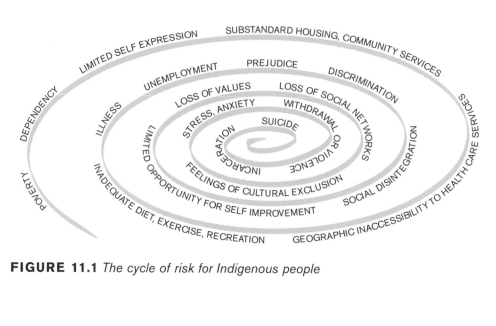

FIGURE 11.1 *The cycle of risk for Indigenous people*

Countering risk:
Indigenous health
for the future

The cycle described above varies among and between groups of Indigenous people, but it is a pattern that occurs more frequently than any society finds acceptable. The question remains: why does it persist? Some explain the cycle of risk on the basis of historical oppression. Oppression of Indigenous people is indisputable. In most cases, land, as the 'soul' of Indigenous people in both North America and the South Pacific, was either taken from them or retained in the early days of colonisation, then taken away by the Crown by force or by legal device (Raeburn & Rootman 1998). Many lost their lands, their culture, their life ways, their livelihood, their freedom and their children to those who colonised them. Yet, in many places, Indigenous people continue to be governed through the lens of a political economy rather than through any serious mechanisms for empowerment or self-determinism. Most Indigenous communities have no sound economic base, restricted job opportunities and little capacity for economic independence. These inequities are magnified by poor skill and literacy levels, overwhelming health and housing problems and unrelenting poverty (Yencken & Porter 2001).

Aboriginal
reconciliation

In recognition of the link between dispossession and the health and well-being of Aboriginal people, many governments have undertaken measures aimed at reconciliation between Indigenous people and non-Indigenous residents of their nations. In Australia, the Australian Council for Aboriginal Reconciliation was established as a statutory authority in 1991. The Australian Council's Bill for Aboriginal Reconciliation was passed that same year as an Act of Parliament (ACAR 1994). The key issues identified as crucial to reconciliation are as follows:

- understanding country—that is, the importance of land and sea in Aboriginal and Torres Strait Islander societies
- improving relationships between Indigenous Australians and the wider community
- valuing cultures as part of the Australian heritage
- sharing histories for shared ownership of the country
- addressing disadvantage to create awareness of its causes
- responding to custody levels to address the underlying issues related to Aboriginal deaths in custody
- agreeing to a document to chart the course of reconciliation
- controlling destinies with greater opportunities for Aboriginal people.

Despite broad political support for the process of reconciliation, many hurdles remain. Native title was recognised by the High Court in 1992 as the survival of a system of Indigenous land tenure, acknowledging Indigenous people as the original owners and custodians of various lands (Yencken & Porter 2001). However, it is not available to all Indigenous people because of 'factors such as the forced removal of people from their lands and of children from their families' (Yencken & Porter 2001, p 42).

South Africa

South Africa has also had a long history of attempting reconciliation between Indigenous and non-Indigenous people. Despite a history of apartheid with its blatant segregation of black and white people, South Africans have been able to negotiate a form of power-sharing, and a deconstruction of oppressive laws and institutions that was formerly thought inconceivable. Since coming into power in 1994, the African National Congress (ANC) has established the Government of National Unity (GNU), which has developed an interim constitution with reconciliation as its central theme. A common theme in the rhetoric is that reconciliation is not about freeing blacks from bondage, but about freeing whites from fear, yet racism continues (Ayers 1999). Fear also continues, as South Africa remains the most violent country on earth. The South African government has been working towards a negotiated solution to Afrikaner self-determination, establishing a 'Volkstaat', or Afrikaner homeland, and has been attempting to end civil conflict in that country, without success. Land remains a contentious issue, as do the effects of the 'Truth and Reconciliation Commission', which has been received with mixed reactions, some believing it to be a legitimised form of revenge, while others maintain their faith in the process of reconciling the past with the present (ACAR 1994; Ayers 1999).

Canada

The colonisation of Indigenous people in Canada was accomplished without the warfare and civil conflict that has occurred in South Africa and Australia. Native title has been recognised in Canada since 1973. There have been numerous treaties and land claim negotiations between the Aboriginal and non-Aboriginal people, some of which have been the subject of protracted dispute. The Canadian constitution was amended in 1982 to recognise the status and treaty rights of Indigenous people. However, its implementation and the processes of reconciliation have not always run smoothly. The treaties have sometimes been devised with insufficient input from the First Nations people and have been the subject of numerous grievances (ACAR 1994; Brady 1995).

Another contentious issue is the right of the federal government, enshrined in The Indian Act of 1867, to define who is Indian (Indigenous) and who is not, and to legislate over Indian people and the lands reserved for them. As a result, Canada's Indigenous people have always been stratified according to whether they are 'status' Indians (those living on Indian reserves or Crown land), non-status Indians (non-treaty or non-reserve Indians) or Inuit. Status Indians historically attracted the majority of federal government resources and have had greater rights to self-government within their Indian bands than either the non-status or the Inuit people. This has created a second and third layer of discrimination for non-status Indians and Inuit, who have sometimes been marginalised by their own people through circumstances not always under their control, such as their place of residence.

Tripartite negotiations between the federal and provincial governments and the Indian people are ongoing, with the ultimate aim of Aboriginal self-government grounded in the constitution. Some forms of self-government exist through negotiation between various Indian bands and the government. The most notable of these is the largest expanse of land (Nunavut) owned and governed by any Indigenous people, which was established in 1999 in the Eastern Arctic Region. In a gesture of reconciliation, in 1998 the Canadian Federal Government offered an apology to all First Nations people for past injustices.

The United States

The American situation is unique in the level of power and authority vested in that country's Indigenous people. The early days of the United States saw many bloody conflicts between Indigenous and non-Indigenous people. At the time of independence, the federal government assumed full responsibility for Indian affairs to protect the native people from the settlers. However, since two landmark decisions in the 1830s that granted nation status to two tribes, the Indian people have existed as sovereign, self-governing entities, subject to federal laws and administrative arrangements (ACAR 1994).

The 1970s saw the beginning of a trend to recognise Indian rights to self-determination and self-governance and many gains have been won. Indian tribal courts now have extensive civil and criminal jurisdictions over matters involving Indians arising on Indian lands. Tribal laws predominate on Indian lands and the tribal courts have exclusive jurisdiction over minor crimes where both victim and perpetrator are Indian, and concurrent jurisdiction over major crimes committed against Indian people. In many parts of the United States, Indigenous people are engaging in discussions currently focusing on environmental management, ecologically sustainable development and Indigenous cultural autonomy.

New Zealand

New Zealand (Aotearoa) was founded on the Treaty of Waitangi, written in both languages and signed by both the Crown and Maori tribal chiefs in 1840. Since then, securing Maori land rights and self-determination has been an arduous process, primarily because of differing interpretations of each version of the Treaty. Both versions were incorporated into statute law by the Treaty of Waitangi Act of 1975 and despite considerable initial litigation over the implications of the Act, it required both parties to act towards the other in good faith.

In recent years, the trend toward litigation between the two groups has been replaced with negotiation, and this has resulted in some satisfactory fisheries and mineral claims. One area of contention has been a government-imposed deadline on land claims which, according to the Maori Congress (a non-statutory body to represent tribes), is contrary to the spirit of shared rights exemplified by the Treaty. Although it is only entrenched in domestic law, the Treaty of Waitangi has been extremely influential in its effect on the position and perception of Maori people in New Zealand. The most visible effect of the 150-year tradition of sharing the two cultures in that country is the pervasiveness of Maori language, symbols and customs in the wider community, encouraged primarily through the education system (ACAR 1994; Brady 1995). The visibility of Maori culture has been attributed to a contemporary worldwide renaissance among Indigenous people, reasserting pride in their traditions and ancestry (Voyle & Simmons 1999).

Progress?

The Australian Council for Aboriginal Reconciliation has made important inroads into closing the gulf between Indigenous and non-Indigenous people in Australia, yet recent policy approaches have contributed to widening the gap, eroding important Indigenous rights, including native title (land) rights (Yencken

& Porter 2001). Few recommendations from the 1987 Royal Commission into Deaths in Custody, or the 1997 Inquiry into the Stolen Generations have been implemented. In fact, the Indigenous population in prison has doubled since the findings were handed down. One study found that Indigenous people were more than 19 times as likely as non-Indigenous people to die in custody, a decade after the Royal Commission (Yencken & Porter 2001).

The refusal by the government to offer an apology for the Stolen Generations has engendered an 'unnecessary and divisive debate in Australian society', which has further traumatised those most affected (Yencken & Porter 2001, p 44). Australia declined to sign the UN Committee on the Elimination of Racial Discrimination Act declaring the right of all Indigenous people to self-determination, which, in conjunction with its refusal to sign the UN Optional Protocol to the Convention on the Elimination of All Forms of Discrimination Against Women, will leave no avenue beyond its borders for resolving discrimination (Loff & Cordner 2000). Despite international criticism, the government's 'directed community services model' continues to vest little control with Indigenous people, and is expected to perpetuate marginalisation and disadvantage (Yencken & Porter 2001).

Although the Indigenous people of other countries in the Americas and New Zealand also suffered from the effects of colonisation, they differ in the extent to which they have benefited from treaties or other social reparations for dispossession (Anderson 2001). The First Nations people of North America have a longer history of negotiating their rights with their colonisers. This has left them with more power over their affairs, and better health status than the Indigenous people of the South Pacific. Health gains among North American Indigenous people after the Second World War have been attributed to the impact of more appropriate health care interventions, and greater access to health care, primarily in reducing the burden of infectious diseases (Kunitz 2000).

In New Zealand, the history of the Maori people shows that their culture and health status have also suffered from colonisation, despite the fact that they have enjoyed the protection, rights and privileges of British citizenship. Their citizenship status is enshrined in the Treaty of Waitangi, now the rallying point for the new Maori renaissance (Voyle & Simmons 1999). They continue to experience poorer health and socioeconomic conditions than non-Indigenous New Zealanders (MOHNZ 2001a). However, the past decade has seen renewed government commitment to the Treaty of Waitangi, with an emphasis on educational goals and the development of culturally appropriate and responsible health services (Gerritson 2001; NCNZ 1996; Voyle & Simmons 1999). A fundamental element for success in the future will be whether or not the Treaty is seen by non-Maori (Pakeha) New Zealanders as requiring their understanding of Maori issues rather than only the other way around (Gerritson 2001).

In Australia there is considerable debate about developing a treaty, but no consensus on what template to use or what distinct rights and aspirations would flow from recognising the status of Indigenous people. The advantages are seen to lie in the opportunity to resolve Indigenous rights by negotiation rather than by the costly, adversarial and ill-suited processes of litigation that have characterised native title decisions (Dodson & Pritchard 2001). In order to foster self-determination it is first necessary to address issues of justice. According to Trudgen (2000) two things are required for effective development: security of tenure and a rule of law. Yet, at present in states like the Northern Territory, where large numbers of Indigenous people reside, the legal situation creates anarchy. The 'land rights' established federally are not recognised or well understood by the local Indigenous people, so they continue to have a divisive effect between different clans (Trudgen 2000). A land council makes decisions about their lands and resources, which for many people creates another layer of disempowerment. These communities are also at the mercy of non-Indigenous laws and systems of justice, which many tribal people neither understand nor assent to (Trudgen 2000). Current debate about Indigenous health is polarised around the issue of welfare. There is no dispute that current circumstances are linked to colonial invasion, dispossession, dislocation, institutionalisation and traditional economies, but some believe that welfare dependency is the major cause of dysfunction in Indigenous communities (Loff & Cordner 2001).

The solutions to the welfarist arguments do not seem to lie solely in providing more financial resources, as this has not been seen as having a significant effect on increasing life expectancy. Maoris, for example, have lower incomes than American Indians, but virtually the same life expectancy (Kunitz 2000). Further evidence dismissing a financial solution comes from examining the pattern of expenditure on health. Currently, the Australian government expenditures on health reflect a 1.22:1 ratio to the advantage of Indigenous Australians. This is an improvement on previous ratios, none of which have demonstrated health gains (Anderson 2001). The yield from this level of investment in Indigenous health may take time, given new government primary health care initiatives, but previous mechanisms for funding Indigenous health became somewhat convoluted within state–commonwealth funding relations, the lack of a national health plan and fragmented access to local health care (Anderson 2001).

Kunitz (2000) argues the importance of financial resources, claiming that high national wealth is a factor associated with greater valuing of Indigenous people's autonomy, control of land, and access to social and health services (Kunitz 2000). This may be cause for some optimism, but the emphasis must be on the distribution of, and control over, financial and other resources, rather than the generation of wealth (Keating & Hertzman 1999). And the path to self-determinism may become more complex in a globalised world.

Globalisation and
the health of Indigenous people

The adage 'think global, act local' may need some reconsideration in the wake of globalisation, especially for Indigenous people. Globalisation is being discussed by many health and social groups in response to what seems to be world dominance by the most powerful nations. The trend towards globalisation has been evolving for several centuries, but over the last two decades there has been growing concern among those at the lower end of the socioeconomic scale about its effects (McMichael 2000; Yencken & Porter 2001). Globalisation is a transnational economic reshaping of world trade and investment, which has occurred simultaneously with revolutions in human mobility and electronic communications. Large multinational corporations have merged to manufacture and market goods, and to pursue new freedoms in trade across borderless markets, including trade in international currencies, without exchange controls (McMichael 2000). The problem is that globalisation has created an international division of labour. The high end is controlled by multinational companies that outsource 'low end' products to poorer countries where labour is cheap and few workplace standards regulate manufacturing or assembly. As a result, there is widening of socioeconomic stratification (McMichael 2000). In practical terms, this increases the vulnerability of some poorer countries, who become 'price takers' while the rich continue to be 'price makers' (Kent 1999). For example, farmers in a poor country may receive less in real terms for a bushel of grain than farmers in wealthier nations for the same amount, because they do not have access to the same means of negotiating prices. Exporting underpriced goods effectively transfers the value of those goods to the control of the wealthy, and gives little hope of escape from a marginalised position.

At the 'big end of town', companies thrive and control commodities in a global marketplace with no trading loyalties. In the poorest urban areas and in the rural communities where most Indigenous people live, people become poorer as a result of global competition, which drives prices down and consigns waste and environmental degradation to where people do not have power to prevent it. The best intentioned policies at the national or global level that allow industrial pollution or land degradation may ignore what occurs at the local level or fail to understand local implications (Mittlemark 2001). Globalisation at its most ruthless both perpetuates the persistent and widening economic inequalities and runs counter to sustainable health, particularly where widespread pollution is tolerated as the cost of economic advancement (McMichael 2000; McMichael, Smith & Corvalan 2000). The challenge, or complicating factor, is the need to create wealth and achieve the greatest good for the greatest number, including future generations (Woodward 2000).

A deeper issue for Indigenous people lies in the extent to which the environmental threats associated with globalisation will further destroy an already degraded environment. In the world-view of many Indigenous people, health and well-being mean integrity and harmony in the interrelationships among all things that constitute people's life ways. Central to well-being is self-determination, and central to self-determination is the right to land and the right to their own laws and customs. To sustain health and well-being, Indigenous people must have both territorial and food security, and this involves having a dignified and meaningful place for all community members, and control over natural resources (Kent 1999; NAACHO 1993; Trudgen 2000).

Kunitz (2000) argues that globalisation will not only increase inequality but will have other deleterious effects on Indigenous people. The issue will be resolved in the way countries will respond to the erosion of sovereignty. Given the fact that national economies are controlled by the flow of international capital, the question remains as to whether or not nations will be willing or able to protect their industries, local employment, workers, the environment or social spending. Once the world becomes a single conglomerate, how will Indigenous people maintain their culture and their very survival?

This question has spawned a new Indigenous people's movement against dispossession, with an emphasis on globalisation rather than the colonisation of past history. Indigenous people in Mexico, Brazil and Latin America, throughout the Amazon, Canada, the United States and the South Pacific are becoming increasingly aware of the need to keep the health and well-being of their people on the globalisation agenda. Kunitz (2000) contends that today's Indigenous activists are better prepared than at any time in history, seeking in-depth understanding of the machinations of large organisations such as the World Trade Organization, which operates beyond scrutiny in making resource decisions. The goal of their counter-offensive is to mobilise international public opinion, even if it means embarrassing governments that acquiesce to a global marketplace without regarding the needs of Indigenous people. This type of activism to assert tribal and ethnic identity has had the positive effect of better connecting Indigenous people throughout the world, which is expected to advance the cause of conservation through resisting the most destructive effects of globalisation (Kunitz 2000).

Many Indigenous people seek to restore tribal ways to rejuvenate the native spirit of community living and counter the individualistic nature of Western society (Raeburn & Rootman 1998). This is a likely outcome of a coherent movement to resist globalisation. But there is a further advantage to this wider connectedness. Kunitz (2000) suggests that sharing of cultures may lead to wider scrutiny of tribal conditions, particularly where oppressive local hierarchies have resisted changing for the good of their people. This is an important issue, and one at the heart of debate on several continents.

---

case study...

Culture can be a health hazard

A decade ago, I attended a conference on women's health in Botswana, and was irrevocably moved when a black lawyer virtually pounded her podium to those of us in the audience who were there to discuss the HIV/AIDS epidemic. 'Why do you reify my culture?' she charged. 'My culture is killing me. It is killing my children. It has killed my brothers. We do not need you to come here to tell us how wonderful it is to be part of African culture. African culture is deadly!'

There was a hush around the theatre. Theoretical papers were shuffled, some of which addressed questions of how health professionals could work with the women of Africa to promote safe sexual behaviours. Others brought show-and-tell presentations from their countries, where behavioural interventions had worked well. None were as powerful as the initial speaker's comments. I have never quite recovered from this awakening, where I sat, troubled throughout the long journey home, re-framing my conception of culture and what it means to the reality of people's lives. I recently returned to Africa and heard many stories of what has transpired over the past ten years. Many more people have died of HIV/AIDS. Male entitlement is alive and well, and keeping the HIV virus on the move.

Many people have no jobs, as the factories are closing, with so few workers and so much recession. The young men available for work are employed as truck drivers, and transport their goods through the main routes of African countries. They are the only ones who seem to be empowered over sexual matters. They trade tomatoes and bread to their many mistresses who come to the designated truck stops. Some of these young women sit in shallow dishes of bleach to dry out their vaginal canals so that their transient lovers will have greater friction, which apparently creates more pleasure. Some already have the HIV virus but they return anyway. Condoms are out of the question as the men claim they do not give as much pleasure.

The next week, at the same comfort stop, the young women will be there again to provide a similar service in exchange for food or other essentials.

Young girls and boys come to the local hospital each day by bus, to visit their classmates who are dying. They come from schools where their teachers may also be ill. They return to homes where the family constitution undergoes many changes, depending on who is sick and who has passed away. Still, we white strangers skirt around the issues, attempting to work within the cultural boundaries, to empower the young girls with knowledge so that they can refuse unsafe sex. For economic reasons, and the rapidly declining availability of men, they listen but do not change their behaviour.

I still hear that woman's rage.

In Australia, as in other countries, there are wonderful, warm Indigenous families. Both the women and men exude gentleness, which is not the way many non-Indigenous people tend to understand them. However, over time, some families have lost their gentleness. Governed by tribal laws, their relationships sometimes get out of hand, particularly where the parties have been drinking alcohol. In these families, violence against women is so prevalent and so serious that the rate of deaths from injury is seven times that for the entire population. It is also responsible for 46 per cent of all hospitalisations among Indigenous women (AIHW 2000). Children are also abused and injured, then sent to school where teachers try to coach them in developing self-esteem in the hope that they will continue their education and break the cycle of violence. At the end of the day they return home, to be abused again. Not so many years ago, in some Indigenous communities, young virgins were taken out to the bush to be gang raped in preparation for a young man's marriage. The reasons for this type of behaviour may have changed, but the fact remains that the rate of interpersonal violence in the Indigenous community is more than ten times that of the non-Indigenous population (Commonwealth of Australia 2001). Pack rapes occur with frightening frequency in some areas, with women hesitating to report them because of fear of retribution by men's kinship networks (Commonwealth of Australia 2001). Women continue to be beaten mercilessly, causing severe injuries to them, their children and the collective psyche of the entire community. I still hear that woman.

Noel Pearson, an Aboriginal leader in Australia, is tired of dysfunctional behaviour among his people. He believes Indigenous Australians have committed three errors in the theoretical analysis of their structural problems.

They have misinterpreted history, they don't understand the dynamics of substance abuse epidemics and they do not understand the reasons for their ill health (Pearson 2000). He argues against those who lay blame for Indigenous people's problems on the fact that they have become victims of a welfare state. In his view, many Aboriginal people were employed and played an important role in society, particularly in the rural areas—the current widespread unemployability followed, rather than preceded, passive welfare, contrary to what some believe.

Pearson contests the view of alcohol as a disease. He believes substance abuse follows five essential factors: cash, spare time, availability of the substance, the example of others and a permissive social ideology. His view is that rather than treat the original causes leading to substance addiction, the addiction itself must be the target.

Pearson's third contention is that Aboriginal people should not place disproportionate blame on the health care system for their poor state of health. Their state of health needs something more fundamental than treatment; namely, a relentless, active intolerance of illicit drugs and alcohol and a society based on work and families. He sees a dysfunctional relationship between families and communities. Social policies focus on the community, which often leads to family rivalries. Aboriginal families are excluded from the spheres of information and education by the low expectations of the rest of society. They have no power, having to negotiate through various community structures for their needs. Being out of the employment loop, there is no sense of self-determinism. Pearson's initial solution is to develop family capacity for income management. Instead of the old people using their welfare money to buy what the family needs, while the young ones spend theirs on alcohol, all welfare payments should come to the family. This would help to overcome the idea among young people that what they receive as income is 100 per cent discretionary. By building skills for income management, which is, in reality, learning about consequences, all family members would be able to understand budgets and the young people would learn to value the types of investments that can be used for work, study or consumer goods other than alcohol, as well as feeling they are part of family maintenance and family cohesion (Pearson 2000).

Trudgen (2000) agrees. In his view, to be healthy is to feel there is something worth living and fighting for. Indigenous people need to create interventions that help them achieve and retain mastery over their lives. They must stand shoulder to shoulder with their non-Indigenous neighbours and work through culturally acceptable ways of creating financial viability, and managing their lands and their laws, and this will require dramatic change, first among the non-Indigenous community. Pearson's (2000) emphasis on family empowerment in this process aligns well with the request of all Indigenous people in the Geneva Declaration on the Health and Survival of Indigenous Peoples (WHO 1999). Their statement revolved around an inter-generational continuum, incorporating four distinct, shared dimensions of life—the spiritual, intellectual, physical and emotional—to interact in dynamic equilibrium with nature. The declaration seeks to regenerate Indigenous families to work towards re-arranging their structural conditions. This has also been the goal of other groups, including those working towards partnership networks in New Zealand to try to better meet the needs of Maori families (Crampton, Dowell & Woodward 2001). The guiding principle in this and other initiatives in New Zealand is cultural safety, a model used also to secure culturally relevant health care for indigenous people in the rest of the world.

Cultural **safety**

The concept of cultural safety was first described in New Zealand in 1988 by the Hui Waimanawa (Ramsden, in Eckermann et al 1992). The concept revolves around recognition of the social, physical and economic elements required by those belonging to the Maori culture, and their rights to partnership, participation and protection (MOHNZ 2001b). Cultural safety encompasses a holistic reflection of the person within the context of family and community, and the customs, attitudes, beliefs and preferred ways of doing things that comprise that system (Eckermann et al 1992). Unsafe cultural practice is any action that assaults, diminishes, demeans or disempowers the cultural identity and well-being of an individual (NCNZ 1992; Williams 1999).

The first step in achieving cultural safety is *cultural awareness*. This includes recognising the fact that any health care relationship is unique, power-laden and culturally dyadic. Once there is recognition of the inherent nature of cultural difference, *cultural sensitivity* can be developed. People can be expected to develop cultural sensitivity once they engage in some form of self-exploration of their own life experience and realities, and the impact this may have on others. The final stage is a commitment to ensuring preservation and protection of others' cultures. Cultural safety is advocacy informed by a recognition of self, the rights of others and the legitimacy of difference (NCNZ 1996).

The principles of cultural safety are similar to the principles of primary health care in that the focus is on social justice. In a socially just, and thus healthy, environment, the relationship between health professionals and the community is one of partnership and mutual exploration of need, rather than one where there is a power differential of provider and consumer. People are free to choose the pathways to health that best suit their needs and customs. All cultures are seen to be equally valid, and both personal and collective views are valued. Both cultural safety and primary health care are not as much about *what* is done by health professionals to promote health and reduce risks, but about *how* this is done (Johnson 1997).

Like primary health care, the cultural safety approach also encourages examination of political processes as they affect health. The overall aim is to empower all people to gain autonomy over decisions affecting their health and health services. The primary goals are to improve health and access to services for all people, irrespective of age, gender, sexual orientation, occupation or socioeconomic status, ethnic origin or migrant experience, religious or spiritual belief, or disability (NCNZ 1996). This can only be accomplished with an understanding that equality means having a right to be *different*, rather than the *same* (Houston 1993).

The major strategy for achieving cultural safety in any community is education. Health professionals must be educated within an ethos of cultural relativism; that is, they must learn to understand and value diversity in cultures, history, attitudes and life experiences. Dowd and Johnson (1996) provide an example of this in their illustration of the health care professional who believes an Indigenous person who sleeps in the desert has become sick because he lives in the dirt surrounded by germs. Cultural beliefs, on the other hand, may attribute his illness to the fact that he failed to look after his land. When we fail to gain this type of cultural understanding, our attempts at helping indigenous people or those of any other culture are doomed to failure. The opposite of this is cultural competence, to know who among the group has *mana* or prestige to walk with the health professional and explore ways of changing behaviour or conditions (David Prentice, Auckland Healthcare Services Ltd, personal communication 2000). Professional ignorance may be seen as professional arrogance, and this interferes with our attempts to advocate for health as a *partner*, rather than a *provider*. The role of the health professional is therefore to understand how power imbalances impede health and how an equitable helping role can be negotiated and changed to provide effective, efficient and acceptable services (NCNZ 1996).

Improving
Indigenous health

Improving Indigenous health status is far from simplistic. Effective health-promotion approaches must include comprehensive and multi-layered strategies that seek to redress the distal, social inequities in all aspects of life, including education, employment, housing, the administration of legal processes and land rights. This must be done in conjunction with strategies to deal with proximal risk factors to prevent suicide, alcohol abuse, domestic violence and smoking.

The HIV/AIDS epidemic is increasing at an alarming rate among Indigenous people (DuBois, Brassard & Smeja 1996; Mill & DesJardins 1996). Tobacco use is a major problem. Canadian researchers report that as many as 60 per cent of Aboriginal Canadians smoke regularly (MacMillan et al 1996). Indigenous people in Australia smoke at twice the rate of the non-Indigenous population (AIHW 2000). The long-term health of young people especially is at risk from the combination of smoking, alcohol and illicit drug use. In the short-term, these behaviours also heighten the risk of accidents, injuries, family disruptions, suicide, infant mortality and bringing young people into contact with the police (Gray et al 1997; MacMillan et al 1996; Malchy et al 1997).

Government agencies have been established in many countries to empower Aboriginal people to meet culturally specific needs. However, some are beset by bureaucratic problems, inadequate placement of Indigenous professionals or managers, misunderstanding of group identity, language difficulties, a lack of coordinated information systems or geographic isolation (Newbold 1997; Tookenay 1996). One of the first things that must be addressed is variable provision and utilisation of culturally appropriate services, and this is attracting government response in New Zealand, Australia and North America (Browne & Fiske 2001; Cunningham 2002; Voyle & Simmons 1999). A further system issue relates to jurisdictional disputes between state or provincial and federal governments, which sometimes create inconsistencies in services or confusion among those needing the services about where to seek help. This should also be addressed, but real change must begin at the policy level and then followed through to the implementation of services.

Goals for
Indigenous health

To address Indigenous health needs, the following goals are important:

- Access and equity in health care
- Greater connectivity between Indigenous people and their advocates
- Cultural sensitivity and cultural safety in all health care practices
- Community self-determinism and self-empowerment on the basis of capacity building
- Public recognition of the unique needs and sensitivities of Indigenous people
- Public awareness of the implications of environmental degradation and globalisation on Indigenous people
- Reconciliation with other people of the world.

Building healthy public policy

The health of Indigenous people is essentially a political minefield. Government policies have attempted to resource Indigenous health strategies, but have had only modest success in reducing the burden of illness, injury and disability. As a result, few claims can be made for self-determinism, empowerment of Indigenous people, or cultural safety. It is an indictment of non-Indigenous policy makers that the most pressing problems, the structural issues, have not been adequately addressed. Government funding for Indigenous health must ensure access to culturally appropriate health services and to the community infrastructure that determines health, including housing, clean water and skills development. This can only be done with the participation of Indigenous people at all levels of government policy so that there is careful integration of physical, emotional, social, spiritual, environmental, political and cultural needs (Golds et al 1997; WHO 1999). Segregating Indigenous health into one policy or separating individual needs from the whole perpetuates fragmentation of services and destroys understanding of the dynamic interrelationships necessary for achieving health and well-being.

Health goals and strategies for Indigenous people must include broad, comprehensive notions of equity. Equity is a two-dimensional concept that consists of horizontal equity (the equal treatment of equal people) and vertical equity, which refers to unequal, but equitable, treatment of people who may not have equal requirements or preferences (Jan & Wiseman 1996). True equity incorporates the right to *difference*, not *sameness*. Equity involves equality of access to and use of health care, without coercion to use one or another service. So there are situations where top-down provision of equitable services may actually be *in*equitable to Indigenous people on the basis of cultural preferences and holistic, traditional definitions of health. Similarly, setting population-based, equal goals for health (horizontal equity) may not achieve intended outcomes, especially if there are disparate needs (Jan & Wiseman 1996). A social justice approach dictates that all needs be considered, even those that fall outside the norm.

Creating supportive environments

The most important elements of a supportive environment are understanding and communication (Arriaga 1994). To understand another culture requires understanding of our own beliefs and attitudes first, then a concerted effort to understand those of the other culture. It is important to know the symbols of the culture and how members of the culture see our symbols. For example, when the health professional is seen as a bona fide community member, a different message is conveyed than when the helper is simply flown in to treat an illness or collect information on the community. Another issue in assessing the need for support is to know how illness is perceived and how its causes and cures are framed within the cultural context. Having at least a cursory grasp of the language is also important to ensure that communication is appropriate. This partly explains the relative success of Maori health initiatives in New Zealand (Aotearoa). Few New Zealanders do not maintain at least a rudimentary understanding of the basic concepts of Maori language. In Australia, few non-Indigenous people even know the name of an Indigenous language, yet when Indigenous people convey their traditions and languages in schools, non-Indigenous students are intrigued by their culture and tend to ask for more cultural exposure. One way to effect reconciliation at this, the operational level, would be to introduce a wider component of Aboriginal culture to school-age children.

When members of some cultures are ill, specific facilities may be required to accommodate religious or other beliefs. Sometimes these may be related to the need for special religious observances, hygiene, diet and bodily contact (Ashkam 1996). Young families may have special needs related to child rearing, such as the need for a hospitalised child to always feel the security of family members, or the need to consult a traditional healer. The family may need to deal with social beliefs about the causes of the problem that may be unfamiliar to the health professional, or to formulate priorities for treatment based on family needs (Bushy & van Holst Pellekaan 1995).

One of the most pressing challenges for health carers lies in meeting mental health needs. The problem of alcohol abuse, for example, is poorly understood and one of the most destructive influences on Indigenous family life (Brady 1995, 1997; Gray et al 1997). Restricting supply is one tactic being used, as is stricter policing at the point of sale. While these may be justified in some cases, they are also regarded as heavy-handed, top-down approaches and have attracted conflicting views. Some see excessive sanctions on the availability or distribution of alcohol as aligned with white colonialist approaches (Kelso Townsend & de Vries 1995). Alternative approaches, where Aboriginal people themselves participate in developing community plans to address the problem, are usually more widely accepted and thus more effective (Brady 1995). These often include reliance on role models who are credible in the cultural environment.

---

case study...

The Feather of Hope

The Feather of Hope is a peer support program for Canadian Indigenous people diagnosed with HIV infection. It was developed by a group of community workers in a small Aboriginal community in northern Alberta, Canada. In the first stage of the program, discussions were held within the community to plan an approach that would be culturally and developmentally appropriate to those who most needed help. The participants identified the need to have an Aboriginal Elder provide a linkage between the older generation and the new. As there was no nominated Elder, an ageing (96-year-old) member of the community was recruited to help plan and oversee implementation of the program. Once the local community of AIDS sufferers was made aware of the program and its focus on Aboriginal culture, a process of guidance and support was begun.

The program's approach is as follows. Each day begins with a traditional Sweet Grass ceremony and prayers to the Creator and Sacred Spirits. The emphasis is first on developing cultural insight into the social, economic and health issues faced by Aboriginal communities and how these are related to development of HIV infection. The educational presentations include

an explanation of the ways traditional methods (healing circles, retreats, sweat lodges and traditional healers) can be used to support people who are HIV-positive. The next part of the program focuses on the development of presentation skills by group participants so that they can all participate in a self-help process and perpetuate the cycle of helping.

All aspects of the program are culturally sensitive. Staff of Aboriginal ancestry have been hired as both staff and board members, to enhance credibility among the community. Because these are local people, they are expected to carry out the local, traditional ceremonies. The philosophy of the program revolves around the belief that disease is a product of both biological and social factors. The illness is viewed as a lesson, not in the sense of a retribution, but as a spiritual teaching. The program is based on mutual support and non-interference, wherein the thoughts, beliefs and decision-making abilities of individuals are honoured. The strategy for learning and understanding is modelling rather than coercion and persuasion, so the older and more experienced people are valued as they are called upon to discuss cultural issues or demonstrate desired behaviours. The most attractive aspect of the program is its basis in empowering the community to develop its potential, an example of a client-focused, culturally sensitive health-promotion approach.

Strengthening community action

Community action in Indigenous groups involves any activity designed to encourage self-empowerment. An empowered community has equitable resources, and the capacity to identify and solve problems, participate in community activities, develop self-confidence and influence social change (Herbert 1996). The role of the health advocate involves enhancing the community's sense of self-empowerment by consulting with them on their need for housing, sanitation, jobs, education, transportation and health care. To perform this role adequately, it is important to become familiar with their problems and needs from an insider's perspective, rather than from the stereotypical assumptions of non-Indigenous groups (Queensland Government, ATSIC Policy and Development 2000).

To understand Indigenous culture with respect to health matters is to recognise that Indigenous people often interpret health issues in terms of relationships between people rather than in terms of medical signs and symptoms (Bushy & van Holst Pellekaan 1995; Eckermann & Dowd 1991). Health-related behaviour change is embedded in the relationships among friends, family members and health care workers, so the health advocate must enhance these interactions and promote greater sharing of information if there are changes to be made.

One misconception that persists among policy makers is that simply adding more resources will fix the problems that conspire to keep Indigenous people in deprived economic and social conditions. Education and skills training are now seen to be the most important elements for strengthening community action. This should lead community development in the direction of appropriately deploying resources rather than simply adding to them, to build local capacity. Equally important is the need to build skills that will help Indigenous communities work towards preventing and overcoming the cultural insult of pollution in their sacred lands (Colomeda 1996). We have a responsibility to help heal these communities by blending information from current research with that of traditional wisdom to work towards a healthier environment for all cultures.

Developing personal skills

Ambiguities persist among Indigenous and non-Indigenous people concerning the extent to which education for the young must be wholly embedded in culture. Some believe non-Indigenous education will destroy the culture, but unless young Indigenous people become articulate and able to argue among professionals, bureaucrats and politicians at any level, they will not attain equitable social and health outcomes (Tsey 1997).

At the same time, there are sensitivities around the notion of the 'museum culture', to be displayed for visitors (Harlem Brundtland 1999). Governments have a responsibility to integrate Indigenous information into the education and health systems in a way that does not objectify Indigenous people as mere museum pieces. Genuine valuing of Indigenous culture respects the terms and conditions within which expressions of that culture are shared.

Indigenous people must be helped to deal with the past before any sense of the future can be anticipated. Many Indigenous families harbour continuous loss and grief from episodes in their histories that have been part of the colonial processes of dispossession, institutionalisation and control. As health professionals, we have a responsibility to adopt a conciliatory approach to their needs by acknowledging the importance of family, community and spiritual harmony to their health and well-being (Golds et al 1997).

Reorienting health services

The most important consideration in attempting to reorient health services towards Indigenous communities is to recognise the primacy of community participation (Golds et al 1997). Self-care is central to community participation and occurs when people are empowered to choose their own combination of health treatments and services. These may be exclusively traditional healing practices, or a combination of cultural rituals, remedies and folk medicine with more contemporary medical treatments (Borins 1995). When health professionals attempt to learn about traditional folk practices and their origins, there is a capacity for building trust within the community and this sends a clear message to the community that self-determinism is valued (Bushy 1992). Accepting folkways and folk remedies for self-care also provides an opportunity to acknowledge the importance of social roles in the culture, particularly those that revolve around the member of the community who may have the responsibility for healing community members. Without knowledge of these practices, a complete assessment of health needs is impossible.

Encouraging people of other cultures to discuss their beliefs about spiritual elements of healing will help us learn more about the things that they believe will or will not work and, in some cases, this becomes a self-fulfilling prophecy. By sharing information, a foundation of mutual respect is established and the health professional may then be able to exchange ideas for preventive actions or assist members of the culture to recognise the need for the type of services that have been omitted from most Indigenous people's health care. These include health screening and immunisation, which are often not considered important by Indigenous people (USNWLC 2001). Genuine valuing of Indigenous culture respects the terms and conditions within which expressions of that culture are shared.

Indigenous health workers in many countries of the world have played an instrumental role in extending modern health services to their local communities (Tsey 1996). These health workers are usually the most effective means of delivering information to families on child care, immunisation, elder care and a range of other issues. However, in some cases the local community health workers hesitate to become involved with intimate 'women's business', such as pap smears. This is usually related to complex kinship networks and the need to separate 'women's business' from 'men's business'. Program planners must therefore consider the gendered context of all health programs and services, and this can only be done with the participation of community members who can act as guardians of cultural interests.

It is not enough to evaluate health and other social investments among Aboriginal people solely in terms of program reach and expected health outcomes (Tsey 1997). It is also important to examine the linkage effects of programs in terms of tangible benefits, such as employment, and intangible benefits, such as well-being and social opportunities. By making these outcomes visible, they may serve as incentives for young people to aspire to improving their educational status and thus being better prepared to ensure the ongoing preservation of their culture.

thinking critically

Aboriginal health

1 Identify the elements of colonisation that predispose Indigenous people to ill health.

2 Describe three major causes of the burden of illness, injury and disability among Indigenous people.

3 Explain the social determinants of Indigenous ill-health.

4 Analyse the effect of globalisation on the health of Indigenous people.

5 Explain four ways in which culture mitigates against good health, and four ways in which it can facilitate good health.

REFERENCES

Allison, K., Adlaf, E., Ialomiteanu, A. & Rehm, J. (1999). Predictors of health risk behaviours among young adults: analysis of the national population health survey. *Canadian Journal of Public Health*, 90(2): 85–9.

Anand, S., Yusuf, S., Jacobs, S., Davis, A., Yi, Q., Gerstein, H., Montague, P. & Lonn, E. (2001). Risk factors, atherosclerosis, and cardiovascular disease among Aboriginal people in Canada: the study of health assessment and risk evaluation in Aboriginal peoples. *The Lancet*, 358(9288): 1147–60.

Anderson, I. (2001). The truth about indigenous health policy. *Arena Magazine*, 32(6). http://www.arena.org.au/arenamag.htm. Accessed 17 January 2002.

Arriaga, R. (1994). Risk management: cross-cultural considerations. *Rehabilitation Management*, Aug/Sep,99(1-1): 131.

Ashkam, J. (1996). Ageing in black and ethnic minorities: a challenge to service provision. *British Journal of Hospital Medicine*, 56(11): 602–4.

Australian Council for Aboriginal Reconciliation (ACAR) (1994). Walking Together: The First Steps. Report of the Australian Council for Aboriginal Reconciliation. Canberra: AGPS.

Australian Institute of Health and Welfare (AIHW) (1998). Health in Rural and Remote Australia. Canberra: AGPS.

—— (2000). Australia's Health 2000, Canberra: AGPS.

Ayers, T. (1999). AAAS reports on health sector role in South Africa's apartheid. *Science*, 283(5402): 707.

Borins, M. (1995). Native healing traditions must be protected and preserved for future generations. *Canadian Medical Association Journal*, 153(9): 1356–7.

Brady, M. (1995). Culture in treatment, culture as treatment. A critical appraisal of developments in addictions programs for indigenous North Americans and Australians. *Social Science and Medicine*, 41(11): 1487–98.

—— (1997). Aboriginal drug and alcohol use: recent developments and trends. *Australian and New Zealand Journal of Public Health*, 21(1): 3–4.

Browne, A. & Fiske, J. (2001). First Nations women's encounters with mainstream health care services. *Western Journal of Nursing Research*, 23(2): 126–47.

Bullen, C. & Beaglehole, R. (1997). Ethnic differences in coronary heart disease cases and fatality in Auckland. *Australian and New Zealand Journal of Public Health*, 21(7): 688–93.

Bushy, A. (1992). Cultural considerations for primary health care: where do self-care and folk medicine fit? *Holistic Nursing Practice*, 6(3): 10–18.

Bushy, A. & van Holst Pellekaan, S. (1995). Footprints, a trail to survival. In: G. Gray & R. Pratt (eds), *Issues in Australian Nursing 4*. Melbourne: Churchill Livingstone, pp 219–33.

Colomeda, L. (1996). *Through the Northern Looking Glass*. New York: National League for Nursing Press.

Commonwealth of Australia (2001). Violence in Indigenous Communities. Canberra: Attorney-General's Department.

Crampton, P., Dowell, A. & Woodward, A. (2001). Third sector primary care for vulnerable populations. *Social Science and Medicine*, 53: 1491–502.

Cunningham, J. (2002). Diagnostic and therapeutic procedures among Australian hospital patients identified as Indigenous. *Medical Journal of Australia*, 176: 58–62.

Daniel, M., Green, L., Marion, S., Gamble, D., Herbert, C., Hertzman, C. & Sheps, S. (1999). Effectiveness of community-directed diabetes prevention and control in a rural Aboriginal population in British Columbia, Canada. *Social Science and Medicine*, 48: 815–32.

Dodson, M. & Pritchard, S. (2001). Pact puts all parties on an equal footing, *The Australian*, 12 December.

Dowd, T. & Johnson, S. (1996). Aboriginal Cultural Awareness Program, Northern Territory Health Services and Institute for Aboriginal Development, Alice Springs, NT.

DuBois, M., Brassard, P. & Smeja, C. (1996). Survey of Montreal's Aboriginal population's knowledge, attitudes and behavior regarding HIV/AIDS. *Canadian Journal of Public Health*, 87(1): 37–9.

Eckermann, A. & Dowd, T. (1991). Strengthening the role of primary health care in health promotion by bridging cultures in Aboriginal health. *Australian Journal of Advanced Nursing*, 9(2): 16–20.

Eckermann, A., Dowd, T., Martin, M., Nixon, L., Gray, R. & Chong, E. (1992). *Binan Goonj: Bridging Cultures in Aboriginal Health*. Armidale: University of New England Press.

Gerritson, J. (2001). Maori health and Treaty of Waitangi. *Nursing Review*, March: 10–11.

Golds, M., King, R., Mieklejohn, B., Campion, S. & Wise, M. (1997). Healthy Aboriginal communities. *Australian and New Zealand Journal of Public Health*, 21(4): 386–90.

Gray, D., Morfitt, B., Ryan, K. & Williams, S. (1997). The use of tobacco, alcohol and other drugs by young Aboriginal people in Albany, Western Australia. *Australian and New Zealand Journal of Public Health*, 21(1): 71–6.

Harlem Brundtland, G. (1999). International consultation on the health of Indigenous people. Geneva: WHO.

Herbert, C. (1996). Community-based research as a tool for empowerment: the Haida Gwaii diabetes project example. *Canadian Journal of Public Health*, 87(2): 109–12.

Hirini, P., Flett, R., Kazantis, N., Long, N., Millar, M. & MacDonald, C. (1999). Health care needs for older Maori: a study of Kaumatua and Kuia, *Social Policy Journal of New Zealand*, Dec: 136–48.

Houston, S. (1993). Opening Address, Council of Remote Area Nurses of Australia (CRANA), National Conference, Broome.

Jan, S. & Wiseman, V. (1996). Equity in health care: some conceptual and practical issues. *Australian and New Zealand Journal of Public Health*, 20(1): 9–11.

Johnson, S. (1997). Cultural safety: from risk to respect. Unpublished paper. Council of Remote Area Nurses of Australia. Alice Springs.

Keating, D. & Hertzman, C. (1999). *Developmental Health and the Wealth of Nations*. New York: The Guilford Press.

Kelso Townsend, J. & de Vries, N. (1995). Aboriginal mental health: a personal view. In: R. Gray & R. Pratt (eds), *Issues in Australian Nursing 5*, Melbourne: Churchill Livingstone.

Kent, G. (1999). Globalization and food security in Africa (draft) http://www.2hawaii.edu/~kent/globaFeb99.html. Accessed 2 April 2002.

Kulig, J. (2000). Culturally diverse communities: The impact on the role of community health nurses. In: M. Stewart (ed), *Community Nursing: Promoting Canadians' Health*, 2nd edn. Toronto: WB Saunders, pp 194–210.

Kunitz, S. (2000). Globalization, states, and the health of indigenous peoples. *American Journal of Public Health*, 90(10): 1531–9.

Loff, B. & Cordner, S. (2000). UN condemns Australia over Aborigines. *The Lancet*, 356(9234): 1011.

—— (2001). Australian Aboriginal leaders tackle welfare of indigenous population. *The Lancet*, 358(9299): 2138.

MacMillan, H., MacMillan, A., Offord, D. & Dingle, J. (1996). Aboriginal health. *Canadian Medical Association Journal*, 155(11): 1569–626.

Malchy, B., Enns, M., Young, T. & Cox, B. (1997). Suicide among Manitoba's Aboriginal people, 1988 to 1994. *Canadian Medical Association Journal*, 156(8): 1133–8.

McCredie, M., Paul, C., Skegg, D. & Williams, S. (1999). Breast cancer in Maori and non-Maori women. *Journal of the American Medical Association*, 282(5): 189–195.

McMichael, A. (2000). The urban environment and health in a world of increasing globalization: issues for developing countries. *Bulletin of the World Health Organization*, 78(9): 1117–24.

McMichael, A., Smith, K. & Corvalan, C. (2000). The sustainability transition: a new challenge. *Bulletin of the World Health Organization*, 78(9): 1067–95.

Mill, J. & DesJardins, D. (1996). The feather of hope: Aboriginal AIDS prevention society: a community approach to HIV/AIDS prevention. *Canadian Journal of Public Health*, 87(4): 268–71.

Ministry of Health New Zealand (MOHNZ) (2001a). Priorities for Maori and Pacific Health: Evidence from epidemiology. Wellington: MOHNZ.

—— (2001b). He Korowai Oranga, Maori Health Strategy, Discussion Document. Wellington: MOHNZ.

Mittlemark, M. (2001). Promoting social responsibility for health: health impact assessment and healthy public policy at the community level. *Health Promotion International*, 16(3): 269–74.

National Aboriginal Community Controlled Health Organisation (NACCHO) 1993). Manifesto on Aboriginal Well-Being. Brisbane: NACCHO.

Newbold, K. (1997). Aboriginal physician use in Canada: location, orientation and identity. *Health Economics*, 6: 197–207.

Nursing Council of New Zealand (NCNZ) (1992). Standards for Registration of Comprehensive Nurses from Polytechnic Courses. Wellington: NCNZ.

—— (1996). Guidelines for Cultural Safety in Nursing and Midwifery Education. Wellington: NCNZ.

Pearson, N. (2000). Misguided policies a toxic cocktail. *The Australian*, 24 December, p 13.

Queensland Government (2000). Protocols for consultation and negotiation with Aboriginal people. Brisbane: ATSIC Policy and Development.

Raeburn, J. & Rootman, I. (1998). *People-Centred Health Promotion*. Chichester: John Wiley & Sons.

Reid, J. & Trompf, P. (eds) (1991). *The Health of Aboriginal Australia*. Sydney: Harcourt Brace Jovanovich.

Ring, I. (2001). Cardiovascular health in Indigenous Australians: a call for action. Conference report. *Medical Journal of Australia*, 175: 351–2.

Statistics New Zealand (2001). Life expectancy and death rates. New Zealand Government, Wellington, http://www.stats.govt.nz. Accessed 14 January 2002.

Stephens, C. (1996). Healthy cities or unhealthy islands? The health and social implications of urban inequality. *Environment and Urbanization*, 8(2): 9–30.

Tookenay, V. (1996). Improving the health status of aboriginal people in Canada: new directions, new responsibilities. *Canadian Medical Association Journal*, 155(11): 1581–3.

Trudgen, R. (2001). Why warriors lie down and die. Darwin: Aboriginal Resource and Development Services, Inc.

Tsey, K. (1996). Aboriginal health workers: agents of change? *Australian and New Zealand Journal of Public Health*, 20(3): 227–8.

—— (1997). Aboriginal self-determination, education and health: towards a radical change in attitudes to education. *Australian and New Zealand Journal of Public Health*, 21(1): 77–83.

United States National Women's Law Center (USNWLC) (2001). US Women's Health, American Indian Health Indicators. Pittsburg: University of Pennsylvania, Oregon Health & Science University.

Voyle, J. & Simmons, D. (1999). Community development through partnership: promoting health in an urban indigenous community in New Zealand. *Social Science and Medicine*, 49: 1035–50.

Williams, R. (1999). Cultural safety—what does it mean for our work practice? *Australian and New Zealand Journal of Public Health*, 23(2): 213–14.

Woodward, A. (2000). Hard choices. *Bulletin of the World Health Organization*, 78(9): 1160–63.

World Health Organization (WHO) (1999). Indigenous and Tribal Peoples: Legal Frameworks and Indigenous Rights. Geneva: WHO.

Yencken, D. & Porter, L. (2001). A Just and Sustainable Australia. Melbourne: The Australian Collaboration.

Promoting
community
competence

Section

Introduction
to the Section

This section extends earlier discussions of community health to the major contexts within which health can be promoted. The section begins with a discussion of the linkages between place and health. On that basis, Chapter 12 outlines the Global Healthy Schools Initiative, and how healthy lifestyles can be invoked by appropriately designed school health programs that set the stage for lifelong health and well-being. Chapter 13 takes this a step further along the developmental continuum, to Healthy Workplaces, where the health and safety of the adult working population can best be cultivated.

In the two chapters that follow, the two major organisational elements fundamental to healthy communities are examined. Chapter 14 examines the evidence-base from which health initiatives can be devised, discussing the type of evidence that should be gathered, and examples of how research evidence has been used in the past to inform the development of community competence. Chapter 15 investigates characteristics of health systems and the requisite policies relating to health systems that are instrumental to health promotion. This is important because, as we seek innovations in health promotion that are relevant in the new century, there is major concern in many parts of the world about the efficiency of health systems and the extent to which they are matched with targets identified through research. This section culminates in an exploration of issues that must be addressed for the future, to assure both policy makers and those working at the cutting edge of health promotion that health for all *can* be achieved with rational planning.

CHAPTER 12

Healthy
schools

ntroduction Healthy communities are a product of healthy organisations, including healthy governments, healthy cities, islands, villages, marketplaces, workplaces, health care institutions and schools (Kickbusch 1997). Feeling comfortable in these communities and recognising the opportunities and resources in each context helps promote a sense of personal equilibrium and harmony, and this is fundamental to health and wellness. It also underlines the social nature of human beings, and the many ways people come to know themselves through their connections with others and their mutually shared environments.

Chapter 1 explained the link between health and place, and this idea is relevant to the healthy schools concept. Individuals, including young people, are linked to their place through three key psychological processes: attachment, familiarity and identity (Thompson Fullilove 1996). Attachment to others in the context of a familiar place is fundamental to the development of self, particularly in cultivating human intimacy and other types of relationships that are important to mental health (Cutchin 1997; Goffman 1995). The theory of attachment suggests that we each have a personal environment that serves as an '"outer ring" of life-sustaining systems complementary to the 'inner ring' of systems that maintain physiological homeostasis' (Bowlby 1973, p 150). Attachment to our outer ring is synonymous with 'place attachment', which is important to our sense of identity, safety and satisfaction with life (Thompson Fullilove 1996).

Healthy places provide the template for the creation of health. For young children, healthy schools set the stage for a balanced life of industriousness, play and social interchange. As adults, healthy occupational settings reinforce this orientation towards healthy living in providing a work life free of injury or occupational illness. At play on healthy golf courses, beaches or ski slopes, healthy patterns of interactions with others are developed in safe environments conducive to physical and psychological well-being. And this extends to health care. Healthy hospitals extend their activities to illness prevention rather than focusing only on illness, and they ensure that the refuse of our tragedies does not perpetuate the decline of our environment. So the 'settings' approach to health promotion has enormous potential.

Worldwide, schools reach approximately 1000 million young people and, through them, their families and communities. Schools are therefore 'the world's broadest and deepest channel for putting information at the disposal of its citizens' (Nakajima 1996, p 3). In addition to information, healthy school environments build health potential, create buffers between young people and their wider social networks, provide intermediary support for them to develop into healthy adults, strengthen the community's protective factors and, in the context of developing skills for lifelong learning, reduce the effect of social gradients (WHO 1997). Healthy schools are therefore one of the most cost-effective health and education investments (Harlem Brundtland 2000).

objectives   **By the end of this chapter you will be able to:**

1   Discuss the capacity of schools to improve the health of young people

2   Explain the links between education and health

3   Discuss three advantages of comprehensive school health programs

4   Identify three barriers to school health promotion

5   Design a school-based program to respond to the physical, social and emotional needs of youth.

The global initiative
for school health

In recognition of the importance of schools in health promotion, in 1995 the WHO established a Global School Health Initiative. The initiative is guided by the Ottawa Charter for Health Promotion and the Jakarta Declaration, with advice from the WHO Expert Committee on Comprehensive School Health Education and Promotion (WHO 2000). The School Health Initiative was designed to serve as a unifying framework for all countries of the world, to work towards strengthening health promotion and education activities at the local, national, regional and global levels (WHO 2000). Its basic premise is that health is inextricably linked to educational achievement, quality of life and economic productivity (living, working and learning). If the appropriate environment for learning and for the development of healthy lifestyles can be provided early in a person's development, there is a greater likelihood of them sustaining health throughout their lifespan (O'Byrne et al 1996).

Since the initiative began, its purpose has become further clarified in relation to the expected outcomes of reducing risk among young people and protecting them against future harm. WHO identified the major causes of death, disease and disability as revolving around six interrelated categories of preventable risk, all of which involve behaviours initiated during youth. These include:

- tobacco use
- behaviour that results in injury and violence
- alcohol and substance abuse
- dietary and hygienic practices that cause disease
- sedentary lifestyle
- sexual behaviour that causes unintended pregnancy and disease (CDC 2001; WHO 2000).

The WHO initiative began with three broad strategies for encouraging health promotion in schools. These included developing the resource materials to advocate for school health programs, mobilising public and private resources through the WHO regional networks, and strengthening national capacities for school health by bringing member nations together to learn from one another (O'Byrne et al 1996; WHO 1997). These strategies have successfully focused on the 'health-promoting school'. Health-promoting schools are designed to encourage caring for the self and others, making healthy decisions, creating conditions that are conducive to health, building capacities for sustainable development, preventing leading causes of death, disease and disability, and influencing health-related behaviours: knowledge, beliefs, skills, attitudes, values, support (WHO 2000).

The Healthy Schools initiative has been markedly successful in the few short years since its inception. The healthy school concept now extends to many countries in many regions of the world, including Europe, the South and Western Pacific, China, Indonesia and the Americas. In recognition of the importance of healthy schools to the health of all people, in 2000 WHO, UNESCO, UNICEF, the World Bank and Education International (which includes Africa) launched a new interagency initiative called FRESH (focusing resources on effective school health). This latter initiative is based on the WHO's 'Education for All' strategy. Its foundation principles are that good health and nutrition are not only essential inputs but also important outcomes of good quality, basic education. This approach to education works towards healthy, safe and secure school environments to help protect children from health hazards, abuse and exclusion, particularly for girls (WHO 2000; World Bank 2001).

Strategies for further development in school health now include the following:

- evaluation research to describe the nature and effectiveness of school health programs
- consolidating research and expert opinion to build capacity and advocate for improving school health programs
- fostering collaboration to strengthen national capacities
- creating further regional and global networks and alliances for the development of Health Promoting Schools (WHO 2000).

Health
and education

The link between health and education has been demonstrated in numerous ways. Creating opportunities for health at school has an important effect on learning. The World Declaration on Education for All is based on the understanding that poor health and malnutrition are important underlying factors for low school enrolment, absenteeism, poor classroom performance and early school dropout (WHO 2000). Young people who are ill or injured, suffer from physical or mental health problems, hunger or malnutrition, pregnancy, the effects of alcohol and drug use, or who fear violence are less likely to learn, irrespective of educational processes (Kolbe, Collins & Cortese 1997; Strauss 2001; WHO 2000). Educational attainment also helps foster good reproductive and sexual health, particularly with an emphasis on HIV/AIDS, which has been estimated to cause 11 per cent of the global burden of disease among school-aged children 5–14 years (World Bank 2001). Literacy also increases a society's resource base, not only in terms of economic growth, but in relation to improved health and quality of life, making an important contribution to human and social capital (Kickbusch 2001).

The most disadvantaged children are the ones who have the most to gain from healthy school experiences. In some countries, children come to school with impaired cognitive abilities from iron deficiency anaemia (IDA) caused by worms and parasites, including those that cause malaria. At all levels of disadvantage, nutrition has an indisputable effect on learning. When children are hungry or undernourished they are less likely to resist infection. Illness may cause them to miss school, or they may become irritable and have difficulty concentrating. Poorly nourished children may also be unable to participate in physical activities to the same extent as their classmates, and therefore tend to be unfit (CDC 1997). Although it is not always possible to supplement children's diets sufficiently through school health programs, some measures can be taken to improve their overall nutritional status. Programs that include regular deworming and iron supplementation, for example, come at a relatively low cost and have shown such positive outcomes as lower absenteeism and higher scores on tests of cognition or school achievement (World Bank 2001).

Providing opportunities for schooling is in itself a powerful way to influence health and health literacy (Nutbeam 2000; Nutbeam & Kickbusch 2000; Ratzan 2001). For older children, learning to avoid risky behaviours or to cope with the consequences of these behaviours ensures better opportunities in life. Many school health programs are now targeted at young, sexually active girls who become pregnant while at school. In the past, most would simply drop out of school, eliminating their chances for gaining employment later on. Health-promoting schools are helping to keep some of these young women studying towards a better life for themselves and their families. This includes one-third of all pregnant girls in Latin American schools and numerous girls in the same situation across the Caribbean and other developing nations. Similarly, healthy schools in the industrialised countries are working towards continuing motherhood programs developed to motivate teenage mothers to return to school

(World Bank 2001). In keeping girls at school, these programs play an important role in supporting basic human rights and in fostering greater social equity (WHO 2000; World Bank 2001). Most programs work towards enhancing psychosocial functioning that will build personal capacity, in the expectation of reducing risks associated with illicit drug and tobacco use, poor nutrition and physical inactivity, suicide, violence, unintentional injuries (playground and sports injuries) and other unsafe behaviours (AHPSA 2000; Kolbe, Kann & Brener 2001; UKHEA 1999).

The evolution of
school health services

Throughout the previous century, the evidence for positive outcomes from school-based health services has been growing steadily. School health centres were originally established to respond to a broadening of the concept of schooling beyond vocational training to encompass the provision of social services (Sedlak 1997). Prior to the era of professionalisation (the early part of the twentieth century), most services beyond the traditional teaching functions in schools were provided by community volunteers. With the development of discrete professions, the number of participants in school health services proliferated; however, their arrival also signalled a fragmentation of function. Health teaching was predominantly relegated to the health or physical education teacher, while the school nurse was primarily concerned with conducting screening tests and responding to playground injuries with first aid services (Leavy Small et al 1995). School psychologists, guidance officers and social workers were also considered an important part of school health services in their role as advocates for positive emotional student health.

During the 1920s to 1970s, school-based health promotion focused on the provision of information, primarily related to hygiene and bodily functions. Little attention was given to environmental or contextual factors beyond the influence of the family. Once research studies began to systematically evaluate these programs, predictably, health-related information being provided in schools was found to have little or no effect on behaviours such as smoking, eating and physical activity (Stone 1996). Gradually, it became clear that healthy behaviours, such as a child's eating habits, were found to be influenced by the interaction between the child and her or his social and physical environments, not simply on knowledge of the healthfulness of foods (Nicklas et al 1997).

As the research data accumulated, the characteristics of an effective health promotion program became clear. The optimal program was based on research evidence, and included developmentally appropriate, culturally sensitive information, presented in a gender-sensitive way (especially for diet-related issues), provided by well-prepared teachers, on the basis of clinical data from health screening, with adequate guidance, reinforcement and follow-up (DeMuth Allensworth & Bradley 1996; Dusenbury & Falco 1995; Fardy et al 1995).

During the community health promotion era of the 1970s and 1980s, the focus of school health expanded to include a more holistic approach with input from all involved in children's educational experiences. A more concerted approach was also timely because of increasing numbers of medically fragile students and those with chronic health problems (Magyary & Brandt 1996). The service was expanded to include screening and immunisation, implementation of HIV/AIDS prevention policies, provision of health education and counselling to students and staff, and participation in the school health promotion team (AAP 2001; Bradley 1997; Leavy Small et al 1995; McClowry et al 1996)

School health promotion campaigns of this time became a team effort and many reported successes in improving health knowledge, attitudes and behaviours—for example, in reducing high sexual risk behaviours (Mullen et al 1995). American, Australian, Canadian, New Zealand and Swedish research studies from this era concluded that school-based programs can serve as a catalyst for broader societal change (Mullen et al 1995). In many cases, especially in the United States, the role of the school health nurse was expanded to that of case manager, a role in which as a coordinator of programs, the nurse provided a 'medical home' for primary health care (AAP 2001). This included dealing with crisis medical situations and providing specialised health care procedures as well as the requisite screening and prevention (AAP 2001). Healthy school programs focused on preventing eating disorders, maintaining cardiovascular health, healthy sexual behaviour, and educating young people about tobacco. These programs were found to be more effective when enhanced by targeted community-wide programs that addressed the role and resources of families, community organisations, related policies (including anti-tobacco advertising) and other elements in the social environment (Beaglehole 1991; Chapman et al 1994; Mackie & Oickle 1997; Mullen et al 1995; Neumark-Sztainer 1996; Nutbeam 1997; Resnicow, Robinson & Frank 1996). Including adolescents in planning such programs and encouraging peer support was also identified as an important element (Komro et al 1996).

In conjunction with the cumulative body of research evidence, a broader approach to school health promotion was spawned by growing awareness that the physical, mental and social health needs of adolescents were often not being met by an increasingly complex, costly and fragmented health care system (Brindis & Sanghvi 1997). Health promotion experts agreed that comprehensive, well coordinated, school-based health promotion programs were the best way to meet the needs of adolescents in a way that could provide confidentiality, respond to their need for spontaneous services, overcome transportation needs, eliminate their loss of study time and even loss of work time for families where, increasingly, both parents were in full-time employment (Brindis & Sanghvi 1997; Resnicow & Allensworth 1996).

Today, school health programs are considered a vital resource for the health of young children. Because schools have the existing infrastructure to link resources for health (education, nutrition, sanitation) they are considered a 'best investment' in sustainable health (World Bank 2001). This increases the efficacy of other investments in children's health and development, in that schools provide an essential sequel and complement to early childhood programs. The combination of the two is relevant in an era where many more young children attend child care than in the past (Sundwall 2001). Schools have the added advantage of an extensive skilled workforce that works closely with the community. This is important in promoting effective intersectoral collaborations for health, such as those between health and education departments and ministries, and partnerships between these departments and parents and community organisations (World Bank 2001). These demonstrate the accessibility of the school as a context for health promotion (Adelman & Taylor 1997).

One additional element that is proving successful in places like the United Kingdom is the 'Healthy Teachers' movement. A number of conferences have been held throughout the United Kingdom to support teachers as role models for good health. Following a series of successful Healthy Teachers meetings in 1999, plans are under way to establish monitoring systems to encourage occupational health among teachers from various schools, to foster greater involvement in improving the health of both the teachers and their workplaces, and to collaborate with school administrators to elevate the profile of health in schools (UK Government 2002). This type of 'spin-off' movement, working in tandem with the UK Healthy Schools Network, helps to raise awareness of health issues throughout the entire community (UKHEA 1999). It is also consonant with the principles of primary health care in that it increases community self-determined initiatives that promote access, equity, cultural sensitivity and the development of human and social capital.

Teachers are also a focus for the New Zealand Health Promoting Schools (HPS) movement. In that country, HPS use the Ottawa Charter as a framework for building the capacity of both the teachers and their school environments (HPS Newsletter 2001).

Health-promoting
schools

A health-promoting school is defined by WHO (1998) as a place where all members of the school community work together to provide students with integrated and positive experiences and structures that promote and protect their health. According to the WHO Expert Committee on Comprehensive School Health Education and Promotion, this type of school:

- strives to improve the health of school personnel, families and community members as well as students
- fosters health and learning with all the measures at its disposal
- engages health and education officials, teachers and their representative organisations, students, parents and community leaders in efforts to make the school a healthy place
- strives to provide a healthy environment, school health education and school health services along with school/community health projects and outreach, health promotion programs for staff, nutrition and food safety programs, opportunities for physical education and recreation, and programs for counselling, social support and mental health promotion

- implements policies and practices that respect an individual's self-esteem, provide multiple opportunities for success and acknowledge good efforts and intentions as well as personal achievements (WHO 1998).

An ideal health-promoting school is an environment wherein the social and physical environments are considered equally important to health, one where pupils, teachers, administrators, family members and others in the community collaborate to develop policies and practices that reduce all forms of violence and adversity, increase equity, respect, caring, self-esteem and opportunities for success in the classroom, the playground and the community. Most importantly, it is a school that is the hub of health promotion, where many sectors (health, recreation, social services, law enforcement, transport, food and commerce) come together to maximise the health, education and development needs of young people (Kickbusch & Jones 1996; Mackie & Oickle 1997). Health-promoting schools display, in everything they say and do, support for enhancing the health and well-being of all members of the school community (WHO 1997).

Comprehensive
school health programs

The areas of preventable risk identified by WHO (2000) are being addressed in the context of comprehensive school health programs aimed at reducing the burden of illness, injury and disability among young people by building physical and psychosocial capacity. Many of these programs are extremely successful, in both industrialised and developing countries, especially in providing for basic needs (safe water, nutrition) and better reproductive health (World Bank 2001). Since comprehensive school health programs began, a number of positive outcomes have been identified, including changes in physical education policies and programs, greater emphasis on managing students with chronic health conditions, and pregnancy and suicide prevention (Kolbe et al 2001). The World Bank (2001) estimates that for every $1 invested in tobacco prevention, drug and alcohol education and family life education, $14 have been saved in avoided health care costs.

A further indicator of the usefulness of comprehensive school health programs is that they fill a gap in service provision for young people who hesitate to access traditional health services (Keyl et al 1996; Walter et al 1995). Confidentiality is a major issue for all adolescents, particularly those in rural areas, where local health providers are often neighbours or family friends (Rickert et al 1997). In some cases, cultural norms or family attitudes prevent them from seeking information or preventive services (Soon, Chan & Goh 1995). Successful school health programs represent an integrated and mutually reinforcing set of experiences for young people that are compatible with the school's educational goals and values and are developed to be sensitive to both family and community-wide public health goals (Nutbeam 1997; Villalbi 1997).

The most effective coordinated school health programs are designed to systematically address risky behaviours through eight interactive components.

1   health education
2   physical education
3   health services
4   nutrition services
5   counselling, psychological and social services
6   healthy school environment
7   health promotion for staff
8   family and community involvement (CDC 2001).

Integration of all eight components means that the school develops as a healthy organisation within a healthy community, with the full participation of students, teachers, parents and others. It also involves ensuring that all teachers are prepared to link their teaching with the development of personal skills to ensure healthy lifestyles. The school environment should be conducive to health and safety, and students should be provided with access to appropriate health services that recognise mental health as well as physical health needs (Nutbeam 1997). Because young people are among the most vulnerable and powerless in society, other forms of action should also be taken to ensure they can utilise their learning in a safe and healthy environment, with opportunities to overcome the limitations of social and/or economic disadvantage. The success of these programs also rests on reinforcement from healthy communities external to the school that are supportive of healthy public policies, such as those governing tobacco and alcohol distribution (Nutbeam 1997).

Evaluating the success of **comprehensive school health promotion**

Comprehensive school health services have been found to contribute to improvements in students' health status and to reduce some risk-taking behaviours. One study found that students who were enrolled in the school clinic were twice as likely to stay in school than non-enrolled students, and another demonstrated their influence on increasing contraceptive use (Brindis & Sanghvi 1997). Evaluation of comprehensive school health programs in Canada identified four factors that contribute to successful implementation of Healthy Schools programs. These include: school readiness, as indicated by a visionary Healthy School Committee; support by the principal, who acts as gatekeeper for the program; community outreach, including the involvement of school councils or home and school groups, community organisations and local businesses; and staff development for public health nurses coordinating the programs (Mitchell, Laforet-Fliesser & Camiletti 1997).

A national evaluation study of school health programs and policies was conducted in the United States in 1994, with a follow-up study in 2000. The researchers found that many health education programs established in primary school taper off during the years when the prevalence of health risk behaviours increases among students (Kolbe et al 2001). They found that three-quarters of the schools following national or state health education standards or guidelines provided instruction on alcohol and drug use prevention, growth and development, nutrition and dietary behaviour, physical fitness and tobacco use prevention. Because these components were incorporated into other subjects, the extent of their effectiveness was not clear. More than three-quarters of middle/junior and senior high schools provided instruction on alcohol and other drug use prevention, HIV/AIDS and other STD prevention, and human sexuality. Most of these schools, however, taught abstinence as the most effective way to avoid pregnancy, and only one in five junior schools, and half of the senior schools taught students how to correctly use a condom (Kolbe et al 2001). They found that, in some cases, mental health and social services staff from the community worked with school staff, but in most cases there was a need for more collaboration.

The trends identified by the evaluation team between 1994 and 2000 showed an increase in violence and tobacco use prevention. There were also improvements in the coordination of physical education policies and programs and an increase in the responsibility of school nurses for providing health services. The three health services that received increasing emphasis were case management for students with chronic health conditions, pregnancy prevention and suicide prevention (Kolbe et al 2001).

The findings indicate that comprehensive school health services are working to some extent, but it is necessary to share both the gains and the difficulties of programs with others. This underlines WHO's push to build capacity through networks and coalitions (WHO 2000). Today's adolescent problems mirror the problems of society, which are primarily within the sphere of mental health and illness (WHO 2001). To be comprehensive, school health promotion services should integrate mental health services along a continuum of care with other services. Holistic and developmental perspectives should focus on individuals, families and the environment, and range from primary prevention and early intervention, through treatment and rehabilitation in the school, community and home environment (Adelman & Taylor 1997). Many components of comprehensive programs require multidisciplinary teamwork, especially in sensitive areas such as suicide prevention. This requires ongoing staff education and school policies that support strategies that confront the issues affecting young people. However, family values sometimes mitigate against what seems to be the appropriate approach to adolescent health promotion, and this is evident in community resistance to such things as teaching condom use.

Healthy literacy, which fosters healthy decision-making and self-empowerment, is an essential part of any successful school health promotion program. St Leger and Nutbeam propose that the health-promoting school contributes to four main outcomes: lifelong learning skills, competencies and behaviours, specific cognate knowledge and skills, and self-attributes (Nutbeam 2000; St Leger 2001). The attitudes that are cultivated through the health-promoting school movement have the potential to develop skills in advocacy and achieve a sense of empowerment. Although the evidence to date is insufficient to establish the 'health-promoting school' as the gold standard in health promotion, the potential remains for schools to achieve the three levels of health literacy mentioned in Chapter 1. Functional health literacy can be promoted through school-based information that increases a young person's knowledge of the factors that inhibit and enhance health. An outcome of this is the student's capacity to contextualise and work through his or her options and strategies for coping with peer pressure. Interactive health literacy, fostered through opportunities at school to become independent and self-caring, sets young people on a pathway to accessing appropriate health information and services. Critical health literacy can be developed through 'classroom and community learning opportunities which address social inequities, determinants of health, policy development and ways of affecting change'. This helps build capacity to participate in community and societal action for health improvements among disadvantaged groups (St Leger 2001, p 201).

Critical literacy can also be cultivated in young people when the community around them believes in their abilities to instigate community change. Finn and Checkoway (1998) examined five case studies of young people's ability to actively participate in 'community building' schemes. They based their analyses on 'youth as resources' rather than 'youths at risk' or 'youths as bundles of pathology' who threaten the social order. They followed groups of young people as they worked collaboratively to build capacity in their communities, to critically question the status quo and to address community needs ranging from peer mentoring to cleaning up the environment. Their observations led them to suggest that empowered young people can have a significant impact on one another and on their communities, whether these are at school or across cultural, geographic or national boundaries (Finn & Checkoway 1998).

In addition to empowered students, St Leger (2001) believes the key to successful programs for health literacy rests with government investments in professional development for teachers, research into school health frameworks and their effects, and dissemination of the prima facie evidence collected thus far indicating that school health programs do work under many different conditions. Kickbusch (2001) urges us to develop indicators for each of the three levels of health literacy to investigate how they are interrelated with general education and general literacy. If a set of indicators could be devised for these relationships, we may be able to measure a new type of health index to complement measures such as the DALYs used for morbidity and mortality. This would help researchers analyse what community factors may be at work reinforcing or constraining general literacy, general education and health literacy (Kickbusch 2001).

Obstacles to success of
school health promotion

Despite encouraging reports from comprehensive school health promotion strategies, some barriers remain. The reviews conducted by Kolbe and colleagues (2001) and St Leger (2001) indicate the need for unequivocal government support for school health programs. St Leger (2001) also underlines the need to disseminate information, which has to date been sporadic. One study in Australia found that, despite Commonwealth policy endorsing a multidisciplinary approach to school health promotion, teachers were unaware of the concept of a health-promoting school, or their roles in implementing health promotion programs (Thyer 1996). Similarly, in North America many schools have yet to translate health promotion ideals into positive classroom experiences. This may require better resourcing for schools, better in-servicing of teachers and a shift in the curriculum to a more socioecological model of health.

Another issue that needs to be addressed is the need for crisis response mechanisms in schools. Unfortunately, the escalating level of violence in society is reflected in the school setting, and few schools are adequately prepared to manage crisis situations (Cunningham & Henggeler 2001). This must be redressed to maintain staff and student morale in times of crisis, and so that children's unresolved reactions to violence at school do not create a downward spiral of poor academic performance (Fiester et al 1996; Kline, Schonfeld & Lichtenstein 1995).

Another barrier to effective school health promotion is related to the typically highly structured and under-resourced nature of school systems. Without staff, space and industrial policies that value health promotion, school-based services will be less than optimal (Nicklas et al 1997). Geographic location may also be a constraint in school health promotion, particularly for schools with little indoor space for physical activities.

The concept of a school-linked community health centre will bear close consideration, particularly for its capacity to bring together many sectors of society interested in community health. Such developments require horizontal cooperative resourcing arrangements at the school and community level as well as vertical cooperative arrangements to ensure that the various bureaucratic obstacles to service delivery can be overcome (Adelman & Taylor 1997). Members of the school community also need to be familiar with the local, external community and its health goals and capacity, to ensure collaborative input and student participation (Landis & Janes 1995).

Another potential barrier to success in comprehensive school health programs is related to the attitudes of either staff or administrators. Because of a lack of understanding or a lack of valuing, opportunities for consolidating health promotion messages may be scheduled during times considered 'expendable', such as in place of physical or health education classes, which are already declining in many places. Similarly, changes in food preparation may be thwarted by staff who have entrenched ways of running school cafeterias (Nicklas et al 1997). Some of these obstacles may be overcome by sensitive approaches to training existing staff, ensuring that appropriate information and materials are disseminated to teachers, administrators and food service staff. There is also a need to maintain consistency in applying policies and practices. To engage the teaching community in nurturing the health of students it is also essential to ensure they have the time for development, delivery and evaluation of the content, so that all work towards health literacy is collaborative and feeds back into the program of general education. Perhaps most important is the need to tailor teaching approaches to the particular needs of students' gender and culture.

case study...

Boys at school

The growing body of research into health literacy suggests that education and environment are the most significant elements in achieving sustainable health and well-being (Nutbeam 2000). This validates the Healthy Schools approach, where the potential for nurturing health and a healthy lifestyle is enhanced by a positive educational experience. Health literacy is both a goal and an outcome of general literacy (Ratzan 2001). From this perspective, a good education in a healthy school environment can provide both the health and scientific foundations for a fulfilling life.

One of the great challenges for teachers, librarians and administrators is how best to help adolescents navigate the journey into adulthood. Educating boys is a particular challenge, especially with declining numbers of male teachers who can act as role models for healthy development. Some high schools have experimented with the 'add human development and stir' approach, others with an integrated curriculum where a resource teacher (usually the physical education teacher) provides curriculum content to other teachers to weave health and human development issues into their subjects. But how effective is this in achieving a balance between physical, emotional and social health and health literacy for boys?

Although students in Canada, New Zealand and Australia demonstrate superior reading skills (surpassed only by Finnish students), boys don't do as well at reading as girls (New Zealand Education Review Office 2000; Statistics Canada 2000). Boys and girls tend to have very different learning styles, which places boys at a social disadvantage. Boys don't put themselves 'out there' as much as girls. They tend to think deductively, rather than inductively, to see themselves as problem-solvers rather than enjoy the ambiguity of such tasks as creative writing. Their attitudes to literature are often linked to its utility, rather than a sense of empathy for either the key characters or the aesthetic rewards of learning. They can be devastated by criticism and being put on the spot (Pirie 2002). The idea of reading to dwell deeply on sentiment or to reflect on the thoughts of others is foreign to many boys. They tend to downplay emotional expression in favour of concrete thoughts and actions, such as in sports, and they tend to shy away from verbal presentations that revolve around their own critical judgements, especially when girls are present. These traits may not bode well for the development of positive mental health and self-caring during adulthood.

The learning styles of boys may be due to a number of factors, including a society that tends to reinforce girls' ability to articulate social and emotional issues, while ignoring the needs of boys to develop similar skills. A Canadian scholar attributes at least some of the problem to the fact that boys associate reading with femininity, which stems from having been read to by their mothers and predominantly female pre-school teachers (Hall 2002).

Teachers have tried to grapple with the differential learning styles of boys, with some success. In the United Kingdom an innovative program encourages fathers or any other male role model to become involved in a range of activities, including joint perusal of newspaper articles and board games to help boys become 'turned on' to reading (UK Literacy Trust 2001). In New Zealand, teachers have tried providing language sessions within a strong activity base, and at a slightly different pace than those for girls. Some have used reading as a vehicle to self-development, promoting interactive group approaches, and a selection of male-oriented materials. In some cases, a collaborative approach has been used to engage the librarians and teachers in staff development activities with wide appeal to boys (NZERO 2000). This approach is also being used in some Australian schools.

One all-male high school in Queensland has developed an innovative program to educate the students for lifelong learning and, in the process, develop an enhanced set of social skills. Guided by the school librarian, they have adopted an 'all of school' approach to boys' literacy. The program includes guidelines and ongoing support for both teachers and parents, who also provide input into the program. The approach includes strong, positive role modelling by published authors who come to the school to talk about their writing. Permission is also sought to invite the boys to email the authors directly to discuss their writing in 'bookraps'. This is accompanied by having the boys attend writers' festivals and running writing competitions at the school, supported by a book club. The boys are also encouraged to attend special writing camps and clinics and to work with peers to design web pages for fiction. The program has proved so successful that it has been adapted at other schools, including coeducational high schools that segregate boys' and girls' reading classes to provide a safe space for boys' learning. This is seen to encourage boys to give expression to their creative development without the judgemental appraisal of girls, or having to tailor their interests to those of the girls. At first glance, this seems to run counter to the principles of equity and equality of opportunity, but in reality it addresses a very serious problem in the differential development of boys and girls. To date, the gendered approach has met with approval from the teachers, students and parents, who are made to feel an integral part of their children's education (personal communication, Helen Reynolds, The Southport School; Alan Trueman, All Saints Anglican School, Gold Coast, Australia 2002).

These outcomes provide affirmation of the role of the school in providing a socialising environment for young people. In a world where the media serves up high doses of violence and unhealthy lifestyles, schools that focus on the holistic development of mind, body and spirit achieve a better fit with the goals of health literacy, particularly those that culminate in the human and social capital of our communities.

thinking critically

School health promotion

1 Explain three essential linkages between education and health.

2 List five factors that influenced the development of comprehensive school health programs.

3 Describe four ways in which the school setting can influence health behaviours.

4 Analyse the facilitating factors and barriers to developing a health-promoting school in your community.

5 Identify the essential components of a school-based program to:

   a) prevent drug and alcohol misuse, and
   b) prevent non-intentional injuries.

REFERENCES

Adelman, H. & Taylor, L. (1997). Addressing barriers to learning: beyond school-linked services and full service schools. *American Journal of Orthopsychiatry*, 67(3): 408–21.

American Academy of Pediatrics (AAP) (2001). The role of the school nurse in providing school health services. *Pediatrics*, 108(5): 1231–2.

Australian Health Promoting Schools Association (AHPSA) (2000). What is a health promoting school? http://www.hlth/qut.edu.au/ph/ahpsa/HPS.htm. Retrieved 14 February 2002.

Beaglehole, R. (1991). Science, advocacy, and health policy: lessons from the New Zealand tobacco wars. *Journal of Public Health Policy*, 22(30): 175–83.

Bowlby, J. (1973). *Attachment and Loss*. Vol. 11, Separation: Anxiety and Anger. New York: Basic Books.

Bradley, B. (1997). The school nurse as health educator. *Journal of School Health*, 67(1): 3–8.

Brindis, C. & Sanghvi, R. (1997). School-based health clinics: Remaining viable in a changing health care delivery system. *Annual Review of Public Health*, 18: 567–87.

Centres for Disease Control (CDC) (1997). Guidelines for school health programs to promote lifelong healthy eating, *Morbitiy and Mortality Weekly Report*, 45(R-R9): 1–40.

—— (2001). School health programs: an investment in our nation's future. US Department of Health and Human Services, Atlanta: CDC.

Chapman, S., King, M., Andrews, B., McKay, E. et al (1994). Effects of publicity and a warning letter on illegal cigarette sales to minors. *Australian Journal of Public Health*, 18: 39–40.

Cunningham, P. & Henggeler, S. (2001). Implementation of an empirically based drug and violence prevention and intervention program in public school settings. *Journal of Clinical Child Psychology*, 30(2): 221–32.

Cutchin, M. (1997). Community and self: concepts for rural physician integration and retention. *Social Science and Medicine*, 44(11): 1661–74.

DeMuth Allensworth, D. & Bradley, B. (1996). Guidelines for adolescent preventive services: a role for the school nurse. *Journal of School Health*, 66(8): 281–5.

Dusenbury, L. & Falco, M. (1995). Eleven components of effective drug abuse prevention curricula. *Journal of School Health*, 65(10): 420–5.

Fardy, P., White, R., Haltiwanger-Schmitz, K., Magel, J., McDermott, K., Clark, L. & Hurster, M. (1996). Coronary disease risk factor reduction and behavior modification in minority adolescents: the PATH program. *Journal of Adolescent Health*, 18: 247–53.

Fiester, L., Nathanson, S., Visser, L. & Martin, J. (1996). Lessons learned from three violence prevention projects. *Journal of School Health*, 66(9): 344–6.

Finn, J. & Checkoway, B. (1998). Young people as competent community builders: a challenge to social work. *Social Work*, 43(4): 335–46.

Goffman, E. (1995). The insanity of place. In: B. Davey, A. Gray & C. Seale (eds), *Health and Disease: A Reader*, 2nd edn, Buckingham: Open University Press, pp 72–8.

Hall, J. (2002). Vancouver Sun Raise a Reader Special Edition Article, 'Boys need to see male role models', http://www/canada/com/vancouversun/specials/raiseareader/boy_role.html. Retrieved 14 February 2002.

Harlem Brundtland, G. (2000). School health and youth health promotion. Geneva: WHO.

Health Promoting Schools Newsletter (2001). November, Auckland.

Keyl, P., Hurtado, M., Barber, M. & Borton, J. (1996). School-based health centers. *Archives of Pediatric Adolescent Medicine*, 150: 175–80.

Kickbusch, I. (1997). Health promoting environments: the next step. *Australian and New Zealand Journal of Health Promotion*, 21(4): 431–4.

—— (2001). Health literacy: addressing the health and education divide. *Health Promotion International*, 16(3): 289–97.

Kickbusch, I. & Jones, J. (1996). A health-promoting school starts with imagination. *World Health*, 4(Jul/Aug): 4.

Kline, M., Schonfeld, D. & Lichtenstein, R. (1995). Benefits and challenges of school-based crisis response teams. *Journal of School Health*, 65(7): 245–9.

Kolbe, L., Collins, J. & Cortese, P. (1997). Building the capacity of schools to improve the health of the nation. *American Psychologist*, 52(3): 256–65.

Kolbe, L., Kann. L. & Brener, N. (2001). Overview and summary of findings: School health policies and programs study 2000. *Journal of School Health*, 71(7): 253–63.

Komro, K., Perry, C., Murray, D., Veblen-Mortenson, S., Williams, C. & Anstine, P. (1996). Peer-planned social activities for preventing alcohol use among adolescents. *Journal of School Health*, 66(9): 328–34.

Landis, S. & Janes, C. (1995). The Claxton elementary school health program: merging perceptions and behaviors to identify problems. *Journal of School Health*, 65(7): 250–4.

Leavy Small, M., Smith Majer, L., Allensworth, D., Farquhar, B., Kann, L. & Collins Pateman, B. (1995). School health services. *Journal of School Health*, 65(8): 319–26.

Mackie, J. & Oickle, P. (1997). School-based health promotion: the physician as advocate. *Canadian Medical Association Journal*, 156(9): 1301–5.

Magyary, D. & Brandt, P. (1996). A school-based self-management program for youth with chronic health conditions and their parents. *Canadian Journal of Nursing Research*, 28(4): 57–77.

McClowry, S., Galehouse, P., Hartnagle, W., Kaufman, H., Just, B., Moed, R. & Patterson-Dehn, C. (1996). A comprehensive school-based clinic: university and community partnership. *Journal of Society of Pediatric Nursing*, 1(1): 19–26.

Mitchell, I., Laforet-Fliesser, Y. & Camiletti, Y. (1997). Use of the healthy school profile in the Middlesex-London, Ontario, schools. *Journal of School Health*, 67(4): 154–6.

Mullen, P., Evans, D., Forster, J., Gottlieb, N., Kreuter, M., Moon, R., O'Rourke, T. & Strecher, V. (1995). Settings as an important dimension in health education/promotion policy, programs, and research. *Health Education Quarterly*, 22(3): 329–45.

Nakajima, H. (1996). Healthy-promoting schools. *World Health*, 4(Jul/Aug): 3.

New Zealand Education Review Office (NZERO) (2000). The 2000 Report. Wellington, NZERO, http://www.ero.govt.nz/Publications/pubs2000/promoting%20boys%20achmt.htm. Retrieved 14 February 2002.

Nicklas, T., Johnson, C., Webber, L. & Berenson, G. (1997). School-based programs for health risk-reduction. *Annals of the New York Academy of Sciences*.

Neumark-Sztainer, D. (1996). School-based programs for preventing eating disturbances. *Journal of School Health*, 66(2): 64–71.

Nutbeam, D. (1997). Promoting health and preventing disease: an international perspective on youth health promotion. *Journal of Adolescent Health*, 20: 396–402.

—— (2000). Health literacy as a public health goal: a challenge for contemporary health education and communication strategies into the 21st century. *Health Promotion International*, 15(3): 259–67.

Nutbeam, D. & Kickbusch, I. (2000). Advancing health literacy: a global challenge for the 21st century. *Health Promotion International*, 15(3): 183–4.

O'Byrne, D., Jones, J., Sen-Hai, Y. & Macdonald, H. (1996). WHO's global school health initiative. *World Health*, 4(Jul/Aug): 5–6.

Pirie, B. (2002). Teenage Boys and High School English. Toronto: Heinemann Boynton/Cook.

Ratzan, S. (2001). Health literacy: communication for the public good. *Health Promotion International*, 16(2): 207–14.

Resnicow, K. & Allensworth, D. (1996). Conducting a comprehensive school health program. *Journal of School Health*, 66(2): 59–63.

Resnicow, K., Robinson, T. & Frank, E. (1996). Advances and future directions for school-based health-promotion research: commentary on the CATCH intervention trial. *Preventive Medicine*, 25: 378–83.

Rickert, V., Davis, S., Riley, A. & Ryan, S. (1997). Rural school-based clinics: are adolescents willing to use them and what services do they want? *Journal of School Health*, 67(4): 144–8.

Sedlak, M. (1997). The uneasy alliance of mental health services and the schools: an historical perspective. *American Journal of Orthopsychiatry*, 67(3): 349–62.

Soon, T., Chan, R. & Goh, C. (1995). Project youth inform—a school-based sexually transmitted disease/Acquired Immune Deficiency Syndrome education programme. *Annals of Academic Medicine of Singapore*, 24: 541–6.

St Leger, L. (2001). Schools, health literacy and public health: possibilities and challenges. *Health Promotion International*, 16(2): 197–205.

Statistics Canada (2001). *The Daily*, 4 December 2001. http://www/statcan.ca/Daily/English/011203/2011204a.htm. Retrieved 14 February 2002.

Stone, E. (1996). Can school health education programs make a difference? *Preventive Medicine*, 25: 54–5.

Strauss, M. (2001). Physical aggression in the family. In: M. Martinez (ed), *Prevention and Control of Aggression and the Impact on its Victims*. New York: Kluwer Academic/Plenum Publishers, pp 181–200.

Sundwall, J. (2001). The journal of school health (origins and early history). *Journal of School Health*, 71(8): 363–6.

Thompson Fullilove, M. (1996). Psychiatric implications of displacement: contributions from the psychology of place. *American Journal of Psychiatry*, 153(12): 1516–22.

Thyer, S. (1996). The 'Health Promoting Schools' Strategy: implications for nursing and allied health professionals. *Collegian*, 3(2): 13–24.

UK Government (2002). 'Wired for Health'. Department of Health and Department for Education and Skills, http://www.wiredforhealth.gov.uk/healthy/healteach.html. Retrieved 14 February 2002.

UK Health Education Authority (UKHEA) (1999). Healthy Schools. *The National Healthy Schools Network Newsletter*, edn 5, Autumn.

UK Literacy Trust (2001). http://www.literacytrust.org.uk/Database/boys.Boysinit.html. Retrieved 13 February 2002.

Villalbi, J. (1997). The prevention of substance abuse in schools: a process evaluation of the effect of a standardised education module. *Promotion and Education*, IV(1): 15–19.

Walter, H., Vaughan, R., Armstrong, B., Krakoff, R., Tiezzi, L. & McCarthy, J. (1995). School-based health care for urban minority junior high school students. *Archives of Pediatric Adolescent Medicine*, 149: 1221–5.

World Bank (2001). *Partnership for Child Development*. New York: World Bank.

World Health Organization (WHO) (1997). Report of the World Health Organization Expert Committee on Comprehensive School Health Education and Promotion. Geneva: WHO.

—— (1998). The World Health Report 1998. Geneva: WHO.

—— (2000). The Global School Health Initiative. Geneva: WHO.

—— (2001). The World Health Report 2001. Mental Health: New Understandings, New Hope. Geneva: WHO.

CHAPTER 13

Healthy
workplaces

troduction Globalisation and the internationalisation of the marketplace have brought many changes to the workplace, most of which result from automation and rapid implementation of information technology (GOHNET 2000; WHO 2000a). Workers throughout the world are today confronted with increased workloads and new organisational structures that require continuing personal and workplace adjustments. New hazards also plague the world of work, and the effects of these have yet to be discovered. In developing nations, the prevalence of physically demanding and hazardous work places half the workforce at risk for illness and injury on a regular basis (WHO 1999a). Workers in industrialised countries are experiencing high levels of work-related stress in epidemic proportions (WHO 2000a). It has been recognised for some years now that keeping the workforce healthy yields benefits for the individual, the industry, families and, in contributing to the creation of wealth, the national and international economies. Equally important is the capacity of healthy workplaces to make a significant contribution to the vitality of the community through the health and safety of workers and their families.

This chapter examines the workplace in the context of healthy settings. It provides an overview of the contemporary workplace as a setting for health promotion, and examines the linkages between healthy and sustainable workplaces in the wider context of healthy and sustainable communities.

objectives **By the end of this chapter you will be able to:**

1 Explain the ecological aspects of workplace health and safety

2 Discuss the links between work and health

3 Explain the impact of globalisation on workers and the workplace

4 Identify the differences in workplace risks for developing and industrialised nations

5 Describe the health potential of workplace health promotion programs

6 Explain the role of healthy public policies in maintaining healthy workplaces

7 Design a comprehensive workplace health promotion program to respond to the needs of employers, employees and the industry.

Workplace health and safety
in the twenty-first century

Work is a major contributor to the health of any population. It is the most important element in generating prosperity, which allows communities to develop the social conditions necessary for health and well-being. Work also has a direct effect on the individual and her or his family, in terms of providing resources for daily living, and the mental and social integrity that contribute to personal growth and a balanced life. Work as an element of society is self-fulfilling in that the economic outputs from work feed back into the potential to create more jobs, better working conditions and greater economic wealth (Marmot & Feeney 1996). The workplace also has the potential for sustainable development of communities, by producing new innovations in low-energy, low-emission, low-waste technologies that have wider applications beyond the workplace. Identification and classification systems for most materials commonly used in the workplace also provide an early warning system for harmful environmental hazards (Pearse 1997).

Because work also has the potential for negative effects on health and well-being, it is crucial to understand how the workplace can act either as an impediment to good health or as an essential mechanism for health maintenance and protection from injury, illness and disability. WHO has only recently begun to investigate the global burden of occupational illness, injury and disability, but extrapolations from Scandinavian and American data suggest that, worldwide, occupational factors are responsible for approximately 2.7 per cent of the burden of illness, injury and disability, which is nearly the same as the risk of tobacco smoking. Work-related injuries kill as many people as malaria (WHO 2001a). Throughout the past two decades, the transfer of technologies into workplaces that are not adequately prepared for them has magnified this burden considerably. Innovations that have led to more part-time workers, more self-employment and an increase in temporary, informal workers have left many employers unprepared or unwilling to assume responsibility for maintaining health and safety at work. This has left many workers either without access to occupational health services, or with inappropriate services that do not provide ongoing support for their illnesses or injuries (WHO 2001a). To date, less than half of all workers in industrialised countries and 5–10 per cent of workers in developing countries have adequate occupational health services (WHO 2001a). This is a deplorable situation, given the nature and volume of workplace risks.

Workplace
risks

Workplace injuries and accidents arise from a range of risk factors, depending on the type of work. For example, the main risks in industrial work are environmental. These include mechanical, physical and chemical factors well known to manufacturing but also prevalent in agricultural work. The organisation of work can also place workers at risk of ill health, particularly in causing stress. High workloads, low autonomy and control over work, shift-work, wage scales and routine repetitive work seem to cause a disproportionate amount of stress, which, in turn, can lead to cardiovascular disease, musculoskeletal problems and other stress-related illnesses (Harnois & Gabriel 2000; WHO 2001a). Over- or under-stimulation and conflict in the workplace can also be a source of stress (Marmot & Feeney 1996). These researchers found that workers whose jobs were classified as high on monotony and low on the possibility of learning new things were also at risk from the sequelae of stress. They conducted a series of studies to investigate the contribution of psychosocial work characteristics to the social gradient in health, and found that high work demands, which are often described as adverse work characteristics, may not be an equal source of stress for those at all levels of the workforce. They speculate that high demands are what make high-level jobs interesting and challenging, and that these can enhance self-esteem. On the other hand, high demands on low-grade, low-variety jobs where skills are under-used may contribute to stress-related illness. This discrepancy may be related to the degree of control as perceived by the employee, and how it is objectively assessed (Marmot & Feeney 1996).

Stress in the workplace has become a serious workplace hazard for 30–50 per cent of all workers in industrialised countries (WHO 2001a). In North America, Europe and the South Pacific, workplace stress has been found to be the greatest cause of stress in people's lives (Kortum-Margot 2001–2). The Association of Canadian Insurance Companies estimates that 30–50 per cent of disability allowances in the workplace are paid because of stress. Their data indicate that once an employee is absent for 'mental health' reasons for three months, it is highly likely that he or she will be absent for more than one year (Harnois & Gabriel 2000).

The amount of stress occurring among workers in the developing countries is also likely to have a major impact on their lives, but it is under-reported for a variety of reasons, some linked to job insecurity. In many of these countries, workplaces have become casualised to the extent of creating significant pressure on those fortunate enough to have employment. This situation is linked to globalisation, which affects workers in developing and industrialised countries differentially. It has led to considerable workplace changes throughout the world as a result of increasing competition, greater cross-national mobility and a new 'mix' of formal and informal work practices.

Globalisation
and work

Since the 1980s, global trade has tripled and trade in services has grown more than fourteen-fold, which has greatly accelerated the production of information, knowledge and technology (Loewenson 2001). Investment flows have been concentrated in about ten industrialised countries, while the developing nations have become increasingly marginalised. This has led to intense competition between smaller countries vying for a shrinking proportion of global investments and markets, which, in turn, has driven down their financial returns. In southern Africa, for example, globalisation has resulted in employment outcomes where the highest-paid 20 per cent of the population controls 10–20 times the income of the lowest-paid, for those who have jobs (Loewenson 2001).

Although globalisation has also enhanced equity in employment laws, there have been major changes to the workplace. Wider spheres of opportunity have increased the number of people in the workplace but most of these have been in industrialised countries, in white collar work environments. There has also been an increase in assembly-line, low-quality jobs, with minimal opportunities for advancement, and growth in insecure, casual employment across the informal sector (Loewenson 2001). This sector involves the manufacturing of 'low-end' products like footwear, garments and toys, and electronic assembly. The work is outsourced to less developed countries where labour is cheap and relatively unregulated (McMichael 2000). Some of these low-end jobs have brought many women into the workforce, to work as casual or home-based out-workers at the cost of increased exposure to occupational risk, decreased rest time, and increased stress. Home workers have also had to assume their own liability for working conditions (Loewenson 2001). Accident and illness insurance is a major problem for most people in developing countries, where less than 10 per cent of the workforce is covered, compared with the near-universal coverage for full-time employees in other parts of the world, especially the Nordic countries (Somavia 2000).

The liberal trade agreements that feature heavily in a globalised world have had some positive outcomes, particularly in eliminating obsolete and hazardous technologies, chemicals and processes (Loewenson 2001). They have also created more tourism markets, and jobs for those fortunate enough to live in attractive locations. But the movement of capital and technology has also outpaced systems for protecting workers' health and deregulated production laws (McMichael 2000). As a result, higher rates of injury and deaths are being seen in the primary and extractive activities of agriculture, logging, fishing and mining, which are some of the world's most hazardous industries (Somavia 2000). Injuries in these and the manufacturing sector occur as a result of mechanical, electrical and physical hazards. Expansion of chemical, electronic and biotechnology industries has introduced new risks, some of which have had a compound effect with the increase in environmental pollutants (Loewenson 2001; McMichael 2000).

The downward spiral of environmental degradation has increased health and developmental risks as well as creating food insecurity and susceptibility to infectious diseases (McMichael 2000). Some of the ill health outcomes include new asthmatic-type disorders, psychological stress, and the ergonomic and visual effects of using video display units (VDUs). Workers in the export processing zones have experienced high levels of machine-related accidents, dusts, noise, poor ventilation and exposure to toxic chemicals. Weak or absent monitoring and regulatory systems have led to the under-reporting of illnesses and injury, related to job insecurity and high labour turnover (Loewenson 2001). At the community level, the global marketplace has eliminated trading loyalties, consigning some exporting countries to continuing, intractable poverty, and in many developing countries it has led to the growth of slums and shanty towns on the fringes of urban areas (McMichael 2000).

Globalisation and the knowledge explosion have also had a profound impact on industrialised countries. The workforce has had to accommodate the need for different skills and schedules to keep up with rapid change. Ongoing education has become part of a typical work environment, in some cases increasing worker stress. Stress in the workplace has exacerbated the financial burden of the economies of many countries. In the United States, for example, health care expenditures are nearly 50 per cent greater for those workers reporting high stress at work than for others (Somavia 2000). Financial pressures are expected to continue as workplaces come to terms with population ageing. Anticipating the retirement of the baby boomers, workplaces will undoubtedly place pressure on the current workforce for higher productivity and greater contributions to pension funds (WHO 2001a). This may already be occurring, as many workers complain of a never-completed workload burden. They feel no sense of closure or satisfaction with a job well done, because the work is never finished.

Stress may be both a precipitating factor and an outcome of a number of other hazards and exposures in the workplace. Besides the physical strain of heavy work, between 10 and 30 per cent of the workforce in the industrialised countries and 80 per cent of those in developing countries are thought to be exposed to physical hazards such as noise, vibration, ionising and non-ionising radiation, heat and other microclimatic conditions (WHO 2000a). Many are also exposed to hundreds of biological agents including viruses, parasites, fungi and moulds. Thousands of toxic chemicals from solvents, pesticides and metal dusts also cause illnesses and injuries. Many of these are carcinogenic, resulting in occupationally induced cancer of the lung, bladder, skin and bone, leukaemia and sarcomas. Minerals and vegetable dusts continue to cause high rates of respiratory conditions and silicosis (CDC 2001; Statistics NZ 2002). Allergenic agents related to some of these substances are causing dramatic increases in allergic conditions, including asthma (WHO 2000a).

The combination of hazardous workplaces and stress has been deemed responsible for gastric problems, headaches, mood and sleep disturbances, depression and disrupted family relationships (Kortum-Margot 2001–2). Some workers have become more vulnerable to infectious diseases because of stress, or turned to tobacco, alcohol, illicit or prescription drugs. Where these have become habitual, further negative consequences have ensued, including decreased work performance, absenteeism and a propensity to suffer from work-related injuries (Kortum-Margot 2001–2). Stress theorists speculate on whether the stress is due to interactive elements of the person/environment interface or the cognitive and emotional factors that lead some to have a propensity to suffering from stress. From either perspective, the problems must be dealt with in the workplace, which is where most people spend the largest proportion of their time.

The organisational causes of work stress include the following:

- *Improper design of tasks*   This includes heavy workloads, infrequent rests, long working hours, shift work, and hectic and routine tasks that do not have meaning for the worker, do not utilise his or her skills and leave little sense of control.
- *Management style*   Management practices that are not transparent or do not include workers in decision-making lead to poor organisation of work. Top-down styles of management usually leave little room for family-friendly policies or practices, so they may compound a worker's problems.
- *Career-related anxieties*   These include job insecurity, lack of opportunities for advancement or promotion, little recognition for work, and rapid change in the workplace.
- *Strained interpersonal relations*   A poor social environment with few supports and little communication between supervisors and workers often leads to ongoing stress in work relationships.

- *Conflicting and uncertain work roles* This may include too much responsibility and too little role clarity.
- *Unpleasant or dangerous work environment* Overcrowding, excessive noise and air pollution, or ergonomically inferior workplaces, can contribute to stress and/or illness (Kortum-Margot 2001–2).

Vulnerable populations
and work

The burden of occupational illness and injury is greater for some populations than for others, especially migrants, women and children. The International Labour Organization (ILO) estimates that of the 250 million children between the ages of 5 and 14 working in developing countries like Asia, Africa and Latin America, nearly 70 per cent work under hazardous conditions (WHO 2000a). Often the only employed member of the family, these children are particularly open to exploitation, either by their own families or by the community. Migrants are another group easily exploited, especially seasonal workers in agricultural communities, who usually have sub-standard housing, limited sanitation, inadequate diet, exposure to pesticides and sun, and a lack of health care (Hahn 2002; UIHC 2000). Some live in unpredictable conditions with a fear of deportation, so they often live much of their lives in social isolation. Many are also illiterate and have little opportunity for self-improvement. Entire families are often affected by a plethora of hazardous conditions that are taken for granted by others (WHO 2000a).

Women workers also have special needs and vulnerabilities. Many women of fertile age are susceptible to specific adverse effects on reproductive health from toxic exposures. They may also incur musculoskeletal injuries from working at tasks with equipment designed for males rather than females. Their stressors also include job discrimination in the form of lower salaries and less decision-making, a double burden of work (home and workplace) and, in some cases, sexual harassment (WHO 2000a). For some women, 'everything they do is work' (Harlem Brundtland 2000, p 5). Large numbers of women throughout the world are now entering the workforce with less education and fewer skills than men, and many readily accept informal work in order to balance family and workplace roles. Illiteracy among women in the developing countries is high, and this multiplies the risk of exposure to substances with labels they cannot read (Harlem Brundtland 2000). Australian researchers have found that, although the overall attributable burden of illness and injury for male workers has been estimated at nearly three times higher than for females, the non-fatal burden of occupational disease is nearly as large for females as for males (Mathers, Vos & Stevenson 1999).

Countering risk:
occupational health for all

WHO, through its Global Strategy on Occupational Health for All, proposes ten objectives for workers' health:

1 Strengthen international and national policies for health at work, developing the necessary policy tools.
2 Develop healthy work environments.
3 Develop healthy work practices and promotion of health at work.
4 Strengthen occupational health services.
5 Establish support services for occupational health.
6 Develop occupational health standards based on scientific risk assessment.
7 Develop human resources for occupational health.
8 Establish registration and data systems that are disseminated to experts and the public.
9 Strengthen research.
10 Develop collaboration in occupational health and with other activities and services (WHO 1999b; GOHNET 2000, p 1).

At present WHO is working to develop three main areas that respond to these objectives. The first is the evidence base for policy, legislation and support to decision-makers, which involves occupational GBD studies. The second is directed towards protection and promotion of workers' health. The emphasis in the current global climate is on small industries and the informal sector, and problems associated with working children. The third area of focus is the infrastructure support and development for human resources and information dissemination and exchange through educational materials, technical cooperation and the creation of GOHNET (GOHNET 2000). This is expected to enhance societal occupational health literacy and promote cohesion between the workplace and the community (WHO 2001b).

Regional networks are also distributing a wide range of comprehensive information to the workplace and the general public. For example, the WHO Regional Office for Europe has released a ten-step guideline on worker and family physical fitness (WHO 2000b). Some offices have worked closely with the ILO to develop good or best practice guidelines—for example, on mental health in the workplace (Harnois & Gabriel 2000). Others have issued guidelines for the development of healthy workplaces (WHO 1999a). Most of these are based on the premise that a regulatory approach alone will not ensure healthy workplaces for productive and sustainable industries. The key lies in complementing regulatory and monitoring guidelines for the chemical, ergonomic and psychosocial factors involved in workplace illness and injury with the corresponding educational inputs (Loewenson 2001; WHO 2001b).

The evidence base is also expanding through both academic programs and collaborations between governments, universities, workers' organisations, employers and non-governmental organisations involved in workers' health (GOHNET 2000). The published literature on health promotion in the workplace indicates that it is a burgeoning field. Recent research investigating worksite health promotion programs on modifiable health risk factors provides evidence that the field is expanding, although there is a need for comprehensive research programs. Some studies continue to address behavioural factors, and these are necessary but not sufficient for improving the workplace. Poole, Kumpfer and Pett (2001) studied the impact of a healthy lifestyle incentive program for workers and their families, finding that smoking behaviour, physical activity, blood pressure and seat belt use improved significantly. However, companion studies are also needed to extend beyond the personally modifiable risk factors to those elements of the workplace that support behaviour change over time, or that focus on prevention of worker illness and injury.

A major literature review conducted on the effect of preventative initiatives in the workplace revealed that, to date, there remains little evidence linking worker health status to improved performance (Riedel et al 2001). Yet this type of investigation is essential in relation to corporate productivity, as it is the employers who are best empowered to make changes. In an age of shrinking resources, productivity arguments tend to hold more weight in the workplace than the quality of life of workers, so many researchers attempt to facilitate change through economic arguments. Riedel and colleagues (2001) examined literature from a wide variety of sources from 1993 to 1998 and drew the following conclusions:

- Evidence regarding the positive effect of early detection on health benefits is strong, especially for short-term health effects.
- Evidence demonstrating a positive effect of behaviour change programs on health benefits is strong.
- Early detection of illness can save and lengthen lives but there is as yet no evidence of cost savings or any negative cost effect.
- There is no evidence of the positive effect of early detection on performance except in the case of depression, which shows a short-term benefit.
- Behaviour change and care-seeking programs show positive cost effectiveness. General exercise and quit smoking programs show positive returns on investment and no negative cost effects.
- Medical cost-benefit is seen in exercise programs for back pain and stress management.
- Five interventions were found to provide short-term savings in medical costs: breast cancer screening, depression screening, adult vaccination for influenza, and care-seeking for minor illnesses and emergency department use. Most of these effected a short-term cost (Riedel et al 2001).

The findings of this study have a number of implications. Apart from short-term benefits, there is still a lack of information on how well workers progress over time when workplace programs have been introduced to improve their health. Many continue to focus on the worker rather than the workplace, and most have measured behaviour change programs in terms of absenteeism rates. The research team argues that the pathway to productivity lies in disease prevention, health promotion, acute and chronic illness management, environmental health and safety, and a healthy corporate culture (Riedel et al

2001). These interventions have the capacity to go beyond reducing absenteeism to improving performance, creativity and motivation, and reducing accidents and health care costs (Riedel et al 2001).

Healthy
workplaces

A healthy workplace is one that:

- creates a healthy, supportive and safe work environment
- ensures that health promotion and health protection are integral to management practices
- fosters work style and lifestyles conducive to health
- ensures total organisational participation
- extends positive effects to the local and surrounding community and environment (WHO 1999a).

These characteristics are achieved through workplace policies for health and safety, good organisational design and management, the physical environment, healthy lifestyles, adequate health services and evaluation of the impact on and of the external environment (WHO 1999a). Healthy workplaces thrive when there is a combination of initiatives aimed at personal development and participation, including family members where possible, and a commitment to sustaining the work environment (WHO 2001b). Benefits include improved worker health, increased job satisfaction, enhanced morale and productivity, cost savings through reduced absenteeism and turnover, a positive image for the company, and competitiveness in the marketplace (WHO 1999b).

A healthy workplace is planned on the basis of its participatory structures, which are empowering in that they include the ideas of workers at all levels of the organisation. It is also comprehensive in that the multiple determinants of workers' health are acknowledged as well as the importance of environmental sustainability. Its multisectoral approach succeeds in valuing the views of all stakeholders, from family members to external experts. In these ways it is congruent with the principles of primary health care (WHO 1999a). This approach has been adopted by the Corporate Health Model of the Canadian Workplace System, which was developed in different versions to be applicable to large organisations, small businesses and family farms (Health Canada 1996). The model is now widely used, primarily because evaluation has shown it to be consonant with the healthy-settings approach and an approach that places considerable emphasis on the workplace as well as the worker. The Canadian model provided the basis for a similar program in Northern Ireland. The Irish program was designed around several principles: ensuring commitment from both the individuals and the organisations; adaptability to businesses of all sizes; coordination of all elements to ensure a coherent approach; a culture of sharing information which includes a 'good neighbour' mentoring scheme for peer support; research, training and education for all interested parties; and comprehensive evaluation (Addley 1999). One of the elements shared by all these programs is commitment to developing a sound base of evidence for research and evaluation.

The evidence base for
workplace health and safety

WHO reports that GBD studies are just beginning to reveal the extent of workplace illness, injury and disability (WHO 2001a). Since 1996, when the World Health Assembly endorsed the global strategy on occupational health for all, the major focus of WHO activities has been on gathering the evidence for policy, legislation and support to decision-makers so that healthy workplaces and the development of infrastructure to support them can be appropriately informed (WHO 2001a). The Global Occupational Health Network was also established in 2000 to disseminate this information throughout the world (GOHNET 2000). The network provides a forum for people to share research findings that have implications for others working towards healthy workplaces, and to develop collaborative partnerships for research and development in the field.

Many areas require substantial research investigation, and some are being addressed in various countries. One of the factors impeding progress in identifying work-related diseases has been the lack of research on women workers. Gender-biased differentiation of work is a universal phenomenon. Women constitute about half the workforce but their numbers are not widely distributed across occupations and industries (Hatch 1996). With the exception of VDU use, most hazards common to female-dominated industries have been virtually ignored. The ethical implications of employing women for certain jobs without sufficient data on the health implications of the work is a major concern. Those currently involved in researching women at work suggest that we need careful documentation of all cases of chemical-related illnesses and gender-oriented exposure registries, especially with so many women now undertaking traditional male occupations (Hatch 1996).

The current emphasis on psychosocial factors in the workplace will also help progress the research agenda for women at work, especially in relation to family responsibilities. One study of female aerospace workers found that those with young children were at a 2–5 fold increased risk of on-the-job injury compared to women without children. The researchers were unable to conclude whether this reflected fatigue or the preoccupation arising from child care responsibilities (Hatch 1996). This type of study should be replicated in other types of industries to build the body of research into women's work in industrialised countries. The implications of parental leave also provides an interesting area for research. Analyses of parental leave patterns show that 120 ILO countries have paid parental leave, the most recent of which was granted to families in New Zealand. Of all the OECD countries, Australia and the United States remain the only ones with no national provision for maternal leave

(McCrossin 2002). The long-term impact of this type of policy is yet unknown, and may reveal important outcomes for children and other family members in relation to what is often promoted as family-friendly industrial policies.

Women in developing countries are being given support for researching the conditions and outcomes of their work through the United Nations. Grants have been provided to women in many countries, to explore the basis of markets for their goods, to improve post-harvest losses without degrading the environment, and to coordinate loan programs. Some of the assistance is targeted to specific industries, such as the banana industry in the Caribbean Islands, and home-based work in Southeast Asia. A grant to be shared across five nations will investigate how women entrepreneurs in Ecuador, the Philippines, Nepal, Albania and Romania can best utilise the internet and other communications tools for e-commerce, distance education and business information (UNIFEM 2002).

The ecological context of work is another area requiring a breadth of research. Environmental approaches to workplace research emphasise context and contingency, describing the connections between workers and their technologies (McEvoy 1996). This type of approach re-frames industrial development in terms of social organisation, allowing us to look at how ecology, political economy and social consciousness interact with each other over time. It is one area where the global network of communications will be helpful to future development. Mittlemark (2001) urges all countries in this globalised world to consider the implications of workplace or industry-based policies on the rest of the world. He cites a case in the 1970s in Iraq where more than 6000 people were hospitalised and 400 died from eating bread made from wheat flour with a high mercury content. United States officials immediately set a recommended maximum daily dose of mercury of only one-fifth that of the limit recommended by WHO. This had a profound impact on those who gain a living from subsistence fishing in remote places like Alaska because the limits of mercury in the fish were set so low that they prevented the continuing viability of the fishing industry. Mittlemark's (2001) conclusion is that restrictive advisories that flow from the workplace have the potential to damage the social, economic and personal well-being of entire villages. This illustrates the interconnectedness of healthy workplaces and healthy communities, and underlines the need to think global but to act on local knowledge as well.

Ergonomic problems in the workplace are also part of the ecological aspects of work. Ergonomics is the study of human abilities and limitations, and the application of this information to the design of the fabricated environment. An ergonomically appropriate workplace is one where workplaces, tools and tasks have been designed to match the physiological, anatomical and psychological characteristics and capabilities of the worker (Stobbe 1996). Many workplace illnesses and injuries are related to ergonomic problems, including cumulative trauma disorders (CTD) related to inadequate ergonomic design, and other musculoskeletal strains that occur in occupations where there is a large amount of manual handling required, and repetitive strain injuries, which affect many women clerical workers (Hatch 1996; Stobbe 1996). Manual handling guidelines cover such things as the weight and frequency of load (in lifting) and posture, lighting and pace of repetitive tasks involved in clerical work (Hatch 1996).

One of the reasons for the persistence of ergonomic injury is that, historically, the approach has been to design a workplace and then try to fit the workers into it through training, worker selection and other administrative schemes. With the rapid rise in CTD disorders, ergonomists are now trying to involve workers at all stages of the design process, including the design of tools, equipment, lighting and ventilation (Stobbe 1996). This represents a more inclusive approach to workplace health and safety that is consultative and based on the experience and empowerment of all involved in the process of work.

Responses to work demands are the product of personal attitudes and values, but also represent work-site norms. For example, some employees have a fatalistic approach to work because of their perception of powerlessness. Workers who feel there is no real protection against risk because employers' priorities rest with productivity rather than safety are often deterred from taking individual precautions even when they are urged to do so by employers (Holmes & Gifford 1997). Certain types of work may also be experienced differentially. As mentioned previously, monotonous work may evoke agitation in some, calm in others. Working conditions that are time sensitive or conflict with personal values may be a source of stress. Ethical dilemmas may also intrude on the workplace—for example, for those selling or promoting a product or service that might be injurious to others.

Identifying and communicating
workplace risk

Although some workplace hazards fit into one or another risk category, workplace injury is best understood as the culmination of industrial, organisation, technical and human error processes (Frye 1997). Many occupational factors are part of an interactive effect between individuals and the tools of their trade. For example, smoking and exposure to workplace chemicals is a lethal carcinogenic combination of risk factors. In such a workplace, smoking may be related to ignorance, personal choice, job insecurity or stress. Inadequate or ambiguous information can be hazardous not only to the worker, but to others in the work environment who have difficulty recognising either the type or level of risk. This again is a special problem for illiterate workers.

Epidemiological data provide information on causal agents and contextual factors in occupational illness and injuries as well as *dose-response data*, or safe limits of substances used in industrial processes. As with other epidemiological research, the web of causation for occupational illnesses and injuries should separate out the modifiable and non-modifiable risk factors.

Despite the contribution to knowledge of workplace health and safety made by occupational epidemiologists, there is a need to broaden the research agenda. Some researchers claim that the type of studies being conducted in the work environment, which are primarily medical and technical, has retarded meaningful workforce reforms. Occupational health activists understand that education goes beyond information to understanding of workers' traditions and goals. Research must therefore examine the actual situations of work, including how workers experience the environment—dizziness, nausea, irritability, menstrual problems—rather than how the statute and regulations define working conditions (Sass 1996). This points to an increasingly global research agenda that would capture the realities of workplace health and safety issues in contemporary society for both developing and industrialised countries.

In addition, there needs to be wider dissemination of research information on workplace health and safety, and this is gradually improving. With research journals, internet access to workplace information and global information networks such as GOHNET, surveillance, diagnostic and evaluative information is more readily accessible than at any other time in history.

In this era of cost containment it is important to gain value for investment and this can best be accomplished by capitalising on the health potential of work. As a first step, we need to ensure accurate and inclusive information gathering and dissemination. The next step is to follow the lead of WHO in investigating good and best practice models of creating healthy workplaces. Finally, workplace health and safety must continue to be at the centre of political activities aimed at sustaining community development. An ecological view of health dictates that the health of the working population be seen as part of the harmonious interaction with the political, economical and social elements necessary for society to thrive throughout this century and beyond.

---

case study...

Good management, good health

In 1991, multinational consulting firm Deloitte & Touche found that women were leaving the firm at a significantly greater rate than men. The firm's senior partners believed this was simply a female choice to stay home and have children, rather than an exodus away from their organisation.

As the outflow continued, the company decided to investigate whether their assumptions were, in fact, correct. This sparked a revolution within the company that has seen a dramatic increase in the number of women managing partners and changed the workplace mix to where women now stay on at about the same rate as men each year. The firm's annual staff turnover also declined from 25 per cent in 1992 to 18 per cent in 1999, as a result of what turned out to be widespread cultural change.

The Deloitte Initiative for the Retention and Advancement of Women grew out of a task force chaired by the then CEO (1992). Thinking this was an 'affirmative action' movement, most senior women argued against it, but once the CEO had become convinced it was an urgent problem for the company, they were encouraged to participate. The task force approached the problem methodically, as if it was one of their consultancies, investigating the dimensions of the problem to prepare a business case. They held a series of intensive two-day workshops designed to bring to the surface the gender-based assumptions about careers and aspirations that had discouraged their senior women from staying on. The next step was the development of a policy agenda that would direct the heads of all offices to monitor the progress of their female professionals. The women began to get their share of the best client assignments and informal mentoring. This was supported by further policies designed to promote more balance between work and life—for both women and men.

The revolution has been successful, and along the way, the firm has learned some invaluable lessons with applicability to other workplaces:

1 Senior management must be front and centre. The Women's Initiative was not driven by the women or Human Resources. Instead it was instigated by top management and continues to be led by the managing partners with close oversight by the CEO.

2 An airtight business case should be made for cultural change. The task force laid a foundation of data which included facts and figures, but also highlighted personal stories. Deloitte had attracted some high-performing women, some of whom were earning higher performance bonuses than men, yet they still left, some of them at a time when they were about to receive promotions. Their stories indicated that this had nothing to do with family issues, and everything to do with the male-dominated culture. For the firm, their resignations represented a major lost opportunity.

3 Publicise the change. Instead of keeping the problem inside the company, Deloitte held a press conference to launch the program. They also appointed an external advisory council, whose members comprised business leaders with expertise in matters concerning women in the workplace. This kept the initiative visible and exerted extra pressure on all the partners to commit to change and deliver results. The council not only informed company members about gender issues, it discovered broader issues. In providing a forum for people to express themselves, they learned that young men weren't trying to achieve what the older men were, they simply wanted a balanced lifestyle. This

came as a surprise to the company, which had operated on the assumption that their young male employees were happy to work long hours for higher salaries.

4 Dialogue is the platform for change. The company discovered that women perceived they had fewer career opportunities than men, but the workshops revealed that many members of the firm were making inaccurate judgements about one another. During the dialogue some of the sexist behaviours surfaced, much to the surprise of the men. The example is given of a comment made by a manager about a female and then a male employee: 'She's not as polished as some. Her presentation skills could be stronger', and 'He's good. He and I are going golfing next week'. The group began to explore subtle variations in language and found that these sometimes sent men and women down quite different career paths. All members of the group agreed that women were unconsciously being evaluated on their performance, men on their potential. Other issues came out in the dialogues, including stereotypical comments that had been made about an Asian worker who was considered 'shy'. This was dispelled when it was revealed that in his culture, success was not measured in being able to 'command a room' or raise one's voice, but in a different management style.

5 The next stage involved putting new attitudes to work, by altering assignments for women, hosting regular networking events for women, then recruiting for the new culture. The company began to promote work–life balance for both women and men, with positive results. Their workplaces are now more family-friendly. Meetings are often scheduled around fathers wanting to get home before their children's bedtime, and both male and female employees opt for flexible starting times, so they can pursue other interests, such as going to the gym (McCracken 2000).

The case study indicates that the types of interactions that occur in the boardrooms and managers' officers are not unlike those that occur on the shop floor. In the final analysis, it is people who create the environments for work, who attend to the importance of the workplace as a place for health and well-being and who consequently rearrange the environment so that the workplace and its cultural, social and physical surroundings are healthy. This is the beginning of what Marmot and Feeney (1996, p 250) call the 'virtuous cycle'. Better working conditions lead to better health (in this case, better emotional health), which leads to better productivity. It is one of the most important goals of the healthy workplace and the people whose lives are enriched there.

thinking critically

Healthy workplaces

1 Give three reasons why occupational health and safety is important to community development.

2 Identify the ecological connections between healthy workplaces and healthy communities.

3 Identify four main features of a healthy workplace.

4 Analyse the impact of globalisation on the workplaces of the future.

5 In an occupational health setting of your choice, discuss the interaction between organisational features, physical and demographic characteristics of the workers, and health and safety hazards in the workplace.

6 Devise a comprehensive workplace health and safety program for a widget manufacturing company of 500 employees.

REFERENCES

Addley, K. (1999). Developing programmes to achieve a healthy society: Creating healthy workplaces in Northern Ireland. *Occupational Medicine*, 49(5): 325–30.

Centers for Disease Control (CDC) (2001). Health, United States, 2001. Washington: CDC.

Frye, L. (1997). Occupational health surveillance. *American Association of Occupational Health Nurses Journal*, 45(4): 184–7.

GOHNET (2000). Editorial. *The Global Occupational Health Network Newsletter*, 1: 1.

Hahn, K. (2002). Migrant families: health-related issues and challenges of women and children in a migratory work force. *Medical College of Georgia*, 1–11.

Harlem Brundtland, G. (2000). Women's work. *GOHNET*, 1: 5–6.

Harnois, G. & Gabriel, P. (2000). Mental health and work: impact, issues and good practices. Geneva: WHO, ILO.

Hatch, M. (1996). Women's work and women's health. *Epidemiology Prevention*, 20: 176–9.

Health Canada (1996). Workplace Health System—Corporate Health Model. Ottawa: Health Promotion Directorate, Health Canada.

Holmes, N. & Gifford, S. (1997). Narratives of risk in occupational health and safety: why the 'good' boss blames his tradesman and the 'good' tradesman blames his tools. *Australian and New Zealand Journal of Public Health*, 21(1): 11–16.

Kortum-Margot, E. (2001–2). Psychosocial factors in the workplace. *GOHNET*, Winter, 2: 7–10.

Loewenson, R. (2001). Globalization and occupational health: a perspective from southern Africa. *Bulletin of the World Health Organization*, 79(9): 863–8.

Marmot, M. & Feeney, A. (1996). Work and health: implications for individuals and society. In: D. Blane, E. Brunner & R. Wilkinson (eds), *Health and Social Organization: Towards a Health Policy for the 21st Century*. London: Routledge, pp 235–54.

Mathers, C., Vos, T. & Stevenson, C. (1999). The Burden of Disease and Injury in Australia. Canberra: AIHW.

McCracken, D. (2000). Winning the talent war for women. *Harvard Business Review*, Nov–Dec: 159–67.

McCrossin, J. (2002). Paid maternity leave: the New Zealand experience. *Life Matters*, 9 November 2001, http://www.abc.net.au.rn/talks/lm/stories/s411926.htm.

McEvoy, A. (1997). Working environments: An ecological approach to industrial health and safety. *Clio Medica*, 41: 59–89.

McMichael, A. (2000). The urban environment and health in a world of increasing globalization: issues for developing countries. *Bulletin of the World Health Organization*, 78(9): 1117–40.

Mittlemark, M. (2001). Promoting social responsibility for health: health impact assessment and healthy public policy at the community level. *Health Promotion International*, 16(30): 269–74.

Pearse, W. (1997). Occupational health and safety: a model for public health: *Australian and New Zealand Journal of Public Health*, 21(1): 9–10.

Poole, K., Kumpfer, K. & Pett, M. (2001). The impact of an incentive-based worksite health promotion program on modifiable health risk factors. *American Journal of Health Promotion*, 16(1): 21–6.

Riedel, J., Lynch, W., Baase, C., Hymel, P. & Peterson, K. (2001). The effect of disease prevention and health promotion on workplace productivity: a literature review. *American Journal of Health Promotion*, 15(3): 167–91.

Sass, R. (1996). A strategic response to the occupational health establishment. *International Journal of Health Services*, 26(2): 355–70.

Somavia, J. (2000). Decent work, safe work. *GOHNET*, 1: 4–5.

Statistics New Zealand (2002). Occupational disease notifications, http://www.osh.dol.govt.nz.

Stobbe, T. (1996). Occupational ergonomics and injury prevention. *Occupational Medicine*, 11(3): 531–43.

UNIFEM (2002). Project Highlights. New York: UN.

University of Iowa Health Care (UIHC) (2000). Program aids migrant and seasonal farm workers with health, education needs, http://www.uihealthcare.com/new3s/news/2000/07/07300migrant.html.

World Health Organization (WHO) (1999a). Regional Guidelines for the Development of Healthy Workplaces. WHO: Manila.

—— (1999b). Fourth Network Meeting of the WHO Collaborating Centres in Occupational Health. Geneva: WHO.

—— (2000a). Occupational Health. Ethically Correct, Economically Sound. Geneva: WHO, http://www.who.int./inf-fs/en/fact084.html.

—— (2000b). Guidelines on improving the physical fitness of employees. Copenhagen: WHO Regional Office for Europe.

—— (2001a). Healthy settings and environment: healthy workplaces. Geneva: WHO.

—— (2001b). The role of the occupational health nurse in workplace health management. Copenhagen: WHO Regional Office for Europe.

CHAPTER 14

Researching
community health

troduction In this era of rapidly changing health care trends, the need for ongoing, systematic research in community health has never been greater. Worldwide, there is an urgent need for close examination of the processes and outcomes involved in building community capacity. To inform the management of health and health promotion strategies, research studies should be undertaken to evaluate the effectiveness of multidisciplinary teamwork and the impact of health sector reforms on communities involved. We also need to study the efficacy of community-based services in relation to demographic and epidemiological data on population health. Most importantly, there is a need to explicate a range of mechanisms for community participation and the extent to which partnerships between various groups of people are effective in improving the health of both the local and global communities.

Research studies are designed by researchers from diverse fields, using a variety of approaches, to address a plethora of health-related questions. Despite the differences in various discipline-based research methods, their common goal is to improve the health of the population, by providing either small incremental contributions to knowledge, or studies of such magnitude as to change the direction of health care. It is imperative that the growing body of evidence for decision-making, quality care, efficiency and effectiveness of the health care system, preservation of the environment, and community participation be given a high profile in our quest for the creation and sustainability of health. This chapter provides an overview of issues related to community health research, and suggests a number of research challenges and strategies that could be used to effect improvements in community health.

objectives   **By the end of this chapter you will be able to:**

1   Identify three major issues that are critical to advancing the evidence base for community health

2   Explain the importance of comprehensive risk factor studies

3   Explain the relative advantage of mixed-method research studies for researching community health

4   Outline the most important ethical issues emerging from new developments in health and medical research

5   Develop a research question grounded in the conceptual foundations of primary health care to respond to a community health issue.

Community health
research issues

As this new century began, health researchers were embracing one of the most powerful moments in research history. The mapping of the human genome was just about completed. A sheep had been cloned. New discoveries in stem cell research were widening the debate into an exploration of possibilities rather than the realities of the present. The global burden of disease had been calculated, and individual countries were beginning to map their own burden of disease in relation to their respective populations and health capacities. The emphasis in health promotion research had shifted from single-factor isolated studies to the comprehensive interactions of many factors. Interdisciplinary investigations that included a variety of research approaches had begun to infuse the research agenda with numerous pieces of information on social relations and their influence on health. Community health researchers began to shift ground from the historical 'methodological imperialism' that had characterised the previous century, to a more eclectic approach that would add realism and utility to the implications of their findings. And among all findings, the unknowns were the most intriguing.

A few years later, we remain on this dynamic threshold, considering a new set of possibilities in the conception of each new study. Our research vision stretches wider than ever before, as we contemplate the dimensions of social relations that shape our socioecological experience of health. Health planning 'targets' that were formerly defined in terms of numerical values now form only part of a wider program of research. The evidence-based practice (EBP) movement has expanded to all health professions, urging practitioners to base their activities on empirical data. Throughout the past decade, there have been new understandings of EBP, beyond previous notions that depicted true 'evidence' as being derived from randomised clinical trials. Today, we embrace a range of methods for collecting evidence for practice, some of which are only recently gaining acceptability across all health professions.

What to
research?

Many researchers have now stopped to wonder about the questions previously asked of health practices, and added more. We know the factors related to poor birth outcomes, for example. Now we question *why* and *how* these affect infant mortality (Berger 2001). We know the magnitude of the global burden of injuries and now ask what use can be made of this information in terms of reshaping the environments within which injuries occur (Krug, Sharma & Lozano 2000). Knowing the relative weight of socioeconomic factors in determining health leads us to question the ways to go about creating equitable conditions from a body of evidence that will be seen to be valid, intellectually sound and scientifically grounded (Pincus et al 1998). Many questions remain. In some cases, we have identified the research questions without explaining how or why they are posed, or we have ignored elements of the research on the presumption that a more inclusive approach would not fall within the scope of competitive funding opportunities (Dunn & Hayes 1999). Research studies are costly, and there are many clinicians and health scholars competing for a limited pool of financial support.

The competitive ethos that surrounds research funding and the separation between researchers and health practitioners shows some interesting differences between the developing and industrialised countries. Evaluation studies are more common in the developing world. This is due to the need for useful, local information to guide change, and the global movement to support community development (McQueen 2001). Research in many developing countries is often designed to capture the realities of what is occurring in short, sharp evaluative studies that will inform immediate strategies for change. These programs of research are often the product of wide-ranging collaborations designed to bring the best information possible to bear on resolution of a problem, and they are responsive to high-level planning authorities. For example, Africa's heads of state have recently collaborated in an economic assessment of the impact of malaria throughout the continent, undertaking a series of interventions shown to be effective elsewhere (Harlem Brundtland 2001). Similarly, international health issues and HIV/AIDS research have become part of the agenda of the United Nations. And mobilising resources for health promotion forms an integral part of the discussions on debt relief for poor countries by the finance ministers of the Group of Eight countries (G8) (Harlem Brundtland 2001).

Undoubtedly the time is right to expand and share the base of knowledge that will move all of us closer to the goal of health for all. The global health promotion agenda is desperately in need of answers to the following:

- What are the effects of globalisation on health?
- What are the implications of the spread of infectious diseases and bio-terrorism throughout the world?
- How can health systems support the needs of political or ecological refugees?
- How does a capitalistic society use wealth in a way that will maintain equity and access in health care?
- Are there ways to overcome barriers to gender equality in promoting health?
- What support mechanisms will create the best opportunities for self-determinism among Indigenous people?
- How do religion and spirituality affect health, and for whom?
- What policies and practices will create the best opportunities for enriched parenting?
- To what extent can adolescents be supported through the crucial time of emerging identities?
- How can housing policies create sustainable neighbourhoods?
- Are there defensible health benefits for rural communities in emerging technologies, particularly telecommunications?
- What healthy policy developments must be made to fund the relative burden of population ageing?

How to
research?

Each of these research questions could be used to guide an entire program of research. However, most researchers know that the most important element in any investigation is the need to pose a manageable question, one that can be addressed in the time frame allowed using a defined pool of resources. It is also important to design research studies within a conceptual framework such as primary health care, and to use the method that best fits the research question.

The greatest challenge for health researchers in the twenty-first century lies in the shift from focusing on formulaic ways of investigating community problems and issues, to a new paradigm that will encourage researchers to articulate a range of problems and solutions. The main objective of community health research must be to help build a high-quality, widely recognised and acceptable evidence base for promoting health (McQueen 2001). This body of evidence must be flexible and inclusive, rather than as exclusively rigid as the classical designs of scientific medical research, which adhered to experimental and quasi-experimental designs. The evidence for community health promotion research flows from analytical frameworks that acknowledge the complexities in working with communities to promote cultural sensitivity, advocacy, partnerships and coalitions for change (Goodman 2000; McQueen 2001). This 'change-promoting' research is applied research, or the type of research commonly known as research and development (R&D). It is pragmatic and guided by the goal of practical application to the wider world (St Leger & Walsworth-Bell 1999).

One area where applied research is desperately needed is in extending the Global Burden of Disease (GBD) studies to community health improvements. On a global scale, life expectancy has never been higher, but we have some major risk factors that impinge on the quality of our lives. These include malnutrition, poor water supply, sanitation, personal and domestic hygiene, unsafe sexual behaviour, tobacco use, workplace hazards, hypertension, physical inactivity, illicit drug use and air pollution (Michaud, Murray & Bloom 2001). Understanding these areas of risk and considering a range of strategies for improvement will be better informed by knowing how the information has been used in other populations. This directs us towards disseminating knowledge to share it with others for the common good of society. For research findings to make a difference, local studies must look further than identifying the burden of disease and disability, to explaining the social conditions that produce inequitable access to resources, and other factors that discourage people from maintaining health where resources are plentiful.

A major gap in knowledge lies in exploring the needs of Indigenous people. The needs of many groups of Indigenous people are not clearly articulated in research agendas that focus on measuring aspects of their quality of life from a monolithic perspective. This attitude assumes that all Indigenous people are somehow alike, so their health needs must be similar. Like non-Indigenous people, each group and each family of Indigenous people is different, with unique issues influencing their health. Until there is a base of research that highlights this uniqueness, 'broad brush' approaches to policy development will not be well informed. For example, in some Indigenous communities government policy relies too heavily on a 'top-down' allocation of funding for health improvements. Money is provided to assist the community to become self-determined. Clearly, in countries like Australia, this is not working. Many Indigenous communities have become neither self-determined nor healthy. Research studies developed in collaboration with community members can help unravel the set of factors that would help or hinder self-determinism. Such local knowledge could be used as a basis for negotiating new or improved health policies that would be culturally appropriate, feasible and manageable for that particular community.

Another area where the design of research studies is important is in examining health policies that have been less than successful. In 2000 WHO established a set of global indicators for judging the world's health systems. The criteria used in this exercise included good health for all, responsiveness to the expectations of the population, and fairness of financial contribution. Some countries like the United States were found to be less than adequate in relation to the global benchmark—that is, in terms of reducing the burden of disease and disability for certain population groups (Michaud et al 2001). Directing research to uncovering reasons for these disparities and then acting upon the findings by initiating new policies would represent a positive response to the WHO initiative. Although conditions differ from country to country, having a point of reference can provide the impetus for research aimed at improving the overall health of the population. Publishing these data improves accessibility to findings by the international research community, primarily through the internet. Dissemination of this information has also precipitated unprecedented growth in international collaborations and created greater sharing of methods and analytic approaches. And analytic approaches have, in turn, become more highly refined, particularly with the Human Genome Project, which has made a remarkable and widely applicable contribution to research methodologies.

Researching
the community:
methodological considerations

Any program of research must begin with a shared dialogue. One distinction that must be made is to understand the difference between research, a research framework, and the application of knowledge to public policy (Dunn & Hayes 1999). These authors define research as the collection of empirical observations. For community health, the focus is on populations and the questions are framed by an interest in the social production of health and the structure of social relations in a specific setting at a specific time (Dunn & Hayes 1999). Situating this knowledge within a conceptual framework helps translate what is observed into a coherent plan for analysis. Within the framework, empirical observations and the processes that mediate them (popular beliefs, cultural expectations, ideological positions, power and authority) can be conveyed to policy makers in a way that makes visible the relevance of findings for community health (Dunn & Hayes 1999).

Designing research studies to be 'policy ready' resonates with the approaches being used to unravel the relative effect of proximal and distal risk factors on avoidable illness and disability (Green 1999; Michaud et al 2001). In the past, researchers tended to gravitate to the more easily measured factors involved in community health, such as tobacco smoking and poverty, but to make a difference, this research must also address the concealed elements in health (Cole et al 1999). It is very difficult to measure community change, for example, and almost impossible to predict the extent to which change is sustainable (Shediac-Rizkallah & Bone 1998). However, much progress has been made in the past twenty years in refining the various interpretive methodologies that complement quantitative measures. Whereas in past times, research in health was only considered valid if it was aimed at testing hypotheses, today many research studies are conducted using qualitative, interpretive research approaches, or mixed methods that combine both qualitative and quantitative data. This is a positive trend for community health research that is typically aimed at measuring inputs or outputs of a program in the context of interpreting the social attributes and meanings held by the members of a group or a community. It also allows evaluation against locally defined goals and those emerging from the broader context of community health (Nutbeam 1998; St Leger & Walsworth-Bell 1999).

When the level of analysis is the community, rather than individuals or a particular risk factor, claims for validity of the findings can only be made under carefully constructed conditions. At each stage, the researcher must be engaged as a participant with the community to explore the research design and findings from a realistic perspective. Community realities are easier to interpret when researchers use triangulation to substantiate their findings. Triangulation is a strategy taken from the field of surveying, where the objective is to take a reading of a location or an object from different aspects or perspectives. Triangulation is used the same way in research. In some cases, triangulation involves the strategic application of different approaches to investigate the same question (Goodman 2000; Goodman et al 1996). Another form of triangulation employs multiple forms of data analysis, which can enrich both construct and internal validity (Goodman 2000). Using a variety of approaches helps the researcher focus on 'how' and 'why' questions rather than to simply identify how the program works. It also allows the researcher to evaluate many levels of outcomes and to pose new questions for evaluation as the study progresses. For example, as a program is being devised, evaluation might emphasise inter-organisational arrangements. The next phase would shift to evaluating implementation of the program and the skills required to deliver various components. The evaluation would then move to a maintenance stage where the focus is on client outcomes (Goodman 2000). Each stage must be carefully devised to employ the appropriate 'mix' of research strategies, depending on what information is being sought.

Mixed-method approaches often address a series of questions, particularly where an evaluation is attempting to record outcomes of certain interventions in the community context. In an ecologically focused study, for example, the researcher would want to measure community change and elements of the environment that either support or constrain the desired change. Methodological triangulation would guide the research team to include some quantitative measurements. For example, the study may ask: Whose behaviour changed? To what extent? With what outcomes? These questions could be answered using a quantitative survey, with responses analysed to judge whether and to what extent any responses were significant, or to provide a basis for predicting future behaviour (predictive validity). Following this phase, or even simultaneously, a more qualitative element would be designed to address the following questions: What factors support the change? Are there cultural barriers to change? What other influences affect the change? How does the physical or social ecology of a community support or constrain the outcomes? Are there financial, policy or geographic barriers to gaining support for the changes?

The latter group of questions require an interpretive approach, and the methods used to gather data would typically include a combination of observations, interviews, document analysis, knowledge of policy and/or social trends. The researcher must secure information that is comprehensive and encompasses the reasons for change or perceptions about the change. There must also be some detailed analysis of the social ecology or contextual factors involved in the change. To accomplish this, the researcher would likely plan a number of in-depth interviews and attempt to extrapolate themes from people's responses that shed insight into the community and its particular areas of need or strength. These data would be analysed in a systematic way to produce *informational* rather than *statistical* significance.

Design
features

Just as interpretive studies require a design that is flexible enough to allow changes as the study progresses, analysis of survey data or quantitative measures may suggest the need for interviews, to guide either conclusions or further data collection. In many cases, there is considerable overlap between methods and this is not a problem if the focus of the research remains on the research question. This type of research has little appeal to purists, who prefer to situate their investigations clearly within one or another paradigm, wherein the data would be exclusively quantitative or qualitative. However, combining techniques and approaches is usually the best way to inform program and policy planning for community health.

Many areas in community health are inadequately researched, for a number of reasons. In most cases, the length of time required to investigate a web of factors or situations is prohibitive. Or the research may be hampered by a lack of funding due to the rigidity of many granting agencies to support broadly based studies. Dilution of interventions in large sites sometimes leads to a lack of clarity in the findings, and this can be complicated by time trend effects. This occurs when the circumstances of the community change over time. A further difficulty arises from the fact that there are few models for participative forms of research and evaluation at the community level (Billings 2000; Gruenewald 1997; Nutbeam 1998). To be true to a partnership model, members of the community should be encouraged to participate at all stages of the research, from designing the study, to analysing the implications of the findings.

Another difficulty in community health research is that there are few norms of expectations or indicators of cultural acceptability. These must flow from local knowledge. Despite these difficulties, there remains a need to identify issues requiring prevention or intervention, and to define a range of community capabilities that would guide feasible health service responses (Omenn 2000). In many community health settings, these issues create obstacles for researchers attempting to inform prevention strategies, particularly when these must be tailored to the needs of the community. Interestingly, this is also the case in the evolving area of genetics research, where research evidence must not only identify genetic predispositions, but guide parents and advocate for children in a way that is sensitive to both community and family concerns (Murphy & Risser 1999). The research agenda for genetic counselling must therefore expect that information may be used as a basis for 'informed refusal' as well as 'informed consent' (Omenn 2000).

Evaluating
process

Despite the obstacles mentioned above, it is crucial to continue to develop the base of evidence for community health promotion, and this requires a repertoire of methods (Patton 2002). Some researchers find primary health care constructs particularly difficult to measure, and choose instead a series of community snapshots which provide local policy planners with local, contextualised information on which to base decisions. Others persevere with studies that are applicable across various communities. Studies of empowerment, for example, are applicable to many different communities. Empowerment is one of the cornerstones of community development and has attracted considerable research attention. Israel and colleagues' (1998) attempt to measure community empowerment was conducted on the premise that it is important to develop measurement tools for concepts like empowerment, which is commonly used in primary health care but not well articulated in the literature. This research group reviewed survey instruments that had previously attempted to measure aspects of an empowering organisation such as participative decision-making, organisational culture and management style. Rather than use these, or simply engage in an open-ended interview format to see whether and why people felt empowered, they designed a new instrument. Their research equated perceived control with empowerment, so they designed the instrument to measure people's perceptions of control at the individual, organisational and community level. The study provided an analytic framework and a research tool that can now be used to measure empowerment over time, or with different populations. Their work provides an important increment in the body of work that has tried to clarify the notion of empowerment and its related concepts.

Laverack and Wallerstein (2001) also investigated empowerment but their perspective is that, although empowerment can be measured as a program outcome, this may limit understanding of how it is actually created in a community. By shifting the focus to measuring the *processes* of community empowerment, researchers can monitor the interaction between capacities, skills and resources at the individual and organisational levels as well as the way changes are supported by healthy conditions, policies and interpersonal structures. In this respect, their work on empowerment demonstrates not only personal capacity building, but the processes of participation. This is somewhat like the goals of participatory action research.

Participatory action research (PAR) is a way of analysing the elements of an activity or program at the same time as it is being developed. As a research method, it provides a context for constructing theoretical foundations for future research, but it is best known for the way the research is grounded in the practicality of problem solving. The techniques of PAR flow from action research, which was originally developed to guide social changes after the Second World War (Titchen & Binnie 1994). Kurt Lewin described action research in terms of a spiral of four stages: planning, acting, observing and reflecting. The PAR method emphasises participation and ongoing evaluation of that participation as well as the way it influences change. On this basis, it has become widely accepted as a model for collaborative partnerships for change (Cruikshank 1996; Titchen & Binnie 1994).

A fundamental element of the PAR approach is building a trusting relationship between the researcher(s) and the community or group (Greenwood 1994). Reflection by the group leads to mutual solutions which are emancipatory because they emerge from the 'bottom up' in the process of investigating and evaluating the problem or situation (Hart 1996). The women's movement of the 1960s and 1970s advocated PAR as a way of involving people in developing their own capacity to become empowered for current and future change and it has continued to be used in feminist research. Techniques have been refined on the basis of several decades of research and today, the PAR approach remains viable as a way of evaluating many aspects of health and health care that form a basis for planning pathways to change (Moody, Choong & Greenwood 2001).

Other methods for evaluation research have attracted considerable interest among community health researchers. However, given the contextualised nature of most evaluation projects, no one method is considered the 'gold standard'. Goodman (2000) describes a 'logic model' wherein a succinct, logical series of statements links the problems to be evaluated with expected outcomes. These statements encompass program assumptions such as the following: training will lead to more skilled staff; information will reach target audiences; when informed, target audiences will attend programs. Goodman (2000) contends that, in order to enhance cultural sensitivity and reduce cultural bias, evaluation of community developments must be contoured to the information needs of each particular community. This approach should span the entire process, from adapting, translating and administering the evaluation measures to analysing the data and interpreting the results (Goodman 2000).

Some researchers recommend a hierarchy of evaluation stages. Nutbeam's (1998) model prescribes a series of six stages. These extend from problem definition, to solution generation, a testing stage for innovations, demonstrating interventions, disseminating the findings and, finally, managing the program. He acknowledges that simplistic, 'reductionist' approaches to health promotion and evaluation have long been discredited, but points to the need to clarify outcomes and their influencing factors. From his perspective, evaluation should be based on measuring change across three types of health promotion outcomes: achievement of personal health literacy, changes in public policy and organisational practices, and changes to the social norms and actions of community members that increase individual control over the determinants of health (Nutbeam 1998). This type of research is well suited to evaluating socially embedded projects such as Healthy Cities, Healthy Schools and Healthy Workplaces but it is a long-term and costly research investment and therefore requires substantial commitment from the communities involved, as well as the research team (Nutbeam 1998).

Most evaluation researchers emphasise the need for sustainability of programs. Shediac-Rizkallah and Bone (1998) use a ten-point guideline for sustainability that includes three types of factors: those that are incorporated into the project design and implementation, features of the organisational setting, and factors in the broader community environment. The first group of factors includes negotiation to secure partnerships, appropriate definitions and measures of effectiveness, adequate finance, training and project boundaries. The next group includes institutional strengths, integration with existing programs and services, and identification of program 'champions' or leaders. The final group of factors include socioeconomic and political considerations as well as the level, type and depth of community participation (Shediac-Rizkallah & Bone 1998). The emphasis on sustainable change must be incorporated into evaluation study designs as a marker of predicted acceptability. Various versions of this type of evaluation research approach are used widely throughout the world, to provide comprehensive, practical foundations for community change.

Aggregating study data
to inform health practices

One problem experienced by many community health researchers is accessing a sample size that has sufficient statistical power to draw definitive conclusions. This problem is almost impossible to overcome when the community itself is the focus of research and yields a sample size of one (Yin & Kaftarian 1997). Where there are distinct factors to be investigated, some researchers lean toward a *meta analysis*, aggregating findings from a number of studies with the intention of securing more reliable results than would be possible from a single study. A meta analysis usually allows for identification of an invariant finding in a group of diverse studies, and defends the appropriateness of the various methods used in previous research (Daly, Kellehear & Gliksman 1997). Because this type of analysis aims to place the findings from all studies on a common basis, the researcher engages in either reinterpreting what has been published, or re-analysing the original data (St Leger & Walsworth-Bell

1999). Although some researchers believe there is considerable merit in this type of research, it has also come under criticism on the basis of aggregating variant data into what may look like a multi-centre study, but without the local evidence to provide a basis for allocating resources (St Leger & Walsworth-Bell 1999). This is also the intention of the evidence-based practice movement.

The EBP movement is based on the notion that providing research evidence for all activities in the health professions ensures accountability to the population for clinical decision-making and subsequent interventions. Since 1995, the UK-based International Cochrane Collaboration has maintained a data base of systematic reviews of research on health care interventions in a wide range of clinical areas (Bero & Rennie 1995; Daly et al 1997). The reviews are held in the Cochrane Database of Systematic Reviews and published through a network of centres throughout the world. In 1998, the 51st Health Assembly of WHO recommended adopting this approach to EBP in health education and health promotion practice. However, to date, only 10 per cent of the 1000 systematic reviews registered in the Cochrane library focus on health education and health promotion (Waters, Doyle & Shepherd 2001). This may be an indication of the difficulty of aggregating community data, particularly when there are so many contextual elements involved. It may also reflect the absence of English-language, published, randomised controlled trials (RCTs) that are typically included in the Cochrane data bases (McQueen 2001; St Leger & Walsworth-Bell 1999). The Cochrane studies, with their emphasis on good science rather than good health, may be too detached from the practicalities of community health to be useful, particularly in responding to the need to study community processes and experience (Baum 1995; St Leger & Walsworth-Bell 1999).

Community health research needs to capture the holistic, comprehensive nature of evidence needed to respond to a complex problem or the unpublished evaluation studies that inform policy planning (McQueen 2001). These provide quite a different base of evidence than that derived from RCTs or experimental research designs. However, there has been a trend in community health promotion towards analysing issues on the basis of research reviews. For example, a review of studies on collaborative partnerships and their effectiveness analysed community studies according to three categories: community and systems change, community-wide behaviour change and population-level health outcomes (Tsai Roussos & Fawcett 2000). The findings of the review indicate a number of challenges for research on community partnerships. One of these is related to the diversity in outcomes, which can be categorical issues such as immunisation, broader concerns such as education and employment; or social determinants of health and community development such as income disparities, trust and social cohesion. Another constraint is the nature of community partnerships, which are difficult to research with any certainty because of the need to establish complex or simple causal connections between partnerships and outcomes (Yin & Kaftarian 1997). Other problems include the complexity involved in most interventions and the difficulty in transferring findings across settings (Tsai Roussos & Fawcett 2000).

A further challenge in community health research rests in the fact that changes are often not detectable for 3–10 years (Tsai Roussos & Fawcett

2000). This time frame often falls outside established parameters set by health planners. There is also an absence of accurate and sensitive indicators for community health concerns. Indicators of progress for the various stages of place-based efforts (for example, in neighbourhoods) may also be difficult to identify. Consequently, many health planners have only superficial understanding of the contexts and mechanisms by which population-level outcomes operate (Tsai Roussos & Fawcett 2000). Multi-dimensional studies are better equipped to capture sequential features, such as the need for environmental changes to occur before population-level outcomes are apparent, but these are often difficult and expensive to undertake.

These constraints have plagued many community health researchers, who find that the best way to research the community is to provide a snapshot illuminating features of the community, its residents, their needs, resources and barriers to health and health care. However, like other evaluations, local snapshot studies are not generalisable to the wider context. A reliable study that can be replicated in other communities requires systematic analysis of the multifactorial, intersectoral elements that establish and maintain community dynamics and personal behaviours. Examples of these types of studies were reported in Chapter 4. They include: studies that examined the relationship between smoking, alcohol consumption and dietary intake (Ma, Betts & Hampl 2000); those that model health behaviour over a number of risk factors (Allison et al 1999); and studies that attempt to examine clusters of environmental factors influencing healthy lifestyles, such as French, Story and Jeffery's (2001) research into environmental influences on eating and physical activity, and Tsai Roussos and Fawcett's (2000) review of the impact of collaborative partnerships on community health.

Some researchers investigating lifestyle factors have also used a multidimensional approach to model how the socioecological elements in society can be modified, for example, to discourage smoking, but these have taken many years and voluminous data from many countries (WHO 1999). Another problem with the data on tobacco smoking is related to the way it is modelled for the future. Researchers have used predictive models for long-term outcomes of smoking extrapolated from current data. The accuracy of these data will not be fully understood until some time in the future, which makes it difficult to persuade policy planners to initiate changes (WHO 1999). The opposite problem can also cause difficulties for policy planning, when policies framed on specific risk factors studied at one level and one point in time fail to adequately address whether and how multi-level contexts of people's lives affect their health (Robert 1998).

One of the most difficult problems lies in trying to undertake evaluations based on non-English-language or non-published reports. The voices of many people from developing countries, even those that have conducted comprehensive evaluation studies, are missing from the most common retrieval systems (McQueen 2001). Empowering communities to make healthy choices is based on the type of knowledge that is local, accurate, reliable and framed within the contexts of people's lives and language (Harlem Brundtland 2001; McQueen 2001).

Research
in the settings

As mentioned previously in this book, health is created and maintained in the settings of people's lives. Researching the processes and outcomes of change should therefore be conducted in these contexts. Although health is promoted in a number of settings, the three most attractive settings for health promotion are health (or illness) care agencies, workplaces and schools. Each of these has considerable differences in culture, physical environment and audience, indicating a need to include in our research as many aspects of the context as possible. Health care sites are a special case. People who use health care services are usually receptive to health promotion information, and trusting of those who provide it, and this combines to produce a setting conducive to effective health education (Mullen et al 1995). Research studies to date reveal positive findings on the effectiveness of health education in health care settings but many questions remain, particularly those related to care and social support issues in the home and community setting (Stewart 1999). A further area for study is the extent to which communities are receptive to community development strategies and factors influencing their participation, especially in rural areas, and where there are many cultural factors to consider (AIHW 1998).

Given the importance of the school as a setting for health promotion, there is also a growing need for studies in the school setting, and this is an area where research has already shown considerable gains. Since the 1980s the relative advantages of comprehensive school health programs have been the subject of several large-scale studies. Studies revealed that curriculum components dedicated to health education have been effective in improving knowledge, attitudes and behaviour related to the use of alcohol, drugs, tobacco, diet and sexual risk behaviours (Kolbe, Collins & Cortese 1997; Kolbe, Kann & Brener 2001; World Bank 2001). As mentioned in Chapter 12, WHO has identified evaluation studies of school health programs as a major priority for the future (WHO 2000). Studying the links between inputs (health education) and outputs (behaviour change) needs to be continued, so that young people's behaviour can be tracked over time, especially in relation to such major problems of adolescence as teenage pregnancy, substance abuse and suicide. Other studies should also be designed to examine the mechanisms for encouraging and evaluating community partnerships and participation in school health programs.

Some of the research approaches being adopted in schools are also appropriate in the workplace setting, particularly studies evaluating the interactive or multiplier effects of a number of factors. Studies addressing the effects of gender are also needed. For example, workplace studies should address labour relations and social factors that support or inhibit women's participation in health services. Workplace stress was also identified in Chapter 13 as an area for ongoing evaluation (Harnois & Gabriel 2000). Stress may be best investigated as part of wider studies on surveillance and monitoring of both physical and social conditions. Workplace factors that interact with social policies should also be investigated to begin to define the elements of a family-friendly workplace. Other studies should address the health of migrant workers, especially seasonal workers in a range of settings. Patterns of injury should also be incorporated into studies of the relative burden of injuries according to various industries as well as population groups. A further area for study would be the bigger picture of globalisation in relation to workplace health (Loewenson 2001). To make a difference to the health of the working community, the use of multiple strategies is important and this guides us toward collaborative teamwork in research as well as in practice.

---

case study...

Evaluating the Leadership for Change program

The Leadership for Change (LFC) program began in 1996 in response to the International Council of Nurses (ICN) member countries' request for support in preparing nurses for leadership roles during health sector reform. Those planning the program envisaged that the twenty-first century would see selected nurses at country and organisational levels equipped with the knowledge, strategies and strength to lead and manage in health services undergoing major change. The focus and the key strategic goals emphasised policy development, management and leadership in nursing and health services, and articulating the role of nurses in preparing future nurse leaders. With support from the WK Kellogg Foundation, the ICN first developed the program for Latin American and Caribbean countries. By 1998, with funding from the New Zealand government, it was expanded to include the South Pacific. Next, LFC began in east, central and southern Africa as a joint venture between the ICN and the East, Central and South Africa Commonwealth Nations (ECSACON), with funding shared between the Commonwealth Secretariat for East, Central and Southern Africa and the ICN. In 1999, the ICN also engaged in a joint venture with the Singapore Nurses Association to institute the LFC program in that country. In the year 2000 another collaborative sponsorship saw the program extend into Bangladesh, largely funded through WHO South East Asian Regional Office (SEARO), with contributions from the Nursing Directorate of the Government of Bangladesh and the ICN.

The basis of the program is that leadership can be cultivated and sustained by strategies designed for self-development, and this capacity can be used to enhance the development of others. The program components include mentoring by experienced leaders, group workshops, completing individual development plans to build leadership behaviours, and team projects designed to mobilise and extend participants' personal knowledge of leadership and strategies for sharing this with others in the program. Workshops are designed around the strategies of action learning to develop leadership potential. Team projects are planned with participant/employer commitment and an agreed responsibility to mentor others in the future. In-country activities revolve around securing funding and delivering accountable health outcomes to the district, country, region and to the ICN.

To develop a strategy for evaluation, the ICN convened an evaluation advisory group. The group spent several days in Geneva, getting to know one another and developing the research framework around team members' various approaches to evaluation research, given their widely diverse backgrounds. This was an important phase of the evaluation, because the strategies being developed would have to be acceptable to a similarly diverse group of program participants, their mentors and their co-workers or supervisors in the various health organisations.

The evaluation strategy began from a brain-storming exercise on the basis of the information required by one of the major sources of funding for the program. The categories of data required by the funding agency included:

1   context/relevance
2   program components
3   effectiveness in meeting program goals
4   unanticipated outcomes
5   efficiency
6   impact
7   sustainability.

The group considered each category, then began to pose examples of what types of information could be aggregated under each. Because of the wide range of projects, evaluation categories had to be flexible enough to capture the realities of personal and organi-sational outcomes that linked personal develop-ments, policy and health care changes and community outcomes.

Many iterations later, each category had a number of component parts derived from inter-rogating a wide range of possible and probable responses. The overarching goal of the exercise was kept in the forefront of discussions: to iden-tify measurable impacts from the LFC program, and then attempt to predict the extent to which these could be sustained, based on the achieve-ments and progress of participants. This refine-ment stage continued, with questions developed for each category and the overall evaluation strategy, broken down into a series of defined steps. First would be analysis of the feedback already provided by participants and stakehold-ers. The next stage overlapped the first. While the documents were being analysed, a survey instrument would be developed to capture missing information from the initial feedback, designed to aggregate responses into coherent patterns. The next stage identified the target group for the questionnaire: those participants

who had undertaken the training and had imple-mented their country or regional programs. Analytic techniques were selected to collate responses in a meaningful way, and the ques-tionnaire was dispatched to gather responses from participants, stakeholders, funders and organisations affected by the various projects.

The data collection tool was guided by the seven categories. Under the first category, questions were asked as to what extent each of the contexts (professional, organisational, legal–political etc) contributed to various out-comes. This required generating a list of explicit outcomes ranging from very general (for example, the timing of the program in relation to national/regional/local health reform changes) to the more specific questions of vision state-ments used and the particular change manage-ment strategies employed.

Once the questions related to each category and a corresponding range of indicators were identified, members of the evaluation group began to 'test' the usefulness of categories by perusing questionnaire responses. This stage was conducted like a pilot study in that it was concerned not only with the data, but also pro-vided feedback on the evaluation strategy. The next phase involved a separate analysis of all documents from four regions (Caribbean, Africa, Latin America and the South Pacific). Results of the documents analysis were compared with the survey results to identify the degree of concor-dance. Further discussion highlighted areas where data were unclear or disparate, to guide the next phase of the study. The next phase involved two case study projects to be con-ducted in each region. The case studies con-sisted of in-depth interviews with participants, stakeholders and mentors with a view towards verifying the data provided in written survey responses and the documents analysis.

Evaluation data are showing that the program is indeed a good way of building capac-ity for change through leadership development. However, much remains to be done to demon-strate sustainability, and this will be the subject of future planning aimed at designing a long-itudinal study. This phase will be extremely interesting, given expansion of the project to other countries in other regions, and refinement of the techniques for data gathering and analysis. The project illustrates a number of issues involved in researching individual, organisational and community change. A long-term commitment is essential. Funders must therefore be made aware that quality information comes at a cost. Researchers must be prepared to work within many different perspectives and contexts. Group dynamics in any collaborative venture are an instrumental part of the research process. Brainstorming sessions are invaluable. Open discussion on a wide range of topics sometimes reveals serendipitous findings that may have been left concealed in a closed, rather than open, forum for discussion. Finally, there is no 'right way' to proceed with evaluation. A sound study uses one or more frameworks at various times in the process of evaluation and these flow from interdisciplinary ways of seeing the whole and the parts, and from a genuine approach to collaboration. The payoff for a program of this magnitude is worth the investment, particularly in illustrating how powerful individual capacities can be when they are designed to inspire capacity building throughout the health care community.

Research
ethics

The major ethical considerations in conducting research studies are universally accepted, and these include ensuring confidentiality and anonymity of research participants, scientific validity, and protection of vulnerable people such as children and those made powerless by institutionalisation. Researchers are ethically accountable to both the researched and the scientific community. This holds them responsible to fully explain to research participants any risks and benefits, regardless of how small, so that participants only consent to their involvement on the basis of being fully informed (Khoury 1996). In all research, there is some opportunity cost for the researched, and this needs to be made explicit, even if it is simply the imposition on their time (Downie & Calman 1994).

Researchers must take seriously their obligation to provide feedback to those supplying information. This ensures that people and the information they hold are not exploited by researchers who simply use the data for their own purposes, whether it is for idealistic purposes (to improve the health of populations), career enhancement (publication), or to guide further research studies. In all research studies, the issue of cultural sensitivity must be addressed. If a research study is devised without full consultation with those being researched, there is a risk of inadequate or inappropriate information being gathered and, in some, cases, misinterpretation of the subtleties that may lead to health problems (Daly et al 1997). The use of interview or observational data poses a particular risk to accurate interpretation. Researchers need to make every effort to grasp the underlying intuitions of those being questioned, as their understanding of illnesses, their causation and treatment is embedded in personal experiences and culture-based meanings (Campbell et al 1997). This is particularly important in research aimed at informing policy development. When the major players are involved in helping to frame the questions, guide the research process and articulate the findings in language that is meaningful to them, there is a greater likelihood that their preferences will find their way into public policies.

Evaluation studies must always be analysed with respect to the intentions of the program, ensuring that the findings, along with any unanticipated findings, are clearly reported as such. Otherwise, there is a chance that researcher expectations or bias will prevent full examination of the full potential of the information, particularly in the policy arena (Cribb & Duncan 2002). Bias can also be a potential problem at the beginning of an evaluation study, where definitional or labelling issues may compromise both the validity and ethical standards of the research. Cribb and Duncan (2002) use the example of research into teenage pregnancy to illustrate this point, explaining that the findings of research into adolescent pregnancy may have focused too much on moral aspects of the problem and inadvertently failed to inform strategies for emergency contraception for teenagers. Their advice guides all researchers towards examining fully and from many different perspectives, any findings with the potential to limit treatment, prevention or further investigations.

Researching
the future

Many questions remain to be addressed in community health. At a 'macro' level, research questions should begin with the effects of globalisation. Research studies should be directed towards identifying how the creation of wealth and appropriate investments in health care can bring about the type of national and international improvements that are vital to sustainable communities. We also need to examine the ways in which various communities have been able to achieve economic, ecological, social and human capital (Hancock 2001). For example, researchers should turn their attention to examining how the newly emerging 'green' businesses that will invest only in socially and environmentally friendly corporations can be supported by the base of evidence that would set an example for other industries (Hancock 2001). This line of research intersects with the social and environmental issues that are so important to a sustainable future. Studies are desperately needed to inform future decisions on climate change, the impact of international decisions on pollution standards, the population mix and migration.

National studies of the policies that support healthy workers and good parenting practices balanced with healthy lifestyles, are paramount. The broader agenda of family research has been neglected to some extent in mainstream public health research, particularly in examining variation in families' perceptions of health and how health is supported within changing family structures. We need to use this information in public debate, to better understand which families use which services, and whether this is based on need, perceptions or convenience, particularly in relation to such things as immunisation

(Seedhouse 2001). Local studies should also attempt to identify what barriers to services exist in the community—such as cost, transportation, time and location. And we should research the extent to which there is unmet need in a given community to inform equitable planning processes, particularly for Indigenous people. This would see research studies designed around unravelling the ' "patterned consistency" of health status, building upon research results on the relationship between health and socio-economic status, ethnicity, race, age and sex' (Kickbusch 1997, p 432).

There is also a need to integrate knowledge of the social environment with what we learn about geographical factors. The work being done through the Canadian Institute for Advanced Research (CIAR) exploring the links between psychoneural and behavioural factors in child development should be replicated in other countries. This would inform the global healthy children agenda from a base of population data (Hertzman 2001). The work of WHO in illuminating the global burden of injuries should also be continued, along with national research into different elements of this burden for workers, and for children (Krug, Sharma & Lozano 2000). Population ageing dictates its own set of studies and these should work towards a coherent understanding for all the world's people of the implications for future planning. And one of the most important areas for global research is to advance the social research agenda accompanying biomedical genetics research.

In addition to the wider issues, there remains little information on locally defined health issues. One important element of the local agenda is health service utilisation. We know a great deal about the provision of health services, but little of the conditions that influence people's access to or utilisation of health care. It is essential that any community health research portfolio includes a series of community 'snapshots' to ensure that, in the true spirit of Alma Ata, health professionals continue to 'think globally' but 'act locally'. As mentioned previously, community involvement in decision-making and the dynamics of participation, should be the subject of further inquiry (Shediac-Rizkallah & Bone 1998).

Questions also remain in various settings. We have witnessed the beginning of evaluation strategies in comprehensive school health programs, but we know little about the perspective of students or their families. In the parlance of contemporary WHO initiatives, we need to know where the best investments in health lie and how we can encourage these to attract ongoing support. This could begin with the recommendation of Green, Nathan and Mercer (2001) to draw inspiration from the success of the tobacco control movement to make changes in other lifestyle areas. This line of inquiry complements Kickbusch's (1997) suggestion to accept the settings projects (cities, health care institutions, schools and workplaces) as standards, so that our knowledge of health technologies includes the social technology of supportive environments for health. Careful evaluation studies of the processes and outcomes of these movements will allow us to validate the standards of best practice in health-promoting settings to build a transferable base of knowledge that can be shared by all communities.

thinking critically

Community health research

1 Identify three research studies published within the last five years that could lead to community health improvements.

2 Explain why the actions of health professionals should be based on research evidence.

3 Discuss the ethical implications of current developments in scientific health knowledge.

4 Construct a feasible research question to investigate each of the following community health issues:
- implications for health professionals of the gradient effect in health status
- interventions with low-SES families to enhance child development
- increasing suicide rates among adolescent males
- relative social disadvantage of migrant women
- continuing fitness for older men.

5 Devise a strategic research plan for examining the adequacy of healthy workplace initiatives.

REFERENCES

Allison, K., Adlaf, E., Ialomiteanu, A. & Rehm J. (1999). Predictors of health risk behaviors among young adults: analysis of the national population health survey. *Canadian Journal of Public Health*, 90(2): 85–9.

Australian Institute of Health and Welfare (AIHW) (1998). Health in rural and remote Australia. Canberra: AGPS.

Baum, F. (1995). Researching public health: behind the qualitative-quantitative methodological debate. *Social Science and Medicine*, 40(4): 459–68.

Berger, C. (2001). Infant mortality: a reflection of the quality of health. *Health and Social Work*, 26(4): 277–83.

Bero, L. & Rennie, D. (1995). The Cochrane Collaboration: preparing, maintaining and disseminating systematic reviews of the effects of health care. *Journal of the American Medical Association*, 274(24): 1935–8.

Billings, J. (2000). Community development: a critical review of approaches to evaluation. *Journal of Advanced Nursing*, 31(2): 472–80.

Campbell, A., Charlesworth, M., Gillett, G. & Jones, G. (1997). *Medical Ethics*, 2nd edn, Belmont, California: Wadsworth.

Cole, D., Eyles, J., Gibson, B. & Ross, N. (1999). Links between humans and ecosystems: the implications of framing for health promotion strategies. *Health Promotion International*, 14(1): 65–72.

Cribb, A. & Duncan, P. (2002). *Health Promotion and Professional Ethics*. Oxford: Blackwell Science.

Cruikshank, D. (1996). The experience of action research in practice. *Contemporary Nurse*, 5(3): 127–32.

Daly, J., Kellehear, A. & Gliksman, M. (1997). *The Public Health Researcher*. Melbourne: Oxford University Press.

Downie, R. & Calman, K. (1994). *Healthy Respect: Ethics in Health Care*. New York: Oxford University Press.

Dunn, J. & Hayes, M. (1999). Toward a lexicon of population health. *Canadian Journal of Public Health*, 90 (suppl): 7–10.

French, S., Story, M. & Jeffery, R. (2001). Environmental influences on eating and physical activity. *Annual Review of Public Health*, 23: 309–35.

Goodman, R. (2000). Evaluation of community-based health programs: an alternative perspective. In: N. Schneiderman, M. Speers, J. Silva, H. Tomes & J. Gentry (eds), *Integrating Behavioral and Social Sciences with Public Health*. Washington: American Psychological Association, pp 293–304.

Goodman, R., Wandersman, A., Chinman, M., Imm, P. & Morrissey, E. (1996). An ecological assessment of community-based interventions for prevention and health promotion: Approaches to measuring community coalitions. *American Journal of Community Psychology*, 24(1): 33–61.

Green, L. (1999). Health education's contributions to public health in the twentieth century: a glimpse through health promotion's rear-view mirror. *Annual Review of Public Health*, 20: 67–88.

Green, L., Nathan, R. & Mercer, S. (2001). The health of health promotion in public policy: drawing inspiration from the tobacco control movement. *Health Promotion Journal of Australia*, 12(2): 110–16.

Greenwood, J. (1994). Action research and action researchers: some introductory considerations. *Contemporary Nurse*, 3(2): 84–92.

Gruenewald, P. (1997). Analysis approaches to community evaluation. *Evaluation Review*, 21(2): 209–30.

Hancock, T. (2001). People, partnerships and human progress: building community capital. *Health Promotion International*, 16(3): 275–80.

Harlem Brundtland, G. (2001). Statement by Dr Gro Harlem Brundtland, Director-General, WHO, to the Fifth Global Conference on Health Promotion, Mexico City, 5 June 2000.

Harnois, G. & Gabriel, P. (2000). Mental health and work: impact, issues, and good practices. Geneva: WHO, ILO.

Hart, E. (1996). Action research as a professionalizing strategy: issues and dilemmas. *Journal of Advanced Nursing*, 23: 454–61.

Hertzman, C. (2001). Health and human society. *American Scientist*, 89(6): 538–44.

Israel, B., Checkoway, B., Schulz, A. & Zimmerman, M. (1994). Health education and community empowerment: conceptualizing and measuring perceptions of individual, organizational, and community control. *Health Education Quarterly*, 21(2): 149–70.

Khoury, M. (1996). From genes to public health: the applications of genetic technology in disease prevention. *American Journal of Public Health*, 86(12): 1717–22.

Kickbusch, I. (1997). Health promoting environments: the next steps. *Australian and New Zealand Journal of Public Health*, 21(4): 431–4.

Kolbe, L., Collins, J. & Cortese, P. (1997). Building the capacity of schools to improve the health of the nation. *American Psychologist*, 52(3): 256–65.

Kolbe, L., Kann, L. & Brener, N. (2001). Overview and summary of findings: School health policies and programs study 2000. *Journal of School Health*, 71(7): 253–63.

Krug, E., Sharma, G. & Lozano, R. (2000). The global burden of injuries. *American Journal of Public Health*, 90(4): 523–6.

Laverack, G. & Wallerstein, N. (2001). Measuring community empowerment: a fresh look at organizational domains. *Health Promotion International*, 16(2): 179–85.

Loewensen, R. (2001). Globalization and occupational health: a perspective from Southern Africa. *Bulletin of the World Health Organization*, 79(9): 863–8.

Ma, J., Betts, N. & Hampl, J. (2000). Clustering of lifestyle behaviors: the relationship between cigarette smoking, alcohol consumption and dietary intake. *American Journal of Health Promotion*, 15(2): 107–16.

McQueen, D. (2001). Strengthening the evidence-base for health promotion. *Health Promotion International*, 16(3): 261–8.

Michaud, C., Murray, C. & Bloom, B. (2001). Burden of disease—implications for future research. *Journal of the American Medical Association*, 285(5): 535–42.

Moody, G., Choong, Y. & Greenwood, J. (2001). An action research approach to the development of a clinical pathway for women requiring Caesarean sections. *Contemporary Nurse*, 11(2/3): 195–205.

Mullen, P., Evans, D., Forster, J., Gottlieb, N., Kreuter, M., Moon, R., O'Rourke, T. & Strecher, V. (1995). Settings as an important dimension in health education/promotion policy, programs, and research. *Health Education Quarterly*, 22(3): 329–45.

Murphy, M. & Risser, N. (1999). Pediatric genetic testing. *Pediatric Nursing*, 25(1): 61–8.

Nutbeam, D. (1998). Evaluating health promotion—progress, problems and solutions. *Health Promotion International*, 13(1): 27–44.

Omenn, G. (2000). Public health genetics: an emerging interdisciplinary field for the post-genomic era. *Annual Review of Public Health*, 21: 1–13.

Patton, M. (2002). *Qualitative Research and Evaluation Methods*, 3rd edn, Thousand Oaks: Sage.

Pincus, T., Esther, R., DeWalt, M. & Callahan, L. (1998). Social conditions and self-management are more powerful determinants of health than access to care. *Annals of Internal Medicine*, 129: 406–11.

Robert, S. (1998). Community-level socioeconomic status effects on adult health. *Journal of Health and Social Behavior*, 39(Mar): 18–37.

Seedhouse, D. (2001). Health promotion's ethical challenge. *Health Promotion Journal of Australia*, 12(20): 135–8.

Shediac-Rizkallah, M. & Bone, L. (1998). Planning for the sustainability of community-based health programs: conceptual frameworks and directions for research, practice and policy. *Health Education Research*, 13(1): 87–108.

St Leger, A. & Walsworth-Bell, J. (1999). *Change-Promoting Research for Health Services*. Buckingham: Open University Press.

Stewart, M. (1999). Social support, coping, and self-care as public participation mechanisms. In: M. Stewart (ed), *Community Nursing: Promoting Canadians' Health*. Toronto: WB Saunders, pp 83–104.

Titchen, A. & Binnie, A. (1994). Action research: a strategy for theory generation and testing. *International Journal of Nursing Studies*, 31(1): 1–12.

Tsai Roussos, S. & Fawcett, S. (2000). A review of collaborative partnerships as a strategy for improving community health. *Annual Review of Public Health*, 21: 369–402.

Waters, E., Doyle, J. & Shepherd, J. (2001). Systematic reviews in health promotion. *Health Promotion Journal of Australia*, 12(2): 171–2.

World Bank (2001). *Partnership for Child Development*. New York: World Bank.

World Health Organization (WHO) (1999). The World Health Report 1999. Making a difference. Geneva: WHO.

—— (2000). The Global School Health Initiative. Geneva: WHO.

Yin, R. & Kaftarian, S. (1997). Introduction: challenges of community-based program outcome evaluations. *Evaluation and Program Planning*, 20(3): 293–7.

CHAPTER 15

Health care:
systems and policy

ıtroduction In all countries, the health care system represents the formalisation of government commitment to the health and well-being of the community. This is demonstrated through each country's capacity for service provision, the generation of resources for health, appropriate financing and good stewardship (WHO 2000a). From the perspective of the community and the health professionals who work with them, the defining purpose of a health care system lies in the provision of good health care, accessible to all in a way that is equitable—that is, fair and responsive to people's expectations. Health care systems, like other systems, must be healthy and robust. It is crucial to ensure that health care systems are efficiently and effectively managed, for to waste resources in health is to compromise the health capacity of the population, and this usually affects those most in need of services. A healthy system of health care is also ethical in its conduct. It is strategic in its endeavours to meet the needs of current and future communities, transparent in communicating its goals and capabilities, oriented towards community empowerment for informed choices, and resourced to the extent that it can support those choices.

Health care systems are an integral part of the wider political agenda. A large component of political activity revolves around resource allocation, and resources are central to the functioning of health care systems. Health policies governing the allocation of resources and the mix of services are therefore critical elements in the policy portfolio. Governments have a finite pool of resources to service the needs of their constituents, and this is typically allocated as a fixed proportion of gross domestic product. However, there are no consistently defined outputs to match specific financial inputs, and outcomes in terms of the health of the population are unpredictable. So financial contribution does not necessarily equate with good health. Various nations also differ in their circumstances and particular threats to health. Health care policies must be responsive to these issues, balancing national, regional and local priorities with appropriate, cost-effective resources. A further layer of complexity is the lack of consensus among policy makers as to what lies within the purview of health. From a socioecological perspective, allocations to health include all funds deployed to conserve the environment, educate families, feed the homeless, construct safe roads and provide incentives for private businesses to build facilities for elder care, or strategies for income security. So strategic decisions in health care affect decisions in all of society. Overarching all these issues is the need for social justice. This chapter provides an overview of how health care systems attempt to achieve social justice in the policy arena to meet the health needs of their populations.

objectives **By the end of this chapter you will be able to:**

1 Identify the most pressing global problems related to health care services

2 Explain current trends affecting both the organisation and administration of health services

3 Discuss the issues that must be considered in planning health services to be responsive to the needs of different population groups

4 Identify at least one major health issue that requires a public policy response at the local and global levels, and the elements it should include

5 Devise a set of strategies to reorient health care systems towards prevention rather than treatment.

The politics
of health care

Although all health care systems have in common the goal of creating and sustaining the greatest good for the largest proportion of people, there is wide variability in the extent to which this goal is achieved. To some extent, this is because of the range of approaches taken by governments to be responsive to needs and demands. Numerous programs compete for government funds and there are many ways to argue health needs. In addition, there is no one best way to organise government departments. Some are managed on the basis of population groups (Departments of Families, for example), while others are managed on the basis of disease categories (Departments of Communicable Diseases), and these structures often determine priorities. Political factions typically influence the flow of strategic activities in the health care system and these also vary. Since the advent of the consumer movement, public lobby groups have also played a role in decision-making, advocating for their particular interests, creating pressure on political decision-makers to allocate more resources to issues such as breast cancer, childhood injury prevention, eliminating drinking and driving, or tough anti-smoking or firearms control. In health care, especially where visible improvements can be made, there is considerable political mileage to be gained from responding to vocal, public interests, particularly if these relate to current, high-profile issues such as HIV/AIDS, the environment or health care for the elderly.

Political tradition also plays a part in the way health care systems are shaped. In some countries, the concept of entrepreneurial health care would be rejected outright, for cultural and historical reasons, whereas in others it is readily accepted. For example, two extremes are represented in the health care systems of the United Kingdom and the United States. In the United Kingdom, the national health services model is characterised by a government-financed and operated system. The United States has an entrepreneurial/market model where the private sector, rather than the government, controls health care. Most health care systems have some mix of public and private health services, and the extent to which they are privatised represents another political element. Commercial partners in the delivery of health care seek returns on their investments. The goals of these vested interests sometimes compete with those of health professionals, but their contribution to the management of health resources can also be instrumental to good health. Private partners make a contribution to health care by acting as a source of benchmarking, particularly in allowing some cross-checking of public efficiencies and quality processes for effectiveness and consistency. They are also important in supplementing what may be deficient government resources for health, and form a significant part of the economic base needed to employ health professionals.

Health professionals themselves have vested interests in the conduct of a health care system. Medical practitioners, especially, spend long years of educational preparation in the expectation of practising in the geographic location and specialty of their choice. Political decisions that limit either intakes into medical education programs or the employment of graduates have the potential to create tensions among the labour force. Similarly, the nursing and allied health workforce have clear expectations of the outcomes of their educational preparation, yet these are sometimes transformed by political processes. For example, decisions that regulate policies related to reimbursing medical practitioners, or that pave the way for the reimbursement of more cost-effective health care providers, challenge the tradition of medical dominance that has existed for many years. Medical practitioners act as gatekeepers to the health care system, exerting control over hospital care, community health services and private medical care. Because they represent a power elite in health care, any challenge to their role as gatekeepers to the system is a major source of political tension.

Another area of contention in the political arena is related to political decisions in favour of continuing or discontinuing one or another program or service. Elected policy makers are sometimes transient and may be intent on fulfilling their personal political visions rather than undertaking innovative and/or unproven approaches to health care. As mentioned in the previous chapter, there is a dearth of evaluative data that would support innovations or changes to health care delivery. Sometimes the lag between developing mechanisms for change and the evidence base that would substantiate that change extends beyond the tenure of a political party or faction. When there is a change in the political party in power, the process of maintaining programs may be left to the vagaries of residual mechanisms, causing uncertainty about whether or not a service will continue. It is important then, in any health advocacy role, to recognise the inherently political nature of health care. The discussion to follow explains the urgency and intensity of developing efficient, effective, responsive and equitable structures and processes to meet health care needs.

Health care:
need and demand

Health systems have existed for as long as people have identified the need to protect their health and treat illnesses. For the past century, there have been many overlapping generations of reform throughout the world, ranging from the development of national health systems and health insurance schemes, to primary health care and its promise of 'universal' care or health care for all (WHO 2000a). Primary health care has been widely embraced by all proponents of community-based services, particularly in developing countries. However, it has also been criticised on the basis that too much rhetoric and too much attention has been focused on perceived *needs*, rather than *demand* for health care. Unlike other systems, health care systems are not strictly responsive to market forces. In the case of illness, each of us would like the maximum treatment possible. So the market for services does not show predictable fluctuations on the basis of the cost of providing the services. Similarly, we would all like to think that we had access to the best available preventive and protective services and information, but these are not always equitably distributed, irrespective of an individual's ability to pay. This poses a set of important ethical issues, primarily around the equitable distribution of resources in ways that allow access to health care for all people.

Throughout the 1990s, the emphasis in health care shifted to a 'new universalism' that re-framed the policy and planning processes from care for everyone (which is often only basic care for the poor), to mechanisms for providing high-quality, cost-effective, acceptable care for all. This new orientation was based on economic advice suggesting that simply assessing needs does not provide a sound basis for efficient strategies for planning and purchasing health services, especially when these assessments do not always capture the severity or priority of needs (Petrou 1998). The 'new universalism' shifts the ideological focus from health service management to individual choice and responsibility. The political focus accompanying this 'bottom-up' approach is to establish clear indications of financial limitations, particularly in light of a potentially infinite demand for care. If services are to be provided for all, then not all services can be provided (WHO 2000a).

Accountability
in service provision

One of the most important elements of the new universalism is accountability. The expanding body of health research, for example, must be considered a global public good. This means that the evidence-base for health systems development should be shared by all citizens of all nations. Given the ease of worldwide communications, best practices can readily be shared between countries; however, this is not yet the case. In some countries, the poor continue to 'buy' health from their own pockets, which simply fills the pockets of policy makers (WHO 2000a). Because many of the poor are also deprived of information that would allow them to better manage their illnesses or injuries, they are doubly disadvantaged. It is important that others understand how this can erode the dignity and well-being of the poor and the many ways information can enhance the potential of a nation's citizenry. With information, consumers can become aware of what is good and bad for their health. Sharing information also allows planners to understand the processes of priority setting, and it helps politicians understand the myriad influences of the market economy, the outcomes of regulatory strategies, the economic and social aspects of training the health workforce, and the utilisation patterns for those accessing health care.

Good and best
health care systems

As mentioned in the previous chapter, a major initiative of WHO in 2000 was to try and unravel the features of all health systems to investigate what works best. Its research showed that there is no 'best system'. It did, however, develop a variety of statistical measures to provide rankings in several aspects of health service delivery, and a composite overall ranking for each country. So, for example, it is possible to benchmark health attainment in terms of disability-adjusted life expectancy (DALE), or the equality of child survival across all countries, and the relative responsiveness of the health care system to people's needs. The WHO research indicates that the most important issue in any health system structure is the extent to which it facilitates the performance of its key functions, which are to improve health (*attainment*), to respond to people's expectations (*responsiveness and fairness*) and to provide financial protection against the costs of ill-health (*performance*) (WHO 2000a). These functions are achieved through *stewardship*, which dictates appropriate decision-making in managing resources equitably.

Health care spending is a complex process. In previous times, there was an expectation that health spending as a proportion of gross domestic product (GDP) was a good predictor of a nation's health. Today, this is challenged by the growing body of evidence indicating that it is the wealthier among us who use health services the most, so the health of the poor is not necessarily advantaged by greater overall spending on health care. Financial modelling of cost-benefits has shown that health improvements can also be achieved for modest cost. For example, WHO estimates that, in terms of return on investment, a $12 investment per person in poor countries would have averted one-third of the burden of disease in the year 1990 (WHO 2000a). A different set of linkages demonstrate the importance of appropriate resource allocation in relation to life expectancy. Life expectancy in Sweden is twice that in Uganda, and some would link this to the fact that Sweden spends 35 times as much per capita on its health system. However, Pakistan spends almost exactly the same amount per capita as Uganda, and yet has a life expectancy almost 25 years higher. This is attributed not to health expenditure, but to Pakistan's achievement relative to resources. In other words, the choices that country has made to use the *actual* health resources at its disposal are the most significant element in health care provision (WHO 2000a).

Another example of variability in health service organisation relates to the maldistribution of medical and health professional resources. The WHO (2000a) report outlines the case of a young, poor woman who visits a rural government health post with a sick infant. There is no medical doctor, and no prescription drugs are available, but a nurse provides the mother with an oral rehydration kit, explains how it is used and makes a follow-up appointment. The nurse sees only six people that day. At the neighbouring community hospital, several hundred patients wait to be seen by a small group of doctors, again with no access to prescription drugs. The doctors, poorly paid, see only a portion of the patients, then hurry to a private clinic to see others so that they can subsidise their salaries. The patients who were fortunate enough to be seen travel a great distance to secure their prescription medications. The others will return the next day, hoping but not always expecting to see a medical doctor. This example illustrates how the low productivity of the nurse, the underutilisation of the hospital, and the financial difficulties of the medical doctors all combine to render the health care system inefficient. In this case, low productivity and patient neglect are the outcomes of poor labour force planning, and a lack of organisation and priority-setting (WHO 2000a).

Health insurance is another area where good stewardship is crucial. Most health care is subsidised by some form of public or private contributions. A fair financing system is achievable only through risk pooling, where the healthy subsidise those who are ill, and the wealthy subsidise the poor (WHO 2000a). To accomplish this requires some form of prepaid financing, or health insurance, to protect the poor from being penalised by out-of-pocket expenses at the time of unexpected illness or injury. A fair system, one that treats everyone in accordance with human rights, is designed to achieve horizontal and vertical equity: to treat alike everyone with the same condition, and to treat preferentially those with the greatest need (WHO 2000a). Most countries have adopted this type of approach, where effective management processes work towards equity. A feature of many of these systems is the separation of purchasing and provider services, which encourages accountable outcomes at the lowest cost, and makes visible the horizontal and vertical integration of services. The health care systems of the Netherlands, Germany, Sweden, Canada, Australia, New Zealand and the United Kingdom have adopted this approach, with the intention of shifting accountability for outputs to providers, in the expectation that they will also be cost effective (WHO 2000b). This type of 'managerialism' is increasingly the norm in health care systems, especially in industrialised countries.

Countries such as Canada and New Zealand have managed the health care system particularly well, achieving cost savings by benchmarking, outsourcing services to be cost-effective and monitoring and enhancing performance with financial incentives. However, there remains a constant need for vigilance even in countries with universal health insurance coverage, on the basis of what is often seen as a disproportionate emphasis on economic rationalism, rather than equitable outcomes or quality of care. In most of the European countries, North America, New Zealand and Australia, equity through individual choice has also become a key objective of changes to health care. Many of these countries are also trying to increase the quality outcomes of cost-efficiencies through national research agendas that will provide the evidence base for continuation or change (Short & Palmer 2000; Thorne 2002).

Irrespective of tighter management structures, even in the 'high performance' countries with sophisticated health care systems, problems of access and equity persist, especially for the most vulnerable people. As long as health care systems continue to fund medical practitioners on the basis of 'fee-for-service' models, economic incentives will focus medical treatment on the 'walking well'—that is, relatively healthy people with minor episodic illness (Kushner 2000). Because these service episodes are relatively inexpensive, and the costs of medical practice are very expensive, there is pressure on the medical practitioner to see as many people as possible as quickly as possible. A further pressure arises from the increasingly litigious environment of medical practice. High overheads and economic performance indicators compounded by exorbitant malpractice insurance costs have led groups of doctors to place boundaries around their practices, in some cases excluding the elderly and other patients with labour-intensive needs. The trend towards litigation also drives a need for defensive medical practice, which has driven many practitioners away from obstetrical care, home visiting and after-hours care (Kuschner 2000). New Zealand has recently developed an innovative, primary health care model wherein communities will have access to primary health care practitioners for services provided on the basis of population needs, rather than as a 'one-size-fits-all' system of care (NZMOH 2001). That country already has a system whereby midwives and nurses provide advanced services to those most in need, such as Maoris, Pacific Islanders and those living in rural and remote areas.

Another side of the health service equation is the identification of needs and preferences by individuals, families and the community requiring services. To develop explicit policies for the rationing of health services there is an ongoing need for a strong evidence base in relation to demographic and cultural factors and health-seeking behaviour. This includes detailed assessment of risk related to the burden of disease and disability, service utilisation patterns, and information on cost related to local prices and contexts (WHO 2000a). Rationing care according to priorities involves considering social, political and cost-effective criteria contextualised to local problems, such as HIV/AIDS in sub-Saharan Africa or adolescent suicide prevention in Australia and New Zealand. However, this type of planning must not be inflexible, to ensure there is scope for innovation as well as meeting the strategic objectives and financial protection as best as can be achieved from the budget allocation. Both innovation and good management are therefore integral to good stewardship.

Good health policies that flow from well-managed health departments define the vision and direction of health care, to exert influence over the implementation of services through regulation and monitoring, and to collect and use the most appropriate intelligence and base of evidence.

Communication of the evidence base is also crucial to good management, especially when there may be difficulties related to language (including the language of research), and to levels of knowledge that are essential for understanding. Communication strategies lie at the heart of informed choices for health. This means that researchers and health practitioners must be mindful of the need to report different levels of evidence and various trends of acceptability. For example, the general public has a right to know dose-response data, such as how much alcohol can safely be ingested, or what cholesterol levels are acceptable, but this information must be presented cautiously, and with the emphasis on the various ways it may be interpreted (Cribb & Duncan 2002). A well-managed health service is therefore one where the emphasis is on coordination, consultation and evidence-based communication (WHO 2000a).

Healthy
policies

From a socioecological perspective, health policy and other public policies are inextricably intertwined. Healthy public policies guide the way governments, communities and individuals address changes that must be made for good health. A good health policy defines the health vision of a nation, establishes benchmarks for its accomplishments, outlines priorities and expected roles of each group involved, builds consensus and informs the public (WHO 2000a). Health policies can reflect global initiatives developed by such agencies as WHO, the World Bank and the United Nations. In a linear process, these would filter down to the national, state and community level, but sometimes the reverse is true. Healthy policies for the national and global community may come from the grass roots or community level. In turn, these are formulated by individuals, who keep watch over the biological, social, environmental, lifestyle and health service factors that serve as the main indicators of the health of the population.

If we accept the evidence on which the model of socioeconomic determinants of health is based (presented in Chapter 4), economic, welfare, health, housing, transport and taxation policies play an important role in the most significant determinants of health. These policies determine education, employment, occupation and working conditions, income and housing (Turrell & Mathers 2000). A responsive health care system acts on this knowledge to develop multilevel healthy policies 'upstream', as well as 'downstream' (Oldenburg, McGuffog & Turrell 2000). These policies should also be multifaceted, devised through intersectoral collaboration to provide access to education and training for those who may have formerly been excluded by race, gender or geography, and to engage with communities through urban renewal schemes and networks. In addition, healthy policies provide structural supports for workplace reforms as well as individual behaviour change. Healthy policies should also include public funding for health care that is economically, geographically and culturally accessible, and that maintains an appropriately prepared and equitably distributed health workforce (Oldenburg et al 2000).

Healthy policies can be both responsive to macro level or 'upstream' factors and seek to influence them. For example, national industrial relations policies can provide a basis for social and family policies that facilitate community development by developing the workforce. Working families are then able to educate their children, which may benefit the whole community by deterring young people from violent behaviour or poverty. Healthy school policies also foster positive pregnancy and parenting, greater productivity and better quality of life, which can build cohesion for the whole of society.

Two of the most significant influences on health policy today are advertising and management policy (Marmor 2001). Advertising by private health care providers creates expectations of the health care system that are sometimes unrealistic. With the managerialism that has gradually crept into the health care arena, the public expects certain levels of efficiency and effectiveness. Because all people want the best health care available, without compromise, this can be difficult to achieve. As a result, health policy makers have a responsibility to inform the public of what they *can't* have as well as what they *can* (Marmor 2001). According to Marmor (2001) good health policy should demonstrate truth value as well as rallying value. This also extends to research, which must advertise the *quality* of evidence-based health care, as well as stating that a new innovation or policy is, in fact, evidence-based (Marmor 2001).

Health-related research needs to be seen as the foundation of healthy policy and funded accordingly. A large proportion of medical research continues to be apportioned to the technological and acute care aspects of the health care system, even though the majority of illness care for chronically ill, disabled, aged, vulnerable and disempowered people is carried out in the home and community. This is significant from a humanitarian perspective, but it also has important financial implications. To explore the implications of this for policymaking, there is a need to articulate a variety of modelling structures to inform strategic planning for such things as community supports and respite services. Kushner (2000) estimates that 70–90 per cent of all chronically ill people are cared for by family caregivers. If even a small proportion of these people withdrew their services, there would be a 20–25 per cent increase in demand for formal services from the health care system.

To date, there are insufficient evaluation data to expedite the flow of resources to help either the aged and infirm, or their carers. Research is also needed to investigate best practices in helping people through the various transitions in health services in a way that ensures continuity of care. So the research base is crucial to policy planning, and evaluation must accompany all policy changes. In those communities affected by changes there must be feedback or monitoring processes built into the changes at specified intervals (Glass & Hicks 1999). Where there are to be dramatic changes, such as hospital closures or reductions in beds, members of the community should be consulted to dispel unnecessary fears and secure meaningful support for the changes (Glass & Hicks 1999). At times, this means involving the community in designing the evaluation so that their concerns are also addressed by the analysis. This consultative approach is particularly valued by rural people and others disadvantaged by distance from the planning process (Ricketts 2000).

One of the most important lessons for policy development is to look to past experience to solve the problems of the future. The community of the future will need a new synthesis that combines the most effective principles and strategies used in the past, with optimal use of the current information base. Poland and colleagues (1998, p 786) caution against accepting the notion put forward during the 1980s that prosperity produces healthy populations. They believe such comments provide convenient cover for those who would 'dismantle the welfare state in the name of deficit reduction'. This sentiment is often echoed by health scholars, concerned that their research findings may be used to justify expenditures rather than to improve clinical processes or reach a wider population. The backlash against the commodification or overt managerialism in health care must be balanced with systematic programs of research that highlight the need for distributive justice and sustainability (Poland et al 1998). Public demand for health care will always exceed the limits imposed by government predictions, so there will always be some rationing of services (Mechanic 1999). The way rationing is undertaken, whether for services or research funding, must be done with accountability by the decision-makers, full consultation and systematic evaluation and dissemination of outcomes to ensure that all populations have access to culturally appropriate, timely and responsive health services.

Good and best practice
in policy development

Policies for good health are most appropriate when they are developed in partnership between service providers, policy makers and the people they serve. Towards that end, a number of initiatives have been developed to establish good and best practice in health, and ensure that information on these practices is widely disseminated.

case study...

Health for All in Europe

In 1994, a group of policy makers in Europe expressed an interest in capturing the practical experiences of WHO member states in relation to the Health For All (HFA) policies and how these had been formulated and implemented across the many nations of Europe. Their analysis tracked both practical applications and policy documents during the HFA era, mainly over the final two decades of the last century. The culmination of their efforts is a significant volume of case studies called 'Exploring Health Policies in Europe' (WHO 2000b). The approach taken to creating such a profile was to ensure that all contributors used a common language for policy making, not in the literal sense, but to create consistent standards for explanation, for example, in setting goals, objectives, policies, strategies and targets. The Ottawa Charter and its language of equity, access and community participation, was used to frame 'like-minded thinking'. The overall focus guided a number of strategic changes for the future. For example, the research team drew the conclusion that countries need to change from implicit values to a clear, ethical framework, from health care inputs to outputs in terms of health status. They envisioned a shift from inward to outward thinking, from bureaucratic administrations to strategic guidance and support, and from control and regulation to consensus and accountability.

Many other issues were shared, including the need to articulate the social determinants of health, to understand patterns of disease, and technologies, to foster greater public participation and intersectoral collaboration, to adopt good governance for health care systems, to deal with globalisation. They confirmed the links between income policy and health, an ecological view of health, and the fact that schools, homes and workplaces were the major settings for health promotion. The utility of the HFA approach was reiterated as a workable framework for the future, with equity acting as the fundamental and linking principle for health policies and a sustainable and ethical future.

WHO made their comprehensive analysis available to all fifty-one member states as a way of finding common links and strategies for the future. As a result of the project, the researchers expect increased public ownership of health issues, greater social inclusiveness and cohesion, a stronger focus on health outcomes, and wider sharing of financial management tools for those administering health programs. The networks that were formed in the process of studying the various country cases created a kind of moral pressure among participants to adopt a universal set of values, that would direct or recommit political efforts towards health for all. They also affirmed the bottom-up or grassroots approach to policy development. A ripple effect has connected members of all countries in the exchange of information, both formally and informally. One measure of success can be found in participants' willingness to provide guidance and friendly feedback to one another. They declared the process irreversible, in that 'returning to a monosectoral, vertical approach to health policy development would be virtually impossible' (WHO 2000b, p 339).

Another health policy 'brainstorming' exercise was carried out in Canada in 2001. Five health ministers, from Canada, Finland, Mexico, New Zealand and the United States, were asked a simple question at the OECD Conference on

Health System Performance Measurement and Reporting, as follows: 'What action are you taking to improve health-service performance in your country and how will you gauge that improvement?'

The Canadian minister related an historic Agreement on Health in the year 2000, wherein a common vision and specific priorities for renewing Canada's publicly funded health system were articulated, with the first of the planned annual reports to be made public by September 2002. The future directions for health care in Canada will revolve around better coordination of the supply and distribution of health professionals, better reporting on performance, including patient satisfaction measures, and improving access to timely, high-quality health services for all, and building on a number of successes in implementing primary health care pilot projects. One area of emphasis will be the health 'infostructure' to expedite sharing electronic and technological innovations in health care.

The Finnish minister explained the high level of patient satisfaction among residents of that country, achieved with almost the lowest financial output compared to other countries in the European Union. The trend in Finland emphasises outpatient care and a shift in government regulation from setting guidelines, to working under legislative processes, financial incentives and information management. Finland's health system is characterised by a remarkable level of technical efficiency and efficient allocation of resources. That country has launched a national health project to ensure that health priorities and divisions of tasks are appropriate and acceptable to the population, with an initial progress report expected in March 2002.

Mexico, a country with a somewhat less developed health care system, provides a contrast to Canada and Finland. The Mexican health ministry is targeting basic care for the poor and a sufficient supply of drugs for treatment. The National Crusade for the Quality of Health Services is attempting to develop codes of practice for health professionals, the use of clinical guidelines in public institutions and certification for health professionals and health units. A new civic culture will see greater government transparency incorporating the perceptions of the public into its health care management and performance.

New Zealand reports an innovative new structure in the District Health Boards (DHBs), which will work with government to set goals and objectives for the priorities aimed at lifestyle factors (reducing smoking, improving nutrition, reducing obesity) and countering prevalent diseases (cardiovascular disease, diabetes), reducing violence in relationships and families, schools and communities, improving mental health and access to child health care services. For each priority, a set of 'toolkits' has been developed with input from specific expert groups. Each of these provides background information and evidence as a basis for treatment or interventions that will affect population health. The New Zealand Ministry of Health has stated unequivocally that the future health of New Zealanders will depend on successful implementation of its primary health care strategy (NZMOH 2001).

The United States, predictably, is focusing on affordable health care, developing innovative health insurance programs for vulnerable people. The health ministry has launched nationwide organ donation and preventative health initiatives, and substantially increased funding for the National Institutes for

Health (NIH), the major research facilities. Priorities also include community health centres, minority and women's health and anti-bioterrorism measures (OECD 2002).

Australia's health care system, like most others, is concerned with efficiency and effectiveness, placing the emphasis on patient outcomes. Australia has developed a National Health Outcome Indicator Framework and a National Information Development Plan, performance indicators in the hospital sector to monitor such things as elective surgery waiting times, costs related to casemix funding (prospective costing of care episodes according to diagnosis) and quality of care (AIHW 2000).

What these examples illustrate is that there are no dramatic reforms occurring in health policy, but a refinement of goals and strategies to bring all countries of the world into a common trajectory: to create sustainable health in the settings of people's lives at a cost they can afford and with the most appropriate use of available technologies. These are the goals of primary health care, and they are now infiltrating health care systems that used to be exclusively focused on the measurable outcomes of highly technical medical treatments, rather than equitable and accessible care for all. However, there remains a pressing need to further entrench social justice into the health agenda.

Policies for
social justice

The research agenda incorporates the principles of social justice through ethical monitoring of proposals and projects, especially in relation to biomedical research. It is crucial in a just world to uphold ethical and socially responsive economic policies governing the biomedical, pharmaceutical and intellectual outcomes of this research, particularly for research in genetics and reproductive technologies (Austin, Peyser & Khoury 2000). The politics of HIV/AIDS research has been instructive. However, policies and laws governing control over patents for intellectual property should now be revamped and subjected to wide, public consultation to prevent large multinational companies from prohibiting parallel developments in countries with the greatest need. A further public health issue in genetic research is related to equity and privacy. One concern is that people, on the basis of possessing genes deemed harmful, will be discriminated against or unfairly stigmatised (Kerr 1996). A further issue relates to the social elements of biomedical research. This will be a growth area for the future, not only in identifying genetic risk but in relation to expression of genes in various population groups. To inform health promotion, research studies must try to unravel factors leading to lifelong well-being in relation to the local and global burdens of disease, disabilities and injuries and personal choices.

A just agenda also asks who will safeguard the dissemination of genetic information, particularly when 'Hyperbole, misinformation and the premature raising of expectations typically surround the press conferences of scientists and accounts in the mass media' (Kerr 1996, p 452). Screening presents another dilemma. Do we screen workers for drugs and alcohol, or HIV, or hepatitis B, or all those who engage in socially incorrect behaviour for mental illnesses (Campbell et al 1997)? What should be the outcome of testing children and adolescents for late-onset inherited disorders? Will there be pre-symptomatic screening for Alzheimer's disease? How will this information be dealt with? What level of risk is acceptable before resources are deployed?

The allocation of resources is also fraught with social and ethical dilemmas, some related to the potential for power relations to prevail over issues of access and equity, and others related to social and/or cultural appropriateness. Health promotion in general poses an area of ethical concern. There is incontrovertible proof that smoking causes ill health, yet rather than blame the victims (smokers), should our health budget include funding for alternative stress alleviation strategies (Downie & Calman 1994)? In addition to health promotion, there are ethical resource dilemmas for caregiving. The very act of coming into care may lead to vulnerabilities for certain patients, even to the extent of exploitation if their cultural identity is not protected (Liaschenko 1997). Indigenous knowledge such as is embodied in the laws of Tapu for the New Zealand Maori, the Dreaming for Australian Aboriginal people, and a range of sources of tribal knowledge of many African, North and South American nations, emerge from non-secular, spiritual beliefs. Any attempts to provide guidance in health matters must therefore be couched in these cultural beliefs (Campbell et al 1997). On this basis, programs that stress 'cultural' treatment models which encourage a sense of Aboriginality should be more efficacious, but there is little research evidence for this. Yet Indigenous understanding is vital if we are to help Indigenous people become empowered to guide and choose appropriate health services.

Another gap in the research agenda lies in the base of evidence for socially just population policies. We live in an era of globalisation, where goods and services move more freely across borders than at any time in past history, but people do not. Given the asymmetry of population ageing in the industrialised nations, and high birth rates in the developing world, would it not be better for the world to free up borders in the more developed countries to greater migration? This would help alleviate the predicted labour shortages and social security strains predicted for the future, and go a long way towards alleviating poverty in the developing countries. Some countries adopt strategies for immigration, population control and education in isolation, and this does not respond well to the contemporary issues affecting all of us. Commitment to human ecology guides us towards demanding greater political accountability and public participation in population policies. How can immigration policies developed during the Industrial Revolution be applicable to the world of today, where there is widespread knowledge of the conditions that cause families to flee situations of oppression, environmental degradation, civil rights abuses and ethnic conflict? How can the natural resource policies of the past suffice when we have clear and comprehensive evidence on the 'cataclysmic' destruction of the world's ecosystems (Suzuki 1999)? And how do the cultures of the industrialised world accommodate the cultures of refugees in ways that are sensitive yet provide protection from harmful cultural practices? The greater depth of knowledge that flows across borders in this era of global communications warrants closer inspection of social justice by all the world's citizens.

Policies for a healthy environment must be holistic in terms of integrating and synthesising the interdependence of people and their surroundings. They must be focused on sustainability, diversity and equilibrium, and responsive to changing needs and knowledge (Lee & Paxman 1997). The failure of the Kyoto Agreement is a global disaster, particularly in the refusal of Australia and the United States to be signatories, as these are among the world's most significant sources of pollution. Developing environmental policies at the local level to recycle non-biodegradable materials will have little effect if our policy makers continue to refuse to set limits on pollution levels in the air breathed by all of us. Likewise, biodiversity is essential to the survival of the world and all its species. Monoculturing the planet with a single notion of development as embodied in the globalised economy ignores evolution's priceless lesson about the value of diversity (Suzuki 1999).

Healthy environment policies are also intertwined with occupational health policies that work towards safe, low-energy, low-emission, low-waste technology and the use of the best available production technology. Policies governing the workplace are based on the dual role of workplaces in providing early detection and intervention for a range of environmental health hazards, as well as being a setting for health and socioeconomic development. Because occupational health and industrial policies are designed to secure the dignity of work for all, they resonate with a social justice approach. Preventing occupational accidents, injuries and diseases and protecting workers against physical and psychological overload implies a parsimonious use of resources, minimising the unnecessary loss of human and material resources.

Towards the future:
room for optimism

Despite the ongoing threats to health, health care systems have also effected some improvements to health. Taken as a global aggregate, there is evidence of rising, sustainable economic growth, decreasing birth and death rates, an overall increase in life expectancy, slowing growth of urban populations, improvement in literacy rates (although there remains a need to improve the literacy rates of African, Asian and Latin American women), decrease in fertility rates and an increase in contraceptive practices in the most populated countries (UNFPA 2000; WHO 1999). These improvements are related to socioeconomic improvements, the growing body of health knowledge and improvements in the delivery of health care. However, the need to continue along this path in health care services is ongoing and has led to greater awareness of system-wide and nation-wide reform.

The promise for the twenty-first century lies in our ability to learn from the twentieth. The policies we have used, the processes by which they have evolved, and the structural features that have enabled their implementation are all instructive. Perhaps more importantly, in the process of creating and sustaining health, we have learned much from one another. Each of us has experiences that reflect differences in gender, religion, ethnicity, socioeconomic background and the endless combinations of these. We have learned much from globalisation, both good and bad. Perhaps this century's major task is to further explore humanitarian imperatives, to achieve equity, in trade relations, in the way we consider other cultures and in disassembling the boundaries between health and all other aspects of society. The most powerful challenge for the future is to create the kind of society in which the meanings of the past can protect and stimulate the future. The Australian Collaboration in conjunction with the Australian Council of Social Services recommends a number of policy directions. For a viable, just and sustainable future, we must:

- close the gap between rich and poor
- generate more and better jobs and spread them equitably
- improve community services
- invest in disadvantaged regions
- educate everyone, particularly the disadvantaged
- provide affordable, eco-efficient housing
- reduce inequalities in health care
- protect Indigenous rights and identity by overcoming disadvantage and building capacity among Indigenous people
- reinforce multicultural traditions and capacities
- protect consumers through food, public health and safety regulations
- make available to all, media opinion, freedom of speech and access to information
- strengthen and protect human rights
- repair land and water resources and conserve biodiversity to protect natural assets
- engage in productivity reforms through environmental modernisation, including pricing reforms
- reduce greenhouse gas emissions
- work towards responsible external behaviours to help other societies (Yencken & Porter 2001).

As we embrace this twenty-first century we need to use the human, social and economic capital created in the last century in creative and visionary ways, to imbue social justice throughout the local and global landscape. The eighteenth century gave us the Enlightenment thinkers, who posited that access to knowledge would create unbeatable arguments against doing wrong (Saul 1997). Yet we have used much of that received wisdom, reinforced over the last century, to justify economic rather than people-oriented decisions. Saul (1997, p 120) describes this as suicidal: 'Simple policy discipline might help us reassert our sense of belonging to a civilization rather than to an imaginary dialectic with inevitable conclusions'. To re-frame the past in terms of a humane future is socially just. Primary health care and the principles that flow from it will help us return to our humanist origins. Learning, working and living by these principles will help us all achieve and sustain health and wellness.

REFERENCES

Austin, M., Peyser, P. & Khoury, M. (2000). The interface of genetics and public health: research and educational challenges. *Annual Review of Public Health*, 21: 81–99.

Australian Institute for Health and Welfare (AIHW) (2000). Australia's Health 2000. Canberra: AGPS.

Campbell, A., Charlesworth, M., Gillett, G. & Jones, G. (1997). *Medical Ethics*, 2nd edn, Auckland: Oxford University Press.

Cribb, A. & Duncan, P. (2002). *Health Promotion and Professional Ethics*. Oxford: Blackwell Science.

Downie, R. & Calman, K. (1994). *Healthy Respect. Ethics in Health Care*. New York: Oxford University Press.

Glass, H. & Hicks, S. (1999). Healthy public policy in health system reform. In: M. Stewart (ed), *Community Nursing: Promoting Canadians' Health*, 2nd edn, Toronto: WB Saunders, pp 156–73.

Kerr, C. (1996). Genetic testing and public health (editorial). *Australian and New Zealand Journal of Public Health*, 20(5): 451–2.

Kushner, C. (2000). Translating principles into practice: lessons from Canada, *Australian Journal of Primary Health-Interchange*, 6(3/4): 10–23.

Lee, P. & Paxman, D. (1997). Reinventing public health. *Annual Review of Public Health*, 18: 1–35.

Liaschenko, J. (1997). Ethics and the geography of the nurse–patient relationship: spatial vulnerabilities and gendered space. *Scholarly Inquiry for Nursing Practice*, 11(1): 45–59.

Marmor, T. (2001). Health Policy. Presentation to University of Queensland Graduate School, Brisbane, 18 July.

Mechanic, D. (1999). Issues in promoting health. *Social Science and Medicine*, 48: 711–18.

New Zealand Ministry of Health (NZMOH) (2001). *The Primary Health Care Strategy: The Future Health System*. Wellington: MOH.

OECD (2002). What OECD ministers are doing for healthcare. *OECD Observer*, http://www/oecdob-server.org/news.../. Accessed 7 January 2002.

Oldenburg, B., McGuffog, I. & Turrell, G. (2000). Socioeconomic determinants of health in Australia: policy responses and intervention options. *Medical Journal of Australia*, 172: 489–92.

Petrou, S. (1998). Health needs assessment is not required for priority setting. (Letters). *British Medical Journal*, 317: 1154.

Poland, B., Coburn, D., Robertson, A. & Eakin, J. (1998). Wealth, equity and health care: a critique of a 'population health' perspective on the determinants of health. *Social Science and Medicine*, 46(7): 785–98.

Ricketts, T. (2000). The changing nature of rural health care. *Annual Review of Public Health*, 21: 639–57.

Saul, J. (1997). *The Unconscious Civilization*, New York: The Free Press.

Short, S. & Palmer, G. (2000). Researching health care and public policy. *Australian and New Zealand Journal of Public Health*, 2(4): 450–1.

Suzuki, D. (1999). Paradise unwound. Chronicles of the future. *The Weekend Australian*, 18–19 December, pp 3–4.

Thorne, S. (2002). Health promoting interactions: insights from the chronic illness experience. In: L. Young & V. Hayes (eds), *Transforming Health Promotion Practice: Concepts, Issues and Applications*. Philadelphia: FA Davis, pp 59–70.

Turrell, G. & Mathers, D. (2000). Socioeconomic status and health in Australia. *Medical Journal of Australia*, 172: 434–8.

United Nations Family Planning Association (UNFPA) (2000). The state of world population 2000. New York: UN.

World Health Organization (1999). The World Health Report 1999. Making a difference. Geneva: WHO.

—— (2000a). The World Health Report 2000. Health systems: Improving performance. Geneva: WHO.

—— (2000b). Exploring health policy development in Europe. Copenhagen: WHO.

Yencken, D. & Porter, L. (2001). *A Just and Sustainable Society*. Melbourne: The Australian Collaboration.

Index